The Boston
Marine Barracks

The Boston Marine Barracks

A History, 1799–1974

John R. Yates, Jr., *and*
Thomas Yates

McFarland & Company, Inc., Publishers
Jefferson, North Carolina

Lieutenant Colonel John R. Yates, Jr., USMC (Ret.),
was the last commanding officer of the Marine Barracks.

LIBRARY OF CONGRESS CATALOGUING-IN-PUBLICATION DATA

Yates, John R., 1930–
The Boston Marine Barracks : a history, 1799–1974 /
Lt. Col. John R. Yates, Jr., USMC (Ret.), and Thomas Yates.
    p.   cm.
Includes bibliographical references and index.

ISBN 978-0-7864-9650-1 (softcover : acid free paper) ∞
ISBN 978-1-4766-1753-4 (ebook)

1. Marine Barracks (Boston, Mass.)—History. 2. Historic buildings—
Massachusetts—Boston. 3. Boston (Mass.)—Buildings, structures, etc.
4. Boston (Mass.)—History, Naval. I. Yates, Thomas, 1961– II. Title.

F73.8.B85Y37 2015   359.009744'61—dc23   2015005455

BRITISH LIBRARY CATALOGUING DATA ARE AVAILABLE

© 2015 John R. Yates, Jr., and Thomas Yates. All rights reserved

*No part of this book may be reproduced or transmitted in any form
or by any means, electronic or mechanical, including photocopying
or recording, or by any information storage and retrieval system,
without permission in writing from the publisher.*

On the cover: the newly and comprehensively renovated Marine barracks,
March 19, 1921; early 1900s mustering (all images author's collection)

Printed in the United States of America

*McFarland & Company, Inc., Publishers
Box 611, Jefferson, North Carolina 28640
www.mcfarlandpub.com*

Table of Contents

Acknowledgments	vii
Preface	1
Introduction	3

Part I—The Fledgling Age

1. Military Obligations Evolve with a Nation	5
2. Marines at Sea, on Land and at War	14
3. Settling in to Normalcy; War Arrives Again	21

Part II—Adolescence

4. The Nation Splits Apart	31
5. The Eventfulness of Peacetime	39
6. Progress Marches On with New Commands	54
7. Major Meade Takes the Helm	67

Part III—The World Stage

8. The Spanish American War and Its Aftermath	87
9. The Era of Col. Pope	101
10. Prison Progress and Changes at the Top	118
11. The Post Exchange Investigation; Wood's Command	130
12. Woes at the Gates	142
13. Samar	153
14. Ebb and Flow of Peacetime	162
15. Shipshape Under Major Hall	173

Part IV—Twilight

16. Lt. Col. Yates, the Vietnam Era, and Memories Preserved   185

Appendix: List of Commanding Officers   195
Chapter Notes   199
Bibliography   215
Index   219

Acknowledgments

Many people have assisted in the preparation of this book. The dedicated persons of the Boston National Historic Park helped in locating material. John Burchill and Peter Steele provided the support of the entire park staff. Phil Hunt and Steve Carlson were always able to lay their hands on anything that was of interest.

Stanley Tozeski of the Federal Archives and Records Center, Northeast Region, Waltham, MA, provided unlimited support and was always most cooperative during time spent researching through the archival material. Appreciation to the entire staff for their assistance.

Dr. William J. Reid, author of *Castle Island and Fort Independence* and former headmaster of South Boston High School, read preliminary drafts and provided very valuable insight and comments.

Leslie DiNanno lended her expertise in navigating word processing nuances. We appreciate her assistance in getting this work to this point.

Preface

The story of the Boston Marine Barracks from its beginning until up to World War II was stored and archived, all musty and forgotten, in the form of typed and handwritten letters. Hundreds of them. Letters written in the nineteenth century were spending eternity unread and boxed away.

That is, until the last Marine Barracks commanding officer, Lt. Col. John R. Yates, Jr., arrived at the National Archives in Waltham, Massachusetts. There he found them: stacks of handwritten and typed letters, the primary communications medium of the day, dating from the very early 1800s up to World War II, all patiently waiting tell their story.

Perhaps unread for over one hundred years, many of these letters were written by the Barracks' earlier commanders. Letters by people of the day writing to the commanders were preserved as well. As Yates read them, times gone by came back to life. What was on the letter writers' minds? What were they trying to say? What were their concerns? How did the Barracks come about? How did it develop? How did the Marines' role on the shipyard change? How did it not change? What did the Marines do? Where did they go? The content in these letters shed new light on their times and their concerns.

Many mysteries remain, however. The surviving letters to be examined by modern times languished in storage. Many stories have no conclusion because there is no record.

This is the culmination of an effort to comprehend and relate each and every letter from that musty old box. Each letter brought long ago people back to life. References to remote place names and events have been further researched to allow the reader to follow along in the Barracks story, but it may be said that this book in large part has been written from the letters.

After World War II any correspondence was lost to the ages. Post–World War II filing and practices left those communications all jumbled up and thrown in with communications from everything else big government had going on.

These letters are all that is left of the story of the early Boston Marine Barracks.

Introduction

Chances are, men who served as Marines from the birth of the United States until 1974 may have been billeted at the Marine Barracks of the Boston Naval Shipyard. They may have participated in some of the most important and thereby historic events in the history of America. The City of Boston grew along with the Navy yard. Boston's infrastructure, its skilled maritime inhabitants, banking resources, and its distribution wherewithal made for a mutually beneficial relationship. The number of Marines stationed at the Barracks ebbed and flowed depending upon need and the mood of the times. A Marine barracks' primary duty was to house detachments of Marines, recruit and train new men and have them ready to set sail with outgoing ships. Incoming vessels undergoing refurbishment disgorged Marines who needed their land legs back. It was a vital place to "freshen troops up" for redeployment. While assigned to the Barracks, a Marine's duty was to guard the Navy shipyard. Ship yards are crucial to commerce. They are also a crucible of military (naval) power.

At sea, while the sailors tended to the sails and the ropes and the guns, the Marines guarded and trained. When closing for battle with enemy ships, Marines perilously high into the upper reaches of the masts and yardarms fired down upon enemy vessels within range. Grappling hooks brought Marines aboard enemy decks into brutal hand-to-hand combat. On some ships, when sailors became potentially mutinous, Marines were stationed in between them and their officers. But one of their most important roles was to leave the ship and assault and hold military objectives. Smaller boats lowered into the water floated Marines to land to take and hold say a land battery, a stronghold of cannons defending a strategic harbor.

Marines from the Barracks participated in every engagement and campaign in which Marines were involved, from the Seminole Wars to the Mexican-American War, the Civil War, the Boxer Rebellion, the Spanish-American War, Samoa, the Second Boer War, Panama, the Philippine Insurrection, Haiti, the Dominican Republic, the World Wars, Korea and the Vietnam War. The Marines housed at the Barracks were trained, rested, and in position to be sent to any hot spot accessible by sea as fast as communications technologies of the day could manage. Navies, throughout history, were seafaring nations' primary military muscle, no matter if in Mediterranean Greco-Romanic times, under Elizabeth I, in Habsburg Spain, or in 19th century Britain. Land armies, which the modern mind equates with military might, had their mobility limitations. Practical air flight was a parlor dream.

Times Change and Politics Don't

The same year the Vietnam conflict officially ended, the Marines' use of the venerable Barracks ended as well. A victim of changing times and the politics of 1972, the shipyard and the Barracks were sent into retirement in 1973. Incumbent President Nixon won a historic landslide reelection to a second term, winning forty-nine out of fifty states, except Massachusetts. This political reality left the Boston Naval Shipyard vulnerable to closure.

Shipyards can be major employers of thousands of skilled labors, prized in any deepwater seaside urban location. This was a consideration. The Boston Naval Shipyard could not expand to accommodate modern ships. Its strength lay in its sailing ship and World War I and II era capacities. Although naval needs are accommodated more appropriately elsewhere, the dry dock remains active to service two of the most heroic ships that ever set sail for the U.S. Navy: the *Constitution* and the *Cassin Young*.

Born as it was during the wooden sailing ship era, both it and the fort on Georges Island, designed to defend against invading navies, faced obsolescence. Many veterans of the Marines who were stationed at the Barracks considered it good duty. I (John Yates) feel especially proud to have been selected to serve as commanding officer for the last three years of the official existence of the Barracks.

Recollections of Thomas Yates

When I was a middle school boy during the early 1970's, my father was the commanding officer of the Marine Barracks. When our family moved into the west wing quarters, we marveled at the size of our "new house." We each got our own rooms. The youngest of us siblings were given the top floor bedrooms. Akin to being assigned the upper bunk on a bunk bed, but that's the way us goofy kids liked it. We often slid down the hand rails, floor by floor, to report to dinner. And it turned out I had the room with a view.

Facing south, I could see Boston Harbor shimmering just a stone's throw away. The USS *Constitution* provided a tall ship foreground, beyond which stood the city skyline of the early 1970's, which sported half the skyscrapers that currently spike the sky today. The John Hancock building, under construction at the time, was having difficulties keeping its windows from crashing onto the street life below.

Next to the *Constitution*, one of the oldest dry-docks in the United States yawned, deep and dry, usually with a ship in service. I may have seen ships come and go from this dry-dock, and appreciated it as much as a middle school child who prefers television would. Huge cranes on rails did, however, capture a boy's attention. Just below the window lay the manicured parade grounds. Us kids would play and run around on the parade grounds. Punctuated on either side by 18th century period naval ship guns, my friends and I would climb on them. And then there was the climbing rope the Marines would use for training. We kids, of course, would swing on it, probably to the chagrin of the "Gunny" in charge.

Every night at dusk, three Marines would march out to the shipyard's flagpole for the official flag lowering. All were to seize movement until the flag was lowered into Marine hands. This was often a challenge for us kids to stop playing. But everybody knew who we were and we would certainly hear about it from our parents! That's not all. The Marines would march back through where we were playing. Little did my friends and I know we were riding our bikes back and forth all around a future national park.

Part I—The Fledgling Age

1. Military Obligations Evolve with a Nation

"No more protected from the rain, than they would be in open air."
—Lt. Caldwell

In 1623, settlers from Plymouth made an exploration trip to what is now Charlestown, no doubt, after learning of another European settlement situated there. At that early date, they found a few isolated settlers who had established themselves for the purpose of trading with the native peoples. The origin of these first European settlers is vague. They were, nonetheless, European expatriates in an exotic land with whom they could relate.

In the years following, waves of subjects of the king of England began to make the transoceanic journey in slow, square-rigged sailing ships more suitable for cargo than for the comfort of humans. With a safe harbor and deep water available in what was becoming "proto" Charlestown, much of this shipping traffic found its way there. The area benefited from this natural resource in the form of settlement and trade. Throughout history and the world, ports became economic and cultural engines. Necessary as well as exotic goods were traded and diverse peoples mingled and exchanged ideas. Colonial Charlestown's economy and autonomy benefited from the vast distances the Atlantic Ocean offered between the town and its imperial master. Square-rigged vessels were able to make the journey, most of the time, though speed was not a virtue or even a priority. Its culture and loyalty were still mostly English; indeed, its residents considered themselves Englishmen.

Trade from the Caribbean grew over the next 150 years in Colonial America. Exotic products found a market in Charlestown and the seafaring traders had no need to venture far from the safety of the East Coast to get it there.

Much can happen in 150 years, especially in 17th and 18th century Europe. England endured its civil wars and Central Europe hardly enjoyed much peace during the Thirty Years' War and the Great Turkish war. Just below the state of war between nations laid the state of competition. Britain and France, both seafaring nations, exported their competition to America. Although Britain had secured the North American East Coast, France made gains in the interior. With its beachhead of New Orleans, the French enjoyed the multiple benefits of the gulf coast, access to the mouth of what turned out to be the greatest river and tributary system in North America, and the Caribbean islands. In time, France consolidated its gains in the interior, inevitably rubbing up against British territory. The independent frontier spirit of settlers and effective diplomacy slowed to the pace of a walking man on muddy, rocky, mountain pass "trails" led Great Britain and France to fight the expensive and long "French and Indian War."

The largest war so far in this land transformed a peaceful and contented Colonial America into a new nation craving independence. Britain and America had been allies during the French and Indian War; however, cultural differences and the backlash of war, and its cost, led relations to grow bitter. Americans were expected to pay for a war fought in America.

New Enlightenment Era philosophies also made their way to the Port of Charlestown. The now familiar notions of equality and freedom either infected or grew like wheat in the minds of the citizens of Charlestown, depending on your point of view. Subjects of the crown, inhabitants of colonial America considered themselves Englishmen, yet they increasingly felt as if they were being treated as natives of a foreign land.

With the commencement of the revolution, Boston Harbor was the first place to feel the hammer blow. British naval cannonade shelled and burned Charlestown to a few houses. Many people's homes were blown up and set ablaze. When Charlestown was considered properly "softened up," on June 17, 1775, British ships disembarked Redcoats to capture Bunker Hill. On another hill just outside of town, Breed's Hill, alerted and massed local forces dug in awaiting contact.

"Don't fire till you see the whites of their eyes!" This suggestion was likely more for the use of the men gathered atop of Breed's Hill. Some were either unfamiliar with guns or not used to pointing them at people. It is no good to fire a weapon if the bullet falls short of the target. And they only had as much ammunition as they could scrounge. It was a good defensive position (a monument stands there today). The men held back three offensives of superior forces until their meager ammunition was spent. They inflicted heavy losses on British troops before making a tactical retreat.

The British evacuated the Boston area and as it turned out never came back; however, contemporaries were never sure of these things.

After eight years of war waged on its own soil by its most productive citizens, the new nation was exhausted, in debt, and leery of a military that might seize power by coup. Small-scale ship and boat building resumed in Charlestown as it had throughout its colonial history.

The Ad Hoc *Future*

The navy was disbanded and its ships sold. The ground troops, the army and the marines were also mustered out. No need for a standing military. The deed was done.

The new nation was essentially a sewn together set of previous individual colonies united against a common enemy and sharing the same coast. Still seafaring by nature and habit, the fledging nation depended heavily on foreign trade. American merchants became serious competitors with established European commercial interests, and aroused the attention of pirates. In 1794 Congress began to rebuild the Navy, and the resurrection of the Marine Corps took place on July 11, 1798, when Congress passed the basic act setting up the corps. The act authorized a strength of 33 officers and 848 enlisted men, specifying the Marines should be employed on sea duty, on duty at various posts and garrisons in the United States and "any other duty on shore, as the President, in his discretion, shall direct."[1]

Site selection for shipyards for the fledgling U.S. Navy—the wood, sail, and rope version—began in earnest and Charlestown was one of several strong candidates under consideration. New London, Connecticut; Newport and Pawtucket, Rhode Island; Portsmouth, New Hampshire; and Portland and Wiscasset, Maine, ports and harbors were also examined. Boston had the advantage of the extensive outer harbor and was found by mariners to be a safe anchorage for large fleets during bad weather. The inner harbor was safe from winds, enemies, and freshets, and could be fortified at a reasonable cost. Boston and Charlestown's harbors were on the neck of lands, which made them defensible by late 18th and early 19th century standards. The skilled labor required of shipbuilding was in place and many seamen called Boston their home port. Seven-foot tides allowed for construction of a dry dock. Local militias were well organized. Late 18th century (1700s) shipbuilding technology was essentially wood and rope. And lots of it. The modern mind may envision the metal navy of World War II. Those ships required access to metal ores, its transportation to the steel foundries, including prerequisite sources of coal and its transportation, the technology to melt the metals out of the ores and shape them, and the skilled laborers to put it all together.

Late 18th century shipbuilding required forests, vast forests, diverse forests. Early America had that; Britain lost its access to them after the Revolutionary War and had to go elsewhere for the wood required for its navy. Solid hardwoods built strong hulls, tall pines became masts, and even irregular shaped trees contributed to the interior structure of a ship. These natural resources dictated the early naval shipyards' landscape. After the commissioning of the USS *Constitution* (which today requires special tree farms for the appropriate timbers) and its five sister ships, the naval complexion of the nation was established, and the development of the early federal navy yards followed closely behind.

Establishment of the Boston Marine Barracks

A Marine detachment was billeted on Castle Island in Boston Harbor in June 1799. As the summer ended and with winter approaching, the subject of a temporary barracks was raised. Secretary of the Navy Benjamin Stoddert was against it, as there were plans for a permanent one at a future date. The following summer in June 1800, The secretary of the Navy began the acquisition of a 10 to 15 acre site in Charlestown. By 1801, a majority of the area now known as the Charlestown Navy Yard was ready for construction. With construction running several months late, the subject of a establishing a temporary Marine barracks was brought to the attention of the Secretary of the Navy Stoddert. Temporary quarters, however, only offered temporary benefits. Shipyards are quite permanent, and it was eventually seen that its security ought to be a permanent function as well. Plans for a permanent facility were already in the planning stage, awaiting funding. The wait would wind up lasting years.

When the USS *Constitution* was laid up in the Boston Naval Shipyard in March 1801, a "small number of naval personnel and a Marine guard of one sergeant, one corporal and eight privates were assigned temporary duty on board." This ad hoc guard of Marines was taken from the small detachment quartered at Fort Independence on Castle Island. On 21 May 1802, the secretary of the Navy wrote to the commandant of the Marine Corps: "A Guard to consist of 1 Sergeant, 1 Corporal and 15 Privates each must be stationed at the navy yards at Boston, New York, Philadelphia, Washington and Norfolk. In cases where guards are already established at any of these places, the number must be enlarged or diminished, as the case may require, so as to be neither superior nor less than the quota above prescribed. We shall soon have vessels arriving at New York and Boston, from which they may be supplied."[2] Until this became boots on the ground, the detachment from Fort Independence remained on board the USS *Constitution* until 14 August 1803.[3]

Although small detachments of Marines were stationed at the Boston Navy Yard at various times from March 1801, a permanent Marine guard was not established until June 1805, when Marine detachments consisting of one lieutenant, one sergeant, three corporals and 15 privates each were ordered to Boston, New York and Philadelphia "to guard the property of the Navy Department in the Navy Yards at those places." At the same time, the secretary of the Navy directed "a small house built for barracks while the lieutenant could be accommodated with a suitable room in one of the warehouses."[4]

The Marines began residency very modestly: in an existing lime shed,[5] a leftover structure from the seven-acre farm of John Harris. Although humble and as comfortable as a tool shed, its location was instrumental to their mission of yard security with its proximity to the waterfront and the main entrance to the Navy yard. There is no information concerning the size or appearance of the lime shed. It was perhaps typical of lime sheds of the late 18th century.

First Lieutenant Henry Caldwell, with Superintendent Nicholson's permission, took possession of the lime shed on the former Harris tract on 14 July 1802. His detachment was better accommodated here than near Hartt's yard on the Boston side. The Marines did their best to make the structure a livable facility. A dozen 8 by 12 window panes were installed in November. The following year, $126.66 of timber and shingles were made available for an addition to the "Marines' house." Most of the unskilled labor was provided by the Marines. The building was in very poor repair from the beginning even though they did all that could be done to maintain it.

When Lt. Caldwell departed for duty aboard the frigate USS *Constellation*, Lt. Newton Keene arrived from the Norfolk Navy Yard. Marine Corps Commandant Franklin Wharton reassured Lt. Keene that he would have little difficulty in repairing the quarters by enlisting several carpenters and purchasing some lumber. Evidently, Caldwell recently complained about the state of the barracks, with repairs over repairs.

Keene was authorized to recruit 20 privates and to be "selective"; in those times, meaning men of good character. Twelve were sent to headquarters, and Keene was to "enlist the guard for the navy yard as established and decline further recruiting." He was to hire just enough to secure the yard and no more.

Uniforms were coming. The first ship bound from Alexandria, VA, brought 20 old type coats, 20 old type vests, 20 caps and plumes (eagles and bands), two pairs of sergeant's overalls, 20 pairs of privates' overalls, 20 stocks and claps, 20 blankets, three knapsacks, and 50 pairs of socks.

The winter of 1804–05 was cold and windy. "Four window shutters" were hung. If the winters weren't enough pressure on the converted lime shed, a situation had arisen over the summer. Men on sick call were sent to the Marine Hospital at the lower end of the yard. There "they were beyond the vigilance of their officers," and while convalescing, they could easily desert if they so desired. Funds were allotted to add to the barracks a room capable for containing the sick. Discussions ensued about a future hospital near the site, but funds never materialized.

Lt. Keene moved on in 1805 and was replaced by Lt. Richard Greenleaf. For 14 months, he was in command of the barracks. Relieved 1 January 1807, he received a staff position to corps paymaster.

The December before, a previous commander was ordered back. Lt. Caldwell resumed his old post. Caldwell's report in March 1807 stated his detachment was in "good order," although it has "suffered a good deal from the inclement season." Apparently he thought the temporary barracks had lasted long enough and had an expert, a real carpenter, come in and inspect the property.

Lt. Caldwell, with the experienced opinion of the carpenter to back him up, held that any sum spent on repair would be a waste of public monies. The carpenter, in effect, totaled the building. Furthermore, several million bricks and "timber going to decay" were available on the yard and could keep costs affordable.

Colonel Wharton's hands were tied by the fact that the secretary of the Navy recently vetoed a request to repair the Philadelphia barracks, so how could he approve Lt. Caldwell's request and not that? Nonetheless, Lt. Caldwell was ordered to bring the Corps to its authorized strength. There was no place to house these recruits.

Headquarters wanted men between 5 feet 4 inches and 6 feet, between 18 and 40 years old and certified by a physician. But why should such prime men want to stay in that dilapidated lime shed? Caldwell believed that if he had "a sufficiency of good clothing and a good barrack," he could recruit 200 by Christmas. Sleeping indoors during winter months attracts recruits. Although he had a small room built for his sergeant and added more bunks for the men and sentry boxes, it still just made do until the awaited funds arrived. Caldwell informed headquarters that his men were "no more protected from the rain, than they would be in open air."[6] Commandant Wharton regretted that he "must support for a short time the inconvenience of the Barracks."

By 1807, it was clear that replacement of the building was necessary. Maybe 1808 would be the year. So in the spring of 1808, Lt. Caldwell again broached the subject. Commandant Wharton was sorry to learn how badly the men were quartered. They could be placed in tents during warmer weather. A private carpenter was hired to examine the structure and make a recommendation as to whether it should be torn down, repaired, or rebuilt. The carpenter reported that the best alternative was to erect a new structure.[7] It was a tear-down.

In 1807, the detachment was excited to learn of their impending new quarters. But when?

The Permanent Barracks

Three years later, on 5 June 1810, the secretary of the Navy announced to the commandant of the Marine Corps that a facility to accommodate 100 to 150 men at the Charlestown Navy Yard as well as a barracks in the New York to house 150 to 200 men would be built. It was to be built "upon the most economical terms," the cost to build both barracks would not exceed $8,000.[8] He also directed Colonel Wharton to make the necessary arrangements for contracting and selection of the sites. With respect to the location of the barracks, he was told to consult with the Naval commanding officers.

Colonel Wharton traveled to Boston in August 1810 and met with Commandant of the Navy Yard Nicholson. They agreed on a site: east of the superintendent's quarters and south of the Salem Turnpike. This familiar location was where structures housed Marines until they shipped out in 1974. The latest building exists to this day. This spot ceremoniously guards the path of where British boots advanced from their ships anchored off of Charlestown to their costly victory on Breed's Hill, remembered in folklore as the Battle of Bunker Hill (Bunker Hill was the objective; however, the bulk of the fighting occurred on Breed's). Heavy shot and shell rained over this property during that horrific blood spill. Over a quarter century hence, many lead and steel pellets were extracted from the ground during the excavation for the foundation.

Colonel Wharton directed Captain Thompson, the commanding officer of the Marine Barracks, to employ local building materials and construction techniques, which explains the slate roof and brick wall construction.[9] Captain Thompson was also informed that the Marines inhabiting the structure would provide the unskilled labor to minimize costs. This slowed progress and necessitated occupancy of the new building on a piecemeal basis.

To keep the back room from being entirely underground, the hill to the right of the commanding officer's quarters would be cut down and a garden laid out. Care was necessary to lead off the turnpike drainage near the fence. The barracks would require 300,000 to 320,000 bricks to complete. Available information suggests that the building was very simple, of course, as a rather rudimentary post Colonial or post Georgian style. Flanking the barracks on the east and west were the three-story wings that served as the officers' quarters. The west wing was the commanding officer's residence, while the east wing provided quarters for the junior officers.[10] Commandant Wharton was pleased at the Marines' willingness to work on their barracks. On November 15 he wrote Thompson, "your men are deserving of much credit in giving so much aid by labour. The comforts of their new quarters will I trust in some way compensate them of their conduct."

On December 20, Captain Thompson, having received furlough to visit the nation's capital, turned over command to Lt. John Brooks. Before doing so, Thompson had seen that two rooms for the Marines were readied in the right wing for the men to move into. Lt. Brooks wrote to Colonel Wharton, "separate in a small degree the officer for his guard, but will contribute much to the comfort of the men." January 14, 1811, Commandant Wharton informed Lt. Brooks that the officers would have to wait until their quarters were finished before moving in. The wait for the Barracks turned out to span from 1802 all the way until the dawn of 1811: nine years.

In late May 1811, Colonel Wharton gave instructions for laying out the parade ground. To establish its perimeter, Lt. Brooks was to take a "certain number of feet from the right of the right wing and left of the left wing ... so as to leave a lane or alley "between the commanding officer's garden and the stables of the commodore for the former and latter to use. He would then run his line toward the Charles River 180 to 250 feet, depending on the configuration of the terrain, as well as the buildings. On July 24, Commandant Nicholson protested that Lt. Brooks, in laying out the parade ground, was "absolutely spoiling the navy yard." To get to the "causeway and communicate with the lower yard, naval personnel had to turn a short corner within 12 feet of the marsh." Yet the grounds stood for twenty years, until the 1830's, when the construction of the ropewalk necessitated a small adjustment.

Wharton commended Brooks' zeal in completing the barracks and grounds. Now he should get back to taking steps to make it more difficult for men to desert. Desertion was a major problem for the Marines, as well as for the Army and the Navy during the early 19th century. Much correspondence focused on this subject. A fence was erected and the rear windows were barred. Apprehension was difficult and punishments were severe. Private Simon Cry, for example, was given 200 lashes.

The Marine barracks, as built in 1810–11, consisted of a central one story block and cellar, with double story wings. Although subject to alterations over the next 160 years, the floor plan of the front façade and east and west elevations of the wings have retained their original form. The structure turned out to be the oldest Marine barracks in the country that is in its original location and which is still in existence.[11] Similar to the commandant's house to the west, the barracks also stood on the high ground in the New Charlestown Navy Yard. A small

Etching of the single story barracks. The brick three story buildings in the background became the commanding officer's quarters, and the commandant of the Navy yard's mansion and office. Marines in possibly Mexican War era uniforms drill with spectators looking on. People came to the yard to watch preparations for war each time a war was commencing.

The officers' quarters on both sides of the single story barracks had probably recently been raised to three stories. Before the Gate 4 road was put in, fresh food from the gardens when in season supplemented the Marines' Diet. The commandant's mansion and office appears in the background.

The new mess room of the Marines at the barracks.

The sleeping room in the single story barracks. The beds were put up for the day to make space for the mess room.

parade ground has since existed between the building and 2nd Avenue, which in 1823 was simply the southern boundary of the Marine Corps property. The layout of 2nd Avenue came in 1828, according to the yard plan of that year.

Now that the new building could house more Marines than necessary for the shipyard's defense, the use of the extra Marines billeted in this structure became part of ships' detachments.

Rotating Commanders

Now that the long awaited Barracks were finally in place, Lieutenant Brooks received orders to take command of the Marine Detachment aboard the USS *Congress* in December 1811. Capt. Caldwell was back—the commander who agitated zealously for a suitable replacement for the lime shed. He spent the last days of his life in command, as he died early March 1812.

Lieutenant Charles L. Hanna, who commanded USS *John Adams* Marine detachment, was named as his acting replacement. Caldwell's widow remained in quarters until she found a place to live off base. Lt. Hanna, however, remained in command of the USS *John Adams* detachment. Colonel Wharton informed Hanna that if the ship departed before his replacement, Captain Archibald Henderson, reported, he was to go ahead and ship out with his detachment and senior Sergeant James McKim would be in charge of the barracks.

Captain Henderson still remained at sea commanding the USS *Constitution*'s Marines. So Lieutenant James Broom received orders to take charge of the Barracks and relieve Sergeant McKim.[12] From December 1811 to August 1812, the Marine Barracks had four commanders.

2. Marines at Sea, on Land and at War

"A ship without Marines is like a garment without buttons."
—Admiral Farragut

High naval officials throughout the 19th century had differing views on how the Marines should be used. The debate may be comparable to 20th century disagreements on how air forces should be used. In the 1890's, Admiral "Fighting Bill" Evan, veteran of the Spanish-American War, did not think that Marines were an unmixed blessing on warships, wrote rather bitterly, "The more Marines we have, the lower intelligence of the crew." However, Civil War era Admiral David Glasgow Farragut asserted that "a ship without Marines is like a garment without buttons."[1] A typical use of early 19th century naval war vessels was to anchor in the harbor of a belligerent and shell a coastal fortification. Fort McHenry is as an example. British warships bombarded the redoubt but failed to take it and put it out of service.

With the addition of Marines, boots on the ground gives the navy a better chance to take a fort, possibly intact. The capture of Santo Domingo without firing a shot is an excellent example. Moreover, for centuries, ship-to-ship fighting consisted of boarding an aggressor's vessel and fighting it out in tough, dirty hand to hand combat. Marines would climb the rigging and fire down on the other vessel. The more fighting men on board the better. One size rarely fits all, however. Not all missions required Marines on board. The use of the Charlestown Navy Yard's Marines no doubt ebbed and flowed by a ship's mission requirements, and by which side of the argument of how to use Marines controlled the money. And then of course the wild card that trumps all: world events.

An example of a type of service that Marines provided to naval ships was exhibited when John Paul Jones captured the HMS *Serapis* in an engagement off Yorkshire's Flamborough Head. American ships deployed Marines on the poop decks and fighting tops during the engagement, their fire kept the British ships' upper decks swept clear. This was of great significance since the *Bonhomme Richard*'s lower deck battery had been put out of action early in the battle, and this helped to restore the balance. Toward the end of the fight, a Marine on an American ship's rigging was able to drop a grenade down an open hatchway on the British ship. The grenade caused an explosion in a supply of gunpowder on the gun deck. The surrender of the British ship quickly followed.[2] Their presence is even interwoven in legend. A British captain, early in a naval fight, called to John Paul Jones and asked him if he wanted to surrender. Jones made his famous reply, "I have not yet begun to fight!" A tired Marine in the upper rigging remarked, "There is always someone who doesn't get the word!"

Frigates under the Union Jack and the Stars and Stripes have met at sea in the years of peace after the Revolutionary War without firing upon each other. However, British ships were stopping

American ships and impressing many of their sailors. This affront, plus maneuverings in the Great Lakes area, reignited naval hostilities with Great Britain that escalated into the War of 1812.

Built at Hart's Yard in Boston, the *Constitution* was one of several ships paid for by federal monies for a new navy. To spread the wealth, Boston was one of several cities awarded a piece of the project. The bold plan on how to build a navy of four ships to match the hundreds of British ships was a modern and breakaway idea of turning frigates into high speed and more maneuverable fighting ships. More sail for its size, and a sturdy build from some of the finest shipbuilding wood in the world, grown in America, a ship of this class had a gun deck capable of holding bigger guns than the British. These ships were to be considered the fastest warships in the world for decades. From its launch in 1798 until 1801, the *Constitution*'s duties were to patrol the East Coast and the Caribbean for pirates.

In the War of 1812, British ships were swarming around the coast of America like sharks, stopping American vessels, confiscating their cargos and either impressing or imprisoning their crews. The *Guerriere*, in particular, had been patrolling up and down the East Coast harassing American shipping.

In high summer 1812 the *Constitution* and the *Guerriere* caught sight of each other. They then engaged in days of pursuit and escape, often on windless days. How do sailing ships escape or close on windless days? One ship and then the other would send small boats out to tow their ships with nothing but the raw manpower of those in the rowboats. Captain Isaac Hull also sent boats out with a sort of hook attached to a half mile of rope for the boat crews to set and the *Constitution*'s crew to haul foot by foot by foot and repeat.

The *Constitution* broke away and briefly docked in Boston's outer harbor for resupply and fresh men after its chase with the *Guerriere*. Out of Boston the *Constitution* sailed north to Halifax to raid British shipping. While there a privateer from Baltimore swore to Hull that he was chased by the *Guerriere*. On 17 August the *Constitution* turned south. A lookout in the tops spotted a hull on the 19th. With favorable winds, it set sail for the yet unknown ship. As it closed, the British had the advantage and tacking, and broadsided the *Constitution*'s bow. This were ineffectual. When the ships were 25 yards apart the Americans loosed their 24 pounders in a destructive broadside that left the *Guerriere* reeling. Marine Lieutenant William Bush went up to the ship's rail, after an hour of maneuvering, and asked Captain Hull if he should board the enemy ship. At that moment, Lieutenant Bush was struck and killed by a shot from a Royal Marine aboard the *Guerriere*. Lieutenant Bush was the first Marine officer killed in combat.[3]

Flush from its victory over the British ship, the USS *Constitution* returned to its hometown of Boston late summer 1812 in unprecedented triumph. The *Constitution* docked for repairs at the Charlestown Navy Yard. By Sept 15, Isaac Hull became the commandant of the Charlestown Navy Yard. The victory's psychological effect was enormous. It was now thinkable and possible for an American ship to defeat a British one.

Punishment

Captain Archibald Henderson was directed to take command of the Marine Barracks on September 7, 1812. Commandant of the Marine Corps Franklin Wharton cautioned Captain Henderson to avoid having any difficulties with the aggressive Commodore William Bainbridge, the commandant of the Charlestown Navy Yard.[4]

By 22 August 1813, Second Lieutenant James R. Broom was in command of the Boston

Marine Barracks. While he was in command, he had obeyed an order by the Army to place a guard over Army prisoners. In those early years, there were disputes over whether the Army had jurisdiction over Marines while serving ashore. The Army as conferring jurisdiction upon Marines serving ashore was a strict interpretation of the act of 11 July 1798. So Lt. Broom wrote his boss, the commandant of the Marine Corps, for clarification of the matter. The commandant responded:

> We act under the Department of the Navy and not the Department of War, unless so specifically ordered by the President of the United States. I have received your letters of the 13th and 14th. I do not know the authority by which you were ordered, and which you obeyed, in detaching from the Navy Yard, a guard for prisoners of the Army. It will be proper at all times to cooperate with the military of our Country for the public good, where the particular service in which we are ordered, and which is more or less Naval, will not be injured or frustrated thereby, but I consider it voluntarily done, and not imperative, as we act under the Department of the Navy and not of War, unless so specifically ordered by the President of the United States.[5]

Even today, the contrasts and similarities of the Marines and the Army can confuse many laypeople. One important point was the issuance of punishment. This made any distinctions more urgent. Marines should be punished by Marines, not the Army. Even the punished thought so. Punishments during this era were severe. Private Oliver B. Trask, a repeated deserter, was court-martialed on March 26, 1821, and sentenced "to walk post ninety nights from retreat to reveille with an 18 pound weight on his back, then to be confined to a solitary cell for 30 days and fed on bread and water only, after which to be put to hard labor until all expenses incurred by his desertion and two dollars in addition to private clothing stolen by him to be paid for, then to be drummed out of the Corps with the Rogues March."[6]

Duels

During this period of history, duels occurred rather frequently. Although they were against the law, they nevertheless happened and witnesses were few and usually mute. A duel took place Saturday morning, September 15, 1819, between Marine officer Lieutenant Francis B. White and a Naval officer, Lieutenant William Finch, on Governor's Island. Both officers were attended by seconds (friends). They paced off between two elm trees. Both officers stopped, turned, and while Lt. White was taking deliberate aim, Lt. Finch cranked off a round and Lieutenant White fell. He was shot through the heart and died a short time later. Lieutenant Finch escaped unscathed and won the duel.

Lieutenant White's body was returned to the Marine Barracks by boat and Captain Wainwright notified the coroner from the City of Boston.[7] The *Boston Gazette* reported that the dispute between the two officers was believed to have been a longstanding one. The *Boston Gazette* further reported that Lieutenant White was buried from the Marine Barracks with military honors.[8] Lieutenant White had a reputation as being a rather troublesome person. He had a dispute with Captain Bainbridge during a card party several years earlier. Bainbridge and White did not agree while betting on "high trumps at doubles." An argument erupted and Bainbridge stormed out of the game.[9]

A possible reason for Lieutenant White accepting the challenge to a duel was the prevailing attitude that Marines were members of a highly specialized organization, and to survive they must build a sense of cohesion and loyalty to their own. Those in authority fostered this feeling.

Very early in the Corps' history, a young Marine officer while at sea was insulted when a naval officer struck him in the jaw. The Marine officer received a stern letter from the commandant, the boss of the Marine Corps, Major William Ward Burroughs.

The lieutenant was informed that he should not accept that kind of treatment and Burroughs actually urged him to fight a duel. Major Burroughs even cited an incident where a Lieutenant Gale was struck by a naval officer aboard the USS *Ganges*. The Marine lieutenant was unable to get satisfaction during the cruise, so when the ship returned to port, Lt. Gale challenged the naval officer to a duel and shot him. Major Burroughs commented, "Afterward politeness was restored."[10]

Riot Control

On 12 March 1824, Major Robert D. Wainwright received a message from the Charlestown State Prison. One of three prisoners scheduled to be publicly whipped in the prison yard captured a guard and subsequently opened the cells of the other two prisoners. The prisoners then locked the guard in a cell. They proceeded to the dining hall and prisoners from other parts of the prison joined them. Major Wainwright dispatched Marines.

Until the Marines arrived, a resolute guard, who had a reputation as a quiet and mild mannered gentleman, faced the unruly prisoners with only a rattan baton and demanded that they return to their cells. The prisoners retorted that they had nothing to lose and refused to leave the hall. The guard slipped out of the hall to safety.

Major Wainwright was requested by prison authorities to order the Marines to fire down at the convicts through the small windows, first with powder and then with ball, until the prisoners were willing to retreat. However, Wainwright decided on a wiser and bolder approach. Wainwright ordered the door to the prison hall to be opened and he marched in at the head of thirty Marines. The Marines formed at the end of the hall, opposite the crowded rioters. Wainwright stated that he was empowered to end the rebellion and he would not leave the hall alive until all convicts had returned to their cells. The prisoners replied that they were ready to die and would fight to the end unless the sentence for the flogging of the three prisoners was rescinded. Wainwright ordered the Marines to load their pieces and to ensure that the prisoners knew that they were loading for real and instructed the Marines to hold their bullets in full view of the prisoners as they loaded. The prisoners still did not back down. The Marines were ordered to take aim and not a prisoner stirred. The major advanced a step or two in the front of the Marines and again urged the prisoners to depart. The prisoners again declared their intention of fighting it out. The stout-hearted major took out his watch and ordered the Marines to level their weapons and aim at the prisoners, but not to fire until they had orders. Turning to the convicts, he declared, "You must leave this hall. I give you three minutes to decide. If, at the end of that time a man remains, he shall be shot dead. I speak no more."[11] A very tense atmosphere enveloped the room as a multitude of desperate men faced the business end of leveled muskets of a small band of well-disciplined Marines. The Marines were ready on the slightest motion or sign from their leader to begin the carnage. The tall commander held up his watch and counted the lapse of the three allotted minutes. For two minutes, not a person, or a muscle moved. Not a sound was heard throughout the quiet hall. At the expiration of two minutes, prisoners in the rear, nearest the door and farthest from the Marines, began to drop out quietly and deliberately through the door. Before the last minute was up, the remaining men were struck by panic and crowded the exit, and the hall was cleared. The steady determination, firmness, and bravery exhibited by Major Wainwright prevented many needless deaths.[12]

The Marines from the Navy Yard did the community favors and supported riot suppressions until 30 November 1833. By then, Captain T. S. English told the selectmen in Charlestown that he could not render assistance or riot suppression anymore unless the president of the United States so ordered.

In August 1824, a very storied and distinguished visitor paid a visit. General Lafayette, the General Lafayette from the Revolutionary War, was received in the Navy yard by an honor guard of Marines, under command of Major Wainwright. The honor guard provided a 15-gun salute. General Lafayette was on a tour of naval stations throughout the United States and by direction of the president was to be received with the highest of honors.

On a hot summer night August 11, 1834, a rioting mob in Charlestown left the Ursuline Convent ablaze. The Sisters of Charity and their students lost everything except the clothes on their backs when they fled the burning convent. Fifteen rioters were caught, arrested and confined in the jail at Lechmere Point.

Sheriff Varnum of Middlesex County was fearful of more violence eleven days later on the night of August 22. He had intelligence that a mob of sympathizers planned to storm his jail and free the prisoners. The sheriff contacted Commandant of the Navy Yard Jesse D. Elliott for armed assistance. Even after the letter to the selectmen referring to chain of command issues regarding riot suppression, Commandant Elliott still provided 70 Marines and 200 sailors for additional security at Lechmere Point. Because of this prompt show of force, there was no further disturbance. For the remainder of the month, however, the Marines were on heightened alert because of concerns that violence could spill over into the Navy yard. By September 10, 1834, the danger passed after the rioters realized that they would be met with force if they threatened any further violence.[13]

The Seminole Wars

The number of indigenous peoples living in Florida declined with the arrival of the Spanish after 1513. British victory over France and Spain in the Seven Years' War, or the French and Indian War as it is known in America, had Spain cede Florida to Great Britain in 1763 as part of the Treaty of Paris. Surviving true Florida natives were taken with the Spaniards to Cuba and New Spain. New Spain was essentially the colonies of Spain located throughout the world. American tribes from the southeast began to repopulate these unoccupied lands. The people called the Seminole were actually members of different tribes, runaway slaves, and free blacks. During the American Revolution, British Florida recruited these Seminoles to raid settlements on the frontiers of Georgia. This made them enemies of the United States.

The treaty ending the Revolutionary War gave Florida back to Spain in exchange for its support in the war. Spain's grip was light, however, maintained only by small garrisons at St. Augustine, St. Marks, and Pensacola, and it did not control the border with the United States.

While Britain and the fledgling United States were fighting the War of 1812, the British landed forces in Spanish West Florida, on the gulf side, and recruited the Seminole again. Spain had no effective means to retaliate.

Also during that war, in 1814 Colonel Andrew Jackson became a national hero after his victory over the Creek Indians in Georgia. The Creek were forced to relocate out of Georgia and out of the country into Spanish Florida. After the war in 1818, General Andrew Jackson invaded Spanish Florida in response to rumors of the Spanish forts selling guns to the Indians, among other things. This complicated matters. Secretary of State John Quincy Adams had commenced negotiations to purchase Florida from Spain, but the invasion, known as the First Seminole War, suspended these.

Eventually Spain did cede Florida, and the United States took possession in 1821. Along with the territory, Florida came with its plentiful "noncitizens" of the United States. This became troublesome to the powers at the time. Reservations for these people to relocate to and live on were the reigning solution. But until a treaty was signed establishing any reservations, the Seminole were unsure where they could plant their crops and even if they could harvest them. Government officials responsible for the task came and went, increasing this uncertainty. The Seminole were also harboring runaway slaves, much to the chagrin of plantation owners.

In 1828, an old enemy of the Seminole, Andrew Jackson, was elected president. In 1830 Congress passed the Indian Removal Act, intended to resolve problems by moving the Seminole and other tribes to the west of the Mississippi River. The accomplishment of this became known as the Trail of Tears.

The treaty of Payne's Landing of 1832 had given the Seminole three years to relocate west of the Mississippi. Realizing the Seminole would resist relocation, the U.S. began preparations for war. Perhaps the Seminole didn't feel like they were part of the United States, having been part of it for only nine years. It would be like someone new taking hostile control of your town and then ten years later wanting you to leave your home. The Seminoles began to attack settlers and ambushed militia wagons, killing soldiers. Large movements of troops were sent into Florida but they were easy to ambush in the lush, thick swamps.

By 1836 the U.S. quartermaster brought a new approach to the war. Instead of large troop movements, he would wear the enemy down. This would require a large military presence, including Marines from the Boston Marine Barracks.

Commandant of the Marine Corps Colonel Henderson volunteered the services of a regiment of Marines from the Barracks for duty with the Army. President Jackson accepted the offer and ordered the withdrawal of all Marines from the navy yards and the Washington Barracks, except for a sergeant's guard (one sergeant, one corporal and 12 privates) to remain at those facilities. The Marines would be ordered to duty with the Army in the Florida Territory. Marines left in the navy yards were to consist of personnel unable to pull field duty. The Barracks must have been a ghost town.

Lt. Col. Freeman was sent to command the Portsmouth detachment and the detachment from the Boston Marine Barracks, and have all proceed to New York City. When Lt. Col. Freeman's battalion arrived in New York City, he took on more Marines from the Brooklyn Navy Yard. Freeman's battalion then shipped out to Charleston, South Carolina. From Boston they traveled between two modern cities. At Charleston they boarded a train, new at the time, from Charleston to Augusta, Georgia. From Augusta, the Marines marched to Fort Mitchell, Alabama, a forward base of operations for the Second Seminole War.

Commandant of the Navy Yard Downes asked the secretary of the Navy for permission to hire civilian watchmen to look after public property in the yard.[14] He had to resort to using civilians as guards due to a lack of Marines while the Marines were serving in the Seminole War.

The Navy sent sailors and Marines up rivers and streams and into the Everglades. Navy Lt. John T. McLaughlin even traveled from December 1840 through the middle of January 1841 across the Everglades in dugout canoes, from east to west. This was to be the first group of whites to complete the crossing. Natives stayed out of their way.

The war began to wind down. It also began to become unpopular. General Armistead had $55,000 at his disposal to bribe chiefs into surrender. Many Seminole surrendered to avoid starvation. Only residual Seminoles remained and were no longer a threat. It was an expensive war for the time. Forty thousand regular U.S. military, including Marines, militia, and volunteers, served. Three hundred of these died in the war.

A treaty was signed between the Seminoles and the United States in Ft. Dade, Florida, on March 6, 1837. Colonel Henderson then received orders to return to Washington on May 22, 1837. He subsequently left two companies in Florida with plans for the other Marines to return to the stations at a later time.

But within two weeks after Colonel Henderson left for Washington, hostilities broke out again and the War Department rebuffed Colonel Henderson's request to return the Marines to their home stations. The War Department felt the need for Marines in Florida was more pressing than their need at the nation's navy yards.

In 1845 Florida became a state. This change did not permanently end the violence. By 1855, a third Seminole war began.

3. Settling into Normalcy; War Arrives Again

"[Recruit] as many good men as you can without delay."
—General Henderson

The critical shortage of Marines at the Charlestown Navy Yard was further complicated by the continuing requirement for the Marine Barracks to provide Marines for ships' detachments. The manpower shortage was somewhat eased with the arrival at Charlestown of the sloop of war *Erie*, which would be laid up for repairs starting September 15, 1837. On October 19, the *Ohio* also dropped anchor at the yard. Both Marine detachments were assigned to duty at the Marine Barracks.[1] Lt. Col. Freeman resumed command of the Marine Barracks, Charlestown,[2] September 10, 1938. The brick wall in the enlisted men's section caved in. A cursory look-see found the foundation had failed. Add to that the need to add a second story to the barracks. Master carpenters Pierce and Turner surveyed the foundation. They framed the first floor at the request of Lt. Col. Freeman. Their jaw-dropping estimate of $2,835 was required due to the extent of the repairs. Funds were never made available and the barracks lingered like this for thirty more years.[3]

Civilian watchmen and not Marines manned security posts. The situation became the new normal after the Seminole War. Commandant Nicholson noticed this when he assumed command of the Navy yard. The Barracks personnel did, however, eventually increase to a point where they were able to resume sentry duties. Their posts were the Main Gate, Dry-dock No. 1, Building H, Building 39 and the lower yard gate.

Only one lieutenant was assigned to the Barracks. Since captains and above were not required to stand duty as officer of the day, this caused a problem. This one lieutenant was therefore officer of the day every day. General Henderson, the Marine Barracks commander's boss, saw the need and rectified this by assigning Lieutenants Edward S. West and H.W. Queen to report to Lt. Col. Freeman.

Brevet Brigadier General Archibald Henderson was the commandant of the Marine Corps from 1820 until his death in 1859. Promoted to brigadier general by brevet in 1837, it was the highest rank of any Marine up to that time. The Barracks received a complement of thirty Marines, August 16, 1842, which brought the Barracks up to pre–Seminole War strength.[4] Lt. Col. Samuel Watson assumed command of the Barracks in October 1842. He was one of the more senior officers in the Marine Corps. The commandant of the Marine Corps considered the Charlestown Barracks key to the organization. Lt. Col. Freeman was sent to command the Marine Barracks at Norfolk.[5]

October 1842, the ship *Ohio* required some Marines. Filling these needs was the Barracks' mission. But this reduced manpower to such an extent that the unit was unable to staff three of the navy yard guard posts. Commandant Nicholson of the Navy Yard wanted eight posts manned by Marines. He requested more Marines from Secretary of the Navy Abel P. Upshur. Nicholson's confidence in the civilian watchmen was very low.[6]

General Henderson got involved and replied to Upshur that Marines were equally distributed at all the Navy yards. At Charlestown, the muster roll listed seven privates on sick call, four on special detail and four on police detail with only thirty left to perform guard duties at eight posts 24 hours every day. In order to meet Commandant Nicholson's request, staffing these positions would require sixty-five ready for duty Marines and each would have to do eight hours on post out of a twenty-four hour tour.[7] Commandant Nicholson needed the posts staffed and realized he wasn't going to get his ideal Marine staffing. In the end he did engage a number of civilian watchmen he found to be "amenable to Naval Law." The watchmen, according to Commandant Nicholson, who may have been pleasantly surprised, performed their duties "quite well."[8]

In summer of 1842, the junior officers of the Barracks made known their concerns regarding their quarters in the east wing. Captain Marston's quarters consisted of a kitchen and one room totaling 304 square feet. The three lieutenants occupied quarters consisting of 204 square feet each. Was the third story going to be used as officer's quarters or as an attic? Lt. Col. Freeman referred the matter to the Navy yard auditors.[9]

At Lt. Col. Freeman's request, the navy yard provided master painter Cyrus Cobb and master joiner Caleb Pierce to examine the east wing. They concluded that the piazza was in such bad condition that it could not be repaired. It would cost $150 to build a replacement. They recommended that the front upper chamber and the rooms in the second story and in the basement be painted and that all the ceilings in the east wing be whitewashed. Three of the rooms required paper. The cost of the painting and papering was estimated to be $85. Lt. Col. Freeman's request for these improvements was forwarded to General Henderson for approval. It was subsequently funded and accomplished before the winter of 1842.[10]

The major responsibility of the Marine Barracks to provide seagoing detachments to naval vessels was gaining momentum. These were going to cause shortages of personnel to cover posts around the yard for years to come.

Commander Lt. Col. Watson went on summer leave 10 August 1843 and Captain Ward Marston assumed acting command. During the commander's absence, the junior officer authorized a detachment for the frigate USS *Cumberland*. To pull this off, he had to solve reenlistment and uniform problems.[11]

The First USS Missouri

Sailing ships still reigned over the seas. By the early mid 19th century, however, the utility of steam technology was gaining wider recognition. Steam powered trains appeared on land connecting cities. They connected locations of raw natural resources and brought this unprecedented tonnage to their processing plants. The steam engine also found its way to sea. At first, ships outfitted with steam technology kept their sails. With new technologies, however, there can be seen and unforeseen dangers. To make steam and to pressurize it required hot fires and boiling water, and pipes, all contained shipboard. Any problems invite an explosion of boiling water and stoked fire, with no place for anyone to run.

The *Missouri*, not the famous World War II battleship, but the first in a series of ships named *Missouri*, was a 10-gun side-wheel stream powered frigate. It was one of the first steam and sail ships. The *Missouri* set sail, and steamed on, a diplomatic mission to Egypt in 1843. Diplomatic missions are replete with gestures, protocol, unspoken messages within spoken messages, and displays of new technologies. The *Missouri* was the latest in naval technology to be shown off at an important diplomatic event. It made the transoceanic journey across the Atlantic and settled safely into British Gibraltar harbor in October 1843.

Things didn't go as planned. A crewman was carrying a heavy container of turpentine, pretty routine stuff. But he spilled it. The spill found flames and a fire quickly grew out of control. The fire engulfed the ship. An alarm was sounded for everyone to abandon ship. The British ship *Malabar* was anchored nearby. Its crew jumped into action and rescued 200 personnel as the *Missouri* burned and sank in the harbor. Relations were cool between Great Britain and the United States throughout the nineteenth century, but humanity trumped any hostilities. The Marines who served aboard the *Missouri* and survived its destruction arrived back in Charlestown via Gibraltar, with only the clothes on their backs. Lt. Col. Watson, on his own responsibility, immediately issued new clothing, and later requested permission from General Henderson, who subsequently approved of the action.[12]

Repairs, Discipline and Rotations

In the fall of 1844, Lt. Col. Watson was cognizant of the need to prevent further deterioration of the barracks. He requested funds for replacement of the platform of the east wing and the portico of the west wing, for rebuilding the cellar, replacing a door and doorframe as well as adding two new pumps. General Henderson forwarded the request and the secretary of the Navy approved $381.25 for the repairs. However, a storm destroyed twenty-six feet of the Marine compound fencing and approval was sought and received for an additional $68 for fence replacement.[13]

On October 16, 1844, the frigate *United States* was laid up and its Marine detachment was assigned to the Barracks. The Marines were sorted out and granted leave and transferred to other posts. The Barracks retained a "fair portion of the guard" in Charlestown.[14]

In June 1844, $109 was stolen from a member of the Barracks. The culprit was apprehended, prosecuted, confined, and dishonorably discharged when he was released from confinement.

Private Samuel Cummings earned confinement for deserting. However, since he only had six months left on his enlistment, Lt. Col. Watson requested permission from General Henderson to discharge him. Henderson concurred and Cummings was discharged.[15]

In September 1845, Lt. Col. Watson requested substantial repairs of the barracks. Three new bulkheads, a new floor for the lobby, two new floors for the east wing, and a new roof for the privy, were considered needed. The total costs of these repairs were $1,020.85, which was approved by General Henderson and Secretary of the Navy Bancroft.[16]

The Mexican War

The collapse of the alliance between the British and Native Americans east of the Mississippi River after the War of 1812 removed considerable enemies from the frontier. Unbelievable amounts of land were gained from France through the Louisiana Purchase. Rich farmlands in the Midwest beckoned. The Jacksonian era philosophy of Manifest Destiny made westward migration okay and "American" in the minds of many individuals. And then there was vast Mexico.

In the 1820's, Mexico encouraged some immigration to settle the underpopulated Texas region. Soon, more migrants from the United States arrived in Mexico to homestead than the Mexican government had anticipated. Constraints on migration began irritating the new arrivals who felt Texas was more the United States than Mexico. In their minds, they weren't settling in Mexico, they were expanding the United States.

Lots happened in 1836. Texas asked to be included in the United States as a slave state. Since this would disrupt the delicate balance of free states and slave states, northern states were in no hurry to annex Texas. Mexico even established that annexation would be an act of war.

That year Texans drove Mexican troops out of what they considered American Texas. Months later, 189 troops garrisoned at the Alamo, a leftover mission from Spanish times, were attacked by 1,800 Mexican forces from February 23 to 6 March. The Battle of the Alamo raged. All of the defenders perished in the fortified mission to the Mexican loss of about 500 casualties. Later that year, the Republic of Texas asserted its independence from Mexico and declared itself a sovereign nation, while it awaited statehood. Mexico refused to recognize its independence.

Boundary disputes existed throughout the lifetime of the Republic. Nonstop violence and feuds within its borders with its Native Americans made a peaceful life a dream to many Texans. Texas was piling up huge debts. These debts were another incentive for Texas to continue to appeal for annexation. Its best chance came nine years later, in the form of a United States presidential election. James Polk became president in 1845 with the campaign promise of the annexation of Texas. On his last day in office, outgoing President John Tyler signed the bill annexing Texas.

Even the border between the U.S. and Mexico was in dispute. The U.S. considered the Rio Grande the border. Mexico considered it the Nueces River. General Zachary Taylor (president four years later) advanced to the Rio Grande on what he considered U.S. soil, April 25, 1846. Mexican troops crossed the Rio Grande and attacked and killed some of Taylor's men.

When the United States annexed the Republic of Texas in 1845, its border dispute with Mexico was now the nation's problem. The landmass beyond Texas containing the future states of Arizona, New Mexico, Nevada, California, and parts of Utah and Colorado, while belonging to Mexico, couldn't be held by Mexico. The annexation of Texas was unacceptable to Mexico, provoking the border incident, and prompting a congressional declaration of war.

Within a few months, the advent of hostilities with Mexico gave Lt. Col. Watson more serious matters to attend to than repairs of the Barracks. It was the most serious international crisis since the War of 1812. At the start of the conflict, the Marine Corps had only 63 officers and 1200 enlisted men total. This was half of the War of 1812 levels. That's the entire Marine Corps.

On May 29, 1846, two weeks into the war, the call from General Henderson came out authorizing Lt. Col. Watson and other barracks commanders to recruit "as many good men as you can without delay." Recruits were informed that the terms of enlistment would be four years for recruits, pay as a private set at $7 a month, and clothing and rations would be provided. Their duty would be "principally at sea." Barracks commanders were further informed that they should advise headquarters whether men could be more readily recruited by setting up "recruiting rendezvous in any part of the city or the vicinity."[17]

Although a recruiting rendezvous might be successful in Lowell, Massachusetts, Lt. Col. Watson thought one in Boston would not. He told his boss, General Henderson, so. Watson thought interested men in the Boston area would rather come to the Barracks to apply. Men came and signed up, so much so that the Marine Corps reached its full authorized strength by early August 1846. General Henderson authorized the closing of the recruiting stations.

But the termination of recruiting was only temporary, since in March 1847 President Polk signed legislation authorizing an increase of 12 more officers and 1000 more enlisted, in effect doubling the size of the Marine Corps, until the end of the war. This war needed men.

Indeed, General Henderson years before the war appealed for an increase in strength but was put down by the secretary of the Navy. The Navy however, now had bigger ships than it could man. The army's troop situation was no less serious. Many of the volunteers' yearlong hitches were about to expire. The situation was dire enough and Henderson had his opportunity. Congress now authorized an increase in troop strength. The legislation would expire, though, at the end of hostilities and troop strength would return to levels stipulated in the act of March 1834.[18] The act of 1834 did settle the land jurisdiction of the Marines. After the act the Marines were under naval authority and no longer under the Army while on land. But during the war, the Marines served under both the Army and the Navy.

General Henderson asked Lt. Col. Watson if he could expand recruiting efforts into other towns outside of Boston. Watson was cool to the idea and did not offer any encouragement. The war wasn't very popular locally (Texas was a world away from Massachusetts and it was a slave state) and competition by army recruiters might hamstring the corps' efforts. Furthermore, Watson opined that the corps may have to provide bounties, or bonuses, to compete, and that since the increase in corps strength levels, the corps may already have everybody who wanted in. Perhaps he grew weary of the recruitment detail. General Henderson did not agree with Lt. Col. Watson. Lt. Benjamin E. Brooke was ordered from Washington to open a recruiting station in Boston, if Watson wasn't up for it.[19] Lieutenant Brooke arrived on the scene. He opened a Boston recruiting office and enlisted forty men within four weeks. General Henderson was proven correct. Lt. Col. Watson was relieved of command. Lieutenant Brooke now assumed command of the Barracks. He continued his duties as officer in charge of the recruiting rendezvous. He also requested "field musics" to be employed to attract the attention of potential recruits. General Henderson agreed and promised to send drummers and fifers "as practicable." The success of the Boston campaign satisfied General Henderson since it showed that the corps "maintains its hold on the popular favour under discouragement and disadvantage."[20]

At the onset of the war, the Navy and Marines were tasked to blockade the coast, in the hopes that a blockade would cripple Mexico. This was no small feat, as Mexico had two coasts. With no Panama Canal, the Navy was required to round hazardous Cape Horn and back to patrol both coasts. The Navy was responsible for thousands of miles of Mexican coastline on both oceans. The California coast was also hostile shoreline during the war. Blockade duty was unenviable. Long, monotonous days, with no port calls, no natural protection from storms, were encountered frequently during this war. Without any contact with the enemy, casualties mounted from scurvy, dysentery, and yellow fever.

One thing the Marines could do that set them apart from any other branch of the service: they could land anywhere ships could anchor and launch shore boats and be a show of force.

Their mobility gave them a flexibility the Army did not possess. This in effect made their numbers appear larger than they were. The Marines' downside: ships could not spare enough of them to hold anything. The nation needed more Marines. This war was the Marines' opportunity to grow.

The manpower situation of the Marine Corps was squeezed by the decision to send two battalions to Mexico to reinforce Major General Winfield Scott's army on its march inland from Vera Cruz to Mexico City. In May 1847, General Henderson was authorized by the secretary of the Navy to organize the first of these battalions. Henderson repeated the method used during the Seminole Wars: strip the barracks in Boston, Gosport, Brooklyn, and Philadelphia of all available personnel to supply as many Marines as possible.[21] On May 18, General Henderson ordered Lt. Col. Watson to command one of these battalions. Perhaps Henderson sensed his old colleague Watson's desire to enter the fight and not be left behind. Watson proceeded to Fort Hamilton in Brooklyn, New York, accompanied by all his effective officers, two sergeants, two corporals and a number of privates. While at Ft. Hamilton, he was to await additional men coming to join his battalion. Three hundred marines gathered at Fort Hamilton under Lt. Col. Watson.[22]

The port city of Vera Cruz had to be taken in order to land the Army and Watson's men for their march inland. Vera Cruz was fortified by a sea wall and two forts to the north and south of the city. Off the coast was the Castle of Juan de Ulloa.

Off the coast of Vera Cruz, the horizon bristled with tall ships. On 9 March 1847, formerly silent U.S. naval cannons blasted away at the castle, just as the Mexicans had expected. This galvanized the defenders' attention. But it turned out to be a diversionary attack. On a strip of beach 2 miles south, 65 surfboats (although 141 surf boats were ordered) carrying 8000 soldiers, sailors, and Marines landed without opposition, the first major joint amphibious operation ever for the United States. Once consolidated, heavy fire from naval guns and shore batteries weakened the resistance of Mexican troops in the Vera Cruz Theater. Twenty days later, 29 March 1847, the city fell after extensive damage.

Two months later, on 1 June 1847, Lt. Col. Watson's men shipped out in a crowded, sweltering ship sailing slowly south bound. They arrived 28 days later at an occupied Vera Cruz. Watson's regiment disembarked and rested and acclimated for two weeks. Then they received orders to march inland under General Franklin Pierce, who would be president 1852–1856. The unit would be under General Winfield Scott's command in the expedition to Chapultepec Castle, gateway to Mexico City.[23]

Back home, the constant demand on the Charlestown barracks for Marine detachments aboard ship and for duty in Mexico compelled the shipyard to increase the use of civilian watchmen in lieu of Marines to provide yard security. They were expensive, however. The chief of yards and docks asked the commandant of the yard, Parker, whether there were any Marines to provide sentries for at least some of the posts to reduce the need and expense of the civilian watchmen. Commandant Parker noted that the continuing requirement for Marines at sea and in Mexico have left all posts in the Navy Yard to civilian watchmen except for the main gate.

During the expedition, since it was the Army's gig, the Marines were kept in reserve and protected the supply train. They persevered through bad weather, deep sand, and harassment from guerrillas. The whole expedition was very risky, and bold. Twelve thousand U.S. troops in a foreign land were up against 32,000 Mexican troops familiar with the land and used to the weather. The risk was huge of being cut off from supplies and reinforcements. Wide valleys, hot deserts and steep climbs tested the troops. In spite of all this, neither man nor beast was lost. Mexicans were defeated in a series of skirmishes and fell back to Mexico City. The expeditionary forces eventually made it to their objective: Chapultepec Castle.

The castle, which sat upon a 200-foot-high hill, was seen as an important defensive position for Mexico City. It was in use as a military academy. Defended by 400 regulars and a garrison cadet force of 100, its high walls give it its best defense. So did the causeways leading up to it, rising from the swamps surrounding the fortress.

On 12 September, a U.S. artillery barrage commenced against the castle. The barrage seized and forces, including Marines, advanced towards the castle on these causeways. The attack stalled as the men waited for assault ladders to arrive. Watson's Marines remained in a ditch along the causeway, awaiting orders. Armchair historians wonder why they didn't just go. Posterity concluded that any rash movements could have risked lives unnecessarily. Once the ladders arrived they were plentiful. Fifty men could climb side by side up the ladders and over the walls. Watson's Marines eventually climbed into the castle and captured 20 to 30 Mexican soldiers. Uncaptured Mexican forces retreated to the city. The American flag was raised over the parapet.

Field batteries attacking Mexico City needed support, so the Marines were called upon. They were in the vanguard of the assault. On 14 September the Marines entered the city. When any city's government falls, a period of lawlessness threatens the peace and well being of it inhabitants. Lt. Col. Watson's Marines were again called upon to restore order. The National Palace was being pillaged. Watson's men were sent in to stop the looting. They succeeded, and they took up residence in the "Halls of Montezuma," the same "Halls of Montezuma" in the Marines' anthem. Lt. Col. Watson was there, one of the Commanding Officers of the Boston Marine Barracks.

This exertion took a toll on Lt. Col. Watson's health. He was sent back to the states but only made it to Vera Cruz when he died on 16 November 1847. He is buried at Vera Cruz to this day. General Henderson was saddened by the loss of his friend: "The commandant of the Corps cannot feel but deeply the loss of a brother officer with whom he had served harmoniously for thirty five years."[24]

The war was over. With the end of hostilities, the United States settled into a postwar pattern that would last until the Korean War: reducing the armed forces to next to nothing. The corps and the Marine Barracks in Charlestown returned to their prewar duties. The two battalions organized for duty in Mexico were brought back to the United States and disbanded. The strength of the Marine Corps was brought to levels before the legislation of March 1847. At the Barracks, the frequent command changes ended when Captain Thomas T. English assumed command for Captain A.N. Brevort. He would command for the next five and a half years.

Focus on Boston

The transfer of Lt. Col. Watson was the first in a series of changes in the command of the Barracks. After Watson, command went to Lieutenant B.E. Brooke. Captain N.S. Waldron took over and then Captain A.N. Brevort was the commanding officer of the Marine Barracks.[25] Captain Waldron's tour was rather brief, since General Henderson designated Captain Waldron to the Second Marine Battalion to ship out to Mexico. He took four sergeants and all eligible privates with him.[26]

During the years 1847 and 1848, the Barracks complex was in a chronic state of disrepair. War money dried up. Lt. Col. Watson complained of the conditions in May 1847, Lieutenant Brooke did in October 1847, so did Captain Brevort in April 1848, and even Captain English did too in October 1848. Repairs had been made but were not enough. After Captain Brevort reported on conditions in the spring of 1848, the secretary of the Navy approved $800.

In June 1848, the end of the war drawdown of personnel to act of 1834 levels caused General Henderson to order the closure of Boston's recruiting station. Recruiting at the Barracks also ceased and reenlistments were referred to headquarters.

The Marine Barracks could focus on its principal function of guarding the Navy Yard and supplying Marines for detachments aboard ships serviced at the Charlestown Navy Yard. Near the end of 1848, reenlistments had enabled Captain English to increase the strength of the Barracks to eight sergeants, two corporals, one drummer, two fifers and twenty-seven privates. Captain English could recruit fourteen more men in 1849.[27] However, Commodore Downes couldn't have as many guard posts as he would like due to the tight personnel ceilings established by Marine Corps headquarters.

Commodore Downes had been shut down before in his desire for more Marines to guard the gates at his shipyard. Captain English had been resisting his requests for more Marines to man these posts. In March 1850, this time Downes knew more Marines have been recruited. Although relations between Captain English and Commodore Downes were amicable, English did it again. He denied Downes any Marines.

General Henderson was even drawn into the controversy. Captain English replied that although more Marines had been recruited, the newer recruits were not adequately trained for sentry duty. Furthermore, should the need arise to provide ships' detachments, which was a distinct possibility, the sentry responsibilities may not be met. Henderson agreed with Captain English. The problem was resolved two months later in May 1850, when the USS *Ohio* arrived at the yard and its 51 Marines were transferred to the Barracks.[28]

Commodore Downes has always preferred Marines on guard posts to civilian watchmen. In August 1851, a civilian watchman broke into an officer's quarters and stole jewelry and other valuables. This galvanized his longstanding beliefs. Naturally Downes wanted the six posts manned by Marines. He felt that government property would be safer with Marines on guard.[29]

William Smith was discharged back in November 1848. Seven months later he approached Captain English requesting reenlistment. Smith was strong, healthy, and of good character, but he was 48 years old. Others were allowed to reenlist despite some physical disabilities and age. This case would need a call from headquarters. General Henderson heeded the request and approved the reenlistment.[30]

A corporal of the guard was in charge of Marines on police detail. Word got back that Marines on police detail ventured out of the yard for drinks. This occurred on several occasions. Worse, the corporal accompanied them on several occasions. Another noncommissioned officer was caught drunk on duty on two separate occasions within two months. Both of these cases needed to be reported to Marine Corps Headquarters. In each case, Captain English reduced the noncommissioned officers in rank.[31]

Supplies were plentiful from 1849 to 1852. In one instance, the quartermaster of the Marine Corps sent a bulk load of uniforms to the Barracks. They sat there in their boxes. But if and when recruiting ever resumed, Captain English was able to provide proper uniform clothing for all new recruits.[32]

The Marine Corps also began a program to replace the flintlock muskets with the latest percussion fire rifles. Flintlocks produced a flint-on-steel spark that lit an exposed pan of gunpowder, which in turn lit the main powder charge, firing the projectile. If it is windy or rainy or both, the system loses reliability. A percussion cap is a very small copper cylinder with a closed end filled with shock sensitive explosive placed on a hollow metal nipple on the rear end of the gun barrel. A hammer strikes the cap and ignites the explosive primer. This was a crucial invention that enabled muzzle loading (to load a round through the front of a gun barrel) firearms to fire in any kind of weather. The Barracks received its new weapons in July 1851.[33]

From 1849 to 1852, there were no substantial improvements or alterations to the structure or grounds of the Marine Barracks. Some minor repairs to the stairway were done. To remove stale air from the squad bays, ventilators were installed. New curtains and some new furniture augmented the commanding officers' office. Drainage improvements were made to the parade field to correct some severe water seepage problems.[34]

Anthony Burns was on the lam for committing a federal crime. To the relief of many he was captured in Boston. This was 1854. And his federal crime was that he was an escaped slave. In 1853 he left his owner and boarded a ship bound for Boston. In 1853, if you escaped slavery successfully, you were free. The Fugitive Slave Act of 1854 was meant to fix that. This became law while Burns was living and working in Boston. Perhaps living in daily dread, he was eventually discovered. Moreover, he was caught in an abolitionist stronghold.

Fortunately this is the United States and he had a right to a fair trial. Or citizens of the United States did anyway. A federal court had to decide whether Anthony Burns had rights, or was chattel, the property of a citizen. The court ruled that he was the property of an aggrieved citizen and must return to slavery. Its hands were tied by the new federal law. Emotions burst into the streets and onto the editorial pages of newspapers. The case of Anthony Burns became a *cause célèbre*.

Anthony Burns needed security. Either for his well-being or to make sure he made it back to servitude, or for show, or for all three, lots of security was provided. To provide his security, the entire Boston police force and the National Guard were called up. Also thrown into the mix, a detachment of Marines from the Charlestown Barracks helped to provide even more security.[35] They came under orders from President Franklin Pierce, a veteran of the Mexican War. President Pierce was the general that Lt. Col. Watson was under during the march to Mexico City. He was virtually their old boss turned president. Pierce gained the presidency by being a northerner from New Hampshire with southern sympathies, and a veteran.

The Fugitive Slave Act of 1854 required all states to return escaped slaves to their owners. Since the colonial days, if escaped slaves made it out of slavery jurisdictions, they were free, and slave owners took a loss. Recently, abolitionists used this to fight slavery. This act was the counter move to that strategy by a Congress with southerly leanings. President Pierce was enforcing this new federal law. Its enforcement also helped avoid war that more and more people were dreading. The heavy security presence by all the local, state, and national authorities may seem like overkill, but on June 2, 1854, 50,000 Bostonians witnessed Anthony Burns being escorted in heavy iron shackles to an awaiting ship on the waterfront.

All was not lost or forgotten for Anthony Burns. After the roller coaster emotional ride the Boston area had experienced, a church soon raised $1,300 to purchase his freedom. In less than a year, Anthony Burns was back in Boston as a free man, to the cheers of multitudes of Bostonians. The Dred Scott Decision was to come three years later.

Facilities problems continued into the 1860's. Major Reynolds complained in a letter to the quartermaster of the Marine Corps about the poor condition of the buildings. He was particularly concerned with appearance and condition of the commanding officer's quarters. He stated that his predecessor had the east parlor tea room papered with "the most grotesque figures you could imagine rendering the apartment exceedingly gloomy." He added that the furniture in the second floor chamber was totally out of place of that which would be expected in an officer's quarters.[36]

In October 1861, Major Reynolds informed the quartermaster of the Marine Corps of his recommendations for the location of gas pipes and gas fixtures for the east wing officer's quarters and the enlisted men's barracks. He also provided estimates for two cooking ranges to be installed in these officer's quarters. He further recommended that the installation of the water system be postponed due to the great expense it would incur since Charlestown was not supplied water beyond that amount which was required for use in the event of fire. There was water in pipes throughout Charlestown, but it only in quantities, pressure, and quality to fight fires. He felt it would be better to wait until the city was able to supply water for all needs.[37]

Part II—Adolescence

4. The Nation Splits Apart

By 1863, the war blossomed into the full-scale blood bath that permanently scarred the nation

A war between the states was dreaded for decades. To put off that problem, the Mason Dixon line was established separating the "North" from the "South," not unlike a shared bedroom with a white line running down the middle. It was a stable solution. But new western lands kept opening up in both the Southwest and the Northwest, and not simultaneously either, rocking a tippy boat low to its gunnels in deep water.

The Fugitive Slave Act was enacted, not to be mean, but to put off an eerily more likely conflict. Kansas and Missouri got an early start on the war. It was distant bushwhacking from Boston's point of view, but horsemen riding through remote villages burning, taking, and killing was brutal stuff.

New western lands coming down decidedly as free states or slave states threatened to tip the democratic balance irreversibly one way or another, forever dooming the new nation as one or the other. Every next thing could decide the ultimate future of the United States. Both sides fully believed they were defending freedom, but from completely different points of view. Compromise wore out its welcome.

The most influential southerners felt the balance was tipping against them. Firebrands awaiting orders to fire those cannons with lanyard in hand blasted away at a lone Union outpost in a southern stronghold.

Batteries of cannons unleashing fire upon Fort Sumter flipped a switch in the minds of every single American, even the unfree. The colossal North, with its modern factories manned by a teeming volunteer immigrant labor force capable of producing a world class output of finished goods, like war materiel, would begin the monumental labors of preparing for war. The South's fixed nonvolunteer labor force mostly continued in its inflexible toils of tending a cash crop of raw goods.

For the smaller of two belligerent parties to strike first is not unusual in history. Japan struck at the U.S. Navy's large number of "eggs in one basket" at Pearl Harbor. Germany in both world wars struck at Russia quick, hoping to subdue it before it could throw its vast population back at Germany. Even America in the early 1980's endured dialogue considering an American nuclear first strike on perceived superior Soviet missile forces.

So the die was cast. Let's get it over with was probably on somebody's mind. The mundane tasks of organizing for total war on a local level began at first in meetings. Recruitment drives needed to be organized.

Methods of military recruiting and administration by the middle of the 19th century were amateurish, haphazard, inefficient, and obsolete for the modern needs of the once federal, now Union, forces. Since contemporaries understandably did not know just what kind of new war this would be, they used standard, accustomed, and practiced recruiting methods at first. Conscription was tried, but it was not very effective. New modifications to recruitment since the last war, such as commutation money, bounties, bargaining in substitutes and irregular recruiting complicated the Union efforts to administer a proper recruiting effort. Two clauses in the Conscription Act also caused unforeseen and considerable problems. One clause allowed any drafted man to gain release by hiring a suitable substitute. The other allowed any draftee to buy his way out of the Army by paying $300 to the government. The value of conscription could not be measured solely by the number of men drafted. But states tried to do just that. Each state was given a quota at each call for troops. Officials tried to meet the quotas ahead of time by swelling their voluntary enlistments. The threat of a draft was an invaluable asset as a constant probe. States and cities that raised more than their share of men could credit the extras to their quota at the time of the next draft. Later, a bill passed by Congress established a system of bounty payments for one-year, two-year and three-year volunteers.[1] The major recruiting effort for the Marine Barracks was to provide Marines for the detachments aboard ship. This effort was hampered by the overall bounty program offered by the states for service in the volunteer forces for duty in Virginia. Major Reynolds complained to the commandant on December 1 1862 that the bounty given by states for volunteers caused Marines to desert for service in the volunteer units in Union forces instead. At this time Marines as well as Navy personnel were not eligible for the bounties. The rationale was that Navy and Marines aboard ships had a potential of sharing in captured prizes.[2]

With the unprecedented amount of recruiting needed for this war, desertions ballooned along with the increase. Lt. Col. Reynolds complained to the commandant that there was not enough cell space for the increasing number of captured deserters. Among other things, cells needed to hold others besides deserters.

A "riotous occurrence" took place aboard the USS *Ohio* on December 8, 1862. There were not enough cells to house these dangerous men. There were 22 mutineers and only three cells. Three prisoners were placed in cells, while nineteen prisoners were placed under a strong guard.[3]

On December 11, 1862, Lt. Col. Reynolds sent a proposal to headquarters for erecting seven cells in the basement of the Barracks in addition to one large cell capable of holding eight or ten prisoners.[4]

With the Barracks' seemingly chronic manpower shortages, these types of desertions were a huge problem. Sergeant William Baker deserted the Barracks the previous April. He also convinced his subordinates to desert with him. Noncommissioned officers (NCOs), the backbone of the Marine Corps, deserting with their men was indeed a very sobering turn of events. The Marine Corps could collapse if this happened en masse. Baker received a commission in a volunteer regiment and merely intended to increase the membership of this regiment. Sergeant Baker was charged with aiding and abetting other deserters from the Barracks. These circumstances were reported to the state adjutant general on December 15, 1862.[5]

Even with the capture of Fort Sumter in April 1861, many in the North and South still expected the war to end after one decisive battle. North and South moved volunteer green troops, many with three-month enlistments, to Virginia. Many troops were sent by train, something new. Large numbers of troops could now be transported quickly and arrive fresh and ready for battle. Spring turned to summer in Virginia with both sides now feeling they had the troop strength to make moves, especially before terms of enlistments ran out.

In July 1861, inexperienced troops from both North and South met at a stream called Bull Run. Many of these virtually untrained soldiers had veteran and experienced leadership from the Mexican War. Not all the commanders were veterans of the Mexican War, however. For hundreds of years, officers were simply the landed gentry; military experience was not a requirement. The battle was a decisive Southern victory. Marines from the Boston Marine Barracks were there. Private Abel J. Wood was captured that day. But the North wasn't going to let this battle decide the war.

Private Wood was later released on parole in Washington, North Carolina, on 15 June 1862.[6] The method of handling prisoners during the first phases of the Civil War was based on a system of exchange. Early in the war the two governments, following long established military precedent, signed a cartel, an agreement providing that at frequent intervals the governments would exchange prisoners on a man-for-man basis. There was an intricate system of values: a lieutenant was worth a certain number of privates; a colonel was worth a larger number, and so on. The bookkeeping became onerous, given the information technology of the day. Many prisoners languished in temporary conditions awaiting exchange.

By 1863, as the war blossomed into the full-scale blood bath that permanently scarred the nation, the system began to collapse. Any pre–civil war gentlemen's agreements began to look like anachronisms.[7] General U.S. Grant discontinued the practice on April 17, 1864. One catalyst was the massacre of black union soldiers at Fort Pillow in Tennessee. Grant felt that the exchange of prisoners of war only served to prolong the conflict.[8]

The war, unprecedented in North American history, indeed, in all of western history until the Great War, naturally caused personnel shortages for the Marine Barracks. Lt. Col. Reynolds told Colonel Commandant John Harris that due to so few officers at the Barracks, he found it necessary to close the mess and allow the remaining officers to take meals outside. He assured the commandant that when he had sufficient officer strength, he would again reopen the mess.[9]

The war spurred modernization, as many watershed events do, so in May 1863, water pipes were introduced throughout the Navy yard, including the Barracks, not for drinking, cooking, or bathing, but for fire protection. Two fireplugs, intended for the Barracks, were positioned one opposite each wing. The water main entered the Navy yard from Chelsea Street through the commandant's grounds to Main Avenue. The Barracks pipeline ran parallel to the Barracks grounds and connected with the main on the commandant's grounds. Lateral pipes were also introduced to all the quarters for family use.[10]

Desertions continued to be a significant problem. Replacements for the deserters from the Marine detachments aboard ships were made more difficult because the Marine Corps could not compete with the bounties offered by the Army.[11]

In the New York City draft riots 120 people were killed and 2,000 were wounded. These riots were the largest civilian insurrection in American history. That the unrest could spread locally was a genuine concern in Boston. The same conditions that caused the New York City conflagration were also present in Boston. That controversial $300 exemption payment was out of reach for thousands of immigrants.[12] A longstanding mission of the Barracks had been to provide perimeter security for the Navy yard. Any draft riots in Boston could threaten the security of the Navy yard. The commandant was fearful that the violence in New York City would spread to the Navy yard and threaten government property. Because of the urgent need for all available personnel, Lt. Col. Reynolds reduced Sgt. Cox in rank for overstaying his liberty by 24 hours. The Marines had been hard pressed and needed all personnel to be available during these dangerous times to resist threatened attacks from rioters. Sgt. Cox was an experienced artillerist and was assigned to one of the field pieces.[13]

Desertions continued to cause a quandary. An alleged deserter, Edwin French from the Marine Barracks in Portsmouth, NH, was arrested in Boston and confined at the Boston Barracks. He assertion is that he had been discharged at Portsmouth and then enlisted as a substitute in the Army, for a bounty, and then deserted and came to Boston. Lt. Col. Reynolds wrote to Lt. Col. Ward Marston, commander of the Marine Barracks in Portsmouth, NH, to verify whether he had been indeed discharged from the Marine Corps.[14]

In January 1864, three hundred Confederate prisoners arrived at the Charlestown Navy Yard. They were confined to a receiving ship, a ghostly brig docked at the yard. The prisoners awaited transfer to the Union prison camp at Fort Warren on Georges Island. Later that year, four Confederate officers and their servants arrived and were confined at the Marine Barracks until travel arrangements were made for their transfer to Fort Warren.[15] Lt. Col. Reynolds sent Lieutenant Lowny in February 1864 to visit several of the commanding officers at local army depots in the Boston Harbor area. Lowny was to ask these officers to examine their rolls and quarters of the depots to see whether any Marines showed up. They might have deserted and then enlisted the Army to avail themselves of the generous bounties.[16]

The wealthy of Boston hired agents to recruit Marines and Army soldiers. Their good intentions were to increase the available manpower for war through volunteers, hoping to make a military draft unnecessary. These wealthy men also contributed a substantial sum of money to provide additional bounties. This enabled the agents to provide an additional $150 to each Marine recruited. The agents also offered to remit to Lt. Col. Marston a further $150 for each recruit. However, Marston declined this; he felt any additional bounty should go directly to the recruit.[17]

In 1864, the War Department, fearful that the ugly draft riots would spread to other parts of the country, now allowed credit against the quotas of the states through enlistment of recruits in the Navy or Marine Corps. Many men of military service age did not want to serve in the war. Similar events repeated themselves during the Vietnam War.

Each city and town had a quota requirement to meet for the war effort. Any person recruited was subsequently counted toward this quota. Cities and towns made sure all residents were accurately counted against their quotas. Whenever a Marine was recruited, for instance, a certificate was sent to the city or town where the individual resided so that the town could be credited with the enlistment. In March 1864, Lt. Col. Marston sent one of these certificates to the board of selectman in Needham so the Town could receive credit for a person recruited at the Barracks.[18] The cities and towns that were not able to fulfill their manpower quotas resorted to hiring agents to pay bounties so that the town's quotas were met.[19]

Recruiting continued to be a major effort for the Marine Barracks, along with providing detachments for ships and shipyard security. Lt. Col. Marston wanted to set up a recruiting rendezvous in downtown Boston. He told the commandant that the Marine Corps was the only service without a recruiting station in Boston. Lt. Col. Marston wanted to send a squad of Marines in full dress with music to parade about the city to attract young men of military age. He also reported that the provost marshals of the ten districts of Massachusetts had received instructions to recruit for the Marine Corps.[20]

The Smith Affair

Bunker Hill Day, June 17, 1864, the secretary of the Navy sent a telegraph to the Marine Barracks ordering the arrest of a merchant, Franklyn W. Smith. A squad of Marines was formed and marched to the hardware store of Smith, Prother and Co. at 102 Federal Street, Boston. They battered down the door of the store, ransacked his office, forced his office safe open, and placed him under arrest. Military authorities took possession of the store. Shortly thereafter, still without a search warrant, they invaded his home on Shawmut Avenue. The home was searched thoroughly, even so far as opening the locked drawers in the desk in Smith's bedroom. The Marines also confiscated Smith's and his wife's personal mail. Smith was a prominent young merchant. Smith was not even given a chance to see his pregnant wife or put on sufficient clothing. He was dragged aboard a waiting tugboat and hauled to Fort Warren on Georges Island and confined. That afternoon, Benjamin G. Smith, brother of Franklyn, was seized in the same fashion at his home in Cambridge.[21] The morning edition of the June 20, 1864, *Boston Herald* reported that the Smith brothers had contracts with the government and that they made large sums of money in a manner that had the appearance of fraud. Senator Grimes of Iowa, in a speech to Congress, claimed the firm was swindling the government in connection with a prominent citizen of Charlestown, formerly a state senator and now holding a very important and lucrative appointment in the Navy yard. He was alleged to be communicating to the Smith brothers when his department would need supplies. When the time arrived, the firm was able to corner the market on the items and thus made a large profit.[22] The pretense for his arrest was an allegation of "fraud upon the United States." Smith, though a civilian, was ordered to report for a criminal trial by naval court-martial in Philadelphia. The Smith brothers were held in confinement and bail was fixed at $50,000, later reduced to $20,000. Surety was raised by a group of prominent businessman and they were released.[23] However, Senator Charles Sumner prevailed on President Lincoln to move the trial to Boston, where Smith would be better able to defend himself. Smith was a very astute businessman. He was also an idealist and reformer. The hostile spirit against him by the secretary of the Navy arose from his repeated and well-documented charges that officials of the Navy Department's bureaus conspired with less than honest contractors to defraud the government through exorbitant prices. He also accused Navy officials of throwing business to favored contractors. The officers in the naval bureaus were indignant that a civilian questioned their integrity. They were particularly incensed by the appearance of Smith before congressional committees and his habit of publishing and widely circulating each charge in pamphlets. The naval court-martial lasted for 115 days. Smith was found guilty and sentenced to two years' confinement and a fine of $20,000. Only the intervention of President Abraham Lincoln saved Smith from ruination. President Lincoln was unwilling to let the sentence stand and be executed, and Smith was freed.[24]

In the Rear

Captain Schererhern was a passenger on a train on his way to Boston. On his trip from Baltimore to Philadelphia, Confederate forces seized the train and captured it. He escaped with only the clothes on his back. All of his baggage on board the train was lost.[25]

Commanding officers of the Marine Barracks at Boston and Brooklyn carried on a minor feud over a carpenter in the summer of 1864. After Lt. Col. Reynolds left Boston to command the Marine Barracks in Brooklyn, NY, he requested that Private Kinzie, a carpenter by trade in Boston, be transferred to Brooklyn as well. Lt. Col. Marston resisted but Lt. Col. Reynolds persisted trying to have Kinzie transferred to Brooklyn. Kinzie was a very good carpenter and they both wanted him. He wrote a very sharp letter to the Colonel Commandant Zeilin questioning Lt. Col. Reynolds' motives.[26]

The tug of war over the carpenter continued. Private Joshua Kyle was moved from Brooklyn to Boston as Kinzie's replacement. Lt. Col. Marston doubted Kyle's competency as a carpenter. When Lt. Col. Marston interviewed Kyle, Kyle stated that he had not worked in his trade for some four years, nor had he worked as a carpenter in Brooklyn. Lt. Col. Marston wanted Kinzie to remain in Boston and said that Lt. Col. Reynolds used a careless manner to have Kinzie transferred to Brooklyn.[27] Nonetheless, On the 28 July 1864, Private Kinzie was transferred to Marine Barracks, Brooklyn.[28]

Private Reardon, a mail orderly, wrote a letter to another Marine's mother. Perhaps this Marine talked of his mother's money. Maybe so much so that Reardon tried to extort money from his mother with this letter. They pressed charges on Private Reardon for tampering with the mail.

Reardon approached Private Mather with a sealed letter addressed to Sergeant Carman (then at sea). Reardon broke open the letter. And then he read it to Private Mather. The letter was from a woman. He scored a very personal and romantic letter to read. Curiously, Reardon then asked Mather to write a letter of introduction to this woman, signing Sergeant Carman's name, and introducing Reardon to this woman instead. Reardon denied all this, but within several days he deserted.[29]

Sweltering on a dog day afternoon, August 22, 1864, Sergeant Baxter approached the officer of the day, Lieutenant Frank Webster, and asked, "Did that Dutchman report me to you?"[30] Baxter complained that men assigned to whitewash were doing a terrible job. He argued with Orderly Sergeant Kroll about the men assigned. Kroll did not like the manner that Baxter was using. Kroll then approached Lieutenant Webster. This aggravated Baxter. Lieutenant Webster, however, was able to calm things down between the two sergeants.[31]

There were occasions when enlisted men who had been "chewed out" for unsatisfactory job performance went over their officer's head for relief. On 26 August 1864, Sergeant Daniel Stoner wrote to Rear Admiral S.W. Stringham and reported that Lt. Col. Marston had called him "a damned impudent puppy." Lt. Col. Marston told Sergeant Sawyer to fall out the recruits in white trousers for parade. Sergeant Stoner interfered and subsequently took over the assignment and paraded the recruits in blue trousers instead. Lt. Col. Marston was irate when he viewed the recruits in a uniform that he had not prescribed and he verbally reprimanded Sergeant Stoner. Lt. Col. Marston also replied to Rear Admiral Stringham and explained exactly what happened.[32]

Corporal Devon from the Marine Detachment aboard the U.S. Frigate *Sabine* went out on liberty. He got very drunk in Charlestown and assaulted a policeman. He was arrested and turned over to the Marine Barracks. At the Barracks, he was confined for six days and reduced in rank by Lt. Col. Marston. R.B. Lowry, the captain of the *Sabine*, complained to Secretary of the Navy Gideon Welles that Lt. Col. Marston had no jurisdiction over Corporal Devon. He further accused Lt. Col. Marston of disrespectful and contemptuous manner and assuming authority that was not his to exercise.[33]

Major Charles G. McCawley assumed command of the Barracks on April 24, 1865. He was the son of a Marine captain commissioned in 1847. McCawley, Sr., served with Lt. Col. Watson's regiment and landed at Vera Cruz, Mexico. He was brevetted a first lieutenant on the field in the Mexican War. Major McCawley later took part in the aborted assault on Fort Sumter in 1863.[34] He went on to serve as commandant of the Marine Corps from November 1, 1876, to January 29, 1891.

Restrooms were not part of the interior of dwellings in those days. Water closets had been installed in the Barracks for the first time in December, Major McCawley reported to Major Slack, quartermaster of the Marine Corps.[35]

Sergeant Francis Broomfield reenlisted at Boston on 2 May. He had been assigned to the USS *Ohio*. Then he received orders to be the 1st sergeant aboard the USS *Canadaigua* on 13 May instead. The following day he deserted. He was found dead at a tavern just outside the Navy yard gate. Sgt. Broomfield had committed suicide. He was buried in the Naval Hospital Cemetery across the river.[36]

On 14 October 1865, Private John Weigand and Private Raupp were on perimeter security duty. They were very good friends and had served together in the war in the same regiment of volunteers.

On this late summer day, Private Weigand was accidentally shot by Private Raupp. His was rushed to the naval hospital with what turned out to be a mortal wound. He was going to die. On his death bed at the Barracks, he asked Major McCawley not to punish his friend Private Raupp. Private Weigand was buried in the Naval Hospital Cemetery.[37]

The War Is Over

The United States did what it does after a war winds down: sending everybody home, even shipyard workers. Boston Naval Shipyard was not immune to the post–Civil War decline suffered by the U.S. Navy. Many shipyards felt the harsh economic practices by the Congress and the secretary of the Navy. A congressional committee even recommended closing the Charlestown facility. The threatened closure was met with heated outcries from newspapers and the local citizenry who were most affected by the action. Cessation advocates in Congress assailed the yard's patronage practices and politics. Many did feel that politicians interfered with the hiring and firing of yard employees. But it turns out Congress did what it often does, it went into gridlock and closure was stalled. Still, the Charlestown Yard and other yards faced a significant reduction in force.[38]

In the years after the Civil War, the Marine Corps' traditional functions divided its personnel between Navy ships at sea and ten shore facilities. The Marine Barracks, Boston, was one of the eight navy yards that used Marines as garrison forces. Approximately half of the enlisted men of the Marine Corps during this period were assigned to shore duty.

Brigadier General Zeilin got an earful when Major McCawley complained that he was forced to suspend recruiting because the Barracks were too crowded. Major McCawley said that there should never be more than 200 privates living in the barracks for sanitary reasons. He had 219 privates living there. The USS *Kearsage* was scheduled to arrive at the yard, along with its Marines. He would be required to billet these Marines as well.[39]

Major McCawley requested that the Medical Department do a survey of the barracks to determine "the cause of sickness at the barracks" and what could be done about it. The surgeon reported the food served was not suitable for good health when vigorous activity was involved in the Boston climate. McCawley's response was that the rations provided were standard fare throughout the Marine Corps: soups and boiled meat. He did see room for improvement, however. The surgeon recommended a bathhouse for the enlisted men, which McCawley conceded was an excellent idea.

Major McCawley recommended to the quartermaster of the Marine Corps that a bakery be built to provide fresh bread and other baked goods.[40] On 6 March 1868, Major McCawley procured plans and estimates from the Navy yard civil engineer and forwarded them to the quartermaster of the Marine Corps. He noted that if they chose to put the bakery in above the canteen instead of in a separate building, it would be very expensive to buttress the supports for the floor over the canteen.[41] On February 8, 1868, Private John O'Shea had the night off and was on liberty. He not only spent his free time getting drunk, he got himself arrested for it. At his trial, he assaulted a policeman, right in the courtroom. The judge threw the book at him and sentenced him six months in the House of Corrections. In a letter to the commandant, Major McCawley stated that this was "another useless man sent from Philadelphia" and requested that O'Shea be discharged from the Marine Corps.[42]

Standing water in the basement festered and ripened every day. Lack of proper drainage resulted in this stagnant water. Major McCawley was convinced that this "primordial soup" was the cause of some fevers among the enlisted men. He recommended putting in new drainage pipes to Chelsea Street rather than tearing up the floors searching for the old pipes. Accurate pipe plans were virtually nonexistent. The water wouldn't go away with pumping either. The continual standing water severely damaged the furnaces, too. Worse, the prison cells were also located in the basement. A very serious health hazard indeed existed.[43]

Brigadier General Zeilin paid a visit to the Navy yard. What he noticed during his inspections were the Marines standing watch in the severe Boston weather. He inquired whether they had proper cold weather clothing. "Arctic boots" were specifically mentioned. The ones made of felt type material provided warmth and protection from cold and wet weather. Major McCawley told the general that two firms in Boston were queried and they offered to supply the "arctic boots" for $2.60 per pair.[44]

5. The Eventfulness of Peacetime

"The command was then given to advance with arms port and bayonets fixed."
—Captain Richard S. Collum

As the years passed, the state of repair of the barracks oscillated between "bubble gum" approaches and serious work, depending on the willingness to disperse funding. The quarters for the Marines, subsequently, were never able to achieve an ultimate state of repair. Small patch-up repairs were the maintenance projects. Poor original construction had been aggravated by the pattern of insufficient maintenance set in habit from back in the late 1830's. That was when strong consideration was given to relocation of the Marine Barracks to a site outside the Navy Yard.

Back in 1837, a determination was made that the Barracks needed either massive restoration or to be relocated. A building to replace it was even in the 1828 master plan for the Navy Yard. This plan involved moving the Marine Barracks outside of the Navy yard. Why? The ropewalk was expanding. And the Barracks were smack dab in the way. (A ropewalk is a building housing the manufacture of naval rope. Twisting the rope fibers and filaments to their proper strength required a building almost a quarter mile long.)

As it turned out, the only suitable site was too expensive, and plans were shelved. This was disappointing news to the Marines. This meant a new structure was not waiting in the wings.[1] Dreaming about appropriate Barracks would have to suffice.

The Boston Marines spent decades dreaming about any proper renovation. The unbelievable time came in the 1870's. It was to be a period of prosperity for Marines and their quarters. Authorization had finally been granted for additional construction on the barracks. The new construction could not be added to the existing building, however. Its foundation was junk. So the original center section of the quarters was demolished. A totally new three-story enlisted section was built in-between the officer wings.

The new Marine Barracks was now a long three-story brick structure with a cellar flanked by the three-story officer wings on the east and west ends. Unlike the appearance of the previous building, it now assumed a unified profile in elevation. It was similar in function with the commanding officer's quarters in the west wing and the junior officer's quarters in the east wing. The south elevation (front view facing the parade field) was the dominant facade of the structure and provided primary access to the barracks. The first floor of the center section elevation was a rhythmic pattern of two windows and a door. An archway that provided access through the building to a rear courtyard defined the center of the elevation on the ground floor. Also along the first story was a flat roof porch that ran the full length of the center section. Entrance to the first floor rooms was from the south facade beneath the single story canopy. The window arrangement of the two upper floors of the center section was a repetitive pattern of double-hung windows with accompanying shutters. A straight run gable was the roof system that joined the gabled roof structure of each wing. The flanking wings served as bookends to the center section. Both wings were three stories with iron railed porches on the second floor, and all windows were equipped with shutters. The only difference between the two wings rested on the ground floor with the doorway to the commanding officer's office in the west wing. Entrance to both wings was on their respective east and west elevations. There were two entrances in the east wing, one for lieutenants and one for captains. The east wing had separate dining and sleeping areas for captains and lieutenants. All building additions and alterations after this period occurred relative to this pivotal 1870 structure.[2]

The Great Boston Fire of 1872

Local situations sometimes developed which broke up the routine of guard duty. The Great Boston Fire of 1872 was one.

On November 9, a fire broke out on Summer Street in downtown Boston. It raged on, getting stronger and hotter, spreading its terrible destruction and danger. By 8 p.m. the fire was declared out of control. Boston firefighters were overwhelmed by the fire's scope. This new scope brought on other concerns as well. People had to be controlled in the fire area.

At 1:30 in the morning the call came in for a detachment of Marines to lend a hand. Captain Richard S. Collum was chosen to command 1st Lieutenants William Wallace and George Welles, three sergeants, two corporals and nineteen privates to provide fire security. The detachment marched to the Boston City Hall and reported to Mayor William Gaston for duty.

The mayor asked them to assist in maintaining order in the large fire zone in the center of the city. Captain Collum and his men were directed to march to the scene of the conflagration. The mayor also gave Captain Collum something else. He gave him discretionary power. He was to "act in the interest of the preservation of public safety and order, as he saw fit."

At 2 a.m. the Marines arrived at Milk Street. There were crowds of densely packed people. And they were in much danger from buildings ready to crumble down. After marching the detachment two hundred yards down the street, Captain Collum faced the men about, forming them in one rank extending from curb to curb. The command was then given to advance with arms port and bayonets fixed.

The men steadily moved in common time. The crowd was driven slowly back before them all the way to the junction of School and Washington Streets. Here the mob was halted and people were held in check until 9 o'clock the next morning. At 6 a.m., 1st Lieutenant J.H. Sherburne arrived on the scene with his detachment of fifteen men from the USS *Ohio*. Captain Collum sent Sherburne with ten men to the junction of School and Tremont Streets. Here Sherburne's Marines were to prevent the passage of all vehicles, and anything else they could prevent. They succeeded to Collum's satisfaction. By 9 a.m. the fire was still raging terribly on Centre Street. Collum sent his command to that quarter. Again they found it packed with people; this time the crowd was impeding the labors of the firemen besides being in great danger themselves. The Marines effectively drove the citizens to Broad Street. The men halted there until their relief arrived at high noon. It was the state militia arriving to relieve them. With their mission accomplished, the detachment returned to the barracks. This first rotation returned to the yard at noon on the 11th. Another shift was sent into the area to provide security.

The next day at 2 p.m. Collum commanded two companies under by 1st Lieutenant William Wallace and Orderly Sergeant Francis Groll of 30 men each and proceed to the sub treasury for further orders. When Wallace's and Groll's men arrived they started to take in gravity of what they were needed to do. The Marines were ordered to guard the removal of government funds from that building to the Custom House. After the funds were safely moved, Collum and his men returned to the Barracks. That same day at 5 p.m. Collum and a detachment of a sergeant, a corporal and twenty-two privates were sent to report to Postmaster William L. Burt for duty. First Lieutenant William Wallace came along.

The Marines were put on post as soon they arrived. The post office building needed security. Its rear was heavily damaged by the fire and lay open to the world. Large amounts of public property were exposed to the depredations of the lawless persons at large in the city. Sentinels were posted in the most advantageous positions with loaded muskets. The duty stood throughout the crisis. "I cannot mention too highly the valuable aid and important services, rendered by Lieutenant Wallace, throughout the whole arduous duty we have performed, and the uniformly good conduct under very trying conditions," Captain Richard S. Collum wrote.[3] Postmaster Burt sent a letter to Lt. Col. Jones several days after the fire in which he commended the actions of the Marines assigned to guard the post office during the fire. He stated, "Their discipline and soldierly bearing were marked and they performed their duties thoroughly, gaining great credit from all our citizens. Please accept for yourself, your officers and men my best wishes for your future success, and thanking you personally for having so promptly responded to my request for this service."[4]

Personnel Shortages

The Marines at the Charlestown Navy Yard spent much of their duty hours manning sentry posts, as they did throughout the nineteenth century. Insufficient numbers of Marines available complicated this primary tasking. This meant only a limited number of personnel could perform any extra duties. The pressure this strain exerted on staffing increased desertions substantially.[5] The manpower shortage during this period created other problems as well. The standing policy of headquarters was to retain recruits at a shore facility for at least a year. While on shore duty, Marines were to receive training prior to assignment to sea duty. This policy was very difficult to accomplish given the requirement for perimeter security monopolizing so much time. Little was left for drills, marksmanship training, and other pertinent subjects. Fortunately it was possible for the recruits to receive training in the use of the latest breech loading rifled musket (the weapon could be loaded from back of the gun instead of the front; rifling was an engraved swirl inside a gun barrel to spin the bullet for a more accurate shot) distributed to the Boston facility in 1870.[6]

During the twenty-five year postwar period of 1865 to 1890, four officers were usually assigned to the Barracks. In September 1882, for example, the Barracks included a lieutenant colonel, one captain, one first lieutenant and one second lieutenant. Enlisted men ebbed and flowed at about one hundred men assigned. In 1883, however, the number of enlisted men consisted of twenty noncommissioned officers and seventy-four privates.[7] The Barracks commanding officer continually complained about the inadequate numbers of Marines assigned to Boston. So much so they were compelled to use civilian watchmen to secure the Navy yard. Colonel Commandant Zeilin felt the pinch enough to bring it up to the secretary of the Navy. Zeilin let it slip that it was necessary to employ "irresponsible watchmen."[8] Perhaps he would prefer the watchmen to answer to him and his men instead of whomever. The commandant of the Marine Corps even pleaded his case to Congress. At the end of the day he was ultimately unable to persuade Congress to increase the size of the Marine Corps. Major McCawley was left but to reject requests from the Charlestown Navy Yard to staff more security posts. And officers were in short supply too. Utilizing a sergeant of the guard to perform duties of the officer of the day might help.

In 1878 the Bureau of Yard and Docks circulated a confidential memorandum to Navy yard commanders. It was a proposal to reduce the number of civilian watchmen and replace them with Marines. The bureau wanted data: surplus watchmen, and the number of Marines required to replace them. Captain Edward McCauley of the Marine Barracks was serving as acting commander of the Navy yard in absence of Commandant Parker. He was in a position to render a Marine Barracks commander's will and opinion in place of a Navy yard commander's will and opinion on the matter. He proposed to reduce the number of civilian watchmen by half, from eighteen to nine. This proposal would require fifteen Marines. Captain McCauley liked having some civilian watchmen at the main gate. They were helpful in identifying workmen entering or leaving the yard.[9]

Commandant Parker returned, and when he learned of the decision made in his absence, he reversed it. He didn't like Captain McCauley's proposal. Parker liked civilian watchmen and wanted to keep all of them. He found them to be honest and industrious individuals with a good standing in the community. They never caused any difficulties for the commandant, which he could not say for the Marines. Marines needed frequent punishment for drunkenness and neglect of duty. Parker let it be known that in his opinion, Navy yards should be regarded as civilian facilities rather than military bases: "The less of the pomp and circumstance of war we have, the better." Parker said that a response to a Yard fire does not have to be a military event. The Marines could be sent elsewhere.[10]

Perennial Discipline Solution?

Marines at the Barracks did need frequent discipline. With increased tempo as well. During a two-day period in 1873, four privates were in trouble. Two were found drunk on duty, and another cursed out a senior noncommissioned officer while drunk. The forth was caught seemingly attempting to desert while on duty as a sentry. During his shift the night of August 4 and 5, 1878, Private Burton abandoned his weapon and his post. Upon his return back to his post as a yard sentry, he was apprehended.[11]

One of the missions of the Barracks not often discussed was to provide custody of Marine and Navy prisoners, to keep them locked up at the Barracks. A small number of cells on the second floor and the basement were used to house prisoners. The ones are on the second floor were fine. The basement cells were another story. The disease-breeding standing water in the basement made this a horrifying solution. That wretched basement was smelly, dark, and cramped, and worst of all, infested with that putrid water. Prisoners would have sloshed about in the filthy stew with no escape. The officers sensed the miasma that engulfed the basement.

In the name of the humanity for the prisoners, the Navy yard commandant and the Barracks commanding officer both recommended to the secretary of the Navy that a suitable prison be constructed in Boston. Of course, funds were unavailable at that time, especially for a project as unsexy as a naval prison. So until this seemingly unlikely project took place, these cells were what the Barracks had available. Of the two sets of cells at the Barracks, the ones in the basement were considered to be the strongest. But the Medical Department frowned on those for glaring health considerations. So much so, these cells were not used and prisoners were confined in the cells on the second floor. But these cells were not intended for long-term confinement. The basement was, but it reeked of a medieval dungeon.

An escape from the second floor's less secure cells occurred in October 1873. It completely demonstrated the deficiencies in these confinement arrangements. Seaman William Walker, under sentence of a court-martial, was confined in one of the second floor cells. The prisoner cut through the door of his cell, lowered himself to the courtyard and made his way over the wall to Chelsea Street.[12]

In August 1878, a board assembled by the secretary of the Navy deemed the cells in the Marine Barracks unsuitable for lengthy confinement, in effect condemning them. But that didn't stop their use. Seven years later in 1884 all six of the Barracks cells were occupied. All prisoners were sentenced by court-martial to confinement. They needed to be put somewhere. Lt. Col. Hebb wanted one cell open and available for whatever comes up. He thought transferring several prisoners to other yards might be a good idea.[13]

Protecting Property and Lives

On 30 May 1873, a fire broke out once again in downtown Boston and this time destroyed the Globe Theater and other valuable buildings. Advancing out of control, it threatened the Boylston Market House. The City of Boston called upon the Navy yard for assistance. Two steam fire engines and a detachment of Marines were dispatched to the area and placed under the orders of the mayor. Captain Collum, 1st Lt. Wallace, 2d Lts. Shailer and Broadhead, four sergeants, three corporals and fifty-five privates, just about everybody, proceeded to the disaster area to protect property and lives, with the last fire as a blueprint. 15 men from the guard of the USS *Ohio* and 21 men from the guard of the USS *Powhatan* arrived to augment and reinforce the Marines. By orders of the chief of police, the Marines cleared Boylston Street entirely of people and formed a line at the junction of Boylston and Tremont Streets. The streets were thoroughly patrolled during the night. No other drama occurred on their watch. Mayor Henry Pierce appreciated the Marines' efforts so much that they were officially recognized and the local Marine officers were invited to a banquet at the Parker House.[14]

Private Charles Serrine was removed from the *Ohio*. He was replaced with a Marine from the Barracks on February 1873 by acting commanding officer Captain Collum. Private Serrine seemed to have "a propensity for gambling," complained the captain of the *Ohio*. Private Serrine showed up at the Barracks in the morning. By the afternoon, he was found drunk in his quarters. He was placed in confinement and his old commander, Captain Collum, opined he should be discharged from the Marine Corps as "worthless."[15]

Private Alonzo Engle was brought to Boston, convicted for desertion and was subsequently confined in the basement for 5 days on bread and water. After his release from the brig, he was placed on duty. What does he do? The day after Christmas 1874, he left his post and entered the junior officers' quarters and stole two overcoats from Captain Collum and

Captain Wallace. He attempted to scale the wall and desert, but was captured. Private Engle was brought before a general courts-martial for all this.[16]

Push and pull about post staffing was constant between the commandant of the yard and the commander of the Marine Barracks. With only 31 privates available for guard duty, Captain Pope believed he could not staff the all the desired security posts. He was forced to close two security posts. Commandant Nichols also requested guards to escort naval prisoners traveling to the federal prison in Connecticut, and the Marines couldn't do that either. So how many privates did Pope need? He said he needed at least forty more privates to man all the security posts the commandant wanted open.[17]

Lt. Col. James Jones assumed command in February 1875. At that time $88 per month was supposed to meet possible needs. Gas for lighting and water expenses ate up most of the sum and little was left for emergencies. Lt. Col. Jones insisted these limited funds were grossly insufficient.[18] He lobbied for more funds to operate and maintain the Marine facilities. He did receive $625 in March to pay outstanding bills. He chided the bean counters for calculating contingency funds for the payment of operations and maintenance expenses instead. Lt. Col. Jones felt that the Quartermaster Department was not utilizing realistic information. This situation caused great difficulty for the Marine officers charged with operating such a large facility.[19]

General Order No. 56, of April 30, authorized a locker or box for each soldier in a permanent barracks. The approved size was two feet long, one foot wide and 10 inches in height. The purpose of the locker was to store a full dress uniform. Each man had to provide his own padlock, however.[20]

Captain Joseph E. Baker was laid to rest. The funeral expenses bill came in from undertaker John E. Perry. Lt. Col. Jones forwarded his charge of $69 to the secretary of the Navy. Jones requested that it be given to the proper accountant for payment.[21]

Sutlers

Before the advent of post exchanges, the modern general stores located on any military base today, sutlers followed armies and sold provisions, beer, tobacco or anything else they could sell to the soldiers. These contractors have been part and parcel of military life dating back to Roman times.

At the Barracks, its sutler employed an agent to be the day-to-day shopkeeper. James Walker was the agent of the sutler who operated the canteen at the barracks. Walker kept the books on individuals owing money. The Marines on the list, however, staunchly denied owing the agent anything and stated that the list was false.

In June 1877, a petition was presented to Lt. Col. Jones asking for removal of Walker as agent for the sutler. Many others in the barracks also expressed a great deal of dissatisfaction about the way that Walker operated the canteen.[22] News about the problems with the Marine Barracks canteen reached the Navy Yard commandant. On 23 July Commandant Parker directed Lt. Col. Jones to investigate the situation and report to him information regarding the operations, for whom is it operated, by whom and by what authority. He also wanted to know what articles are sold and whether for cash or credit. He also wanted a full statement of all liquors, either distilled or fermented, that had been sold over the past thirty days.[23] Lt. Col. Jones replied to Commandant Parker's concerns the following day. The authority for operation of a canteen was indeed contained in Army regulations. Canteens had a purpose. Their purpose was for the sale of toiletries, tobaccos, periodicals, clothing, footwear, and spirits to the enlisted men for their necessity and comfort. This merchandise may not be available otherwise to these men whose travel is considerably restricted, and often they are far from home. The chain of authority started with a council of administration with the approval of the commanding officer. The canteen was located in the basement under the offices of the officer of the day, the same basement that was shared by the ripening sitting water that wouldn't go away and the horrifying jail cells housing prisoners languishing in squalor.

The sutler herself was Jane Dulany, widow of Colonel William Dulany, and she resided in Baltimore, Maryland. James Walker was from Boston and was appointed by Dulany to be her agent, and he operated the canteen. The canteen was only opened during the hours of 11 a.m. to 3 p.m. and closed for 15 minutes an hour. However the reliefs posted at 10 a.m. and 2 p.m. were permitted to get their refreshments before going on posts.

The items for sale in the canteen were combs, brushes, blacking for shoes, suspenders, and other articles that may be required by the men, in addition to pies, cakes, and other desserts, pending their availability. Marines were not permitted to have more than two glasses of ale at any time the canteen was opened. The articles were sold to the men on credit, which was collected by the sutler on the first payday ensuing. No one was permitted to use the canteen who was not a member of the command or the Marine detachments of the ships in the yard. In regards to credit, Lt. Col. Jones issued an order that no one should be allowed a credit exceeding one half of his monthly pay within the same month. One man's case concerned Jones. Walker had violated the order by selling goods to one man for nearly his entire month's pay.[24]

The Hebb Era

Water waste did not drain well from Captain Wallace's quarters, where his family lived and slept. The problem "caused very offensive odors producing continual headaches and nausea." He acknowledged, however, that it would be very expensive to dig up and get at the cause, and did not want to proceed with repairs until headquarters gave proper authorization. But if the problem persisted, he would have to move his family out of the quarters. He and his family were very fearful of diphtheria. Cholera also broke out sporadically but tragically in places.[25]

The plumbing was bad and only getting worse. Lt. Col. Hebb described the condition as intolerable. There was a stoppage in the cesspool. An estimate to repair the stoppage of $40 was sent to headquarters. Hebb told them he found a plumber willing to wait until July for payment when the appropriation was resolved.[26]

The parade grounds were a work in process in these early years. After heavy rains or spring thaw, the grounds were a muddy mess. Water collected; drainage was a considerable problem. In high summer July 1878 the Navy yard civil engineer, a man named White, assessed the problem. The parade ground's average grade was 4½ inches in 3 feet. But at a distance of 87 feet, this amount of fall was determined to be the cause of the washouts of the parade grounds during heavy rain. White's recommendations: either the grounds be paved with concrete, or the grade improved. While they were at it, a fall of six inches from the barracks to the crest of the slope was included to allow rain to drain away from the building. The estimated cost of the grade improvement was $1,600. The major cost was 1,434 tons of gravel at seventy-five cents per ton ($1,075.50). The remaining $525 of the estimate was to re-lay the pavement, and fill, and then sod the grassy slope.[27]

Yard Commandant Ransom ordered Lt. Col. James Jones to "discontinue the sounding of any horn or trumpet by any person of your command at any time between sunset and sunrise, and likewise dispense with all reveille and tattoo performances." Lt. Col. Jones was perhaps in great askance about how to respond to this order that basically repudiates Marine military tradition. He went to his boss for input and appealed the directive to the Navy Department.

Months later, by December, Secretary of the Navy Thompson had taken notice of the situation and asked if Commandant Ransom could please explain "what purports to be your order of July 10, 1879" and if he could clarify "under what authority & for what reasons the order was issued?" The secretary of the Navy apparently did not agree with Commandant Ransom. The secretary of the Navy then enlightened Commandant Ransom that "as the order is in violation of the Navy regulations, you will please revoke it." The debate as to whether the Navy yard carried on military airs or civilian airs continued as a constant, given the dominant presence of civilian shipyard workers.[28]

By the summer of 1880, the agent of the sutler, James Walker, turned over his keys to Lt. Col. Hebb. The agent said to Jane Dulany that he could not afford to keep it open any longer.[29]

On 4 October 1880, the commandant of the Marine Corps, Colonel McCawley, came to inspect the Navy yard. The Marines also came under his inspection. He also inspected the other Marine detachment from the United States Receiving Ship (USRS) *Wabash*, a floating barracks, the cheapest solution to Marine Barracks overflow. Fortunately, all went well. He was very pleased with his visit.[30]

The following spring in April, Colonel McCawley expressed his opinion to Lt. Col. Hebb about another matter. The numbers coming in to him about desertions from Boston, compared to other barracks on the East Coast, got his attention. He wanted to know what was going on. Hebb was ready for this. First: beer had been prohibited in the canteen. The sutler couldn't make it pay without the sale of beer. So the canteen wasn't open anymore. And the desertion rate had increased because of it. Second, an important point too, men transferred without being paid ended up leaving and owing money to the sutler. Further, Hebb saw that when the men got paid too often, they were less responsible with their money.[31]

By August, trumpeters were in very short supply. Lt. Col. Hebb had to give up his only trumpeter to the USS *Minnesota*. This left the Barracks without any bugler to sound the calls. In his view this was an intolerable situation.[32]

During October 1881, Lt. Col. Hebb was intrigued about setting up a recruiting rendezvous wherever he thought one might work the best. He liked Haymarket Square. It was a hub of public transportation. A one room in Haymarket Square was available for $20 a month. Another on the corner of Friend Street and Hanover Street was $22 a month. Lt. Col. Hebb reminded the colonel commandant that offices needed to be furnished and this one would require funding for chairs, writing desks and a stove.[33]

The Kimberly Brothers, the authorized contractor for food services, had not been paying their suppliers. These same suppliers consequently didn't want to deal with the Kimberly Brothers. That is unless Lt. Col. Hebb paid them directly, rather than through this authorized contractor. Hebb complained to Quartermaster Slack that no supplier trusted the Kimberly Brothers. He also claimed that Kimberly Brothers had allegedly swindled companies in California, too.[34]

Lt. Col. Hebb had two prisoners sentenced to one to two years in cells that were 6 feet, 11 inches long, 5 feet, 4 inches wide and 8 feet, 9 inches high. That's just over 6 by 5 feet. It was the only room a prisoner got for at least a year, in the dank, dim, swampy Barracks basement jail, illuminated by occasional gas lamps. It was truly a medieval dungeon. And it was full. In November 1881 Hebb had six of these cells, for seven prisoners. He insisted these cells were never intended for containment of prisoners for long periods of time, rather for punishment for minor offenses, and the facilities reflect that.[35]

Usually when a ship arrives at the Navy yard for long-term repairs, its Marine detachment is transferred to the Marine Barracks for duty. This was not the case when the USS *Saratoga* arrived. The Marine detachment was indeed moved to billets in the Barracks. But the commanding officer of the USS *Saratoga* wanted to retain command of these Marines. Lt. Col. Hebb complained to the commandant of the Navy yard, but he offered no help. Lt. Col. Hebb then asked the secretary of the Navy why there was no provision in the law for temporary transfer of ships' Marine detachments.[36]

In January 1882, Private Rosemond transferred from the USS *Tennessee,* took some leave and spent it in Boston. That is normal. This time though, the Barracks administration received a letter from the Boston Board of Health. It was official notification that Private Rosemond was hospitalized at the Boston Smallpox Hospital.

Alarmed, Hebb responded by requesting that the yard surgeon provide vaccinations for all members of the Marine Barracks. Hebb asked the board of health in Boston for prior notification of the release of Private Rosemond. The smallpox hospital advised Hebb that upon his release, Rosemond should be given a two-week recuperative leave prior to his return to duty. Hebb promptly agreed. He notified Private Rosemond that either he take a two-week leave, or he will be hospitalized at the Chelsea Naval Hospital for the same period. Rosemond agreed and went on leave prior to returning to duty at the Barracks.[37]

Some Marines signed on and enlisted but lived in their civilian homes. Ten Marines lived in the Boston area. All ten overstayed their liberty and reported for duty under the influence of alcohol. Lt. Col. Hebb seized upon an opportunity regarding this issue. The USS *Saratoga* needed Marines, as it was ready to set sail. He knew just who to choose. For the good of these particular Marines, Hebb felt that "a change from their old associates would be beneficial to the service and themselves," and assigned them to the USS *Saratoga*. This idea came with a sacrifice. He was short of personnel and needed more personnel to fulfill his guard responsibilities for the Navy yard.[38]

The west wing junior officers' quarters continued to experience troublesome sanitary conditions and smells. The junior officers went to their boss about it in March 1882. They asked him to ask the commandant of the Navy yard to get the yard surgeon and civil engineer in to take a look and make recommendations to correct the waste drainage problems, hopefully once and for all.[39]

A year later the food service contractors Kimberly Brothers were still giving Lt. Col. Hebb problems. The Kimberly Brothers didn't have any credit with the local providers. This means the brothers couldn't get locally fresh foods. They weren't paying their local suppliers. Fresh fish, some of the best in the world, off the docks, meat, and daily baked fresh bread weren't getting to the men.

On his responsibility, Hebb went into town to get that "caught this morning fish" and those still warm loaves of bread to feed his men meals worth sticking around for, and maybe think twice about deserting. He was responsible for payment, too. Lt. Col. Hebb told his boss that the Kimberly Brothers should not have a contract. The Marines lost money on this contract.[40]

In 1880 the United States elected James A. Garfield as their next president. A veteran of the civil war, he was a general in the Union Army. His skilled oratory got him elected to the House of Representatives. Nine times. After serving in the house since 1863, in 1880 Ohio elected him to the U.S. Senate. But 1880 was also a presidential election year. The more prominent Republican candidates failed to gain critical mass support. Garfield came on as the compromise Republican candidate, which was very much Lincoln's party at the time. He went on to defeat the Democratic candidate. Garfield thus far has been the only sitting representative to be elected to the presidency.

Only months into his presidency, on 2 July 1881, President Garfield was traveling to give a speech at his alma mater. Waiting in the wings was a disillusioned federal office seeker. This office seeker's aggressive behaviors had previously gotten him banned from the White House. Unsuccessful at gaining government employment, he then stalked Garfield for weeks and began to think he needed to remove Garfield for the benefit of the Republican Party.

At 9:30 a.m. the president was walking through the Sixth Street train station in Washington, when the office seeker seized his opportunity. He shot Garfield in the back and in the arm.

All stops were pulled out for the first president shot sixteen years after Lincoln. Alexander Graham Bell specifically designed a metal detector to find the bullet in his body. It was promising and proved to work perfectly later, but this time the signals were distorted by the bedsprings. Modern medicinal techniques and practices could have saved the man. Sterilization was not fully accepted yet. Garfield became increasingly ill over the next several weeks from infections.

He spent his presidency and his summer bedridden in the White House with fever and in extreme pain. The hot, dank, Virginia summer was also weakening Garfield, who was from cooler Ohio. An airblower was installed over six tons of ice; the air was dried by being blown through a series of cotton screens and succeeded at times cooling the room 20 degrees compared to outside temperatures.

All summer long, the country and much of the world was sympathetic to the president. On 6 September the ailing president was moved to the Jersey shore for fresh air and quiet. In hours, the locals completed a special rail spur to get the president to his cottage. Thirteen days later, 19 September 1881 at 10:20 p.m. he suffered a massive heart attack and an aneurysm, following blood poisoning and pneumonia. He died two months before his fiftieth birthday. He was the second youngest president to die in office after Kennedy.

He served for only six months, from March to September. Only William Henry Harrison's presidency was shorter at 31 days.

When winter thawed in April 1882, six months after the passing of the president, the Garfield Monument Committee in Washington, D.C., began to erect a monument for the late President James A. Garfield. Lt. Col. Hebb sent $41 and listed the names of the officers and men who contributed to the memorial.[41]

The local bugler was buttonholed to teach drummers John Hughes and George Wills how to play the bugle. It wasn't going well. Since these men already had more musical ability then anybody else, Hebb requested that they be sent to Washington, D.C., for training. The steamer USS *Tallapoosa* just so happened to be bound for Washington, D.C., and was scheduled to stop in Charlestown. They could hop aboard.[42]

In April 1882, the colonel commandant of the Marine Corps received a letter from deserter Private Kenny. Filled with allegations of offenses by Lt. Col. Hebb, it "recommended an investigation of Lt. Col. Hebb's modus operandi." Hebb had his suspicions as to the letter's authenticity. He first compared the handwriting of the real Private Kenny to the handwriting on the letter signed by Private Kenny. No similarity at all. Hebb suspected Private John O'Byrne.

The letter went on about how the Marines were not being fed enough meat, the rations were of poor quality and that Hebb was substituting vegetables for meat. This was probably about the same time as the issue with the food service contractor. He did recall that when he first assumed command, the men weren't getting enough meat. Hebb denied everything; after all, he did bring it upon himself to provide for his men proper fresh local food.[43] The putrid smells in the homes of the junior officers were finally stopped in May. Gas from the main sewer line was emitting from the drains and into their living spaces. The drain line from the kitchen to the cellar was fixed.[44] That the junior officers were very relieved that the terrible smell was gone is probably an understatement. The personnel strength of the Barracks in November was reported to the commandant of the Navy yard as follows: 3 officers, 10 sergeants, 7 corporals, 1 drummer, 1 fifer and 67 privates. Also attached to the Barracks were 7 privates who were hospitalized at the Chelsea Naval Hospital.[45] Lt. Col. Hebb reported to Commandant of the Navy Yard Badger his reasons for the misconduct of so many Marines. In particular, the drunkenness, the overstaying of liberty, and the desertions, Hebb was pretty sure happened because the men were paid too frequently and there was no canteen to buy beer. Lt. Col. Hebb based his opinion on 26 years of experience in the Marine Corps. He recommended paying the men quarterly. That way they would only get drunk once instead of three times. He also indicated that since there was no canteen to buy beer or other items such as towels, blacking for their belts and brushes, they were required to purchase these items on the civilian market and thus contracted debts outside of the yard. When payday arrived, those who owed large sums tended to desert.[46]

The Marine Barracks continued recruiting. In November, Lt. Col. Hebb renewed an advertisement in the *Boston Herald* for recruits as follows: "A number of young, able bodied, unmarried men, between the ages of 21 to 35 years, for service in the U.S. Marine Corps, apply at Marine Barracks, Navy Yard, Chelsea Street, Charlestown District."[47]

Adjutant-Inspector Major Nicholson from Headquarters arrived to inspect the Marine Barracks. Some unflattering things came up, and these ruffled Lt. Col. Hebb's feathers. Major Nicholson's report alleged dirty areas and cobwebs on the ceiling. The inspector was also concerned about improper food served to the men. Again the shadows of the food service contractor were cast upon the Barracks.

Hebb responded to these findings in a letter to his boss, the colonel commandant of the Marine Corps. The inspector got it wrong, he insisted. The officer of the day routinely inspects all barracks areas on a daily basis and reports any discrepancies to the commanding officer. There have been no reports from the officer of the day finding the barracks areas other than satisfactory. Insofar as the cobwebs, he explained that these were actually small cracks in the ceiling, which looked like cobwebs. Finally, the adjutant-inspector's report contradicted the inspection reports of the commandant of the shipyard and the secretary of the navy. They both inspected the Barracks in preparation for Major Nicholson's visit several weeks prior and found everything shipshape.[48] Could Hebb have ruffled the adjutant's feathers somehow?

In December 1882 junior officers Captain Pope and Captain Wallace of the Barracks sailed the Boston Harbor. Not quite yachting season is the month of December. They docked at each of the harbor forts. Marines quartered at the Barracks needed a place to retain their proficiency with their weapons, a place to shoot their guns. But island after island turned them away. Hebb reminisced about his days on Mare Island, California. There the Marines were able to target practice and not worry about putting civilians in danger or noise. But he didn't have any place like that in the Boston environs.[49]

In December, more feathers were mussed between Hebb and yet someone else, his boss, the colonel commandant of the Marine Corps. Colonel McCawley went to his boss, the secretary of the Navy, about matters of a very serious nature against Hebb to consider.[50] Why was Hebb alienating his boss, too? James McKendry of Charlestown plied the Boston harbor in his modest boat. In the still daylight hours of 6 to 7 p.m. on March 20 one of the last days of winter, McKendry had people over to his home. Private George West, whom he knew from the yard waterfront, and Andre Hay came over for a visit. At one moment in their conversations, Private West glanced at a possibly more mature Mr. Hay, and then asked McKendry, "Can this man be trusted?" McKendry replied, "yes."

West then confided: "I have a lot of lead, at least 500 to 600 pounds at the lower sea wall of the Navy Yard." West was offering to sell it and have McKendry take it away on his boat.

West had it all figured out. He knew the guard on post, Private Cooney, and he was all right, and West would be there also. Hay turned to McKendry, "You had better not have anything to do with it." McKendry, it seems, trusted Hay's advice enough to have him over to be there for this exchange, so he declined the offer. Private West shrugged and said he would get another boatman to do it. McKendry dragged his feet until April and then reported the conversation to Hebb. The evidence was apparently strong enough for Hebb to request Private West be tried by general court-martial. He could be housed in that horrible dungeon in the basement for over a year if convicted.[51]

In May, the cellar of the men's quarters flooded for several days. This wasn't just the teeming pool of bacteria and disease languishing since the old days. A stoppage in the soil pipe leading from the enlisted men's vault into the Chelsea main sewer service caused a back up of raw sewerage. Excrement covered with grease stagnated in the vault and rose to the height of several inches.

Feeding his family on the proceeds, a contractor won the enviable job of removing this most unimaginable and disagreeable fetid waste and cleaning out the pipe. A small brick trap adjoining the kitchen was also replaced. The pipes leading to the brick trap were also replaced.

Hebb sighed in relief that they dodged an outbreak of disease because of it. He spent this money for the contractor without headquarters' prior notification, so he had to answer to Quartermaster W.B. Slack. Hebb hoped the quartermaster could understand what its like to suffer the unending, night and day, intolerable terrible smell his men had to endure to get the rest they required for the yard duties and sea duties. He had to hire the contractor on this emergency basis, as this was indeed an emergency situation. He included the plumbing contractor's bill with his letter.[52]

A father of a Marine recruit at the Marine Barracks wrote a letter to the secretary of the Navy. He accused Lt. Col. Hebb of having signed up his son while he was drunk. Hebb was frustrated. He had to respond to this tiresome situation, as the letter went to his boss's boss. His reply is that he had never enlisted or reenlisted any man who was intoxicated. To back up this case, he enclosed a letter from the Navy yard surgeon, Winslow. He examined Private Burke only minutes prior to his enlistment. The examination showed no indication of intoxication of the enlistee.[53] Hebb had to reply to accusations made by civilians in Boston if his leaders heard about it. By May 1883, fewer Marines were on hand to meet security responsibilities. Hebb asked the colonel commandant for 15 or 20 more privates to staff all the required guard posts in the Navy yard. Out of his 54 total privates, 11 were sick in the Chelsea Naval Hospital, 3 were sick in the Marine Barracks, 3 were confined, 9 were absent without leave, and 2 were cooking and couldn't be touched. Another one was on fire and lamplighter duties, and one carried meals and policed the guardroom at the Main Gate. This took 30 of these Marines off the table, leaving only 24 available for guard duty. This commandant of the Navy yard preferred Marines at the guard posts rather than civilian watchmen, and they were short one of them too.[54] There still was no canteen for the men to purchase personal items. Now that the men were only paid once a month, much to Hebb's preference, they still needed hair grease and shoe polish and they needed a place to purchase these items on a more frequent and convenient basis. Hebb requested the secretary of the Navy in July 1883 appoint a post trader to the Marine Barracks. It would improve discipline and morale, lower desertions, make the men more content, and improve reenlistment.

Lt. Col. Hebb appointed a council of administration of junior officers and senior noncommissioned officers to recommend a suitable person as the post trader. They had the job of interviewing and selecting the post trader.

The council recommended Peter Higgins, who had applied for the merchant vacancy. Hebb approved of the council's choice. The secretary of the Navy wanted to be in the loop.[55] After all, he paid the Marines and a post trader was authorized to withhold debts from this pay.

The method of payment to the post trader originated from an order Brigadier General Zeilin issued to Barracks Commander Lt. Col. McCawley in 1869. It authorized the post trader to sit at the pay table with his books and accounts. Money owed to the trader by the men would be withheld from the men's pay. An officer must witness the transaction.[56] The Barracks was short of noncommissioned officers: sergeants. Hebb requested more from the colonel commandant in July 1883. He had only 3 sergeants for guard and 2 sergeants were required on a daily basis. He was forced to substitute a corporal for the sergeant of the guard. Of the corporals, only 6 with 2 acting corporals were available for the guard, requiring 4 corporals per day. Corporals were on duty on a day on, day off basis. These guys were working a lot. Further, the enlistments of the first sergeant and the drill sergeant were due to expire at the end of July and they made it clear they would not reenlist. Sergeants and corporals were the backbone of the Barracks. They kept the organization running smooth.[57]

In July 1883, having a post trader at the Barracks became a reality when the secretary of the Navy approved the appointment of Peter Higgins. Hebb requested that the colonel commandant provide instructions for the post trader.[58] In September 1883, the yard surgeon had recommended that the men be provided with more living space. The sleeping areas were comfortable enough in August when the windows were open. In winter, however, when the windows were shut tight, the air was fetid and close. More men became sick in the winter because of this poor ventilation.

The proposed changes, however, would only provide the enlisted men with little more than half of the minimum allowance of air space adopted by the Barracks Commission in Great Britain some 20 years prior. After considering what do about this, just about all the staff could do was to move clothes back to the old clothes room, but that still left the barracks crowded. They could also move the sergeants to the upper floor to be closer to the men. They were housed in one room downstairs, too far from the troops' dormitories to provide any influence. They recommended that the opening to the new sergeants' quarters have glass doors and windows to provide better visibility to the troop areas.[59]

Recruiting continued. In October 1883, Hebb renewed the following advertisement in the *Boston Herald*, "Wanted at Marine Barracks, Navy Yard, Boston, Mass, a number of able bodied, unmarried, sober and honest men between the ages of 21 and 35 years, who can read and write to serve in the United States Marine Corps for a term of 5 years."[60]

Now the Barracks was bursting at the seams. Interested in bringing the numbers down, Hebb queried the colonel commandant whether the USS *Shenandoah* needed Marines from the Barracks. He also wanted to know whether headquarters was going to send men to the other posts and stations. If headquarters could not send recruits to other stations, the Boston Marine Barracks would need more bedsteads to sleep the many men presently located there.[61]

On October 26, Hebb volunteered the colonel commandant that he had 20 privates to for the detachment aboard the USS *Shenandoah* when it was commissioned. He added they were a batch of good ones; the newly recruited Marines were well drilled and all ready for sea duty. And Hebb would still have 50 privates left over for guard duty.[62] On November 20, the newly appointed Peter Higgins resigned as post trader. The council of administration, the junior officers and noncommissioned officers reconvened and went through another series of interviews. P.T. O'Toole rose to the top of applicants.[63] The colonel commandant of the Marine Corps took Hebb up on his offer of men. The commandant assigned the recruits to sea duty with the USS *Shenandoah*. He also sent some to other posts. This sent staff numbers plummeting at the Marine Barracks in Boston and now it was short of privates. Hebb asked for at least ten more privates for guard duty. He would not have any new recruits trained and ready for duty for at least three or four more weeks.[64]

Captain R.C. Mead submitted his morning report. Hebb sent it back. He questioned its accuracy, and he wanted it corrected. Captain Mead must have been miffed. He disagreed and huffed, "It suits me, you may write anything that you chose there," and continued, "I write my own reports and will not be dictated to by you as to what I should write." Hebb brought the secretary of the Navy in on this situation.[65]

The tiff between Captain Meade and Lt. Col. Hebb was resolved. Hebb appointed 1st Lt. Elliot and 1st Lt. Spicer to a board of survey. They were to determine disposition of furniture in Captain's Meade's living quarters. Captain Meade vacated his quarters and was transferred.[66] On June 12, 1884, Private Philip Robinson was crushed to death at the public bathhouse float near the Washington Avenue Bridge. How does one become crushed at a public bathhouse? It is likely when the floating dock came back together with the secured dock, perhaps Private Robinson was in between the two. City officials determined the death to be accidental.[67] Hebb passed along the city's findings to the colonel commandant.[68]

Marines transferred to the Portsmouth Marine Barracks before they cleared their debts with the post trader. Lt. Col. Hebb sent a list to the commander. On 28 June 1884, he requested that that the money be collected from these men.[69] The adjutant-inspector from headquarters was back. He was ready to do another inspection. Did he like the skirmish drills? No. However, 16 of the 28 privates were new recruits. That's most of them. And half of the new recruits were only up to 3 classes into their training and the other half had no training at all. Four more had come off guard duty that morning. Hebb told the inspector this.

The inspector also reported "the general appearance of the command was untidy." That's because the inspector asked to have the men dressed in their fatigue jackets. Again, probably exasperated, Hebb explained that the men perform all their police duties in their fatigue jackets and are more apt to soil them rather then their full or undress coats. It isn't mentioned whether this was the same adjutant-inspector as last time.[70]

5. The Eventfulness of Peacetime 53

Personnel strengths in September 1884 reached goal. Hebb asked the *Boston Herald* to discontinue the advertisement for recruits.[71]

Peter O'Toole, the appointed post trader who withstood the rigors of the board's review, was confined in a jail in Boston. From his cell, he wrote to Hebb telling him that he did not want his brother-in-law, Henry McAughre, to look out after the post trader store. Hebb was puzzled. O'Toole had selected McAughre. And the Navy Department approved O'Toole's selection.

McAughre came with papers. McAughre approached Hebb with a bill of sale. It said McAughre would pay O'Toole $300 per year for five years. Hebb fired back the transaction was a violation of the law. Hebb believed O'Toole knew that it was a violation of the law. The Council of Administration was unable to locate the books or invoices for the purchase of goods sold to the men of the Barracks. The Council of Administration then did the obvious. It recommended O'Toole's appointment as post trader be revoked.[72]

In December, after an eventful tour of duty as commander of the Barracks, Lt. Col. Hebb received orders for transfer to the Marine Barracks in Portsmouth, NH, effective 31 January 1885.

He was not happy with the orders. He gave the colonel commandant the following reasons: First, he would have completed the customary five years by May 5, 1885. Second, a move after 31 January was during the most unseasonable time of the year, especially to a place with a more rigorous climate than Boston. February was the worst time, he emphasized, for transferring a family with small children. Hebb reminded the colonel commandant of his desire to take a January vacation in Florida before the move, and that he had arrangements to be at Mount Dora in Florida by mid–January. Hebb had 5 to 6 weeks' leave saved up, as he had not taken more than six months' leave in his entire 24 years of service.[73] On March 30, 1885, the fruit of another, getting to be a habit, convening of a board to appoint a post trader was unveiled. Louis DeBock was chosen as the post trader for the Marine Barracks.[74]

6. Progress Marches On with New Commands

"...by those who wish to dine in a button-up coat."
—Colonel Clement C. Hebb

Lt. Col. J. L. Broome assumed command of the Marine Barracks, Boston, on February 2, 1885.[1] During the Civil War, Broome served under Admiral Farragut with the Western Gulf of Mexico Blockading Squadron. Broome commanded the four-company battalion, which included 300 Marines. Back on April 29, 1862, Broom's battalion landed at New Orleans. They raised the Union flag at the customhouse and they held it until the Army arrived.[2]

Lt. Col. Broome wasted little time finagling orders to ship out when a rebellion began in Panama. He asked the secretary of the Navy to be given command of one of the battalions preparing for service in Panama. His reasons included: He had more official letters of thanks than all the other officers in the Marine Corps. The late Admiral Farragut expressed his desire that Lt. Col. Broome would one day command the Marine Corps. He claimed that Admiral Farragut made that statement to him on his last walk he ever took on a bridge of a ship July 4, 1870, at Portsmouth, NH. Admiral Farragut died shortly thereafter. Also, he had remained on deck while wounded in not one but two different battles.[3]

When a rebellion flared up in 1885 Panama, it threatened to impede rail traffic between the Americas. It also threatened the work of the French company building the Panama Canal.

Centuries ago, Panama's position at the narrowest stretch of land between the Americas assured its importance as a gold transport route to Spain. But by the mid-nineteenth century, the exclusivity it enjoyed as an interoceanic route had waned. Steam made travel around Cape Horn more practical and the transcontinental railroad provided an overland alternative. With the success of the recently opened Suez Canal, a canal across the isthmus was the most promising path to restored prominence. Between 1863 and 1886, for twenty-three years, the isthmus had twenty-six presidents. Coups d'etat and rebellious violence had been virtually continuous.

In 1885, a revolt headed by a radical liberal general became a fight noticed by Washington with its violence and property damage, virtually destroying Colon. By April, all available Marines at Boston were ordered to Brooklyn, New York. They were to join up with Marines from other units along the East Coast. They would coalesce into two battalions and ship out to Panama.

United States forces occupied both Colon and Panama City. They guarded the railroad until Colombian forces could take over. The Marines stayed in Panama until May 1885, when Colombian troops assumed responsibility for law and order.[4]

6. Progress Marches On with New Commands

In May 1885, Captain E.C. Reid returned from duty in Panama aboard the USS *Omaha*. He had in tow his detachment of 2 officers, 4 sergeants, 3 corporals and 34 privates. But Reid left the Barracks last month on 2 April with 2 officers and 59 enlisted men. They did join up with a detachment from the USRS *Wabash,* that floating Barracks off the docks at the shipyard, of 1 sergeant, 1 corporal and 15 privates at Brooklyn, New York.

Most Marines made it back home but not Private J.C. Murray. Murray was left behind in Brooklyn. He couldn't leave Brooklyn, as he was confined there. He was awaiting trial for the murder of a seaman in Panama.

Other than that, Captain Reid said that he could not speak highly enough about the men under his command, Company D, 2nd Battalion. He commended the noncommissioned officers most highly. The only reportable incident was that three Marines got drunk and became in dereliction of duty.[5] Lt. Col. Broome requested 30 more Marines to be assigned to the Barracks for use as guards. It was June and time for the Bunker Hill Day parade. He asked for some Marines to participate in that annual anniversary celebration of the Battle of Bunker Hill. He stated that many high city, state and local officials would be there. It behooved the Barracks to be there, as it would be most beneficial to the image of the Marine Corps.[6]

With preparations well under way for the parade, suddenly twenty-six Marines were abruptly sent to the yard doctor's office. Speculation was of a cholera outbreak at the Boston Marine Barracks.

The Marines did not participate in battalion drills in preparation for the Bunker Hill Day parade. Since the Marines were not in the parade, the mayor was upset and people were very disappointed. The outbreak panic and its effect on the festivities caught newspaper attention. Boston newspapers reported this large number of sick Marines probably in alarmist tones to all. The story came to the attention of the colonel commandant. His office dashed off a telegram asking why so many Marines were affected in mid June 1885.

Broome reported that 26 men were indeed taken to the doctor's office at the Navy yard. That didn't necessarily mean they were all sick, it was just that Broome wanted to make sure as many Marines were checked out as possible for their well-being. Most of these men were not placed on the sick list and went back to their shift rotations. Not everybody was spared, however. Five men were indeed diagnosed with sporadic cholera. They were promptly admitted to the Chelsea Naval Hospital just across the Mystic River. The medical officer determined that the cause of the sickness was the unsanitary conditions at the Barracks, in particular the prisoners' cells.[7]

Immediately after the cholera breakout, Lt. Col. Broome assembled a panel to examine condition of the cells on 15 June 1885. Captain Reid, 1st Lt. Jackson and 2d Lt. White, the junior officers, filled out the board. They were to determine the cleanliness and any presence of foul smells in the cells. The panel was to find ways to keep the cells clean and in good condition. Also to be determined was how the prisoners were kept clean. Did they bathe regularly? How often did the prisoners change their clothes? And then there was the prison bedding. How often was it aired out and were the beds inspected on a regular basis? The Board was to compile data and report its findings.[8] The investigation singled out the night buckets. How long were they in use? Who emptied them? Were the men who emptied the buckets volunteers? Were they detailed? Or was it a punishment?

During this naval era, punishments for infractions of rules and regulations were astonishingly severe. A summary court-martial was often used as punishment. Convicts could be confined on bread and water, with a full meal only on every third day. If that wasn't enough, the prisoner could be kept in two sets of irons for the period of confinement.[9]

July 1885 Lt. Col. Broome could use more bodies. Broome asked headquarters for 25 more privates to be able to man all the guard posts. Five Marines were transferring to the USRS *Wabash* and shipping out with the USS *New Hampshire*. And then there were ones who were on the rolls but not there. The deserters—6 or 7 deserters further depleted the existing strength. With hat in hand, Broome suggested he could man all the posts by August 1 if his request for personnel were granted.[10]

The colonel commandant basically said to Broome that if you want more Marines, recruit them yourself. And don't ask for any from other posts. They are struggling too. To give Broome something, McCawley gave him authority to advertise for more recruits.[11] Broome ran with it. He advertised in the *Boston Herald* on July 27: "Recruits for the United States Marine Corps, unmarried, able bodied men to enlist for 5 years. Only those of sober habits, who can read and write English will be enlisted."[12] Recruiting went very well. In fact, by the end of September, recruiting was suspended because the Barracks had run out uniforms. The advertisement in the *Boston Herald* was suspended until further notice.[13]

Chelsea Street brought Charlestown to the bridge over the Mystic River to Chelsea. It was a busy street in its time. So much so that horse drawn street cars, trolleys on rails pulled by horses, carried people up and down Chelsea Street. In modern times, it is that quiet street in between the Barracks and the Mystic River Bridge.

These horse drawn trolleys passed close to the rear of the Barracks property. That's life in the big city. But there was a slight rise on Chelsea Street immediately behind the commandant's house. This slight rise was locally referred to as Commodore's Hill. Trolley operators had a habit of speeding down the rise past the Barracks. Horse drawn trolleys were speeding in front of the barracks. Broome thought the drivers were operating the trains in a very dangerous manner.

He brought this to the attention of Charles Powers, the president of the Middlesex Railroad Company. Broome told him his drivers were speeding down Commodore's Hill on Chelsea Street endangering people in the area. Broome wanted the drivers to operate the trains at a more moderate speed. He advised Powers that if he observed trolley drivers operating in a dangerous manner, he would arrest them and confine them until civilian authorities interceded.[14] The prison cells at the Barracks were always full of prisoners serving sentences of courts-martial. In November 1886, Broome reported that all six cells were full. No vacancy. Four were confined serving sentences of general courts-martial and two were serving sentences of summary courts-martial. He reported to Commandant of the Navy Yard L.A. Kimberly that he would have to relocate the summary courts-martial prisoners to a temporary location in case more prisoners need confinement.[15]

The Naval Prison

In 1886, the solution for the lack of cell space for prisoners was nearing completion. Building 38, built in 1854 for use as a packing house and cooperage, was converted and ready to house prisoners in six months.[16] There were lots of details to tend to: security, maintenance, oh, and staffing. Broome provided the staffing numbers—how many non-commissioned officers and privates would be required to provide security for the new prison in the Charlestown Navy Yard—to headquarters. He saw that the floors were made of wood boards instead of an iron floor with a wood overlay. The prisoners could cut through the wood and escape through the cellar he thought. Because the "prison was so flimsy, the physical force of the guards must be depended upon rather the strength of construction. Due to this construction reality, Broome submitted that one officer, one provost sergeant, one sergeant of the guard, three corporals and 30 privates were required. If, however, the prison were more structurally secure with stronger windows, floors and walls, it would only require 15 privates, not 30. The guards could be detailed from the Barracks on a daily basis. The recommendation for a commissioned officer be on duty with the guard at all times would require two more officers to be assigned to the Marine Barracks. No room was available for them at the Barracks, but they could be billeted off base.

With a secure exercise area, guards would not have to carry rifles. If the prisoners were taken outside for exercise, guards would need rifles and could endanger bystanders should a prisoner attempt to escape. So he recommended a proper exercise yard be added with the following dimensions, 80 feet long, 20 feet wide, with a wall from 18 to 20 feet high.

He thought guards should carry muskets at guard mount. While on post inside the prison, they should carry side arms. Side arms were reserved for noncommissioned officers, officers and those of rank or position. So only the most select guards could be used inside the prison. Meals for the prisoners could be prepared at the Barracks mess with an alternate galley in the prison.[17] Broome was still trying to get the pension that was offered by Congress for those who served in the war with Mexico forty years before. He wrote to the colonel commandant in February 1887 and reiterated his service in that campaign. He noted that he had served as a 2nd lieutenant in Company F of the Marine regiment commanded by Colonel John Harris.[18] Lt. Col. Broome had 18 privates sick in the naval hospital. This left him very short of personnel. Decoration Day was coming and the Marines were scheduled to march in the parade. But with 18 privates down, few were left to assemble. Broome was anxious to have a battalion for the parade and make a good appearance. The parades were a really big deal in Charlestown and Chelsea, and went over really well. It would be a shame and a missed opportunity to keep the enthusiasm alive in case recruiting comes up to not march in the parade.

The 1886 Bunker Hill Day was a grand one. Charlestown got the Salem Cadet Band to march in its parade. The Barracks helped out and had the band report to the Barracks where these youngsters got to hang out with the Marines all day long. Charlestown later provided an "elegant" collation for the Marines at Monument House to show their appreciation of the Marines' contribution to the big event that kept attention on their city. The City of Chelsea also employed a first class band, which also stayed with the Marines throughout the day. Chelsea provided a lavish banquet at the G.A.R. (Grand Army of the Republic) Hall. Marines were seated handsomely at decorated tables and were waited on by the women of Chelsea. Broome made sure he let the colonel commandant know of all this gratitude. He felt it was very important to gratify the wishes of the people in this area. The Marines should make a good turnout, which was why he needed more personnel.[19]

Broome's request for more personnel was met by this response received May 18. Was there was an epidemic in Boston? So many Marines were in the naval hospital. Oh those men? Some men sick in the hospital regularly go out on convalescent leave, get drunk, and get involved in riotous conduct. The commandant of the Navy yard did, however, authorize Broome to arrest any sick Marines found out in the streets. He felt this incentive might hasten their recovery in the hospital and would prevent them from getting hold of liquor, which tended to delay their recovery.[20]

The parade grounds were looking threadbare. He asked the quartermaster for permission to purchase 150 pounds of fertilizer. There were too many bare patches of grass all over the parade grounds. The fertilizer he wanted to use was the same stuff used on the Boston Common and the Public Gardens, and these areas were wonderful show places in Boston. He wanted the parade grounds to be as well kept as those areas.[21]

Broome was unable to get enough recruits just by advertising in the Boston newspapers. Over the last period of advertising, only one recruit was enlisted. He felt it would be more effective to set up a recruiting office in Boston with the services of an attending examining surgeon. After all it was the eighties. Broome felt that the Marines could get 20 or 30 applicants a day and be able to select 2 or 3 men per day. He assured the colonel commandant that he would provide his personal attention to the matter.[22]

Private Louis Guyor was received from the USS *New Hampshire* with a bad character report. He earned the label "liberty breaker." He has been arrested for drunk and disorderly conduct on the streets of Boston and was confined by civil authorities. Earlier correspondence with headquarters had noted his bad character paper trail. The letter from the colonel commandant was read to Private Guyor and he was counseled that he must behave. Broome considered Private Guyor to be "an utterly worthless man for the services, as he was an incorrigible drunkard and habitual liberty breaker." He recommended his discharge.[23]

Recruiting was still very slow and done the old way, through newspaper advertisings. Broome complained again to Colonel McCawley that the present recruiting program was not working. He had only 15 privates for guard duty at the time. He felt it was useless to attempt to enlist new recruits at the Barracks. They had been unable to get any suitable applicants for 63 days and there did not seem to be a scarcity of sound men in the area.[24]

The Constitutional Centennial Celebration was scheduled for Philadelphia, Pennsylvania, on 15–17 September. The Marine Corps had detailed one 1st lieutenant, 2 sergeants, 2 corporals, and 2 field musicians to participate in the celebration. Because of this large outlay of personnel coupled with the paucity of men, Broome had to cut down the number of guard posts in the Navy yard that would be manned by Marines.[25]

The lights were too low in the Barracks. Before electricity, gas lines threaded throughout the building provided indoor light. The gas pressure in these lines was too low. Broome wrote a letter to the president of Charlestown Gas Company telling him this. Repairmen from the gas company arrived at the Barracks twice but there was no improvement. The Barracks would have to use candles or oil lamps for lighting if it continued.[26]

The Barracks post trader, Louis DeBock, appointed in 1885, left Boston on August 29, 1887 on a train to New York with his wife and four children. He was scheduled to board a ship on September 3 at Jersey City to Brussels, Belgium. The chief of police of Jersey City, New Jersey, found this suspicious enough to bring to the attention of Commanding Officer Broome. No reason was ever given as to why he was leaving Boston and he did not resign as post trader.[27]

A long awaited moment in the Marine Barracks' history was near. The naval prison was almost ready for occupation. They could finally get these men out of that horrible filthy dungeon. By autumn 1887, provisions for the naval prison in the yard were being ordered. The Barracks ordered 50 sanitary buckets, 50 buckets for drinking water, 50 buckets for washing, 50 spoons, 50 small pans, 2 large mess pans, 3 large kettles and 1 large dish pan for use in the prison. Broome also asked that a sanitary sink ("a toilet") be provided for emptying the sanitary buckets each morning. Sanitary buckets were absolutely essential in the cells. The prisoners could not be removed during the nighttime hours to go to the head.[28]

On December 1, 1887, Broome reported that he had assigned a sergeant and six privates as guards at the new prison.[29] With the new prison coming a reality, the administration of the prisoners was examined. Broome asked the judge advocate general of the Navy for instructions on the proper inspection of letters written by prisoners. These letters couldn't just be handled like regular mail. Broome had to open other people's letters, something few people do. But since these people were prisoners of the U.S. Military, their rights were different. Sets of regulations for the operations of naval prisons were forwarded to the commandant of the Navy yard for his recommendations and approval.[30]

Christmas Day is a quiet and lonely day to be on guard duty. Sometimes the Christmas spirit moves people to set aside the usual rules and regulations. Sergeant of the Guard Bernard Duddy allowed a woman onto the Navy yard and into the guards' break room at the Main Gate. What's more is that Sergeant Duddy allowed Private Long to leave his guard duty post and visit this woman in the break room. Officer of the Day 1st Lt. H.C. Haines came down to the Main Gate to check on things. Haines must have been quite surprised to find the woman and Pvt. Long on the table in a compromising position. Subsequently, Lt. Haines placed Sergeant Duddy in confinement pending judicial action by the commanding officer.[31]

The naval prison was established in the Navy yard. This was an unbelievable and long awaited event. The prisoners could now be warehoused appropriately. At first the Barracks must have been happy to staff this facility that finally emptied the basement of prisoners.

After the newness faded and the responsibilities of running a prison became more clear, Broome found the prison increased the staffing burden on Barracks personnel. Broome complained that he was very short on personnel. He needed 3 sergeants, 6 corporals and 15 privates, and the reason for the increased requirements was the burden of the added staffing at the prison. Broome stated that he only had a sufficient number of sergeants to mount the guard and in the event of casualties or sickness, he would not have a sergeant available to fill the vacant position. He further stated that he had only 8 corporals and needed at least 6 more, and he was short 5 privates for guard duty.[32]

The need for guards at the lower end of the Navy yard became more clear, but there were barely enough Marines available to mount the guards for the present posts. Broome agreed with the commandant of the Navy yard that there certainly was a strong need for the additional posts; trespassers were very likely in that area. Adding two more posts would require all available manpower, including recruits who were not yet fully trained. To add the two additional posts would require at least 15 more privates. This was not possible to support.[33]

On January 2, 1888, Lt. Col. Broome received a letter from the missing post trader Louis DeBock. He was on a leave of absence granted by the secretary of the Navy from September 1887 to January 15, 1888. DeBock wanted an extension to April 15, 1888. Broome, who had a post trader but didn't really have a post trader, probably coolly suggested to DeBock that he must make his application to the secretary of the Navy.[34]

DeBock never returned from Belgium. Secretary of the Navy W.C. Whitney revoked his appointment as post trader. This was at the behest of the Council of Administration, which requested the revocation of his appointment after DeBock was absent for five months.[35]

On the eve of 1st Sergeant Joseph M. Cassious' retirement from the Marine Corps, Lt. Col. Broome wrote a glowing recommendation for the 1st sergeant. Broome was boundless in his recommendations of Cassious' abilities. After all, Sgt. Cassious was in charge of the Barracks' money and kept it sound. He said that 1st Sergeant Cassious should be rewarded for all attention to detail.[36]

Major Houston

It was Major George P. Houston's turn as commanding officer. First of all, he did not look at First Sergeant Cassious quite the same way as his predecessor. In fact, Major Houston asked the colonel commandant for his transfer. The major did not think he was fit enough to be the 1st sergeant of the Marine Barracks. He didn't trust him. Sgt. Cassious wanted sea duty anyway and that was all right with Major Houston.[37]

Things got intense when it was learned that Cassious had cashed check #2856. He had cashed the check and then signed a memorandum confirming receipt of the correct amount of money. First Lieutenant White and Major Houston saw the memorandum and were stunned to see Cassious had indeed signed it. First Sergeant Cassious had taken the commander's paycheck and forged the name of Major George P. Houston on it.[38] The cashier at the bank knew Cassious and stated that he had indeed presented the check for payment.

How did Cassious get the check? He also possessed the key to the commander's post office box. When Major Houston assumed command and requested a new key be made for him, Cassious retained the old key. With the old key, he was able to get access to the check.[39]

With the money in hand Cassious deserted on March 27, 1888. The following day, Major Houston placed First Sergeant Cassious under arrest. But to arrest someone they need to be accessible. Cassious was nowhere to be found. They had to search for him.

He didn't get far. Civilian authorities soon discovered Cassious in civilian clothing.[40] He was taken into custody. After he was processed and booked, Major Houston got his turn with him. He personally reduced him in rank and without missing a step, requested his discharge.[41] The Secret Service sent Detective Drummond in to investigate the forgery case. He interviewed Major Houston on April 24, 1888. The investigation revealed that the name Cassious was an alias. Cassious' real name was Joseph A. Morse.[42]

Months later Major Houston received a communication on October 11, 1888, from Owen D. Galvin, the U.S. attorney. He informed Houston that Joseph M. Morse, alias Joseph M. Cassious, had been convicted of forgery. He was sentenced to five years imprisonment at the Charlestown State Prison, not to be confused with the Navy yard prison.[43]

The body of Private Robert H. Walsh was found floating in the tidal, brackish waters of the Charles River. On May 3, 1888, the Boston police notified the Barracks about this matter. He had been dead for at least four months, the report stated. How he had met his death had not been determined. When asked to explain this to headquarters, Major Houston reported that Private Walsh had deserted on January 4, 1888.[44] That's about four months prior.

Perhaps he escaped across the marsh during low tide when he deserted. January leaves the marsh a landscape of snow and ice (accumulated snow at low tide, and then higher tide waters absorb into the snow and freeze) creating truly arctic conditions with thick chunks of ice flowing back and forth upon frigid saltwater and settling were the lowering tide leaves them. Alone and isolated in the marsh, Pvt. Walsh might have been trapped as water everywhere rose around him and lifted these mighty little icebergs. When seawater had risen to higher than a man could stand, the deadly jostling of these floating virtual rocks might have slowly crushed Pvt. Walsh in its glacial grip, and then pushed him under into the bone chilling waters below the blocks of ice all grinding together, leaving him drowning and dying a slow, cold, crushing death.

Telephones were installed for the first time at the Marine Barracks in October 1889. It was a significant improvement in communications for the Marines.[45] The Marine Corps provided men from all posts and stations to man the guard the Paris Exposition of 1889. Boston provided Sergeant Berry and 8 privates. They were ordered to proceed to Brooklyn, New York, to join with other Marines from other posts and proceed farther to the Paris Exposition.[46] The new naval prison was filling up quickly. Major Houston explained to the commandant of the Navy yard that he had 43 general courts-martial prisoners and only 41 cells available. He was forced to double up in cells 29 and 30. He stressed that it was detrimental the health of the prisoners confined in such tight quarters. He recommended the early release of some prisoners to make the necessary room. Any prisoner serving a sentence of less than a year should not be sent to the naval prison in the Charlestown Navy Yard.[47] Major Houston was sizing up his new command and his new responsibilities. The prison was a burgeoning one. Prisons have their harsh realities. Major Houston had one thrust upon him. He came in with fresh eyes and saw some crummy things. One was when prisoners were released from confinement, they owed the prison money for clothing and $2 a month for prison expenses. Major Houston thought this practice was not in the best interests of the naval service. With a little more oomph he declared, "This habit is an outrage against humanity."

The real outrage was what happens when prisoners were discharged into the City of Boston without a penny. They can only become dependent upon the State of Massachusetts for aid. The case of Private Rackliff illustrates this reality. Rackliff was discharged from the naval prison penniless. Ultimately the Commissioner of Charities classified him as a vagrant and had him returned to his family in Baltimore.

To end this inhumanity Major Houston recommended that general courts-martial prisoners be paid on discharge the full amount allowed by the sentence of the courts-martial. No checkage against their pay accounts should be allowed.[48]

A merchant, Patrick Quinn, operated a shop in Charlestown in the Navy yard area. Quinn felt persecuted enough that he complained to Major Houston. No word about the origin of all this friction. What remained for posterity to see was that Major Houston explained to the secretary of the Navy that Quinn and his wife were rather eccentric individuals. The Quinns had a particular dislike for Private Walsh, the baker at the Barracks. They promised that they would do their best to put him behind bars. Mrs. Quinn even threw kerosene on a Marine and ruined his uniform. Quinn had also written threatening letters to Captain Fagan and to Lt. Col. Houston himself stating they would do them both bodily harm. Lt. Col. Houston just placed the store out of bounds for all Marines to reduce all the drama.[49] The recruiting office downtown turned in its routine report. This one stated that a "colored man" came in to apply for enlistment on November 15, 1889. The sergeant of the office informed the surgeon, Doctor Winslow, that he had an applicant for examination. It didn't go very well.

The report contained some allegations that the surgeon did not like the man. The surgeon told him that he was not accepted. The applicant became incensed, witnesses present stated. The man said to the surgeon, "Do you reject me on account of my being a colored man?" The doctor replied, "I do not." and walked away. The applicant subsequently left the recruiting office.[50]

Hebb Era II

Colonel Clement C. Hebb returned to reassume command of the Boston Marine Barracks at the beginning of March 1890. The Barracks was at it again. Col. Hebb convened a Council of Administration to select another post trader. On March 14, 1890, the secretary of the Navy asked the board to interview Thomas F. O'Rourke of 34 Moulton Street, Charlestown, for appointment as post trader. The Council on Administration was to see if he would be a good fit and stick around.[51] Electric lighting was going in for the parade grounds and the arcade area. Hebb considered electric lighting more cost effective. For years the parade grounds were lit by gas. The gas lines grew old and unreliable. Lighting suffered. Night after night of disappointing lighting probably ground away at Hebb. The time had come. Either replace the old gas lines with new ones, or try out this intriguing new technology, at a much lower cost. He wouldn't miss the difficulties maintaining proper gas pressure.[52] The Marines at the Barracks were saddened by the death of 1st Lt. Samuel Jackson on October 27, 1890. His funeral was held at St. Paul's Church on Tremont Street in Boston. The funeral cortege included a parade of Marines marching at half step from St. Paul's Church to the Boston and Albany Railway Station. Permission was granted by the City of Boston for the funeral procession to proceed as requested.[53] Flags were flown at half-staff at the Boston Navy Yard.[54]

Leaders at the headquarters of the Marine Corps decided to discontinue the mess jacket as an authorized uniform item. Hebb wrote to the Uniform Board and requested that it not be done away with "by those who wish to dine in a button-up coat." Colonel Hebb considered these gentlemen at headquarters as the ones who wanted to do away with the mess jacket. He owned one himself, and it was quite expensive, but it was handsome and very useful. He encouraged all who wanted to wear the mess jacket to feel like they could. It was necessary for members of the British Military, and even members of the United States Army and Navy. Colonels, majors, lieutenants and officers alike delighted in wearing the mess jacket at the mess and afterwards. The mess jacket was distinctively military, he insisted. It always made the Marines stand out while serving aboard ship; indeed, it was probably the cleanest jacket they had at sea. It would be a great misfortune to discontinue its use. At the very least, those who had one should retain it with the addition of the sleeve devices as worn on the full dress, so as to have some continuity with uniforms. He ended his letter: "We should not let one barrier fall, but rather stand by our guns."[55] Colonel Hebb wanted to set up a room in the Barracks for use as a library and reading room. He wrote the quartermaster of the Marine Corps that it would be in their best interests and would provide a wholesome atmosphere for the men.[56] Payments to vendors for supplies and repairmen for maintenance were all too often very slow, since all payments had to be made through headquarters. In August 1890, Colonel Hebb told headquarters that Miss Richards, the landlord for the recruiting rendezvous office in Boston, wrote to the Barracks twice to collect the rent money for June—two months late, lawfully owed to her. This put the commanding officer in an awkward position. He felt that Richards was a very good landlord and didn't deserve this.[57] Electric lights were installed in the arcade area. These finally replaced the frequently malfunctioning gas lights in the arcade area and on the street in front of the Barracks. It was welcome news to everyone in the area when the Electric Light and Gas Company approved the installation of the new electric lights.[58] Retiring the mess dress raised many eyebrows and sent opinionated officers into gear. In response, in November 1890, headquarters wrote to all posts and stations and asked for recommendations for uniform changes. Captain Fagan replied to the invitation for recommendations as follows:

> 1. Any changes should not require a couple of baggage wagons to transport the extra uniforms of 50 Marines suddenly ordered to service, would be a change for the better. 2. The present full dress hat for officers and men should give way for a helmet. The helmet could be used by the addition of a white cover for all seasons and climate. 3. No more than 2 dark coats should be

allowed. The epaulets as now worn for enlisted men could be attached to one coat for full dress occasions. These epaulets are the great features which make a hundred Marines look in line as there were fifty more and make the round shouldered recruits in ranks appear the equal of a veteran. They could be securely fastened which now is the only objection. 4. Dark blue trousers should be worn by officers and enlisted—a welt of orange to be worn by officers and a broad stripe for sergeants. 5. The present arrangement of chevrons strips should not be interfered with and orange remain as the distinguishing color of the Marine Corps. 6. White trousers should be abolished and a white jacket be adopted for warm weather. This would avoid the distressing appearance of men on shipboard in soiled white trousers, impossible to launder properly and when called on suddenly, the men could appear instantly in showy white jackets. 7. Shoes should be fitted with buckles so that men could quickly appear in ranks in case of fire or alarm on active service. 8. The waist belt plate should have stamped on it the motto of the Corps "Semper Fidelis" and the cap device restricted to the hat. 9. On no account abolish the officer's "shell jacket." It is worn by foreign officers at state dinners and balls and is invaluable to an officer loving the military life and its amenities. The full dress device as now worn on the sleeves of the full dress coat should be permitted to be worn on the sleeves of the said jacket and a low cut vest of blue with gold cord around the edges be allowed. The mess jacket should not be made obligatory to those who prefer a buttoned up coat for eating, but it should not be abolished."[59]

Colonel Hebb received orders to be president of the Retiring Board in Philadelphia and he was detached from the Barracks July 9. Major Percival C. Pope became the new commanding officer.[60]

Major Pope

In the summertime when garbage takes on it particular inclusive and ripening smells, swill and ashes from the Barracks piled high on public carts was not getting collected. Major Pope complained to the city health department. He wanted it removed on a daily basis. To do otherwise created a health hazard on top of being absolutely unpleasant to have around. The Barracks was a large facility and generated lots of refuse.[61] The Marine Barracks historically had been strapped of men. Multiple gates requiring rotating shifts of men were a push and pull on staffing since the beginning. Ships all patched up at the shipyard and setting sail often required even more Marines. Some times the Barracks' "ship comes in" and Marines disembarking from incoming ships filled bunks and staff shore duty slots. Now naval prison staffing became a very real competitor for available Marines as well. It became a reality, just sinking in to everybody, that a prison was plunked down right here among the shipyard community, and was there to stay. It was supposed to be the solution to the Marine Barracks "dungeon." But solutions often breed problems of their own. Major Pope, having assumed command of the Barracks, also gained the naval prison's attendant responsibilities. One of them was to communicate with the secretary of the Navy concerning the conduct of a prisoner serving a sentence of general court-martial.

On Valentine's Day 1892, Private Hugh McFadden was "talking and whistling and lighting a piece of paper from a gas light" and was reported for it. Eight days later Pvt. McFadden was again "lighting a piece of paper from a gas light and being disrespectful to the corporal of the guard." Word of this behavior got to the secretary of the Navy. To paint a more complete picture of Pvt. McFadden, Major Pope also reported that his record of deportment otherwise was good.[62]

Major Pope's concerns went beyond misbehaving Marines. Misbehavior, however, is preferable to news of a death of a Marine. Private Matthew B. Ryan, USMC (Retired), living on Bunker Hill Street in Charlestown, had passed away. Major Pope sent officers from the Barracks to make a condolence call with his family and to make the necessary arrangements for a funeral. Major Pope, informed through a telegram from headquarters, that $30 was allowed for the destitute widow to help defray funeral expenses and subscription.[63] Recruitment advertisements in the newspapers asked for single men. Often, however, married men who needed work and a steady paycheck were the ones enlisting. To get the job, they felt the need to obfuscate their status. July 1892, Private James Miniham enlisted at the Barracks and stated that he was single. Then a woman showed up. She claimed to be his wife. And that he had two children. She wanted him discharged immediately because he was their only means of support. Major Pope asked the colonel commandant what he should do.[64]

Around that time 150 enlisted men lived in the Barracks. Many started to realize that the Barracks might be infested with bedbugs. The insects came out the woodwork while they were sleeping. Many suffered a lack of sleep because of them. Major Pope contacted an exterminator to start the process of trying to get rid of the pests.[65] Major Pope's tight manpower numbers were also affected by accidents. Nowadays, highway casualties are our transportation related numbers of sorrow. In the 1890's, railroads took their toll. Private Frank Horn was killed in a railroad accident in Boston. Major Pope described this in a letter to Isa A. Horn, the next of kin of Private Frank Horn. Pope's main concern was if she would like his remains or should the government provide burial for him.[66]

Distraught parents wrote to the colonel commandant when their sons did not send money home as they may have been required to do. The mother of fifer Arthur Ratcliff was destitute. He was supposed to provide support for her, explained a letter sent to the commandant. Fifer Ratcliff was remonstrated, and he pledged to send $5 a month to his mother. To ensure that Ratcliff was able to send the money to his mother, Major Pope withdrew his privileges to use the post trader.[67] Marines were not allowed to borrow or loan money because it caused all sorts of problems. Drummer Charles W. Blush came to Major Pope stating that his mother was terminally ill. He commenced to cry and asked Major Pope to loan him $10 so he could travel to his mother. Major Pope arranged to advance him $10, taken out of his next pay. Blush then went to the post trader and attempted to borrow $3. Then he went to another enlisted man and attempted to borrow $2.

Time passed. Major Pope noticed Blush had not paid his debts. The colonel commandant got wind of these things. He had heard of an order Pope gave when he took command. Something about no loaning money. Major Pope explained to the colonel commandant that he had indeed issued an order when he assumed command that forbade anyone to loan money. Further, the post trader would not be allowed to loan money. If he did then the canteen could be closed.[68]

It was a very busy time for Marines stationed at the various Navy Yards along the east coast in 1892, in a spread thin kind of way. Barracks everywhere were reduced to skeleton status because of the tremendous demands for their services in other areas of the country. A Marine guard was assigned to participate in the opening exercises of the Chicago World's Fair. The guard was to remain as a permanent guard at the Chicago Exposition during the summer months. Marines were also assigned duty at the quarantine station at Sandy Hook, New York. And all the while, the New Great White International Navy was burgeoning, built to protect and financed by the growing American commerce, now exporting its goods throughout the world. Larger, metal, steam and coal fired, freshly commissioned ships of the Navy required whole new numbers of Marines for seagoing detachments.

An 1893 *Boston Herald* recruiting advertisement in February read: "Wanted—for the U.S. Marine Corps: Sober, able-bodied, unmarried men between the ages of 21 and 25 years and from 64½" to 72" in height. Pay from $13 to $16 per month, clothed, fed and medical attendance free. The military duties are generally performed at Navy Yards and on board men-of-wars, and offer excellent opportunities for young men to travel and visit foreign countries. Recruiting office is at 6 Canal Street and Haymarket Square, Boston and the Marine Barracks in Charlestown, Mass."[69] Locating a suitable place for target practice was becoming a long, uncertain endeavor. Seems nobody wanted bullets flying around and the noise that got them there in their back yards. A site in Framingham managed by the state came up as a possible location in a letter Pope wrote to the adjutant general, Colonel William J. Chase.[70] Nothing came of it though. A suitable target practice area was eventually found in the harbor on Lovell's Island.[71] Someone must have sighed relief, as it was accessible by boat, the means of the day, and a shipyard had a few of these floating around.

Remember the trouble the horse drawn trolleys caused in front of the Barracks at Commodore's Hill? Problem solved. Electric trolley cars were introduced to Chelsea Street, or the Salem Turnpike, depending on if you are from the local area or north of Boston. Electric trolleys had more range and now Boston could be even more linked to Salem. Chelsea Street was no longer just a connection between Charlestown and Chelsea. Nor was it the lifeless alley between the great Mystic River Bridge and the Navy Yard of the 1970's. Or even the "back-to-life" feel it has today. Salem Turnpike bridged the north shore, Salem, Lynn, and even East Boston to Boston. It was an important throughway of commerce and people right in front of the Barracks.

The wires for propulsion of the trolley cars were installed on the same poles as the telephone lines. These very strong electrical currents, literally inches away from the substantially lower voltage of communications electricity, caused telephone problems. An annoying buzzing interfered with conversation when people used their telephones. Major Pope complained to the commandant of the Navy Yard.

Standard telephone technology for many years was what is generally called a "ground circuit." It works similarly to a school science class light bulb and battery circuit. When a caller picks up a receiver off a telephone cradle, it grounds and completes the circuit (turning on the light in science class) or in this case, sending a signal to the switching office. At first these were managed by the iconic telephone operators. The signal to the switching office triggered a return signal, manifested by a dial tone. After the phone number was put into the system by a caller's finger riding the rotary dial, a new circuit opened. This sent a signal back to the switching office. It had the authority to ring the bell on the receiver with that number. When that receiver was picked up, it opened that circuit, allowing for two way voice communications. Even modern technology shares the same basics. High speed Internet does the same but in nano form, and swifter transmit ions, allowing for more data in the circuits.

Major Pope wanted to change from the "ground circuit" telephone wire system to a "special metallic transmitter." This would cost $156 per year and "it would be worth it as it was necessary to have good communications." The Navy yard commandant agreed and approved the request on July 28, 1893, and Major Pope relayed the request to New England Telephone and Telegraph Company.[72] Hooligans brutally beat Private Thomas M. Walsh to an inch of his life on Chelsea Street in Charlestown, on July 26 1893. With a severely fractured skull, he later died of the injuries. His remains were transferred to the city morgue and the Barracks was later notified of his death. Two men were arrested in connection with the death of Private Walsh, as reported in the July 29 *Boston Globe*. The two men were held under $1,500 bail and charged with manslaughter.[73] When Marines were transferred and were indebted to the post trader, the commanding officer was able to correspond with the new station to require the Marine to pay his just debts. Major Pope felt that the washerwomen who did the men's laundry were entitled to the same protection. These hard working women were losing too much money when transferred Marines did not pay up on transfer, he noted in a letter to the colonel commandant. They just might quit washing. He wanted an order issued that would provide the washerwomen with the same protection regarding indebtedness as the post trader.[74] The old coal burning furnaces were filthy, labor intensive, and couldn't keep the enlisted men's quarters warm in cold weather. All the furnaces were unsafe and needed major repairs. The time had come to have the old coal furnaces removed. It was the era of steam. Steam was proven and the state of the art in interior heating. On 28 September 1893, Pope decided to install a steam heat system in the Marine Barracks. Pope quoted the estimate of $2,300 for installation to the quartermaster and said that the system had been reviewed by the yard civil engineer. The quartermaster was invited to visit the Navy yard and inspect the old system and be briefed on the new steam heat system.[75]

The latest books, magazines and newspapers were available to the men at the Barracks. Such items for the health and welfare of the men were purchased through a company fund that came from a percentage of the profits of the post trader. When command of the Barracks passed from Major Pope to acting Commander Captain Francis Harrington, the balance was receipted to Harrington and he became responsible for the $743.46 company fund.[76]

Recruiting was successful in 1893. Maybe too successful. There was no place to house all these recruits. Captain Harrington requested that 15 recruits be transferred to other posts and stations to relieve the overcrowding.[77]

Privates William H. Conway and John F. Hayes came back from liberty drunk and disorderly on December 22, 1893. Sergeant of the Guard Francis M. Fox confronted them. Belligerence reigned. He must have given them a hard time, as the misconduct report stated one of them called him "a whore's bastard!" and "a son of a bitch!" among other things. Private Conway even threatened to rip Fox open with a knife if he ever saw him on liberty.

Conway was ordered to confinement. He resisted. He became so obnoxious and violent he was placed in irons and led to the Barracks cells, the dungeon. As Sergeant Francis Fox, drummer John Hughes and acting Corporal Michael McKenna were escorting him to his cell, Conway broke out of his irons and threw a cup at a window in the cell's passageway, smashing it. Upon receipt of this information, Captain Harrington recommended that Private Conway be tried by general court-martial. That could land him in the new naval prison, a block away.[78] Recruiting throughout the Marine Corps turned out to be a very successful endeavor. Recruiting no longer needed to be pursued. Captain Harrington notified the landlord, Eugene Buckley of No. 6 Canal Street, Boston, that the rooms would not be required for enlistment offices after February 28.[79]

7. Major Meade Takes the Helm

"I respectfully decline to make myself responsible for the 'fullest success' of any untried experiment at this station."
—Major Meade

Decorated Civil War veteran Major Robert C. Meade assumed command on January 15, 1897. Back during the war thirty-four years prior, he was part of a daring night attack upon Fort Sumter on September 8, 1863. Since Sumter is accessible only by boat, that was only way to attack. And his unit attacked at night because, it being a Confederate controlled harbor, stealth and surprise were most necessary. He was brevetted there a first lieutenant for "gallant and meritorious service." But the next day, stealth and surprise proved fleeting and Confederates captured Meade and his men. From that day forward, Meade languished as a prisoner of war. He was uncertain about when he was ever, if ever, going to go home again. Men were dying there. Why not him? But December 2, 1864, after 15 months in Confederate custody, he secured release.[1] It was perhaps this memory and what he took from it that informed Major Meade to keep the barracks library well stocked with current newspapers, magazines, and pamphlets such as *Boston Herald*, *New York Herald*, *Detroit Free Press*, *Army and Navy Register*, *London Illustrated News*, *The Pilot* and many others less familiar to the modern reader. All subscriptions were paid from the Company Fund. The Marines enjoyed the library.[2] The only chaplain around on the Navy yard was Chaplain Alfred L. Royce of the U.S. Navy. But he was with the detachment from the USRS *Wabash*, the floating barracks tied up down by the docks. Major Meade asked if Chaplin Royce could perform his priestly functions at the Barracks at 2 p.m. in the Reading Room. Again possibly echoes of his prisoner of war days, he also asked if the chaplain could hold services immediately afterwards at the naval prison. Chaplain Royce was very happy to accommodate the request.[3] Recruiting had been curtailed throughout the Marine Corps. Similar to our age, as the modern military's guidelines restructure according to need, so did the Marines in contemporary times as well. Only higher quality people could pass muster and get in.

Like anything else, there were exceptions, for exceptional people. Major Meade's son, an aspiring 16 year old musician, he came of age in the life culture of the Marine Corps and desired to enlist, but he also came of age during tight recruiting times. Major Meade sought the assistance of the colonel commandant. The commandant's approval came back happily for examination by a medical officer. Accompanied by his parents, Meade's teenage son arrived at No. 6 Canal Street in Boston to start the process. This was stated in a letter to Fred Helger, 384 Huntington Avenue, Boston.

As a sort of a savings plan for the youngster, his pay would be $12.80 per month for the

1st and 2nd years, for which the government would retain $4 per month in the 1st year. Then there would be an increase of $1 per month for the 3rd year, $2 per month in the 4th year, and $3 per month in the 5th year. The government would retain all these monies until his enlistment expired. By then he would be 21 years old and an accomplished musician with money in the bank. The station for the apprentice musicians was Washington, D.C.[4] What a thrill it is hook up our households to cable TV and high speed Internet for the first time. Contemporaries were giddy with excitement anticipating the arrival of the latest means of communication, finally coming to the navy yard. And it was within the Barrack's grasp to have this latest technology. Telephones. What was its first use? This was game changing ability to communicate, and Major Meade chose to have a telephone line installed between the Barracks and the naval prison. The distance between the two locations was considerable. Communication by messenger was the Barracks' current system and it required staffing. Telephones eliminated this staffing issue. Prompt reporting of fires and other quickly unfolding occurrences were also held up as huge considerations to justify the monies spent on this luxury.[5] Three more apprentice musicians were recruited 18 February 1897. One was Charles Ruger of 547 Main Street from Woburn and the other two were from the same street in Boston, James Lee of 14 Fellows Court and James McLaughlin of 3 Fellows Court.[6] Budgets allowed recruiting to begin once again. The notice out went to the public that exams would be held at the Marine Barracks from 10 a.m. until 1 p.m. every duty day.[7] After the earlier attempts at improving the parade grounds met with mixed results, Major Meade asked the secretary of agriculture for a suitable grass seed to cover an acre of land. He wanted a seed that was both durable and would provide an attractive appearance. He also requested a few varieties of flower seeds to beautify the grounds.[8] Civilian hooligans had been tearing up the bricks from Water Street at the Main Gate and throwing them at the windows of Navy yard buildings. Major Meade went to the local police for this one. Meade submitted that the perpetrators of this destruction were civilians and therefore outside the jurisdiction of the Navy yard. The Marines couldn't act and the punks knew this. Major Meade, with hat in hand, asked Captain White of the 15th Precinct if he could take preventive measures to end these occurrences. It is uncertain what occurred next, but Meade told Captain White that if he couldn't provide a solution to this matter, non-commissioned officers could be sworn in as special constables without pay, within his authority, and do the job for them, in their own precinct.[9] For a potential enlistee, recruiting opportunities often can be boom and bust. By March, recruiting was once again on the boom pendulum swing of the cycle. The colonel commandant gave Major Meade the green light to recruit without limit. Like recruitments before, the business of recruiting required an office downtown. Meade requested a different office than last time. The last one at the No. 6 Canal Street location was too noisy for the surgeon. Recruiting gets disruptive at the Barracks.[10]

Authority to open a recruiting office somewhere else in Boston was granted. For Major Meade one office is as good as the other. Since Surgeon E.P. Stone had to work in this office, Stone was going to help Meade find another one.[11]

Ninety-eight Court Street made the final cut. Rent was $32 a month. Ninety-eight Court Street couldn't have come at a better time. They wanted to begin recruiting April 1, 1894.[12] Nobody missed the No. 6 Canal Street storefront. Advertising began in the *Boston Globe* in early April. Word needed to get out about the Marines' new location.[13] On the chilly and stormy gray seas of March 1894, Captain Harrington was en route to Norfolk, Virginia, on a Merchant and Miners Line steamer out of Boston. Making the trip even more unpleasant, about 30 Navy enlisted men were disturbing the passengers. Like they owned the place, they acted with utter disregard for rules and deportment, doing as they pleased, smoking over all parts of the ship, and taking possession of the smoking apartments to the exclusion of the 1st class passengers. These men were under the charge of Blacksmith Dixon. One man had himself locked up for the night by Captain Harrington himself. Liquor was smuggled aboard. The sailors showed no respect for Captain Harrington or Blacksmith Dixon. They congregated around the windows of the staterooms in spite of the protests of the occupants and regaled their ears with profane and obscene stories and songs. Blacksmith Dixon lamented he had no control over the men. He even had to strike a man in the main salon to enforce an order. The incident was referred to the commandant of the Navy Yard.[14] The 1st sergeant of the Barracks was ready to retire in April. Major Meade appreciated the service of First Sergeant Martin Downey. He wanted to place on record that he was a very capable, upright and most honorable soldier. Meade had the most heartfelt gratitude for his service and regretted to see him leave. Downey was from Ireland and had spent some 27 years in the United States. The Marine Corps were his life. He had made no friends outside of the corps. But he did have a brother in Ireland, and wished to live with him.[15] The Marine Corps changed the method of paying the men from cash to checks. Major Meade didn't like this one bit. He complained that he received a package of checks for payment of the troops on April 20, 1894, and that this was very annoying and inconvenient. He stated that he had never consented to this method of payment and was insulted that he was not trusted with cash. It was also foolhardy to issue individual checks to men who had never handled a check. That it involved an immense amount of labor to get the check cashed and it would make it difficult to get the men to settle up with the post trader, laundress and barber. The men needed training on how to endorse a check.[16] But the colonel commandant directed that Meade would have to accept the idea that the men would be paid by check.[17] Meade strongly protested one more time with the same points as in a previous letter to the colonel commandant.[18]

Prisoners at the naval prison were put to work. Major Meade thought this could make the prisoners feel useful, lessen the cost of their maintenance and could possibly make the prison self-sustaining.

Rumors spread that the prison employed prisoner laborers and chain gangs, and that it may be a labor camp. This attracted a congressional inquiry. Prisoners working while in confinement got the attention of Congressman W.M. Curtis of the U.S. House of Representatives. Major Meade considered the original order, which he wrote, and he defended it. The Navy yard commandant, however, promptly struck down the working requirement from the order, for he considered it "convict labor." Major Meade responded that there was no valid reason why the prisoners should not make themselves useful to the government under proper guard. He was a former war prisoner himself and might have seen things from a prisoner's point of view.

That the federal government had the same right to prevent escape of prisoners that the states possessed was also stricken from the original instruction. This meant that a loaded pistol with the authority to use it was not given to prison guards. Meade felt it was folly to give a soldier an empty rifle, and to tell him that if he loads and uses it, he is a murderer. This nullifies a soldier's usefulness as a prison guard. So any punishment given to a soldier when a prisoner escapes, under these conditions, was a rank injustice to the soldier.

The Boston Marine Barracks prison's present system of confinement without proper exercise or work wasn't as severe as the brutal solitary confinement of the Eastern Penitentiary in Philadelphia. Philadelphia was even cruel enough to damage the health of a prisoner.

Although opportunities abounded for the prisoners to read as much as they pleased, they weren't reading. Meade felt these men did not come from the classes to whom books were a solace and who never tire of reading and study. Meade was convinced prisoners wanted to work, no matter how trivial the work may be, like painting rocks for example. So he earnestly felt that some system of prisoner employment must be adopted.[19] A system of commutation of prisoners confined under the sentence of court-martial was developed by the Secretary of the Navy in the early 1890's. But providing commutations of sentences for a quarter or even a third of the detainees in the naval prison was not in the best interests of the naval service, complained Meade to the commandant of the Navy yard. Prisoners were not entitled to the clemency of the government. He gave four examples of individuals who either got into trouble or deserted shortly after their commutations by the secretary of the Navy. Prisoners began to feel it was a right and not an act of clemency to have their sentence commuted. This situation was unsettling feelings in the naval prison.[20] After a diligent search, a suitable rifle range was established on Lovell's Island in Boston Harbor. It was a fantastic range. The maximum distance was 500 yards. Meade could get the yard tug to ferry the Marines out to the island every Tuesday and Friday. He also asked colonel commandant about allowing Marines to wear their firing badges proudly on their uniforms.[21] Major Meade was not happy about how the 1894 Bunker Hill Day parade went down. Two companies of Marines from the Barracks participated in the parade, even though there was no requirement for them. The heat of that Bunker Hill Day was intense. Four Marines were stricken with heat exhaustion. Although the state of Massachusetts had a large number of militia units available to march, the units were conspicuous by their absence. The straggling, partially uniformed bodies of mostly boys were substituted instead. The civic section of the parade was composed of just a few GAR (Grand Army of the Republic) people, firemen, masons and even letter carriers. Seems only the Marines cared, he wrote to the colonel commandant.

That these two companies participated was a big deal. Usually, drills, instruction and other training occupied "day off" duty status and the off time of the Marines. If volunteers were requested for this parade, there would be none. No sailors from the Navy yard were involved in the parade. While the Marines were ready to participate in any legitimate function, "a paltry affair of this nature was beneath our dignity." The mayor of Boston did not even honor the Marines with the courtesy of determining whether it was possible for Marines to participate before writing to the Bureau of Navigation.[22] On July 13, 1894, authorities overlapped when the sergeant of the guard at the Main Gate thought the Navy yard captain of the watch had interfered with his duties.[23] A clarification was in order. Here is the attempt: For any violation of orders or regulations relating to persons or property coming and going through the Main Gate, the captain of the watch should report to the captain of the yard. This was a general order issued the following day by the captain of the yard, Captain Albert Kantz. In the absence of the captain of the watch, the noncommissioned officer at the Main Gate (the sergeant of the guard) will then be responsible for enforcement of the regulations. The captain of the watch and the noncommissioned officer on duty were both admonished that wrangling is not in the best interests of anything and that punishment will come swiftly.[24] The replacement of the obsolete hot air heating system was underway. The specifications for installation of a steam heating system were forwarded to the quartermaster on July 23, 1894. A few days later, the bid of Lynch and Woodrow was forwarded to headquarters for approval.[25] The twice weekly boat trips to Lovell's Island for target practice sounded great on paper but in practice it did not always work out. Weather may be great on Thursday but not on Friday for example.

7. Major Meade Takes the Helm

The Marines had a great place for target practice, but they couldn't get there. Meade requested on August 22, 1894, that yard boat transportation to Lovell's Island be provided as many times per week as possible.[26] The new toilets installed in the barracks were a huge improvement, but not all the bugs had worked themselves out yet. A simple thing we take for granted: toilet paper, people were not accustomed to yet. They were not ready to buy and pay the high cost of the toilet paper, nor were they ready to understand the necessity of having it and using it. Only toilet paper, called water closet paper back then, could be flushed down the toilet without causing expensive stoppage clearing. If anything else was used, the result was massive clogs of the sewer pipes. The Barracks was forced to purchase for the first time toilet paper for use from monies in the Company Fund. Meade recommended that toilet paper be purchased by the quartermaster and issued to the Barracks.[27] Men sleeping at the Barracks longed for completion of the steam heating system. But to some military contractors, the steady "endless work" was longed for. Lynch and Woodrow were making modifications to the project as they went along. More and more, it got to the point that Major Meade had to warn them that if they kept this up, the Barracks would have to stop work on the job. Or they could continue the way they were going and Major Meade would for their edification provide some free expert assistance to ensure that the steam heating system project was faithfully executed, and not strung along for the sake of milking the Barracks, as some may have been grumbling. But the Barracks simply did not have the proper expertise available to monitor the work. So it would have to bluff that it might. The contractor was taking advantage of the Barracks' lack of expertise, because he thought that it didn't have it.[28] Modern headaches. A pile of firewood was so much simpler. The gas pressure has been inconsistent. The Barracks finally advised the supplier, the Charlestown Gas and Electric Company, that they had one month to improve service or the Barracks would seek another supplier.[29] The steam heat installation still required attention. The contractor's people were installing steam heating coils in the officer's quarters and complaints were made to the contractor about this. Major Meade wanted radiators installed in all officer's quarters instead of the heating coils.[30] Good call. The system ended up lasting decades and decades. The operation of a naval prison, by its nature, created many anxious moments. The guards tried to keep the prison safe. After all, a prisoner's punishment should be as advertised: time served in custody. Their lives should be secure during this interlude. Otherwise imprisonment could be a death sentence. General court-martial convict Frank M. Grant, 3d Class apprentice USN, was found attempting to kill himself October 1894. If the prison was so safe, how did he get this far? He saved bits of string over a long period of time. The day came when his collection became strong enough to hold his weight.

An alert guard rescued him from death. Posterity found out why this convict took such action. He had a bad toothache. He must have been in constant pain for all the time it took to accumulate this remarkable string collection. The surgeon could not give him any relief. To ensure that Apprentice Grant did not try again, he was denied possession of anything that could possibly be used for that purpose.[31] There is no record, however, as to whether he received any relief for this toothache, which precipitated the attempt in the first place. A roof ignited in flames on the building next door to the prison. Normally, occupants of a building can egress, but prisoners are locked down. And to remove them, as painstaking and time consuming as it is, also provides an opportunity for escape and increases the chances for harm to themselves, their guards, and the public. It was huge that an alert Marine guard was able to extinguish the flames.

What caused the fire? Construction was in progress on that building. The investigation published October 6, 1894, revealed that the plumbers were using an open brazier for melting lead to solder piping. The use of this open flame device by any contractor was expressly prohibited in the specifications of that job.[32] Noncommissioned officers (NCOs) are almost always in short supply. They can be the most effective personnel in any military in any time in history. But perhaps due to its own myopic priorities, Headquarters Marine Corps exacerbated the problem by sending out a directive that substantially encumbered the ability of commanding officers to promote qualified NCOs. Major Meade needed more NCOs to run both the Barracks and the prison. He complained to Colonel Heywood on October 16, 1894, that he was hard pressed without them. He has been required to transfer NCOs, too. He asked for the ability to promote Marines in order to fill the requirements for more NCOs. He also provided a list of all of his NCOs and their assignments.[33] Lynch and Woodward had eyeballs on them since the beginning of the steam installation project. By the fall of 1894, heating season was approaching. Major Meade wanted a fixed date of completion, as it was almost time to turn the heat on. He wanted pressure exerted on the contractor by Headquarters Marine Corps.[34] To reduce loss and misuse of issued items, Major Meade devised a system for accounting for knapsacks, haversacks and canteens. Rifles were typically numbered and could be accounted for very well. So he advocated a system of numbering haversacks, knapsacks and canteens much the same way. Each Marine would be issued those items with a number assigned to each. Marines would not be allowed to utilize items that do not correspond with the proper number issued. Major Meade felt that this system would considerably reduce the loss and misuse of these items.[35] Sometimes long discharged Marines request financial considerations. Thomas Murphy used to be posted at the Marine Barracks. He claimed a pension for injuries received during his service. The agency rejected the claim. Murphy put on his initial enlistment that he had rheumatism prior to entering the Marine Corps. But Murphy was on his third enlistment when he was injured. For all other service he was perfectly healthy. Major Meade, going to bat for Murphy, felt that the government was not acting in good faith with enlisted men, so he complained to the William Cochran, commissioner of pensions, Washington, D.C., on December 3, 1894. Murphy was in excellent health when he was injured. The injury he received caused paralysis, making him unable to work. Major Meade was concerned that he was deprived of his livelihood and was now destitute. A medical board subsequently examined Murphy. Meade was convinced that Murphy was being punished for his truthfulness on his initial enlistment, which unfortunately often happens, and wanted the commissioner of pensions to please reconsider the plight of Murphy.[36] The Barracks contracted with a firm to paint bathtubs in the officers' quarters in the summer of 1894. Major Meade was unhappy with the results. He complained to contractor Frank A. Titus that the work was improperly accomplished and left his officers without the use of their bathtubs for two months. So Meade refused to pay Titus for the work. Turns out that only one bathtub was poorly painted and needed to be redone.[37] In December 1894, Major Meade again refused to pay a contractor for work he felt was substandard. A bill for repair of a coffee boiler charged eleven hours of labor. He wrote to S.P. Hicks and Sons that the bill was excessive since it only needed an iron ring around its upper edge fastened together and copper soldered over the broken part and then the handle required securing only. He was convinced it was a simple job, certainly not requiring 11 hours labor. The bill would not be paid until such time as it was modified to the agreement of Major Meade.[38] Improvements to the naval prison came in fits and starts. With the installation of electricity, the prison made an important leap towards modernization. But like many other things around there the electrical wiring did not proceed smoothly either.

An examination of the electrical drawing revealed that there was only one switch controlling the electric lights in all parts of the prison and the guard room. Major Meade objected to this plan. It was a serious defect: all of the lights going on and off in a prison, all at once. Each section of the prison needed control over its own lighting for security, including the guard room. If the original electrical plan was followed, then even the guard room would be dark along with each section of the prison.[39] Violent confrontations between Marines were beginning to seem routine. On February 11, 1895, Private Walter Conway barged his way into the sleeping room of the guard at noon. He menacingly aroused Private John Smith from sleep. Conway then belted Smith. As if reaching to hug the man after he smacked him, he moved in as if about to kiss him, he opened his mouth, bared his teeth, and bit off a portion of Smith's ear. Not enough, Conway then attempted to throw Smith down a stairwell. But before he could, other Marines in the area seized him. Private Conway was confined and held for action of higher authority.[40]

Guards securing prisoners on details outside prison walls around the Navy yard could no longer carry loaded weapons, the commandant of the Charlestown Navy Yard so ordered. Of course Major Meade didn't like this order. As if stating the obvious, he explained that it would be very difficult to apprehend an escaping prisoner under those circumstances. The guard would have to give chase to an escaping prisoner with the advantage of no heavy clothing or accoutrements. Without a loaded weapon, the guard only has his "powers of persuasion," a tall order against a fleet footed prisoner.[41] Punishments for infractions of regulations, or "breaking regs," were quite severe under Major Meade. Private Nicholas Kenny made a scene in quarters one night; he was drunk, he resisted arrest, and he used abusive and obscene language at the sergeant of the guard. Kenny was confined in double irons for ten days. Meade went through channels for the authority to discharge Kenny as unfit for service.

This wasn't the first time Kenny was "brought to attention." Kenny made a filthy mess on his post, enough to make report, on October 18, 1894. On November 22, 1894, he misappropriated government clothing.

On April 21, 1894, he was 3 hours late returning from liberty. The same day, probably still stewing from the tongue lashing he must have endured, he was caught writing obscene graffiti on the woodwork of the sentry box—while on duty about his commanding officer and other officers of the Barracks.[42] Perhaps because he knew his Marines all too well, Major Meade made inquiries to local penal institutions as to whether wayward Marines, missing from the Barracks, might be serving sentences for civilian crimes, accounting for their absence. The letter asked the superintendents to inform him of any Marines confined and the offense involved.[43] Major Meade received a pencil written letter from a group of prisoners from the naval prison in June 1985 requesting spiritual aid for prisoners of the Catholic faith. Meade swiftly contacted the priest of St. Mary's Church in Charlestown and asked if he could conduct a Catholic Mass in the naval prison on Sundays. It was important to Major Meade to provide the prisoners with as much spiritual comfort as was possible,[44] as he was a prisoner of the Confederates himself back during the war. The books must have piled high, as the Barracks hired a librarian for its library. Major Meade explained in a letter to Colonel Heywood, although the librarian issued the books and accounted for them, Meade was the real librarian. Ultimately, at the request of the Marine Corps inspector general, the librarian was out and the care of the books would be placed in the hands of the post treasurer.[45] The cook at the Barracks was paid extra for his services. This got the attention of the inspector general in a visit to Boston. Meade explained that the cook actually prepared nine meals per day. The mess area was too small to seat the entire command and the cook had to prepare two breakfasts, two dinners and two suppers for the Barracks on a daily basis. He was also required to provide 3 meals each day for the naval prison. Major Meade was paying the cook for the extra work which required him to be on duty form 0300 until 1800 each day. That's 15 hours a day.[46] A July 2, 1895 advertisement in the *Boston Globe* said: "Wanted—For the U.S. Marine Corps: sober, able bodied, unmarried men, between the ages of 20 and 25 years and from 65 to 72 inches in height. Pay from $10 to $16 a month. Clothing, food and medical attention provided in full. The military duties are performed at Navy Yards and on board men-of-wars. The service offers excellent opportunities for young men to travel and visit foreign countries. Must apply in person at the Recruiting Office, No. 98 Court Street, Boston, Mass. None but men of good character need apply."[47] Naval prisoners could look forward to a daily life of picking up trash on a Navy yard in an era before littering was an issue. This took a lot of guards. Especially since they were carrying unloaded weapons. Major Meade needed to staff them regardless. The Barracks were almost always short of personnel when they just had to ship out Marines or use them for guard duty, and now they had to staff a prison too. He wrote to headquarters and asked for more corporals.[48] As dire as that sounded, the Barracks was down and out for men. It could truly use a boost. There was recruiting. After all, Meade was paying for an office. Meade was paying for newspaper advertisements. And it happened to be the year 1895. Men signed up. They were filling bunks. They were filling all the bunks. Major Meade could now proudly offer 15 recruits for headquarters to use to fill vacancies elsewhere.[49]

High powered, long-range rifle training was great stuff at Lovell's Island out in the Boston Harbor. It was one of the finest facilities in the Marines, when they could get out there. Then there were handguns. Do Marines have to go all the way out into the Boston harbor just to shoot those? Who carries handguns? Generally officers carried handguns. A gentleman's gallery to retain proficiency would be appropriate. There were unused buildings as the Navy recently changed from wood to metal ships. Meade requested use of the old Mast House. It was long and the best choice in the yard to fire side arms indoors. He assured the commandant of the Navy yard every precaution would be taken against accidents.[50] Plenty of recruits were available, but corporals were in short supply that summer at the Barracks. Boston's Marine Barracks had the rather unique function compared to other Marine Barracks of staffing a naval prison. Corporals were better suited to guard prisoners, as they were more seasoned and accomplished military men when compared to recruits who were fresh off the streets. Meade explained this to headquarters. After all, regulations required these corporals for prisoner work details.

Meade had to scrimp and use privates in lieu of corporals for prisoners when they were out and about the yard, outside of their cells and walls. Meade knew, however, that it was much safer to guard prisoners with experienced Marines. Prisoners with more military experience than their guards, outside of their cells and prison walls on work detail, especially if the guards couldn't use their weapons, was frighteningly dangerous. Meade had to bluff the prisoners to get by.[51] The policy of requiring unarmed guards on the prisoner work details was a thorn in Meade's side. If a prisoner decided to bolt, guards could only give chase, and leave the rest of the labor party under guarded. This indeed happened. A prisoner escaped from work detail. Ordinary Seaman William Bryant bolted while cleaning streets in the officers' quarters section of the yard. He ran towards the waterfront, dove into the water, and tried to swim across the river. Private Cain, on duty at Post 6, spotted him. He quickly took a small boat out and captured him. This event was recorded August 24, 1895, nice time of year for a swim.[52] Punishment for the escape attempt by Seaman Bryant and the disruption it caused, in the name of good order and discipline, was a general court-martial recommended by Meade.

That incident prompted Major Meade to advocate once again for guards to carry loaded weapons when overseeing prisoner work details. Meade was working with a potentially dangerous ratio of 30 prisoners to 10 guards on these work details. If command wants to have unarmed guards, they will have to get more of them in order to reduce any danger to staff, the local population, and the prisoners themselves. Either arm the guards or hire more of them was the big question. Guards needed to surround prisoners armed with shovels and other heavy instruments as potential weapons in order to quell any violence or escape. Sometimes personnel issues, long considered the province of the young and newly enlisted Marines, also occurred among the most experienced. Private John Doyle had served 28 years in the corps and was two years into his third re-enlistment. He was a hopeless and irredeemable drunk in the opinion of Major Meade. Meade, however, was perplexed. Doyle had so much service, yet he felt that he could no longer pass over his acts. Doyle even had chronic diarrhea and was hospitalized for it for 262 days during his previous enlistment. He recently had been released after 175 days in the hospital and was placed on light duty. And when he returned from liberty from this light duty August 21 he was too drunk to perform any duty. So thereafter, Doyle wasn't trusted to go on liberty, because he would get drunk.

And after all this, he was caught smuggling liquor into the barracks. For punishment, he was denied privileges at the post traders store. And once again he resorted to having smuggled liquor provided for him. Major Meade included all the information in a letter to the colonel commandant and asked for disposition on Doyle's case.[53] Meade provided descriptions to his boss, Colonel Heywood, September 1895 of all the security posts in the Navy yard and the requirements of the manning the naval prison. He was convinced that Boston needed two first sergeants, 17 sergeants, 34 corporals, 6 musicians and 120 privates as a minimum permanent force to man the Barracks and the naval prison.[54] Major Meade also requested an additional officer be assigned to Boston. The naval prison was a real working prison. Prisons are usually run by their own administrations, not part-time as an extra duty assignment. The Marine officer of the day was constantly required and taken away from his other duties in order to fill a position. A once part time post was now a full time responsibility. The additional officer would be assigned for prison duty only.[55]

Growing numbers of skilled laborers needed a standard means to enter and egress the shipyard on a work-a-day basis. Military personnel on authorized liberty also needed access. This could only happen at the Main Gate. It was not the only gate into the yard, however. Private Harbaugh of the floating Barracks USRS *Wabash* tried to leave through Gate 4 but was rebuffed; Gate 4 to Chelsea Street was a private gate only.

The story goes, he had returned with Chaplain Tribon of the USRS *Wabash*, who told the sentry that he must allow Private Harbaugh to pass through, on "his (Tribon's) authority" as a commissioned officer in naval service. Major Meade countered that although Chaplain Tribon has some authority as a commissioned officer, it does not extend to disregarding the orders of the commandant of the Navy Yard.[56] It was a triumph for Private Harbaugh, Meade grumbled, to have a commissioned officer try to circumvent Navy yard orders. The act seriously affected discipline at the post.

The Tail Wagging the Dog

Nobody wants to fund a naval prison. Major Meade expressed his views to the commandant of the Navy yard October 3, 1895, about getting legitimate money to run the Prison. Not a one time funding either, the prison needed its own budget. It was unrealistic for the Barracks to continue to have the prison as its sole responsibility, as it had grown unsupportable. The prison grew from just a few holding cells back in the sailing ship days into a more "industrial" facility for an industrial age. The bureaucratic age's benevolence was overlooking the prison. The naval prison wasn't under any particular bureau's authority in regards to repair and maintenance. Congress appropriated no special sum for any support either. Consequently, prison facilities decayed and bills went unpaid. To cover this, the "bubble gum and masking tape fix" was to charge all expenses, not actual repairs, to "Pay Miscellaneous" or "Contingency: Secretary's Office." Some repairs could come partly under the Bureau of Yards and Dock's authority. But some didn't come under any particular bureau at all, and were hard to fund. To release these monies, the Navy Department needed to submit a request to Congress for a separate sum to maintain the naval prison. That was over the commandant of the Navy yard's head.

Until 1894, the Barracks provided the necessities used by prisoners in the naval prison (sailors or Marines alike) because they were needed. But problems arose when a prisoner was confined and there was no money available for subsistence.

The nature of the naval beast was that when a ship docked at the yard, its men were transferred to shore. Indeed, the Barracks' mission was to take in and use these men for sentry and prison duty and to release Marines for sea duty. When authority was transferred from ship to shore, lines blurred, however, especially when it came to money.

In the case of the floating Barracks USRS *Wabash*, its pay clerk would not pay for rations for prisoner Sayre recently off the *Wabash*. He claimed the prisoner was ashore and no longer aboard the *Wabash*. Well sort of, but a prisoner is not useful staff. Prisoner Sayre ended up subsisting in the same manner as other prisoners with an allowance given by the court for "prison expenses." Meade appreciated guidance as to whether it was to cover health and cleanliness, or whether it was to cover subsistence.[57]

On December 24, Christmas Eve 1895, Prisoner Evans was on a working party. First Sergeant Edward Yates directed him to go and pick up some swabs (mop heads). He went to get the swabs, but Corporal Barnett forbade him to take them. As prisoner Evans turned to go empty handed down the stairs to rejoin the working party, Corporal Barnett sprang at him and struck him in the face with a clenched fist. Barnett bellowed, "You go to your cell! I am running this place as long as I am here!" Corporal Barnett then locked prisoner Evans in his cell. First Sergeant Yates of the prison came up the stairs looking for Evans. Corporal Barnett replied that he was locked in his cell. Sergeant Yates ordered Evans released, and then asked Corporal Barnett why he did not honor his request for Evans to pick up the swabs. Corporal Barnett replied that he "did not give a damn for him [Yates] or for the Major." After an investigation, Corporal Barnett was placed under arrest (prisoner at large). He subsequently broke arrest status twice and was confined himself.[58]

A smothering report on the sanitary conditions of the Marine Barracks and the naval prison was submitted to Major Meade on 26 January 1896. It found the ventilation in particular was very poor and to fix it would be difficult. The report also indicated that they were presently only allowing 390 cubic feet of space per man. That was not enough. Six hundred cubic feet per man was needed to provide for better ventilation. Although bunk beds were new and quite practical, they had to have reasonable ceiling space. If the ceilings were too low for them the man in the upper bunk cannot even sit up in bed let alone breathe. The report also recommended electric lighting be installed in the barracks areas to alleviate pollutants from candles, kerosene lamps, and whale oil lamps.[59]

Sergeant John De La Doer died suddenly 1 April 1896 and nothing could explain his death. Nonetheless, Major Meade began efforts to locate his wife, since he was sure that she would want him buried in a Catholic cemetery. Just in case Meade couldn't locate Sergeant De La Doer's wife, he requested authority to bury him in the naval hospital cemetery. The funeral unfolded 2 p.m. on 3 April.[60]

The deceased leave behind matters and assets needing resolve and possession. Sergeant De La Doer had an account in the Warren National Savings Bank in Charlestown. But Meade was not able to locate a bankbook, so he wrote to the bank. In the interest of the widow, the Marine Corps wanted to settle his affairs.[61]

Private George Emerson fell ill. Major Meade sent Pvt. Emerson to the surgeon of the yard to be checked out and treated. Once Meade got the surgeon's report he must have been flabbergasted. All the surgeon did was take Emerson's version of the story, and put that into his report, Meade complained. The surgeon should have given more consideration to other circumstances, he must have murmured. The major wrote on the notes which accompanied the report of the surgeon, "I therefore disagree with the Surgeon who has not taken any evidence whatever than that simply stated by the man and who is, therefore an incompetent judge."[62] A tugboat crewed by Marines to transport Marines to Lovell's Island for rifle practice was desired by Major Meade. He wrote to Headquarters Marine Corps for one on July 21, 1896. But Colonel Heywood said no. He recommended the Marines continue to use the yard tug *Iwana* to travel to Lovell's Island, no changes. Meade was cautioned to avail all opportunities to use the range for target practice. In other words: get scheduled as often as possible. He was assured headquarters would not have any complaint with him in that regard.

Colonel Heywood suggested that the Barracks start to take steps to begin to establish a gallery range in the yard. The District of Columbia National Guard was held up as an example of a successful galley range at the brigade armory in the District. He urged Major Meade to find out from his yard contacts to determine whether there are any buildings suitable for that purpose.[63] Massachusetts Naval Militia were good guys, or so it seemed. The Barracks thought it was all right to lend them out items. And then what happened? The naval militia didn't return what the Barracks had loaned. Militias are organized but non-state supported military styled groups. Perhaps they felt entitled to the loaned equipment. Meade asserted if this happened again he would deny them the use of any training materials. He would be done with them.[64]

Thirty-six prisoners made life for their companions and their bosses a job. Twenty-five misbehaving sailors and 11 recalcitrant Marines ended up on the daily head count as prisoners in the naval prison for the month of August 1896.[65]

Thought you heard the last of the bickering between Major Meade and the Surgeon? Major Meade's remarks on the surgeon's notes in the Emerson case opened the flood gates of vitriol between the two professionals. Meade didn't have any foul motive; he just implied a lack of effort to find the truth, a proper investigation in the case of Pvt. Emerson. Probably his real peeve, Meade claimed that the Surgeon never consulted him for any information whatsoever. Meade had appropriate information that he felt should have been included in the surgeon's report. He could have supplied the surgeon with information concerning the origin of disease which might have been important to the diagnosis.

Meade even gave an example. Surgeon Rogers, who certified that there was "no evidence" that his disease originated in the line of duty, sent Private Andrew Price to the naval hospital on June 27, 1896. Meade contended that the "no evidence" statement was not true since there was every evidence immediately available that the disease was directly chargeable to the duty he was performing. Indeed, the Medical Board, which discharged Private Price from the service on the 4th of July, found that his duty was the absolute cause of the disease. Major Meade contended that Surgeon Rogers should not have signed documents stating the disease was not caused by duty, without a proper investigation to determine the absolute truth. Medical records are very important papers went it comes to determining pensions. They cannot be too closely scrutinized and guarded by commanding officers, as Meade felt he was tending his responsibilities.[66] Headquarters ordered the Barracks in Boston to transfer ten Marines to the USS *Brooklyn* on August 29, 1896. Boston was assured replacements from the Marine Barracks in Newport, R.I. But Major Meade complained to the commandant of the Navy yard about the quality of the replacements that he received when they arrived, and he only received six Marines from Newport, not ten. Out of these, Captain Cochrane of the Newport Marine Barracks recommended one of them for discharge as unfit for duty. He was locked up in a jail at a local police station. Another's record showed scarcely anything other than delirium tremens. A third had such a record of offenses he could not even be placed on duty. A forth was a habitual drunkard. Only two men were fairly respectable. The Marines that were sent to the USS *Brooklyn* were men of high value. Major Meade reported Captain Cochrane to the secretary of the Navy for unloading worthless men upon Boston Marine Barracks.[67] Marines stationed at the Barracks for very long periods of time and likely had no other home caught the interest of Major Meade. This concern was heightened when Sergeant James Harnan died at the naval hospital. Major Meade requested that Sergeant Harnan be buried at the naval hospital cemetery, since he apparently had no home other than the Barracks.[68] Corporal of the Guard John G. Quigley, on his barracks inspection rounds, discovered Private George B. Hanna in the lower passageway of the barracks. Private Hanna was wearing civilian clothes. His seabag was packed with his uniform clothing and other articles. It was clear he was actively preparing to leave the barracks. Corporal Quigley tried to place Private Hanna under arrest. Hanna resisted arrest and attempted to strike Corporal Quigley. It was necessary for Corporal Quigley to use his bayonet to defend himself and place Hanna under arrest. While the sergeant of the guard was preparing the cell for Private Hanna, Hanna struck Corporal Quigley again. Corporal Quigley was obliged to use his bayonet again to subdue and confine him.[69]

Misunderstandings occurred between the naval hospital and the Marine Barracks. One concerned the Private John Doyle case, discussed earlier. The secretary of the Navy asked for an explanation why Private Doyle had been in the hospital for 26 out of 33 months of service. Why was Private Doyle, in view of his extended hospital stays, retained for service, on October 27, 1896?[70] Three days later, the Barracks asked the naval hospital the same thing.[71] He was retained at the naval hospital since admission on September 14, 1896, for the following reasons: (1) he had long and faithful service for over 28 years; (2) the origin of disease was determined to be in the line of duty; (3) The nature of the disease was "chronic diarrhea," it might have been Giardia; and (4) On April 9, 1896, a board of medical survey recommended his retention in the hospital for further treatment.[72] Several days more, the matter was referred to the commander of the Boston Marine Barracks for endorsement.

But Major Meade's endorsement stated that "he had nothing to add, except perhaps so far as the word 'faithful' applied to Private Doyle's service and this word I cannot accept. His record is very bad indeed and on August 30, 1895, I laid his whole case before the Colonel Commandant. Private Doyle is utterly worthless of trust as his last duty fully proved. He came from the hospital on August 12, 1895, ostensibly cured and was regularly posted as sentinel on August 29, 1895. He was perfectly sober when he was mounted on guard duty, however he was able to smuggle liquor while on post at the gate and got hopelessly drunk." Meade had known Doyle for years and he always exhibited the same characteristics as a confirmed and habitual drunkard.[73]

General court-martial prisoner and coal passer Herbert S. Moore escaped from a prison work detail November 3, 1896. An experienced and trustworthy prison guard, Private James S. Barrett, was in charge of a prisoner sweeping the walkway in front of the officers' quarters at the lower end of the yard. Seizing an opportunity, Moore sprang over the wall to the street below. An alarm was sounded. The local police were notified and furnished with a description of the prisoner, and the $50 reward.[74] Private Doyle again came to the attention of disciplinary proceedings. For disrespectful language toward a superior officer, he was tried by general court-martial. He pled guilty and was ordered confined to await sentence of the court.[75] Major Meade did not want to handle the pay accounts of the Marines at the Barracks. He wrote to the secretary of the Navy and requested that the pay accounts of Marines be transferred to the pay office of the Navy yard. Meade felt that as a line officer, he should not be held responsible for pay accounts. The Navy Pay Office always handled Marines aboard ship, why not on shore too?[76]

Headquarters was still concerned over the lack of yard based rifle range practice facilities. A suitable building should be assigned to the Marine Barracks for use as a galley range, and this was requested by Colonel Heywood on 7 January 1897. He explained how important weapons training was to the Marines throughout the corps.[77] Recruiting was suspended February 1897. The Marine Corps was full. Reenlistments could continue, however.[78] On February 24, 1897, Marines from Boston were dispatched to Washington, D.C., to participate in the inaugural parade of President William McKinley on March 4.[79]

McKinley defeated William Jennings Bryan after a "front porch" campaign about "sound money" based on a gold standard and high tariffs. McKinley was the last president to have served in the Civil War, starting as a private and rising to brevet major. He was also the first except for William H. Taft and Teddy Roosevelt of the modern clean-shaven presidents. Positive economic maneuverings by his administration, the victorious conclusion of a very important war, and the annexation of Hawaii as a territory marked his first administration. McKinley defeated Bryan again in the 1900 election on a campaign based on imperialism, prosperity and free silver.

Corporal Herrington, on duty as corporal of the guard at the Main Gate, allowed two women "of ill fame" to ply their trade in the bedroom attached to the guardroom. The officer of the day discovered the arrangement and as this was against policy, placed Corporal Herrington under arrest.[80]

Another Marine got a newspaper reporter into the Barracks to do a story on the Corporal Herrington affair. The story hit the *Boston Globe*. Major Meade scoffed and referred to the reporter's story as "a scurrilous and false report." Private Howlett was disciplined for bringing this reporter on post.[81]

Major Meade enlisted a recruit and sent him to the Marine Barracks in Brooklyn, New York. However this recruit was missing a little finger. The commanding officer of Brooklyn complained and subsequently wrote to headquarters about this matter. When word about these communications got back to Colonel Heywood, he chided Major Meade when he admitted to having made "only a cursory examination" and did not discover the loss of a finger. "You should make more than a cursory glance before forwarding him to a surgeon," Colonel Heywood responded, "it is part of the responsibilities of a recruiting officer."[82] It came up that Major Meade had been awarding contracts to enlisted men. An investigation commenced. Protocol dictates that the adjutant and inspector of the Marine Corps spearhead the inquiry. The major explained that he did indeed utilize this method. He also knew of many very prominent Marine officers who also practiced the same. Colonel Heywood agreed that it was customary for commanding officers to purchase materials on the open market and have the required work done by enlisted men. After the report came out, Colonel Heywood, perhaps responding to heat, declared to the major that he had never heard of the practice and told him to desist immediately.[83] In April 1897, Private Speers, a general court-martial prisoner, complained about the quality of the prison food. Meade replied that the prisoners were provided the same food as the Marines at the Barracks. Even in modern times, state correctional facilities often purchase and provide the same food as state run universities. Major Meade even huffed and ventured the assertion that Private Speers probably received far better food in every respect than he ever had in his life before. Speers, in his statement, said that there were 40 or 50 hungry men in the prison. Meade smirked that they existed in his imagination only.[84]

The USS *Constitution* ruled the seas at the turn of the 19th century. Nearly a hundred years later, sails gave way to coal and steam and then to oil. The iron and steel ships of the Great White Navy replaced wooden sailing ships. These new technologies were affecting life aboard naval vessels. With these new realities in mind, in April 1897, the secretary of the Navy sent a circular letter throughout Navy and Marine Corps stations all over the world to invite comments concerning some changes to naval discipline and regulations. In particular he asked if age old punishments—the use of bread and water diets, loss of pay and the use of extra police duties as punishment awarded by summary courts-martial—were appropriate in these more modern times.

Major Meade, always with something interesting to say, offered his opinion: In the case of Marines on day on and day off guard duty, it would be impractical to impose "extra police duties" as punishment. On his "day off," a Marine has a certain amount of fatigue duties to perform, in addition to drills, recitations, and other exercises. Bread and water diets for long periods of time degrade the quality of a serviceman's health and subsequently affect his timely return to duty, or his employability in the civilian world. The loss of pay did more to punish the innocent families rather then the delinquent himself. Citing Article 30 Naval Regulations: "extra police duties may be added to solitary confinement not exceeding 30 days" for example, and Major Meade thought that punishment would, in ordinary cases, meet all the requirements of service, in place of bread and water sentences. Senior medical officers, as newly realized nutritional facts emerged, were further convinced that bread and water sentences were invariably prejudicial to the health of even the strongest men. The major was fine with remodeling the law retiring bread and water sentences and substituting something better, ending hundreds of years of a discipline tradition in a tradition bound Navy. But he would be disappointed to see more "extra police duties" added to the work of Marines doing guard duty.[85]

In spring 1897, corps personnel strengths fell below authorized levels and Boston was authorized to resume recruiting.[86]

Colonel Heywood sent an officially worded letter to Major Meade on the issue of giving contracts to enlisted men for work, illuminated in the adjutant and inspector's report. Colonel Heywood's explicit instructions to him in response to this report: "Commanding officers are also informed that they have no right to award contracts of any kind of government work at their posts to enlisted men of the Marine Corps serving under them, such an award being unauthorized and of questionable legality."

Unofficially the thinking was that the practice wasn't unique to Boston and it provided overtime for the men. It wasn't policy, however. It was just one of those customs that exists until it ends up in a report. An official response is expected to rectify the matter.[87]

On June 5, 1897, Major Meade sent a list of officers on duty at the Marine Barracks to the commandant, Charlestown Navy Yard: Meade, Robert, Major, Commanding Marines Commanding Naval Prison Commanding Recruiting Office; Kelton, Theodore, Captain, Duty Officer at Barracks OIC Clothing, Armory, etc.; Kane, Theodore, 1st Lt., Duty Officer at Barracks; Fuller, Ben, 1st Lt., Duty Officer at Barracks.[88]

The naval prison was getting on in its years and needed improvements. So Major Meade enumerated recommendations to the commandant of the Navy Yard as follows:

1. Enlarge the prison yard for prisoners to have a place to exercise. Although the prisoners were sent out on working parties in the Navy yard, it was not always beneficial exercise.
2. More reading material. The chaplain was an important benefactor to the prison, accommodating the need for books and magazines within his capacity.
3. The kitchen range in the prison galley needed replacement.
4. Provide the guards with loaded weapons. Guarding prisoners with only a cane when prisoners carried crowbars, axes, picks, or hatchets was a dangerous practice. Just carrying an unloaded pistol, as long as those who were guarded were not aware, was better than a cane.[89]

Meade asked permission to use the public stables as temporary living quarters for Marines. Plans to renovate the living areas of the barracks were nearing fruition. These stables were between the Barracks and the Commandant's Quarters (mansion) and exist today; they were occupied by wagons not draft animals. The stables would only be used for housing during the most disruptive phase of the work scheduled for the summer months until October 1, 1897.[90] Bids for installing electricity were sent to the quartermaster of the Marine Corps on August 19, 1897, for approval.[91] Major Meade exhausted all possibilities for housing his Marines before he grudgingly settled on the stables. One idea was to move the garrison to Lovell's Island during the summer months. A reasonable solution, he thought, as long as they had the necessary tentage and supplies.[92]

Drug use became a problem, or seemed to become one with the emergence of the operation of modern machinery and pharmaceuticals. Private James Davis was an "opium eater of long standing," Meade reported. Private Davis would consume two bottles of morphine per day, enough to kill ten to fifteen people. Although he had this drug habit for a very long time, Davis gave no outward signs of drug addiction and was an excellent man and merited nothing but commendation.[93]

The guardhouse at the Main Gate was in deplorable condition. The Marines wanted it completely replaced but understood that it would take some time to get the project approved and have the appropriations provided. So Meade requested funding for "masking tape and bubble gum" repairs to the guardhouse for minimal habitability until replacement of the entire guardhouse could be achieved.[94]

The post exchange or as it is known in the vernacular, the PX, was and is a popular destination to many. It is the place to buy just about anything most people could want on base—magazines, candy, soda, soap, coffee ready or not—often in remote locations. In modern times they are seen as places to buy items not subject to local taxes.

Before the PX there were the post traders. Remember the trouble they caused the Barracks' commanders? They were basically shop keepers set up in the bowels of a military facility. This secretary of the Navy was ready to replace the post trader with something more modern and appropriate.

At the turn of the twentieth century, naval power was the predominant military power a country could project. The Navy was a better investment than the Army at the time. Consequently, the Navy had grown into a military industrial colossus. This colossus certainly had the bureaucratic wherewithal to manage the exchange's logistics and finances more efficiently than private concessionaires. Marine Barracks in Boston was selected as the test market location for the first post exchange.

Theodore Roosevelt, the assistant secretary of the Navy at the time, spearheaded the establishment of the post exchange system. He came to Boston to have a look around. Major Meade met with Roosevelt in the office of the commandant of the Navy yard in the commandant's mansion. After the meeting, Meade volunteered he "had a full and free conversation with Mr. Roosevelt."

Meade was not very enthusiastic about replacing the post trader system. He felt that his current post trader was a good man and served the Marines very well over the years, and was about to lose his job. Boston newspapers became aware of Major Meade's grumblings. His grumblings filled space on newsprint. These caught the attention, of all people, the Assistant Secretary of the Navy Theodore Roosevelt.

Since this was Roosevelt's baby, he disagreed with Major Meade's opinions that made the press and shot back two letters at him. Major Meade denied he originated the newspaper articles and emphasized that he had presented these same concerns to Roosevelt himself at their meeting earlier.

Roosevelt informed Meade that he must make the post exchange the "fullest success," and it will be his responsibility to make it one. To which Meade, in a most lawyerly way, replied, "It is my intention, and it has been my intention from the first, to do all that lies in the power of a single man to further the wishes of the Department. But I respectfully decline to make myself responsible for the 'fullest success' of any untried experiment at this station. If there is a 'success' in it, I will find it but I promise no more and with due respect I say no more could reasonably be expected of me." Major Meade went on to request that a court of inquiry determine the facts in relation to the post exchange matter. He felt that he was burned by irresponsible newspaper writers and falsely represented.[95] The establishment of the post exchange became a reality with correspondence from headquarters, Marine Corps to Marine Barracks, Boston, on September 18, 1897. The following articles established the first post exchange in the Marine Corps:

1. By direction of the Secretary of the Navy, under date of 17th instant, and for the purpose of further testing the relative merits of the system of post tradership as it exists in the Marine Corps and that of the post exchanges as existing in the Army, you are authorized and directed to establish a post exchange at the marine barracks under your command, to be conducted in all respects, so far as practicable, in strict accordance with the laws, regulations and rules governing the conduct of post exchanges in the United States Army, a copy of which is herewith, being General Order No. 46, Headquarters of the Army, A.G.O., July 25, 1895. 2. You will designate a competent officer as the officer in charge of the Post Exchange, to be assisted by such attendants as the business may warrant, to be selected from the enlisted men of your command. 3. The officer in charge will make to the commanding officer a monthly report, in detail, of the conditions of the exchange under his charge, whether beneficial to the command, or otherwise, with such suggestions and recommendations in regard thereto as may, from time to time, seem to him

advisable. Such reports to be forwarded without delay, to the Colonel Commandant, by the commanding officer with such remarks as he may desire to make regarding the results of this experiment. 4. At the end of six months the officer in charge of the post exchange will make to the commanding officer a full and complete report, including the financial condition of the post exchange, with a statement of receipts and expenditures, with his opinion as to its effect morally and economically, as well as its advantage or disadvantage to the command. The commanding officer will forward the same to the Colonel Commandant with such remarks and recommendations as he may have to make regarding the advisability and practicability of continuing the same at his post. 5. On the first of October 1897, the system of post tradership at your post will be abolished.[96]

On October 30, 1897, Headquarters Marine Corps sent a telegram to Major Meade and informed him that the post exchange at the Marine Barracks, Boston, would be established on December 1, 1897.[97]

Major Meade was assigned to command a battalion of Marines in a Boston parade in the fall of 1897. He said he was going to try to be mounted on horseback for the parade. He was a field officer after all and a mount was a part of his uniform in a parade.

And then Admiral Sicard issued an order that there would not be any horses in the parade. Major Meade protested to Roosevelt's boss, the secretary of the Navy, about the order. Meade had a precedent in his pocket: another parade in New York City. Major Huntington was in command of a battalion of Marines for a parade in conjunction with a naval officer in command of a battalion of sailors. The naval officer could not ride a horse. Since the naval officer could not ride a horse it was determined that a marine officer wouldn't ride one either. Major Huntington protested to the secretary of the Navy. The secretary directed that a naval officer who was able to ride a horse should be provided with a fine steed or a captain of Marines would command the battalion. There you go.[98]

President William McKinley won re-election in 1900. Only months into his second term, September 1901, he was assassinated by an anarchist. Former Assistant Sec of the Navy and Vice President Theodore Roosevelt, whom Meade annoyed, became president.

The work on the addition of the fourth floor was completed by late October 1897, allowing the Marines to move back in before the winter season.[99]

As the nineteenth century was closing, the Marine Barracks became one the most imposing structures in the yard. It was this period the building was raised to its full height of four stories. The overall appearance of the south façade (the front of the building) was much the same as it was in the preceding period except for a fourth floor. It featured hip roofs on the wings, shutters on all of the windows, and a large awning that covered the center half of the second and third floors of the building. A wooden porch had been constructed on the west facade of the west wing and it was in plain view from the south as well. The wooden porch has since been enclosed and was once a TV room.

The basic functions and layout of the building were similar, though numerous modifications were made to the basic plan. Three of the major improvements were the addition of the central heating system, electric lighting, and indoor toilets. Each portion of the building obtained its official designation. The west wing or commanding officer's quarters was designated House H. The center section or enlisted men's quarters was House I, and the east wing or junior officers' quarters was designated as House K.[100]

Electrical wiring of the Barracks was completed in November 1897. But that didn't mean they were ready to turn on the hi-fi or smelt aluminum. Getting the lackluster electrical power, not like today, from a significant power transmission problem made the lights weak from lack of proper voltage. Service was uncertain at best. On one day after installation, electrical service was available for only seven hours. The Barracks wanted 24 hours of reliable service. Major Meade warned the Charlestown Gas and Electric Company that if they did not receive reliable electric power, the Barracks would disconnect from the commercial power and connect to the power generated by the Navy yard which was providing 24-hour service.[101]

Headquarters was concerned with the practice of commanding officers requesting the discharge of Marines as "unfit for service." This was getting to be on a wholesale basis. It made the radar. So when the commanding officer of the Marine Guard on board the USS *Lancaster* requested authority for discharge of 3 Marines as "unfit for service," the colonel commandant took issue with the request and transferred the men to the Marine Barracks in Boston. Colonel Heywood wanted the wholesale discharge of men as "unfit for service" to be stopped. He informed the commanding officer of Boston's Marine Barracks to keep the men under observation for a period of time and report his opinion to the headquarters after they had been given a full trial on shore.[102]

The new post exchange was high visibility with headquarters. In December 1897, the colonel commandant informed Major Meade that he may allow credit in the post exchange of up to one-third of a Marine's monthly pay.[103]

It became the end of the Meade era when he was detached on December 20, 1897. His post exchange wrangling with Assistant Secretary Theodore Roosevelt undoubtedly hastened his departure. His career didn't end there, however. During the Boxer Rebellion he commanded the First Marine Regiment's attack against the Tientsin native quarter on July 13, 1900.[104]

The Boxer Rebellion

Major Meade was as far away from Boston as he possibly could be, in Northern China, in 1900.

For a year and a half, just about all of the European great powers: United Kingdom, France, Italy, Russia, Japan, Germany, Austria-Hungary, and not to be left out of the action the United States, converged on China. China, once one of the greatest empires in history, was reduced to being fought over as spoils by the 19th century great powers. China at the time was more of a tradition bound region than a nation. With no strong central government, it was ripe for any plundering imperialists looking to enlarge their colonial footprints in a world with rapidly decreasing unclaimed lands.

In a separate flash point, China not only lost Hong Kong to Great Britain, it also was required to purchase its opium. The pre–World War I rise of Nationalism politics engendered this reality.

Not only prestige-seeking countries rushed in to China. Settlers, merchants, and missionaries moved in as well, claiming ownership of its lands. A similar historical pattern was the American West. Settlers, merchants, and missionaries moved onto Native American land and claimed ownership of it. Where the similarity ends is that China had a substantial population, unlike the sparsely populated American West.

Great navigable rivers made substantial portions of inland China accessible to westerners by boat. This was key for a major region lacking the railroad infrastructure of modern western nations. Settlements grew up along these rivers. The settlement near Tientsin was one of these. At first, the close location of the city of Tientsin was beneficial to the pioneering settlers. U.S.

Navy boats plied the rivers and serviced these communities for one hundred years, until the rise of Mao Zedong in 1949.

Foreigners forbidding increasing amounts of prime ancient lands to the multitudes of subsistence farming peasants widened the gulf of understanding between the two interests. This resentment grew into the Boxer Rebellion.

Tientsin, a walled city one mile square, where one million Chinese lived in or near, had a treaty port along the Han River composed of 700 foreign, or European, men, women, and children. But now they lived under the increasing threat of the Boxers, a militant, anti-foreign and anti–Christian peasant movement. Most were merchants and missionaries, but there was one American notable who also resided there, Herbert Hoover and his wife Lou Henry.

Six countries with interests in China sent 2400 troops to guard these settlers. On June 15, thousands of Boxers from the countryside converged upon Tientsin. They rioted through the city killing Christians and destroying churches. On the 16th, the inconsistently armed Boxers moved toward the settlement. Defenders were waiting and drove them off with solid fire. The Chinese army was also present. It awaited orders from Peking—whether to support the foreigners or the Boxers.

But as a result of battles elsewhere, Peking chose the Boxer side and ordered the army to attack the settlements. Complete with its 19th century heavy artillery, the Chinese army bombarded the settlement on the 17th. Defenders were stretched thin and communications were cut off from the allied fleet for days. Fifteen thousand Chinese troops and boxers armed with swords, spears, and antique guns massed. Defenders braced for attack. Instead they began to endure a siege. The Chinese army's primary action was a daily artillery barrage. In all, 60,000 shells rained on the settlers. Most did not explode, however. Corruption at the munitions plants reduced their quality.

Nonetheless, everyone knew the settlement needed reinforcements. After four days of organizing an allied expeditionary force, regiments, including Major Meade and his Marines, made their way, on foot or beasts, up the railway tracks from the coast towards Tientsin. Herbert Hoover, a mining engineer with a local knowledge of the terrain, rode out to meet the Allied forces. Together with the U.S. Marines, he guided three columns of French, British, American and Japanese troops to defendable approach points to the south gate of Tientsin.

Entry by gate was the only option, as it was a walled city defended by artillery and modern water-cooled machine guns. An assault left the allies pinned face down in muddy open swamps. The Chinese army fought with unexpected valor. A Japanese commander with combat experience against the Chinese emphasized that the Chinese would fight fiercely until the end if trapped, but would retreat if given an out. The allies took note.

Several attempts were made by the Japanese to blow up the gate with explosives, but defenders simply cut the fuses. It took a courageous Japanese soldier to bring in a short fused bomb. He was killed in the explosion (a suicide bomber is a contemporary version) but the gate was taken out.

Japan first and then the allies, including Meade's Marines, rushed into the walled city. Just as the Japanese commander assessed, the Chinese army retreated. Due to the lack of any coordinating leadership, the attack soon became a looting and pillaging disgrace. Russians and Germans perpetrated the worst atrocities. Undisciplined conscripts raped, and then bayoneted, their victims. The Marines were disgusted and made attempts to quell the horror, but some Marines were injured by this action.[105]

As a result of this pivotal battle, the allies reassessed their view of the Chinese army's valor. This they planned for in subsequent campaigns and quelled this rebellion. Rebellions are revolutions that didn't succeed. Revolutions are rebellions that succeeded. That is why these events are known as the Boxer Rebellion in Western history books.

But the desire to break up large holdings of land and divide it among subsistence farmers, although unknown at the time, was a harbinger of things to come: Marxist and Communist land reform movements. Where the Boxers failed, Mao Zedong succeeded. His was the revolution.

An important overarching problem with far reaching effects of this whole affair was that with so many nationalities, there was no overall commander. This undoubtedly left behind bad blood among the allies. Japan and Russia went to war five years later and the European players nine years after that.

With the dawn of 1898, the opinionated Major Meade was gone from the Boston area. Former duty officer Captain Allen C. Kelton became the commanding officer of the Marine Barracks.

One of his first acts was to appoint a sub-committee of enlisted men consisting of Sergeant Thomas McCabe, Sergeant Edward Clifford and Corporal Timothy Sugrue. Their task was to see if the needs of the enlisted men were being met with the new post exchange system.[106]

In January 1898, headquarters requested that Captain Kelton report on sales, including beer in the store. A price list of articles sold was also required and a pay day statement showing each man who had patronized the post exchange. The report covered the 15th to the 15th of each month and was expected on a monthly basis.[107]

Incorrigible prisoners were a lingering problem and gave the new Commander Captain Kelton a thorn in his side. A group of general courts-martial prisoners were continually at odds with prison guards and the administration. The trouble making prisoners were duly warehoused in solitary confinement, but they would revert back to their previous bad behavior immediately upon release. Captain Kelton recommended that prisoners who would not properly behave be transferred to state prisons and should wear distinctive uniforms while serving sentences, making it more difficult for prisoners if they attempted escape.[108]

Private John Doyle was once again the subject of official correspondence. Private Doyle died at the naval hospital on April 4, 1898, and Major Pope appointed 1st Lt. T.P. Kane to inventory his personal effects.[109]

PART III—THE WORLD STAGE

8. The Spanish American War and Its Aftermath

"Your son Fred S. Cutter is here on duty and is a very good boy."
—Lt. Col. Pope

Cuba was a colony of the aging and retreating empire of Spain. Since the Columbus era around 1492 until the contemporary times of 1895, Spain was a great power for a remarkable span of almost 400 years. But very competent competition in the Caribbean by British, French, and now the United States navies weakened any Spanish follow through on promised reforms in Cuba.

Unrest erupted in 1895 as those awaiting these forlorn reforms began to feel neglected. The brutal treatment of the Cuban people resulting in over 100,000 deaths by Spain received wide publicity, mainly through reports that appeared in the New York newspapers. U.S. citizens were living in Cuba, some with extensive property interests. They witnessed this brutality themselves and became concerned for their own safety, and were affected by the extensive property damage caused by the suppression. All U.S. trade with Cuba was halted. The Spanish prime minister attempted to settle the conflict in 1897 by negotiating with the insurgents, but they would not settle for less than complete independence. Perhaps the horrible treatment by Spain ended any chance of compromise. Back in the United States, popular demand for intervention gained support in the U.S. Congress. The violence ground on. A series of incidents eventually precipitated U.S. intervention. U.S. battleship USS *Maine* arrived 25 January in the port of Havana to protect U.S. citizens and property after receiving reluctant permission from Madrid to do so. No shore leave was granted to avoid trouble. Officials on location felt the ship's presence had a calming effect and recommended sending another ship when the *Maine* was scheduled to depart.

After 20 days of anchorage in the harbor, at 9:40 in the evening of February 15, 1898, a tremendous explosion tore open the *Maine*, rocking the usually tranquil waters. Two hundred sixty lives were blown sky high. Five tons of gunpowder ignited, obliterating the forward. Captain Charles D. Sigsbee and his officers survived because their quarters were in the aft of the ship. Spanish officials and the crew of a civilian steamer nearby acted quickly to rescue survivors, allying initial fears it was a hostile act.

Underwater twisted metal wreckage and the lack of any technical expertise gave the four-week investigation flexibility to tailor its findings. The fact-finding committee published its official conclusion: a mine was placed under the ship. When this was announced, the American public reacted with outrage. Positions hardened. April 21, President McKinley ordered a blockade of Cuba. Spain responded with a declaration of war the next day. The committee's report served to send the nation to war with a European great power.

Wild rumors circulated about an impending attack on the eastern U.S. coast by Spanish naval forces. In more modern times, wild rumors spread about ground forces landing on Hawaii after the Pearl Harbor attack. Even at the onset of Desert Storm, military facilities far inland, such as Eaker Air Force Base in Arkansas, braced for terrorist attacks. The crisis with Spain left the East Coast inhabitants in a state of high anxiety. Congressmen and governors echoed their constituents' demands for protection and applied pressure on the U.S. Navy to provide defense of port cities.[1]

War fever affected the Marine Barracks, too. Many Marines shipped out for sea duty. With many more battalions embarking for Cuba, America was indeed preparing for a real war with the venerable empire of Spain and bracing for its vicissitudes. On April 6, 1898, the first sergeants and corporals were ordered to Norfolk, Virginia, for ship duty.[2] Two weeks later, 2 more sergeants, 4 corporals, 2 drummers and 20 privates were moved to Brooklyn, New York, to board ships there.[3] Orders came on the same day these troops left Boston for another draft of an officer, 4 sergeants, 2 corporals and 50 privates all ordered to Brooklyn for sea service.[4]

The new Great White Navy was sailing the high seas. As the 20th Century dawned, the United States owned a world-class navy, waiting for something to do, just as the bills came in to pay for it. The moment for America to assert its authority over European powers in the Western Hemisphere had arrived: the U.S. will do the colonizing here, thank you very much. A period of difficult economic times had also descended on America after the 1890's had started off so promising. The war with Spain in 1898 provided just the impact the American economy needed to turn things around, a positive vicissitude indeed. And the U.S. Navy, its opportunity to serve had arrived on a very timely basis. It provided the Navy the chance to test its new warships, its modern organization and its ability to provide for its logistical requirements, and to season its leaders in naval combat. The war helped to reinvigorate the Boston Naval Shipyard as a principal ship-building and repair facility for the Navy. During the 1898–1899 period, the yard provided repairs to over fifty naval ships. The increase in work necessitated a large workforce, more skilled and well-paid jobs for the Boston area.[5]

Until 1898, the yard had always been open to visitors. No pass was required and visitors could even go into the various shops and watch the goings-on. This ended here.

The responsibilities of the post exchange at the Marine Barracks required a monthly report be made to headquarters, war or no war. Captain A.C. Kelton's assessment in his report was that it seemed to work rather well. More men utilized the post exchange than they did the post trader. The benefits that accrued to the command were certainly very well received. They were able to purchase pool tables and items for the post library with what would have been the post trader's income. He also reported that although beer was served in the canteen, there did not seem to be any abuse of alcohol. His overall opinion was that the system was advisable and practical.[6]

Sinking of the *Maine* brought about a strong anticipation of war with Spain. This excitement increased the visitors to the yard. The visitors wanted to watch the preparations for war up close. All well and fine until there is an accident: a small child fell into a dry-dock. However, the dry-dock was full of seawater. Fortunately the child was unhurt; it nevertheless caused great concern.[7]

With more and more visitors, folks began to become concerned about saboteurs and spies mixing in the throngs. Additionally, many Marines from the Barracks had already been sent to war. Fewer were left to guard the Charlestown Navy Yard. The last day for casual visitors to the Navy Yard was April 11, 1898. The commandant of the Navy Yard ordered that visitors to the Navy yard would no longer be permitted, unless they were on official business or a guest of families residing in the yard.[8]

The daily life of shipyard routine provided distractions to the war. A member of Congress requested a reduced sentence for a general court-martial prisoner. Major Pope was horrified and forcefully replied to Congressman Cummings that personal favoritism has injurious effects upon military service, especially in the prisons. The applicant must earn the reduction through his own good conduct. It should all depend on the prisoner. The prisoner was urging the representative to do what Major Pope didn't want to do himself.[9]

Major Pope received orders to command the second battalion of Marines dispatching to Cuba. He then made arrangements with the paymaster of the Marine Corps for his wife to receive a portion of his pay while he was away. He left the Barracks on April 22, 1898, to join up with the second battalion of Marines.[10]

The movement of Marines from the Barracks gained momentum. On April 22, two sergeants were ordered to Brooklyn, NY, for duty with the Marine battalion.[11] Two days later, Sergeant Edward Clifford was assigned to duty as 1st sergeant of the Marine detachment aboard the USS *Harvard* in port in Brooklyn.

With major Pope gone, this order was signed by a lieutenant commander of the Navy, commanding Marines, with Marine Barracks letterhead.[12] The lieutenant commander was the only available ranking officer around to sign a letter that deploys troops. Three days after that, 1 sergeant and 30 privates were dispatched by railroad to Washington, D.C.[13] In three more days, 20 more privates were transferred to Brooklyn for duty with a battalion of Marines.[14] Once again, on May 2, seven more privates joined this battalion.[15] And on May 5, Sgt. Louis Ebers was ordered to report to Brooklyn for duty with that Marine battalion.[16]

Routine requests for services by retired Marines had to be honored amid the war preparation efforts. Retired Marine Private Charles McKeough requested to enter the naval home in Chelsea. Captain Wallach verified his service. He had been disqualified for further service due to a physical disability on his last enlistment. At the time of McKeough's rejection for further service, a former colonel commandant informed him that the naval home was open to him. However, for family reasons he did not take advantage of the opportunity. Now he was 74 years and no longer had a family, and was ready to be admitted to the naval home. Captain Wallach forwarded his request to Headquarters, Marine Corps.[17] No further correspondence indicated how the matter was resolved.

In mid–May the transfers began in earnest. Two sergeants, 3 corporals, 1 drummer, 1 fifer and 20 privates were ordered for duty with the Marine detachment aboard the USS *Lancaster*.[18] Again on the 17th, 1 sergeant and 6 privates were transferred to Norfolk, VA, for duty aboard the USS *Newark*.[19]

Large numbers of Marines were leaving for sea duty and assignment to the battalion of Marines, causing a rapid depletion of personnel. The Marine Barracks was authorized to advertise for new recruits in the *Boston Post* and the *Boston Herald*.[20]

Movement of Marines from the Barracks continued into June. On June 3, fifty more privates were transferred to Norfolk for sea duty.[21] On June 15, another draft consisting of 1 corporal and 15 privates was dispatched to Washington, D.C., for duty.[22]

Wartime brought increased ship activities to the shipyard and many different peoples together. And sometimes these people didn't like other, even though they were on the same side. Private McQuade got into a shouting match with an unknown sailor right in front of the commanding officer's quarters on Chelsea Street. They were told to go away by the Marine on Post 2 sentinel duty. They didn't like that. Instead of shouting at each other, they now shouted verbal abuse at the sentinel. The sergeant of the guard was called. When he arrived he opened the gate and tried to drive the agitators away from their boss's home. But as soon as he opened the gate, McQuade and the sailor rushed into the yard. McQuade punched the sergeant of the guard and the sailor right hooked the sentinel.[23]

Recruiting was smooth. Except for one thing. Maybe one office was plenty. Captain Wallach wanted to "centralize" his recruiting efforts at 98 Court Street. He notified the landlord, Thomas H. Armstrong, esquire, that the extra office at 30 Portland Street would be vacated on June 30, 1898.[24]

A person was behaving in such a manner as to have attracted the attention of those on watch. He was taken in June 28. His papers showed him to be a citizen of Portugal. Why was he there at the Navy yard several months after the new access policy? Well, language barriers delayed that investigation. The Marines had to do something with him until the local Portuguese consul arrived. They put him in the Barracks dungeon in the meantime, by order of the commandant of the Navy yard.[25]

Marines were transferring in and out of the Barracks with increased tempo. This turnover took its toll on routine and vital tasks of maintaining the Navy yard. Anytime peacetime military routine is disrupted by war, what were once high priority duties get superceded by even higher priorities. Or a stellar individual is transferred for the greater war cause, but ends up doing something less urgent than what they were doing before they were transferred. Captain Wallach asked the commandant of the Navy yard to use his influence to have Corporal James S. Barrett transferred back to Boston from the Portsmouth Naval Shipyard in New Hampshire. Corporal Barrett had been in charge of the prisoner work detail for the past three years. These maintained the walks, grounds and trees about the yard. Corporal Barrett's leadership was solid and he was sorely missed. What he was doing in Portsmouth was not as important or interesting as his duties at the Boston yard, in the opinion of Captain Wallach.[26]

Thirty more privates shipped out to Norfolk for sea duty on the August.[27]

The prison fund was important and interesting monies enough that the commandant of the Navy yard wanted to know where it was and what was being done with it. Captain Wallach explained. The money was designated as the U.S. Naval Prison Fund and was deposited as such in the Bunker Hill National Bank in Charlestown. The commanding officer of the naval prison was the custodian of these funds, as the prisoners were not allowed to have any money in their possession. These financial resources were administered for the benefit of the prisoners as necessity may dictate.[28] Checks were drawn against the prison fund and signed by the drawer (Captain Wallach) as commanding officer of the naval prison. The funds were received from receiving ships at the Navy yard and from the paymaster of the Marine Corps. These comprised the monthly allowance of the prisoners. The prison also used whatever cash the prisoner may have possessed commencing confinement.

Prisoners in the naval prison slept on straw or hammock mattresses on iron bunks. It even sounds uncomfortable. To minimize this discomfort, in times when there were more mattresses available, a second mattress was issued to inmates to soften their beds. Hammock mattresses were so thin that the iron slats on the bunks once deranged a man's hair in the mattress, on top of making a very miserable bed. Straw mattresses were lumpy, scratchy, and very uncomfortable indeed. To modernize the naval prison at the turn of the century, Captain Wallach recommended that mattresses of better quality be sought as replacements.[29]

On July 18, 1898, the Spanish government requested a settlement with the United States. The war seemed to be over, after only several months. What started as an intervention into the closely watched struggle for Cuban independence became one fought in the Caribbean Sea and the Pacific. That is were the assets of the U.S. and Spanish navies happened to be and could get at each other when hostilities commenced.

History repeated itself in America's favor. As the brand new USS *Constitution* defeated the HMS *Guerriere* back in the War of 1812, the brand new Great White Fleet swiftly defeated the aging and tired Spanish fleet all around the world. Local inhabitants sided with the Americans against their long time Spanish rulers.

At once exciting but also filled with great responsibility, a nation proud of its anticolonial heritage suddenly gained colonies of it own. With U.S. naval ships controlling the Spanish territory ports of Puerto Rico, Guam, the Philippines, and Guantanamo Bay, these territories became American "prizes" Spain was unable to win back. The Spanish Empire was effectively over. The loss of Cuba, seen as a province of Spain (like Hawaii is to the United States) and not just a colony, hurt and caused a national trauma in Spain eventually leading to the Spanish Civil War. In the lives of the Marines of the Marine Barracks, these place names would soon come to mean many things.

With the war over, Marine Corps Headquarters notified Captain Wallach that recruiting should be reduced and the *Boston Globe* should suspend recruiting advertisements until further notice.[30]

Lt. Col. Pope returned to the Marine Barracks as commanding officer in August.

Post Spanish-American War Period

The electrical power plant in the Navy yard was undergoing renovations that would provide dreamed about increases in electricity. Lt. Col. Pope wanted the quartermaster to make arrangements with the Bureau of Yards and Docks to provide electrical power to the Marine Barracks, too.[31]

Prisoner Private Barber on work detail was making the walls in the Barracks basement look brand new, whitewashing them in September. This general court-martial prisoner went on his "bathroom" break. Instead of returning to beautifying the dungeon, he climbed up and out the washroom window. He climbed the Navy yard wall and escaped onto Chelsea Street.

Not all naval prisoners from the prison were as familiar with the Marine Barracks as Barber. He had been stationed there before incarceration. The guard responsible for Barber was Private John Sweeney. He was also responsible for three other prisoners at the time of the escape. What happens to a guard when a prisoner escapes? Private Sweeney was confined. At least Lt. Col. Pope supported Sweeney in his letter to the commandant of the Navy Yard. He said Sweeny was an excellent man and it just seems the prisoner slipped away in the darkness of the basement when the guard turned his back.[32]

By September, Marines who had served with the 1st Battalion during the war were returning to the Boston Barracks. They were ready to go on leave. A large number of them had requested what Pope described as a "well deserved furlough."[33]

Marines were coming back from war and were once again filling bunks. Gates closed during the war because everybody was gone could now be opened again. Lt. Col. Pope though this might be a good time to request monies for repairs of the guardroom. Glass also needed replacement and doors repaired. Cars and trucks began passing through the main gate everybody uses. It wasn't designed for this new traffic and it wasn't safe. On September 20 Pope established a post in the rear of the Main Gate (Gate 2) to handle this modern traffic. This was going to become an important post, he said, and he wanted a new sentry box for it. Without a sentry box a driving rain or sideways snow or unrelenting sun could knock out a gate's sentry, rendering the gate unguarded.[34]

Parents of Marines wrote to the commanding officers from time to time concerned about the welfare of their sons, especially when they had not heard from them for a long period of time. One response to such a letter was written to Mrs. Cutler in October 1898. Lt. Col. Pope wrote: "Your son Fred S. Cutler is here on duty and is a very good boy and stands on our books as a first class man in conduct. I called him into my office this morning. He said that he has written to you and that he will write again tomorrow when he is off duty. He is very well."[35]

Congress authorized by the acts of April 26, 1898 an additional pay of 20 percent for those who served in action during the Spanish-American War. Lt. Col. Pope provided a list of 49 Marines who had served with the 1st Battalion of Marines in Cuba to the auditor for the Navy Department.[36]

Memories of what was now becoming known as the Spanish-American War were still fresh, but things were returning back to normal. Routine tasks once again became priority.

Across the harbor in South Boston, unable to get back to the Barracks himself, lay Private John J. O'Keefe prostrate from an illness. He had been kept at 22 Ellery Street since September 20, possibly for quarantine against those late 19th century communicable diseases. Over a month later a horse drawn ambulance from the Navy yard was dispatched 29 October 1898 to finally go get him and put him in the naval hospital.[37]

First Lieutenant Charles S. Long became the new post exchange officer, relieving Captain A.C. Kelton of these duties November 18. His orders were to follow the regulations, in particular General Order No. 46, created by Army Headquarters on July 26, 1896. That one was a biggie. All orders for merchandise and beer required 1st Lt. Long's signature: the lieutenant needed to sign for everything. This caused issues in the past. Delivered goods required vouchers to establish an appropriate auditing paper trail.[38]

The December 1898 issues of *Boston Globe* and the *Boston Herald* began to run recruiting advertisements. They ended up running for the next three months.[39]

The Marines on sentry duty and local cops on a beat often became familiar to one another. Sometimes they could help each other out professionally. A local policeman was talking with the sentinel at the Chelsea Street gate near the Chelsea Bridge, on yard grounds. The officer of the day saw this. Regulations are regulations. Sentries cannot speak to anyone outside their line of duty. Lt. Col. Pope got the Boston police chief involved. The sentry was going to be punished for this infraction. In fairness's sake, Lt. Col. Pope wanted the chief of police to take action against the beat policeman as well.[40]

The new possessions won from the Empire of Spain had U.S. Marines heading to new place names. First stop: Guam. Probably contemplating a dreary boring tour, Pope wanted the men to bring along some baseball equipment, games and other amusements for while they were there. They had the money to do it too. The commander moved to get authorization for an expenditure of $50 for these items from the post exchange "Profit Fund" monies. This money was readily available and designated for benefit of the men. Indeed, the fund had accumulated to $700. Headquarters approved the expenditure. However, headquarters also reminded the commander that the object of a post exchange after all was to use these profits for the good of the command and that such large sums of money should not be left to accumulate.

It is reasonable that this money accumulated, however. The command was not used to this new wealth. The commander could have asked for and gotten even more funds for the men transferred to Guam since they had contributed to the profits themselves.[41]

The USS *Marblehead* had some serious disciplinary problems, so bad that its miscreants were confined to the naval prison in chains. Pope, not having a dog in that fight, requested permission to remove the chains from the prisoners. Perhaps he didn't want to set a precedent that may ultimately make him look bad. After all, Boston would want to know why he kept "all" his prisoners in chains. Not only that, the USS *Marblehead* was still feeding these prisoners. Pope was unsure what century the *Marblehead* was living in, so he doubted the quality of food given the prisoners' state of chains. He wanted them to get their meals from the Marine Barracks in the same fashion as the other prisoners.[42]

Lt. Col. Pope received orders to command a battalion of Marines on the island of Guam, by 1898 a U.S. territory. Guam had been formally ceded to the United States by Spain in the terms of the peace treaty just signed in Paris an ocean and a continent away on the 10 January 1899. Boston was instructed to furnish one first sergeant, 4 sergeants, 2 corporals, 1 fifer and 30 privates for the battalion of Marines due for Guam.[43]

On an island archipelago in the South Pacific, Guam is only thirteen degrees of latitude north of the equator. It is perhaps one the most remote places on this earth. Home to some of the best scuba diving in the world, it could be a tropical paradise, but it lacks the trade winds of Hawaii, making Guam very hot and sticky. It does, however, have fresh water and an excellent harbor.

Pope was probably concerned he would have nothing to read, so he requested that a library be loaned and moved to the island of Guam. He supported his request by illuminating that it was a very lonely and isolated outpost indeed, and the Marines would need a bountiful supply of reading material. And there just happened to be a ship available to send this library, the USS *Yosemite,* which was scheduled to transport the troops to the area.[44]

The silk battle flag for the battalion of Marines now commanded by Colonel Pope (newly promoted) was sent to the Barracks in error. Captain Kelton forwarded it the unit en route to the Pacific.[45]

Men were also transferred to the battalion of Marines at Cavite in the Philippines, also recently ceded to the United States in the peace treaty. Captain Moses requested the commander of the Marines in Cavite to collect the money that was owed to the post exchange in Boston and was heading to the Pacific. These monies were not properly left behind.[46]

The Barracks won two handsome silver trophies against Battery G, 7th U.S. Artillery. One silver trophy was awarded for being second to none in proficiency in physical drill, bayonet exercises, and company drill. The second silver trophy was for winning the tug of war. Winning matching silver trophies was a good way to spend a fine May day in 1899. The brigadier general commandant at the event expressed his heartfelt appreciation for the work done by the folks who got the events to go off without a hitch and how a good time was had by all. He emphasized that the day's results reflected very well on the officers and men. The efforts illustrated the drill and discipline of the post.[47]

Newburyport once thought it was in competition with Boston to be the major shipping port of Massachusetts very early in the 1800s. Treacherous waters at the Merrimac River's mouth put the kibosh on that ambition. A lighthouse was in operation at this river mouth on Plum Island in Newburyport. It helped guide mariners through the shifting tidal brackish waters, sandbars and rocks, and surf, often at night.

Ever vigilant, the lighthouse keeper was looking out upon the bay when he discerned a rather unpleasant sight: a lifeless body of a person, floating out with the tides in the Merrimac River. As the body got closer, the lighthouse keeper could make out that the cadaver was clothed in a Marine uniform. The body was also quite decomposed. How word got back to Pope about this was the lighthouse keeper's handwritten letter, dated 9 May 1899.

Subsequent inquiry revealed that it was the body of Private Michael Kelleher. He was a member of the Marine Detachment aboard the USS *Castine*. He was lost falling out of a train while it was crossing over the Merrimac River in Newburyport at 8 p.m. November 20, 1898. This meant his body has been floating back and forth in the incoming and outflowing tides for months. The panel's findings left nothing to posterity as to how the private fell off the train.[48]

It must have been just like in the movies. Someone leaping or falling or thrown from a train just as it crosses over a river. It looks great. This happens in the movies all the time. The story plot's usual objective is to allow a character to exit the scene without killing them, or leaving their fate unknown for future use. That's the way it usually works in the movies. This time, however, Michael Kelleher was killed by the whole experience.

Lt. Col. Cochrane

Lt. Col. Henry Clay Cochrane assumed command on May 15, 1899. He came with battle experience.

Back in 1882, Egypt was governed by a combined British and French protectorate (a form of colonialism). Nationalist leader Arabi Pasha had an anti-colonial agenda with unclear grassroots supports which threatened the stability of that government. The threat was serious enough to concentrate the British Mediterranean Fleet on the port of Alexandria in June 1882. The new Suez Canal was at stake.

Along for the adventure sailed a token U.S. squadron, three ships waving the U.S. flag, and the screw sloop *Lancaster*. A screw sloop was the latest technology of the day, a sail ship with steam power that ran screws (propellers), the modern propulsion mechanism of any modern navy today, replacing paddle wheels. This was an opportunity to try out this new equipment and give volunteer Marines a chance to try out their training.

Although lightly armed compared to the non-portable army, the Marines' mission has been to amphibiously land anywhere the Navy can take them from the sea and achieve a beachhead. Marines were also trained in dreadful ship-to-ship, hand-to-hand combat.

British bombardment of the ancient city of Alexandria, founded by Alexander the Great, commenced on July 11 1882. After three days of cannonade, the city was softened up to the leadership's satisfaction; men climbed into landing boats and rowed ashore. The Americans sent a landing force ashore several days later on the 14th under the command of future Barracks Commander Captain Henry Clay Cochrane.

Cochrane had been Lincoln's aide at Gettysburg and was present the day the president made his speech. With such eloquence in his background, Captain Cochrane calmly declared his landing party would "stick by the British and take their chances." By the time American boots were on the ground, over four thousand British troops had all but taken over the city.[49] The Arabi Pasha revolt was beat down and the affair began what was to become a 40 year British occupation of Egypt.

One of Captain Cochrane's first concerns at his new post was to improve the security of the naval prison. He recommended to the judge advocate general that the fence around the prison exercise yard should be raised 3 to 4 feet for a total of 12 feet. It could be done with light iron wire grating (a forerunner to chain link) he said, and it would also improve the appearance of the yard. Also, if the fence were raised, it would eliminate two guard positions.[50]

It was time for telephone service to be provided on a twenty-four hour basis between the two important gates (Main Gate and the East Gate) and the Barracks. Lt. Col. Cochrane requested such service to his superiors.[51]

Lt. Col. Cochrane, an astute man, looked for the recruitment notices he requested advertised when he received a copy of a newspaper. He discovered this particular paper had put the ad in the "legal notices" section. He knew, since he commanded such men, that the class of men that the Marine Corps desired to reach were not interested in legal notices. So he notified the Journal Newspaper Co., 264 Washington Street, Boston, and asked them to run the advertisement in the "situation notices" section instead. This is where men seeking a steady, reliable and a fairly remunerative job would more likely find the ad. He added that he would be very pleased if the newspaper would place the advertisement in the proper location where it would do the most good.[52]

Rotations of Marines on Guam and Cavite, remote details to be sure and anyone stationed there probably did not want to be marooned there either, were being filled with replacements from the Barracks. On August 8, one officer, 2 sergeants, 1 corporal and 35 privates were transferred to Brooklyn, NY, to serve with the 2nd Battalion of Marines.[53]

The Marines at the Barracks were having difficulty training with the Lee rifle. The Lee rifle was the latest weaponry technology of its day. Weighing almost 8 and a half pounds with a barrel length of almost a yard, its effective range was 600 yards. It was introduced to the Marines just before, or to some it felt like as soon as, the outbreak of the Spanish-American War. Its lightness enabled the mission of the Marines to land and hold beachheads. The Marines who served in Cuba used this rifle. On their way to the Caribbean, the troops were hurriedly given lectures and field stripped their new rifles, and were given ten rounds to shoot for familiarization. But the troops on the USS *Panther* under Lt. Col. Huntington stopped in Key West for two weeks of target practice. This practice proved worthwhile when contrasted to the experience of allied Cuban guerrillas. The guerrillas encountered initial difficulties when they were handed fresh guns out of a wooden box.

The Lee rifle's flat ballistics, accuracy, rate of fire, and the light weight of its ammunition proved beneficial in mountainous jungles and against massed Spanish troops. The ability to carry extra cartridges allowed the Marines to continue their assault even though their re-supply was disrupted.

But in subsequent campaigns in the Philippines, many felt the small caliber of its cartridge lacked the shocking or stopping power of a .30-caliber against crazed bolo welding guerrillas at close distances. However, at the battle of Teintsin, the advancing Marines armed with Lees were able to transport 10,000 rounds and never ran short of ammunition, unlike the other Western forces that had to capture the imperial Chinese arsenal to continue fire.

Back at the Barracks, daily routines did not sync up with prescribed training on the Lee rifle. It was very difficult to carry out the Army firing regulations with personnel on a day on and day off schedule of guard, Cochrane explained to the assistant adjutant and inspector for rifle practice at headquarters. The curriculum required by regulations contemplated progressive and systematic instruction by thoroughly trained officers. An effective regimen to be sure, however, but it also required uninterrupted attention by a command with 5 or 6 nights in bed and some degree of permanence. In order to accustom the men to the Lee rifle, Lt. Col. Cochrane was placing new recruits within 3 days of enlistment in the shooting gallery and giving all a turn at practice camps. He found the results encouraging, and the 40 volunteers for the Marine Manila battalion were ready to take the field on arrival.[54]

Lt. Col. Cochrane responded to a circular letter (addressed to Barracks commanders) from the assistant adjutant and inspector of rifle practice at headquarters by complaining that facilities for either gallery (indoor) or range (outdoor) practice at the Boston yard were inferior at best. The gallery range was partitioned off in the extreme northeasterly end of the yard, far from the Barracks, and could not be heated. It contained five regulation iron gallery targets placed too close together, although two iron revolving targets were entirely satisfactory. The building (Bldg. 122), however, was of ample size and well lit. The field range on Lovell's Island was eight miles out in Boston Harbor. The range had been heavily damaged by gale force winds and required substantial repair. The yard tug required for transportation to and from Lovell's Island had many other duties, and they interfered with routine transport of Marines to the island.[55]

The School of Application, a campus inculcating entry level Marine officers in leadership, professionalism, and officership, was not able to accommodate all the young men appointed as second lieutenants. Although ideal training, classes were full so headquarters sent 4 young lieutenants to Boston to complete their training there. Boston was tasked to provide special and theoretical as well as practical instructions to qualify them for their future duties as leaders of men.[56]

When retired Marines passed away, the Marine Barracks commander was responsible for making the necessary arrangements for services and burial when there was no next of kin. Private W.D. Cranith, USMC (Ret.) of 11 Princeton Street, Charlestown, passed away at the age of 72 on August 20, 1899. Lt. Col. Cochrane requested permission to have the yard chaplain hold the funeral service and have him buried in the naval hospital cemetery.[57]

Private Herman W. Kuchneister was being groomed for promotion to the rank of corporal, but he failed to pass the exam. Cochrane was in askance as to why this man was being singled out for promotion, after all, Lt. Col. Cochrane did not notice any thing special about him. Headquarters informed Cochrane that Captain B.H. McCalla, of the U.S. Navy, was recommending Private Kuchneister for promotion.

He conspicuously displayed bravery as a member of the crew of USS *Marblehead* when he helped cut the cables off Cienfuegos, Cuba, during the Spanish-American War on May 11, 1898. Private Kuchneister was severely wounded in the head during the battle. It was the desire of the brigadier general commandant to reward his highly meritorious conduct, however, not his injury. This clarified why Cochrane was instructed to give him ample time for preparation and re-examine him for promotion to corporal.[58] There's more. A bronze Medal of Honor came in the registered mail to be awarded to Private Herman W. Kuchneister. General Order No. 521, Navy Department, authorized the Medal of Honor. Colonel Cochrane himself was directed to present the medal at a formation of all personnel of the command in full dress uniform.[59]

Recruiting started to occur outside the Boston area in September. The Marine Corps opened a recruiting office in Springfield at 294 Main Street, and the *Springfield Republican* was informed of this.[60] Recruiting efforts were fruitful. Lt. Col. Cochrane wrote to Headquarters Marine Corps and stated that the limits of accommodation of recruits in the present facilities had been reached. He requested that the surplus recruits be transferred to other posts.[61]

Admiral George Dewey visited Boston in October. His victory in the Battle of Manila Bay in the Spanish-American War was one of the best-known events of the war. He was the only person in history of the United States to achieve the rank of admiral of the Navy. His extensive Civil War naval experience was proper preparation for this honor. After the Civil War he commanded the USS *Constitution* when it was berthed at Annapolis Officers' School as a training ship. In 1880 after returning to the peacetime sea duty of inspecting lighthouses, Dewey was assigned to Washington, D.C., as a bureau officer of high rank and became one of the most popular men in town.

Spring 1898 found Dewey outside of Manila Bay, the most important harbor in the Philippines. Orders came in that America was now at war with Spain and its ships were targets. To get at the enemy he needed to enter the bay. But the bay was fortified. The only way to get past the shore batteries was to enter the bay at night, an extremely hazardous endeavor. Inside the harbor, however, awaited a variety of obsolete Spanish vessels and inexperienced seamen. On May Day 1898 Admiral Dewey made a command decision.

Curiously, the Spanish fleet awaited confrontation out of range of the Spanish land batteries of cannons, the same batteries that were keeping the U.S. fleet from entering during the day. These could have augmented and provided cover for the Spanish admiral's forces and evened the odds, but its commander stayed in the harbor and had his fleet anchored at shallows instead.

Where the Spanish fleet anchored did, however, spare the shelling of Manila and would allow his inexperienced sailors to swim to shore if they survived a fight with the superior American navy. Dewey knew of the state of the Spanish defenses and preparedness. This knowledge probably influenced his decision to enter the harbor at night. At first daylight, the Americans proceeded to dismantle and disorganize the Spanish fleet. A battalion of Marines was provided for a parade in Admiral Dewey's honor.[62]

On Thanksgiving, November 25, at 9:20 p.m. a couple of guys tried to get in the lower yard gate. The sentry asked who they were; they said they were ship keepers. The sentinel turned them away. They headed away down Chelsea Street toward the bridge. Not the massive and dominating Mystic River Bridge, but its humble predecessor whose purpose was to simply link Chelsea to Boston.

Forty minutes later, a man had a ladder to an open window on Building 77 and was just starting to climb. As this sight wasn't puzzling enough, the Post 6 sentry couldn't resist challenging the man: he bolted. The guard sounded the alarm.

Local policemen joined in the chase. They caught and arrested James Murphy near the Chelsea Street Bridge. Murphy wasn't just standing around doin' nothin'. Valuable metals, 45 pounds of them, were in his possession. The Post 5 sentry identified Murphy as one of those "shipkeepers." The search for his buddy was cut short by a fire coincidentally breaking out in the yard at the same time.[63]

Private Donald E. Ferris had gotten ahold of 50 pounds of tobacco, yes, 50 pounds of tobacco. All that is known is that he wanted to unload it. He tried to December 8 at a store at 326 Hanover Street. He offered to sell the tobacco to the shopkeeper. The shopkeeper instead reported him to the police. Lt. Col. Cochrane requested that Private Donald E. Ferris be tried by a general court-martial.[64] That's a stint in the ancient Charlestown Naval Prison if convicted.

James Murphy, the guy who took the valuable metals, was not acting alone after all. Seems Patrolman Jeremiah Haggerty got him to name names. On December 9 James Carroll and Bernard Dougherty were rounded up as accomplices. Cochrane recommended the chief of Boston police recognize this officer's success.[65] Unrecorded was if the fire was related to the crime.

That it was beneficial America won territories from Spain is undeniable. Also undeniable was the need to garrison them with Marines. This affected the Barracks staffing. Two sergeants, 2 corporals, 1 drummer, 1 trumpeter and 50 privates were transferred to Brooklyn, NY, on August 29. They were to set sail with the 3rd Battalion of Marines to the port city of Cavite in the Philippine Islands.[66]

On November 30 privates (recruits) were sent to Washington, D.C., for duty.[67] In January 25 men were transferred to Norfolk, VA.[68] Sixteen days later 15 more recruits were transferred to Portsmouth, NH.[69]

For the Paris Exposition of 1900 a "poster child" Marine was wanted for a sweet duty. Headquarters asked Boston to furnish someone who was fluent in French, presented a trim appearance, well behaved, and a good-looking Marine. This Marine would be assigned to the naval exhibit at the Exposition.[70] Private Eugene Chevalier was nominated. His recommendation indicated that he possessed good manners and presented a fine appearance.[71] A Marine's Marine.

Good news: Recruiting was going very well. Bad news: this overtaxed the sleeping facilities at the Marine Barracks; twenty men were sleeping on the floor. Cochrane wanted to transfer twenty recruits to another post and asked headquarters for approval.[72]

A typical tour for a Marine overseas was two years. This, Lt. Col. Cochrane had to clarify to a fiancée of one the Marines stationed in Manila. He would not likely be there longer than two years, unless he volunteered to stay.[73]

A fact of Barracks life: 25 men were transferred to the Marine Barracks in Washington, D.C., in February.[74] And then in March, another 25 recruits were also moved to Washington, D.C.[75]

Private Jeremiah Crowley deserted the day he enlisted. An investigation revealed more than meets the eye. It discovered he had a wife, two children and a drinking problem. So much so his drinking compelled his last employer to lay him off until he sobered up. Private Crowley continued drinking anyway. Perhaps in an alcohol haze he ended up in Boston and enlisting in the Marine Corps as if he was getting a tattoo. He had claimed to be single when he enlisted.

The standard punishment for deserters was a court-martial and imprisonment. But this would end up punishing his family far more than Private Crowley. Cochrane recommended to headquarters that his enlistment be cancelled and no further disciplinary action taken.[76] Lt. Col. Cochrane could show appropriate compassion to those caught in the middle of military discipline.

Forty-two-year-old Second Lieutenant S.A.W. Patterson had been on a bender. These benders were becoming all too routine. It was affecting work. Twice before he had been placed on the sick list, for related reasons. Perhaps all this was getting to him. When he was home in his quarters, Patterson made the decision to slit his right wrist with a razor. His colleagues Lieutenants F.E. Evans and McDougal were nearby.

Did this factor into his decision? To put on a show? Have help nearby if he reconsidered after the attempt? Or go for it anyway and use his colleagues as a "trust fall?" They came to his rescue, perhaps as expected, and they discovered him in time. The junior officers immediately administered first aid and placed a tourniquet near his wound. Patterson was transported across the Mystic River to the Chelsea Naval Hospital for treatment.[77]

Marines misbehaving in different states can become bureaucratic hot potatoes. Private Patrick J. Griffin, a Marine stationed in Boston, and the responsibility of Lt. Col. Cochrane, was expected to be received by the Charlestown State Prison.[78] However, the warden of the Charlestown State Prison was concerned enough about this transfer that he contacted the secretary of the Navy in regards to the receipt of this general court-martial prisoner.[79] The warden was doubtful whether he had the right to receive a prisoner from another state. The private was after all apprehended and convicted for a civil offense in Maine.

Prisoners are expensive. States do not want to contain and feed another state's inmates, especially if they are unruly. The state prison warden cited an old state law which limited prisoners receivable to those convicted within Massachusetts' borders to support his position. The warden was going to run the question up the flagpole to the attorney general for an opinion on this case.

Colonel Cochrane

Recently promoted Colonel Cochrane was in his office working at his desk well into the admirable hour of 9:45 p.m. when he heard three unskilled blasts of a bugle. The bugle blasts could be heard as far away as the main entrance. This was unusual. He suspected that it was probably some Marine returning from liberty drunk.

The sergeant of the guard and the officer of the day, Captain Moses, were sent to get to the bottom of this incident of 18 May 1900. They reported back that it was a stranger instead: a student undergoing initiation into a society at Harvard. The shenanigans had been required by this student's voluntary initiation. The gag was to come to the Barracks, unknown and uninvited, and perform goofy and silly things. What also came out of the investigation: when the youngster, about 20, arrived at the officers' quarters, Captain Moses assisted in the tomfoolery by sending for a scarlet full dress coat, white belt, sword and Marine bugle for the student to wear. While arrayed in this finery he led the student into the guardroom to use the telephone. He needed to call an upperclassman student to verify his challenge. A stunt like this is best with an audience, and Captain Moses provided one. Needless to say Captain Moses was in difficulty with his commanding officer over the matter.[80]

Colonel Cochrane visited another island in Boston Harbor he might use for a training camp. Cochrane stepped onto Peddocks Island in May, as it looked suitable for a summer training camp for target and boating practice. The rent was accessible; the owner offered a lease of $25 per year for the camp and rifle range. The owner placed no restrictions on the Marines. He asked only that the Marines not interfere with the other tenants living on the island.[81] It wasn't specified if this interference included the noise a rifle range would entail.

The citizens of Charlestown were very good to the Marines and had always showered them with great generosity. So in appreciation of the Marines' participation in this year's Bunker Hill Day Parade, the grand marshal delivered to the Barracks 1400 glass bottles of ginger ale, sandwiches, and over 25 cigars as refreshments for the naval brigade and the Marines who marched in the parade. This wasn't just any year. This was 1900. This was a turn of the century celebration. All of the recipients were very pleased with this gesture of kindness. Colonel Pope even chortled that it would take some time to smoke all the cigars.[82]

The placement of general court-martial prisoner Private Thomas A. Griffin finally was resolved, with unexpected results. He was to serve his sentence at the Connecticut State Prison at Wethersfield. Sergeant Henry J. Bray and Private Eugene Smith were ordered to escort Private Griffin to this facility.[83]

The Barracks continued to provide personnel for the new battalions of Marines overseas. On June 21, 2 sergeants and 18 privates were transferred to Marine Barracks in Brooklyn, NY, for duty with the 4th Marine Battalion organizing for service in the Philippines.[84]

Post Exchange Officer Second Lieutenant Wadleigh was ordered to the 5th Marine Battalion for duty in China. Second Lieutenant D.C. McDougal became the next post exchange officer. McDougal was reassured that he was taking over a post exchange in good accounting order and in the black. Indeed, post exchange business revenues exceeded $1,000 per month and Colonel Cochrane advised Lt. McDougal to pay close personal attention to the exchange to insure its continued success.[85]

Colonel Cochrane was convinced Quartermaster Sergeant Thomas McCabe was not able to refrain from overindulgence in intoxicating liquors. This affected his reliability and therefore not worthy of his present rank. Colonel Cochrane recommended that his warrant as quartermaster sergeant be cancelled.[86]

June 28, Quartermaster Sergeant Thomas McCabe shot himself in the head with a revolver and died. He was due for discharge in several days.[87] Colonel Cochrane explained to his sister Mary McCabe in his letter of notification that McCabe had in fact been drinking for several days. But it did not reach such a level which would have alerted others that he would take such desperate steps. Mary McCabe was assured that her brother would be buried with military honors at the naval hospital cemetery if she did not exercise the option to have his remains removed to wherever she desired.[88] And in the event that she was the sole survivor of QM Sergeant McCabe, she could make claim to whatever possessions he had, after executing the proper affidavits.[89] Another letter informed her that all her affidavits were in order. Any money discovered or due at death must come to the heirs through the auditor of the Navy Department. Quartermaster Sergeant Thomas McCabe did not appear to have any debts.[90]

Lavatories in the naval prison were horrifying. The plumbing needed repair immediately. The automatic faucets in both lavatories required considerable overhauling and replacements. Pipes were leaking and required packing, and new washers needed installation. One washbowl was cracked and unfit for any use.[91]

In July 1900 the 5th Marine Battalion was being organized in Boston and destined for service in China and the Boxer Rebellion.[92] Colonel H. Clay Cochrane would command the Battalion. Captain L.H. Moses, friend of the Harvard bugle boy, would command one company. Lt. Col. Meade was already over there. Boston would also provide Second Lieutenants Charles B. Taylor and Douglas C. McDougal in addition to 1 gunnery sergeant, 4 sergeants, 5 corporals, 1 drummer, 1 trumpeter and 113 privates. They would also receive 1 sergeant and 4 corporals from Marine Barracks Portsmouth, NH. The USS *Massachusetts* was assessed 1 sergeant. All were assigned to the 5th Battalion of Marines.[93]

Marksmanship training for the Marines again became more difficult when the rifle gallery in the yard was destroyed by fire on July 19, 1900.[94]

9. The Era of Colonel Pope

"The U.S. Government is not so hard up for men as to oblige its officers to resort to trickery to retain men in the service."
—Captain Williams

On August 4, 1900, at 10:30 in the morning Colonel Percival C. Pope assumed command of the Marine Barracks.[1]

The naval prison needed updating to the 20th century. The facility still used good solid wooden doors on the cells. But they closed the cell shut tight. These seriously interfered with proper ventilation. Colonel Pope recommended these wooden doors be replaced with iron doors with bars on cells in the center corridor of the prison. They should be the same design as those on the outer corridors of the lower floor of the prison. He requested that the yard civil engineer make an inspection and determine the cost of the project.[2]

Bedbugs, cockroaches, ants, and spiders in the barracks living quarters caused considerable discomfort to say the least, and raised sanitation and health concerns. G.C. Brenner of 25 Crown Street from Brooklyn, NY, was requested to estimate the costs of exterminating these pests from the confines of the entire barracks, guardrooms and even the officers' quarters.[3]

The civilian coal passers working for Messrs. J.E. Lewis and Co. of Chelsea took all day to shovel 20 tons of coal into the coal bins at the barracks. Colonel Pope complained that the loading took from early in the morning until 9 p.m. Pope found this unacceptable, as it caused great inconvenience to all at the barracks. If the coal could not be loaded in a more expeditious manner then he would have to order coal in smaller quantities.[4]

Three Marines from Boston were transferred to the Barracks in Washington, D.C., to ship out for duty in the Philippines with the 6th Battalion in September 1900.[5] Headquarters instructed that they be fitted out with leggings, white helmets, white belts, cartridge boxes, and campaign hats and suits. Full dress uniforms were to be placed in storage.[6] Something was afoot.

The First Philippine Republic officially declared war over a year earlier against the United States on 2 June 1899. The First Republic struggled to gain independence following annexation by the United States. A virtually forgotten conflict by modern U.S. citizens, the effect of the war's tens of thousands of Filipino casualties changed the cultural landscape of the Philippines. The Catholic Church was no longer the state religion. English replaced Spanish as the primary language of education, government and business.

Why isn't this conflict remembered as much as D-Day or Pearl Harbor? The war was not fought with a European power or Japan. It was a tough, dirty fight with atrocities committed by both sides. Local inhabitants were herded into concentration camps surrounded by free fire zones. Disease took its toll in these overcrowded inadequate makeshift camps. American troops were disemboweled with bolo knives.

This three year, seemingly endless slaughter was the result of miscommunications, unauthorized or reversed promises, and harsh suppressions by the U.S. A nation, which by the way, proclaimed to champion nations colonized by the yoke of the European powers.

So Boston's Marines were headed to their "Vietnam." After a trip that took them to the other side of the world by sea, they arrived at the Philippines. Here they dropped their duffle bags off at their new assignment in Cavite City, a port town in Manila Bay.

Soon, together with sailors and Marines from the USS *Baltimore,* they all converged on Imus. Their attack led to the capture of insurgents. Five days later, under Lt. G.F. Elliot, the Marine battalion from Cavite City took Neveleta.

The secretary of the Navy ordered all prisoners, except those serving general court-martial sentences, to be removed from the naval prison—wonderful news to those confined to the poorly ventilated old world dungeon. But to those managing the facility, these inmates with short sentences now needed a place to go. They couldn't go back to the old barracks jail cells. A medical board had condemned these confinements. There was no place to hold prisoners for short periods of time. The prison filled that role.[7]

Colonel Pope commented to Brigadier General Heywood that deserters usually turn themselves in when civilian work dries up. He noticed they seem to return to military jurisdiction when winter arrives. Going to prisons where they will receive good food, warm beds and enough work to keep them healthy becomes their plan. And when their term of confinement ends, they even receive a sum of money, more in fact than they could earn working in a factory for small wages. In cases like those, Colonel Pope recommended that they be discharged as unfit for service rather than confinement.[8]

The usual method of transporting troops at the turn of the century was steam ships out of Fall River, MA. It was still cheaper then rail transportation. Sometimes the railroads were used. A mentally ill sailor needed to be transported to Washington, D.C., for treatment. Colonel Pope, in a telegram to headquarters, stated, "Do not think advisable send crazy men via Fall River, recommend be sent by rail arriving Washington in early evening. The escort can return via Fall River. Naval Commandant approves."[9] Mental illness only recently received its due recognition as a serious condition. It was often rendered manageable through regimens of strong medicines, but these regimens must be custom suited to each patient through a trial and error process.

Time eventually renders modern technology obsolete. The state of the art of communication in contemporary times, the telephone at the Barracks, needed replacement. The existing equipment did not operate well and it was unable to receive proper volume. Colonel Pope was stunned by the toll charges for long distance telephone service. Pope was not funded to pay for all these calls. Were Marines using the telephone to call family and friends from far away? He wanted all operators to stop making connections that might trigger any toll charges.[10]

The naval prison couldn't wash its own dishes. After meals the dishes were brought some distance to the bathrooms and washed there. Yuck. Colonel Pope wanted an enamel sink installed in the prison. The status quo was not sanitary.[11]

Two officers from the USS *Amphitrite* were walking to the Main Gate. The sentry acknowledged them and made requests. They disregarded the sentry when they were challenged and walked away without paying any attention to the sentry. They blew off the sentry, who challenged them three times.

Colonel Pope let Captain E. S. Houston of the USS *Amphitrite* know that these officers violated the directives of the secretary of the Navy and the commandant of the Charlestown Navy Yard. All persons were required to treat sentinels with proper respect at all times. Officers of the naval service are supposed to be examples of correctness to all.[12]

With the colder weather approaching, measures had to be taken to ensure that the recruiting office at 98 Court Street in Boston be kept warm. Homes may have had some sort of heating but offices and store fronts were catch-as catch-can. Captain John A. Lejeune requested that Colonel Pope provide a wood burning stove and a supply of wood to him.[13]

Young Captain Lejeune was just beginning what was to become a very distinguished career in the Marine Corps. He served just about everywhere any Marine could have served during that period. Lejeune became the commanding general of the Second Division in France during World War I. He later served as commandant of the Marine Corps for nine years and then retired in 1929.[14] Camp Lejeune in North Carolina is named in his honor. Camp Lejeune is a massive training base with 14 miles of beaches for amphibious assault training and is located between two deep water ports, allowing for efficient deployment. He was the "Greatest of all Leathernecks," a "Marine's Marine."

Marines at the Barracks protected the American Legation in Peking, China, during the Boxer Rebellion in 1900. The commandant of the Marine Corps forwarded a letter he received to Colonel Pope. This letter came from the U.S. minister to China, the honorable B.M. Conger. It stated that American missionaries back in Peking passed a resolution. The missionaries commended the Marines for the security of the legation in Peking. Colonel Pope was directed to read the citation to the men at parade formation.[15]

Dust clouds from Chelsea Street would find their way onto the bunks in the barracks if the windows were open. Colonel Pope contacted the superintendent of streets of the City of Boston and complained about the condition and cleanliness of Chelsea Street. The dust was a menace to good health. Thus the windows in the barracks, already ventilation challenged, were not opened, even during hot weather. Recent repairs of the trolley car tracks were covered with sand and the passage of trolleys caused the sand to be ground up into very fine particles and dispersed into the Barracks areas.[16]

Colonel Pope received a letter from a G.M. Elliot of Brunswick, Maine, concerning buy-out procedures for a member of the Marine Corps. Colonel Pope replied that buy-outs of enlistments may be granted by the Navy Department. One year of enlistment must be served before a discharge can be purchased. The price for drummers, trumpeters and privates on a first enlistment was $100 during the 13th month and $1.50 additional during each month. The maximum price was reduced $3 per month during third year and $4 per month during fourth year. Minimum price reached during 48th month remained the same until expiration of enlistment. For noncommissioned officers, the price prescribed for a private with the following amounts added for corporals ($5), sergeants ($10) and those above sergeants ($15).[17]

By November an increasing prison population was causing unsurprising trouble. The prison became so congested that two prisoners were recommended for restoration to duty to provide room for incoming prisoners.[18]

Court-martial punishments apparently were changing. The Navy Department letter 6774-00 relative to Private Charles Bader, USMC, indicated this possible change. It stated that Private Bader, a general court-martial prisoner, was "restricted to the limits of the Navy Yard, Boston." Colonel Pope must have scratched his head after he read this policy so he asked, "Did it just mean no liberty?"[19]

In mid–December Colonel H. Clay Cochrane, the former commanding officer of the Marine Barracks, was assigned to command of the 1st Regiment for service in Cavite City, the navy yard in the Philippine Islands.[20] Cavite City was virtually becoming a remote Boston Marine Barracks.

There was serious infestation of insects in the barracks, again. Waltham Chemical Company was hired to eliminate the problem in December.[21]

Lots of Marines were on hand for staffing. Official strength was 324 men. But living space for these men was very tight. So tight they had to resort to "hot bunking," where those off duty occupied the beds of those on duty. Imagine sleeping in someone else's bed and they are sleeping in yours. Colonel Pope wanted some recruits transferred to other posts to make sufficient room in the barracks.[22]

The prison was overcrowded too. Colonel Pope recommended that 10 general court-martial prisoners be released for either restoration to duty or discharged from the service. This was necessary to make sufficient room for newly sentenced prisoners.[23]

An epidemic of diphtheria broke out in the Barracks and the naval prison in late January. The medical officer advised Colonel Pope not to transfer any men from Boston until further notice.[24] Diphtheria is a respiratory illness and is very contagious, spread by physical contact and aerosolized secretions (largely eradicated in industrialized nations since through mass vaccinations). Headquarters was notified on the first of February that the Barracks was under quarantine.[25]

But new recruits kept coming. They couldn't be sent to the quarantined barracks either. Adjutant and Inspector Colonel George C. Reid appropriately reached out and offered assistance to this diphtheria dilemma. Reid instructed the recruiting officer the Boston office at 98 Court Street to send all new recruits to the Barracks at Newport, RI, or to Portsmouth, NH, instead. Colonel Pope was instructed to keep the recruiting officer posted and inform him when conditions become safe at the Boston Barracks.[26]

The quarantine was lifted February 7, 1901. The routine of the Marines at the Barracks and the naval prison returned to some semblance of normalcy.[27]

Prison overcrowding is a perennial problem, for civilian penitentiaries and for naval prisons. Crack down and get tough policies eventually lead to prison overcrowding and discipline issues. Too many men with bad attitudes fit too tightly together are fissionable. Fortunately not all cases are the same. So Colonel Pope requested clemency and release of 18 prisoners to reduce the pressure.[28] Again on March 15, 1901, Colonel Pope requested 16 more prisoners be released to make room.[29]

Officers were ordered to shore duty for a year at Boston by Brigadier General Heywood until April 2, 1902, including Captain Dion Williams, First Lieutenant Yandell Moore, Second Lieutenants F. Udell, F.S. Wiltse, W.D.A. Junkin, H. Colvocoressess and H.A. Herbert Jr.[30] They would regain their land legs.

Due to this new influx of junior officers, there was soon to be more chiefs than Indians around the Barracks. And now headquarters ordered 28 privates and their requisite sergeant and 2 corporals to join a detachment forming in New York for duty at Cavite City, Philippines, at its Navy yard.[31] The list of those shipping out was posted April 10, 1901.[32] In late May Colonel Pope complained to the Waltham Chemical Company, sent to get the bugs out, that they didn't fulfill their contract. Rats and mice over ran the Barracks. Those pests, in addition to bed bugs, cockroaches, ants, and spiders were still there, and probably hornets too.[33] It was hard to sleep with all that company and be fit for duty.

The prison was still overcrowded. Granting clemency only went so far. Plans were reviewed for outfitting the facility for more albeit temporary capacity. An obvious option was using the guardroom for more cells. This plan in front of the board was to divide the 25 by 23 foot guardroom into five 10 by 11 foot cells. Five more cells available would a good thing, but there would be no ventilation. The medical officer submitted using this space like that would be unsanitary. No ventilation is unsanitary. His opinion swayed the judgment of the board surveying the prison. They would not move forward with this plan to increase capacity. More plans needed exploration.[34]

The prison was still overcrowded. Every day it was still overcrowded. Colonel Pope once again used the clemency option to reduce numbers in the prison in April.[35]

Fire in the chain shop occurred the middle of the night, of course, at 2:55 a.m. in Building 42 on April 18. About the only one awake and around to see it was an alert sentry. He notified his sergeant and the Marines turned out to fight the fire. In his report Colonel Pope stated the Marines fulfilled their duty and all Navy regulations were carried out, except for ringing the Navy yard bell.

A military staple throughout the ages: a near disaster was averted, but what people remember is that one checklist item was missed. Colonel Pope explained that the Marines were unable to ring the bell because the rope connection on the bell outside the building was out of order. He wanted it highlighted that the Marine sentinel was vigilant and the other Marines arrived at the scene promptly, over that regulation detail.[36]

The population of the naval prison was increasing at an alarming rate. Colonel Pope requested more personnel from headquarters to administer and guard the prison. He already had 107 prisoners in his responsibility and expected at least fifty more prisoners coming through the pipeline.[37] On May 7 he reported that there were now 120 prisoners with 20 more expected when the naval prison completed its project to enlarge capacity.[38] Finally in June, Colonel Pope asked that the other half of the building used by the general storekeeper be considered in the planned expansion of the naval prison. Move the general storekeeper out and it would practically double the space for cells to warehouse prisoners.[39]

Occasionally choice duty assignments provided a break from the day-on and day-off guard duties. One such prime duty occurred when 1 corporal and 5 privates were detailed to report to Marine Barracks, Brooklyn, NY, for duty at the Pan-American Exposition held in Buffalo, NY, during fine May weather.[40]

The bed bugs were still biting at the Barracks. Colonel Pope continued to complain to Waltham Chemical Company that he was not satisfied with their extermination program. Exasperated, he snorted that the bugs seemed to thrive on the powder that the exterminators applied. Bed bugs get everywhere. In spite of their name, their extermination must be comprehensive. Rats and mice continued to rule over the Marines' quarters. Indeed, 5 rats were caught in the traps in the east wing of the barracks, prompting the letter to Waltham Chemical Company the next day.[41]

Colonel Pope requested the release of 16 more prisoners to help alleviate overcrowding.[42]

On holidays such as Memorial Day, the Barracks was deluged with requests for Marines to participate in the various ceremonies. Navy Department directives proclaimed that Memorial Day was a holiday for enlisted men. It was a day off. So when Marines were wanted for parades on Memorial Day, the men could not be detailed to march unless they volunteered for the assignment.

The Grand Army of the Republic (GAR), an organization keeping the spirit alive of that victorious Union Army from the Civil War receding benignly into the past, requested Marines at their various encampments that day.[43] Colonel Pope replied to the GAR that the Navy Department could not detail Marines for parades on Memorial Day unless they were volunteers. Pope said he told any possible volunteers it would be a lot of fun and all expenses would be paid, but he could get only eight volunteers and was very sorry that he could not accommodate their request.[44]

This was not the only letter that needed to get out. Word about the directive was just trickling out to outlying organizations and committees. Other letters needed to be sent to various Memorial Day committees who also requested Marines for each of their observances. That is a lot of Marines. These replies explained that the Barracks was unable to provide all these firing details for all their different encampments because of the recent Department of the Navy directive. Only volunteers could participate in the various programs and that Marines could not be detailed.[45]

Other uses of Lovell's Island had now prohibited its use as a rifle range. Summer season of 1901 brought summer residents. Weaponry practice at this range had been proven decisive so far at Tientsin, Cuba, and the Philippines. The range was indispensable. Where were the Marines to practice for their annual requalification for firing at 200, 300, 500 and 600 yards?[46] With hat in hand, Colonel Pope inquired to the managers of the range at Walnut Hill, the Massachusetts Rifle Association, that the Marines were unable to locate a suitable site in the Boston environs.

Again the quickest, easiest thing to do under Colonel Pope's control to ease prison crowding was to early release more prisoners. A list of 15 general court-martial prisoners was sent for early release.[47] Colonel Pope even reached out to the sheriff of Middlesex County, John R. Fairburn. Fairburn said that he could help him out by taking as many as 50 to 70 general court-martial prisoners, but only a temporary basis—if he could pay the per diem cost per prisoner of 30 cents, and provide official documentation from the secretary of the Navy to the Board of Prisons Commission, his superiors. Colonel Pope was concerned enough about the prisoners under his responsibility that he traveled to inspect the prison facilities in West Cambridge. To his satisfaction, he found them neat and clean.[48]

There were other rifle ranges around. But who would take on the Marines? Another range in Medford, increasingly farther out from Boston, was given attention and its managers queried. Colonel Pope of the U.S. Marines, again hat in hand, asked Captain Clark of Company E, 5th Regiment, a Massachusetts Volunteer Militia unit for the use of their range only during the months of June, July and August.[49]

The long awaited expansion of the naval prison was approaching fruition. Colonel Pope sent a list of general court-martial prisoners with long sentences to headquarters with the recommendation they be sent to Middlesex County Jail while the naval prison is undergoing alterations.[50] The prisoner count at the naval prison on 1 June listed a total of 114 inmates, 82 sailors and 32 Marines.[51] Ten days later the first group of five general court-martial prisoners were moved to the Middlesex County Jail in West Cambridge.[52]

Was it really necessary to enlarge the capacity of the Barracks? Colonel Pope thought so and stated his case to headquarters. The brigadier general commandant replied that more fact finding needed to be done as to exactly how to increase the Barracks' capacity.[53]

Until now, the Charlestown Gas and Electric Company provided electricity for the lights at the Barracks in the arcade, the outside area. There wasn't yet indoor electricity. The service was lackluster, too. There were from the start considerable problems with consistent voltage and with it, proper lighting. Colonel Pope had had enough. He was done. Colonel Pope formally asked the electric company to remove all its wiring by June 30. From July 1 on, the Navy yard electric plant would provide the electricity for the lights under the arcade.[54]

Bedbugs were still in the barracks. The Waltham Chemical Company was once again notified on June 24, 1901, to send an exterminator to the barracks immediately. Colonel Pope was very distressed with their inability to eradicate the problem.[55]

The plans to enlarge the naval prison provided for cells to accommodate 150 prisoners. Colonel Pope reviewed the plans and sent his comments to the commandant of the Navy yard.[56]

A bright moment occurred in the search for a place for the Marines to practice their gunnery. The Massachusetts Rifle Association approved the use of their rifle range at Walnut Hill. Colonel Pope replied to their approval with vast appreciation. He told how important rifle range practice was to the training of Marines, and probably how it proved useful in the wars. He assured the association that the Marines would observe all safety regulations and provide a trained officer to be in charge at the range.[57]

The naval prison August 5 census showed a decrease. There were 58 Navy personnel and 17 Marines for a total of 75 prisoners.[58]

Among the Marines in Boston were some fine sharpshooters. A standout was Sergeant W.G. Smith. He was hand picked and sent to Annapolis, Maryland, to join the Marine Corps Rifle Team to compete for the "Hilton Trophy."[59]

Although overshadowed by other cups in prestige, it represents a major achievement. Henry Hilton donated the trophy to the National Rifle Association in 1878. Teams from the Army, Navy, National Guard and reserves as well as militia and volunteers from foreign countries compete for it even into modern times.

Ten more privates from Boston were sent by headquarters to report to Camp Heywood for the Pan-American Exposition in Buffalo, New York. This put a severe strain on the barracks and its ability to provide security at the Navy yard and the naval prison.[60]

Electric lights were installed throughout the barracks, its offices and the officers' quarters in August. This included indoor electricity. Colonel Pope asked the commandant of the Navy yard for the assistance of the Navy yard naval constructor to monitor the wiring efforts of the contractors. He wanted somebody he could trust looking over the project. His concern was that the work should be accomplished properly, safely and expeditiously.[61]

J.C. Becker, a helper in the Steam Engineering Department, was leaving the yard through the Main Gate at quitting time, 5:20 p.m. on August 23, 1901. The sentry noticed his bulging satchel. An amazing amount of copper lay crammed inside. The sentry ran this up his flag pole to his bosses, Sergeant O'Day, the sergeant of the guard, and Corporal Doherty. They took over from there and eventually turned him over to civilian authorities.[62]

The insects were still there living in the Barracks along with their friends the rats and mice. Colonel Pope explained the problems in a strongly worded letter to the Waltham Chemical Company. He could not make any payments until the situation improved.[63] In another letter, this time an angry one, dated October 16, Pope told the Waltham Chemical Company that their work was to be discontinued since there seemed to be no eradication of either insects or rodents. No improvements had been observed.[64] The Waltham Chemical Company was probably just as frustrated as Colonel Pope.

A trolley car struck and killed a pedestrian on the Chelsea Street Bridge November 10,

1901. The conductor, most likely in an agitated state after accidentally killing a person, ran to the guardhouse at Gate 5 at the east end and demanded to use the telephone. The sentry probably wanted to help but could only explain that his phone was not connected to any outside telephone lines. The telephones at the guardhouses were only connected to the main guardhouse at the barracks. The conductor in his excited state began to use abusive and threatening language toward the sentry. It was necessary to expel the conductor from the Navy yard.[65] No word was left whether the conductor received any assistance.

Personnel availability ebbed and flowed at the Barracks, as it has for its already one hundred years. Now it was ebbing. There was too much going on overseas. Colonel Pope requested more troops but General Heywood couldn't give him any. General Heywood thought Colonel Pope's 68 Marines on daily guard seemed like a very large guard. He should try to reduce what the guards were guarding.[66]

Items disappeared in the yard and then were subsequently discovered installed at the Marine Barracks. In this case, a radiator was stolen from the yards and docks machine shop. An investigation found that radiator installed at the Marine Barracks. The yard civil engineer wanted to know who did it. It was policy that no government property be removed without authority and used elsewhere.[67] One can imagine the scenario. "Where did you get this?" "Don't ask!"

Having sentries watching the shipyard for 24 hours seven days a week had its benefits. Steam engines for cranes blow off steam. Routinely. On December 8, 1901, the sentry at Post 6 noticed that a crane engine near the lower ship house was blowing off steam in an unusual manner. The sentry alerted his boss, the sergeant of the guard. Sergeant Pearson then summoned off duty Fireman Sawyer. Sawyer came in and inspected the crane engine. The steam gauge was registering 120 pounds of steam pressure. That was in the red: there was little or no water in the boiler.

Sawyer extinguished the fires in the boiler and prevented the boiler from exploding.[68] Steam boilers exploded much too often back then. These were particularly nasty events, especially for those nearby. Hot metal shrapnel, boiling water, and fire exploding everywhere made some stalwarts miss the days before steam.

The secretary of the Navy awarded 8 medals of Honor and rosettes (ribbons) to Boston Marines for their service in China and the Philippines: Gunnery Sergeant Peter Stewart, Corporal Reuben J. Philips, Drummer John A. Murphy, Private William I. Carr, Private Henry W. Davis, Private Daniel Daly, Private David J. Scannell and Private William Zion. Each man was also entitled to a gratuity of $100. They were to apply to the auditor of the Navy Department to receive that amount.[69]

Naval prison population in January 1902 was on a decline. The report listed 58 prisoners, 42 sailors, and 16 Marines in confinement.[70] But by the middle of March the prison population began ticking back up again. The March 15 prison report showed 45 sailors, up by three, and 16 Marines confined.[71]

Corporal Alfred Tietze was promoted to sergeant in recognition of his faithful and meritorious service in Samoa, a remote archipelago in the South Pacific.[72]

A Dutchman first sighted the Samoan islands for the first time in 1722. Contact was limited until English missionaries and traders arrived in the 1830s. The island cluster happened to be located along the most favored route across the Pacific Ocean. Although its natives were living as they always did before contact with Western cultures, they gained a reputation among the French, German, British, and Americans as savages. They were known to engage in headhunting. A warrior would take the head of a slain opponent and deliver it to his chief.

The islands were either blessed, or cursed depending on your point of view, by a harbor and fresh water in a very remote stretch of the vast Pacific Ocean. This attracted the interest of colonial powers that could project their navies. The Americans in the late nineteenth century saw Samoa as a coal refueling station for its new ships, placed in between home and its new possessions on the other side of the world. The United States began laying claim and set out to form local alliances. The British sent troops to protect their harbor rights and businesses. This activity triggered an eight-year civil war with Britain, the U.S., and Germany supplying aid to the belligerents. In March 1889 all three colonial powers sent ships into Apia harbor and a more serious war seemed at hand. But a massive typhoon scattered and destroyed the ships, ending the conflict. The question over who should control Samoa remained unresolved.

The Siege of Apia in March 1899 ten years later provided the opportunity for resolution. A larger force of Samoan rebels besieged Samoan forces loyal to the prince. Landing parties of Marines from British and American ships supported the prince and defeated the rebels. The Tripartite Convention of 1899 partitioned Samoa into two parts. The eastern island group became a territory of the United States and is known today as American Samoa.[73]

The Philippines conflict required 20 more privates and their 2 sergeants, and 2 corporals from the Boston Barracks.[74] These troops were transferred to the Barracks in Washington, D.C., where they were to ship out for overseas duty. Perhaps they were relieved to leave the bed bugs and rats behind.

Private Billy Smith was confined in the naval prison for desertion. But he got a "get out of prison card," and a free ticket on a steam ship. Gunnery Sergeant John A. Logan was going along as his escort. He and Logan boarded a Merchants and Miners Transportation Company steamship bound for the District of Columbia. They had an appointment with the surgeon in charge. They were going to meet and discuss his stay at his new home at the Government Hospital for the Insane at Anacostia in the District of Columbia.[75]

In March there were fewer prisoners behind bars. Colonel Pope informed the commandant of the Navy that the shipyard's naval prison could handle 10 more prisoners.[76]

Again in April, 15 more privates and their 2 sergeants and 2 corporals were dispatched to the Marine Barracks in Washington, D.C., for assignment to the Philippines.[77]

It was time to update the naval prison uniforms. Taking a cue from the state penitentiaries, Colonel Pope asked Fred Pettgrove, chairman of the Prison Commission of Massachusetts, for a sample of the cloth used at state facilities. He also asked for the cost per yard of the material and the cost of the finished garment.[78] Within a short time, the Barracks received a prison uniform used by the state. It was too conspicuous for Navy Yard surroundings, Colonel Pope thought.

The naval prison was undergoing a complete change. Population was down to 50 men. They were confined in an upper loft over the prison. New cells were to be ready for occupancy by the middle of June. Pope invited the Prison Commission to make a visit.[79]

The Naval Prison

The welcome arrival to the shipyard was of all things the prison ship *Southery*. Perhaps its presence was a belated response to Colonel Pope's pleas for assistance in the prison overpopulation problem.

The *Southery* was a steamer built in England in 1898. It was later converted into a collier right there at the Charlestown Navy Yard. A collier is a bulk cargo ship designed to carry coal and to sail alongside coal fired warships. Noted for their flat bottom hulls and sturdy construction, the first aircraft carriers were colliers fitted with a large elevated flat deck. Oil fired warships were coming on line and rendered colliers obsolete. Placed out of commission at the Norfolk Navy Yard, it underwent conversion there into a prison ship. It was then moved to Boston on April 6, 1902. Eight days later 9 prisoners were transferred from the naval prison to the USS *Southery* for confinement under the terms of their sentences.[80] This became a significant safety valve for a crowded prison. On April 21, fifteen days later, Captain Dion Williams, acting commander of the Marine Barracks, reported that there were 49 prisoners under his responsibility and now the newly renovated prison could accommodate up to 60 prisoners. He requested that 11 prisoners be transferred from the *Southery* to the naval prison.[81] The unit went from overcrowding to surplus in a matter of days.

When you are a commander of the Barracks, be ready for anything. This time the fate of a rented piano needed to be resolved. George H. Champlin and Company owned a piano it rented to 2d Lieutenant Woog. But 2d Lt. Woog had been assigned aboard the USS *San Francisco* and shipped out. The piano, however, was still in Lieutenant Woog's old quarters. Captain Williams strongly urged Champlin that he had better get in touch with Lieutenant Woog if he wanted his piano, or the rent.[82]

Sometimes the parents of Marines can be misinformed by their Marine sons. And the commanding officer has to hear about it. A notable correspondence was from the mother of a Marine who complained that her son said he was transferred to the Philippines in order to deprive him of the opportunity to obtain his discharge. Captain Williams replied that her son had volunteered for duty in the Philippines and certainly was not detailed to go. He added, "The U.S. Government is not so hard up for men as to oblige its officers to resort to trickery to retain men in the service."[83]

The recently renovated prison could now house up to 60 prisoners. Colonel Pope recommended that whenever the census went below 60 prisoners, the commandant of the Navy Yard should order transfer of prisoners from the *Southery*.[84] Perhaps he felt it would be better for the prisoners, and it would also justify and fill his new prison.

The Navy yard benefited from having sentinels on 24-hour watch. There was always an alert set of eyeballs around to report any incidents or fires. Fires occurred with relative infrequency at the turn of the twentieth century. A shipyard was especially vulnerable to fires. A fire did start in Building 71. A sentry did discover it. The Marines were turned out and subsequently extinguished the fire. The fire got out of control when flames grew from ambers in a charcoal bin and spread from there. Colonel Pope was concerned this time because the fire was near the paymaster's office. Freight train cars stand there, practically blocking the entrance to the yard. City firemen complained that if they had to use one of their larger fire trucks, they would not have been able to enter the yard because the freight train cars were blocking the entrance. He recommended that the railroad cars be moved and in the future parked somewhere else.[85]

Opposite, top: Turn of the century funeral beyond the aging barracks, on the site where the tennis courts now stand. Chelsea Street in the back shows its life before the modern sized Mystic River Bridge wiped out the life of Chelsea Street to make way for its dominating presence. The old officer-of-the-day shack is pictured before its replacement was built.

Bottom: The Barracks, September 20, 1902, with a good view of the old officer-of-the-day Office and Chelsea Street buildings.

9. The Era of Col. Pope   111

October 25, 1902, the Barracks with obsolete ship guns gathered, possibly for meltdown of the metal.

The commanding officer of the Newport RI Marine Barracks requested recruits from Colonel Pope. But Colonel Pope subsequently had to decline. The Philippines demanded too many Marines from the Boston Barracks. Even Boston had to borrow 30 privates from the Brooklyn Marine Barracks to help ease their personnel problem. Colonel Pope did not have enough men himself to man all the security duties in Boston and few recruits were coming to Boston at the moment.[86]

A Marine's mom, Mrs. Edward Flagg of Washington, D.C., asked Colonel Pope for her son to be transferred nearer to her. He said he tried but his boss the commandant of the Marine Corps had disapproved of the transfer because of the paucity of Marines in Boston. So she wouldn't get discouraged, he suggested Mrs. Flagg take up the matter with Brigadier General Heywood.[87]

Again, Colonel Pope had the painful task of sending a Marine to an insane asylum. In June, Sergeant Michael O'Day and Private Thomas Breen were detailed to escort Sergeant Gustaf W. Stenberg to Government Hospital for the Insane in Washington, D.C. They boarded a Merchants and Miners Transportation Company steamer on its way to Washington, D.C.[88] They would see that he got to his new home safely.

The USRS *Wabash* had arrived on the scene.

A classic wooden sailing ship, the *Wabash* nonetheless saw extensive service during the Civil war. After the war, the *Wabash* was overhauled at the Boston Navy Yard. Re-commissioned, it served as a flagship in the Mediterranean squadron. It cruised throughout the Mediterranean

Sea from 1871 to '73. After only a couple of years, in 1874 it was bought to the Boston Navy Yard and decommissioned again.

The shipyard workers worked their magic and converted her into the U.S. receiving ship *Wabash*. The USRS *Wabash* was a nonpropelled receiving ship, meaning that it didn't go anywhere. One of its first and longstanding missions as the USRS *Wabash* was serving as temporary housing for the Boston Barracks from 1876 to 1912. All this command belly aching about lack of housing and lack of personnel to do the job, here it was all along, rooms. The Navy simply took an obsolete ship, a surplus ship that cost more to dismantle than to restore, that made its way to the shipyard. They converted it into a "cruise ship" without the propulsion.

For 36 years there were virtually two Marine barracks. One floated like a duck. That was enough time for slight nuances of difference to emerge from the two barracks. Then they weren't so slight. Even though the Marines at the barracks in the Charlestown Navy Yard and the Marines in the detachment aboard the USRS *Wabash* were supposed to be contiguous (they get the same training and train on the same weaponry), there still could be problems with the same equipment.

The Marines aboard the USRS *Wabash* were armed with the Lee straight pull rifle. The land barracks used the U.S. magazine rifle, .30-caliber. For parades, whenever some Wabash Barracks volunteers could join in, they could only be given what the Barracks used, the U.S. magazine rifle. Pope must have thought this was ridiculous and out of hand. He recommended that the Marine detachment aboard the USRS *Wabash* be armed with the U.S. magazine rifle.[89]

The Boston Barracks received 60 Marines from the barracks in Brooklyn, NY. Colonel Pope acknowledged this and extended his sincere thanks to its commanding officer.[90]

Major General Heywood assigned 43 privates and their first sergeant, two sergeants, and three corporals to Boston after serving in Samoa with Major L.W.T. Waller's battalion. Colonel Pope was authorized to grant 15–30 days of leave to each member of the Samoa returnees.[91] The U.S. couldn't have gotten Samoa without the new Navy and didn't need Samoa but for the new Navy. The territories from Spain felt like Christmas gifts. Now Samoa was a necessary way station needed to tend these new far flung territories. With Marines shipping back and forth from the Philippines and Guam, the U.S. needed a "gas station."

That summer in July, Private Hugh Boyle, after serving only four days, went AWOL, shot himself and died. Colonel Pope requested that a medical officer be sent to Peabody, Massachusetts, where his body was found and report back. The 1st sergeant was also dispatched to Peabody and made a positive identification.[92]

There was no burial allowance for Marines whose death occurs while absent without leave, especially suicide. Pope noted that there were no funds to recompense the family for burial expenses. On top of that, Private Boyle had only served for four days before he deserted, and because of the short time he had served and the uniforms and equipment he had been issued, he probably owed money to the government.[93]

On August 6, Boston received a draft of men who had completed their tour of duty in the Philippines. It consisted of one sergeant major, one gunnery sergeant, one first sergeant, 1 sergeant and 17 privates.[94] That's a good thing. The Barracks needed them.

The expansion of the naval prison allowed 30 more prisoners to be transferred from the *Southery*, that prison ship lurking off the pier. The July prisoner report showed 52 sailors and 7 Marines in the slammer, a wooden door slammer at that, 59 in total. A month later, the August 31, 1902, prisoner report showed a dramatic rise to 89 prisoners: 81 sailors and 8 Marines.[95] Those confined that crisp autumn climbed to an astounding 147 prisoners—124 sailors and 23 Marines.[96] The numbers dipped a bit by mid November but to a still stratospheric

129, including 115 sailors and 14 Marines.[97] November ended with numbers rocketing up to 148 prisoners, comprising 131 sailors and 17 Marines.[98] It was dangerously close to capacity; 150 prisoners were all the naval prison could stomach.[99]

Panama

Colonel Pope needed 15 privates and asked headquarters for them. Instead, headquarters replied that the Marine Corps were raising troops to form a battalion. This battalion of Marines would ship out for the Isthmus of Panama. Something was going on. Other Marine Barracks up and down the East Coast were getting hit up too. Within a few short days of headquarters' answer to Colonel Pope, he was ordered to provide or give up 24 privates, one quartermaster sergeant and 4 sergeants for duty in Panama.[100]

A passage over the Isthmus of Panama had been a dream for hundreds of years. The first modern solution in 1855 had a railway connected from Atlantic Ocean to the Pacific Ocean. It was a lot of packing and unpacking. An all-water route was seen as the ideal solution.

Twenty-six years later in 1881, the French began to try to construct a sea level canal. This was a very tall order given the terrain. The endeavor was difficult. The French effort ultimately cost 22,000 lives and went bankrupt by 1890, nine years later.

America became interested in a canal project. After all, it just commissioned a new international Navy. The U.S. learned from French mistakes. New engineering studies found that a lock system might make the canal possible. It was less expensive and faster to build than a sea level version.

The Hay-Herran Treaty was signed on 22 January 1903 and allowed the U.S. control over the land of the proposed canal. The French had issues with the Colombian government. The U.S. wanted no foreign government getting in the way of this national security project. The U.S. Senate ratified the treaty but the senate of Colombia did not. Unrest developed. Taking advantage and seizing the opportunity, the U.S. supported Panamanian rebels with money and troops, including Marines from the Boston Barracks.

On 2 November 1903, U.S. warships blocked sea-lanes to prevent Colombian waterborne attempts to put down the rebellion. Dense jungle took care of any land-based attempts. The seas were the only way Colombia could assert its authority over the isthmus. And the U.S. Navy ruled them. Resistance withered. Bribes succeeded in getting lingering Colombians to lay down their arms. Panama declared its independence and the U.S. quickly recognized it.

In 1904 the U.S. bought French equipment and excavations for $40,000,000, paid the new country $10,000,000 a year, and work began in May. Eventually to secure a lasting peace, Colombia was paid $10,000,000 and $250,000 for several years after that for the recognition of the new country of Panama.

New thinking about general court-martial prisoners appeared evident by the circulation of Navy Department Letter 5755-6-02 dated 30 June 1902. The Navy Department would not be averse to exercising extraordinary clemency in special cases. Acting Commander Captain Long compiled and provided a list of prisoners whose conduct while confined had been excellent. He recommended that the unexpired portion of their sentences be remitted and that they be discharged from the service.[101]

Private James Reynolds deserted. And then came back and surrendered. Why? Acting Commander Captain Charles H. Long, while Colonel Pope was away on leave, thought he knew why. Reynolds deserted and found existence quite rough. Institutionalized life in a prison, Reynolds might have pondered, could be a better deal. Imprisonment just might indeed be a step up in some deserters' living experiences. Captain Long asserted all along that some deserters shouldn't get confinement, the usual punishment.

Acting Commander Long even commented on Reynolds' appearance when he surrendered, "an appearance which indicated that the world had not dealt very kindly to him since his desertion. It was evident to me that this man surrendered not because he wished to remain in the service, but rather to secure comfortable shelter from the rigors of winter, such as could be assured him if he were tried by court-martial and sentenced to a term of confinement. I am of the opinion that the severest punishment that could be inflicted is to turn him out of the gate." He recommended that Private Reynolds be discharged as unfit for service.[102]

Seems deserters did indeed want to come in out of the cold. Again on December 19, deserter Private Thomas H. Mitchener appeared at the Barracks. Mitchener seemed more of a hobo than a Marine. He seemed the type that deserted in the summer and returned when winter closed in. Long recommended that Private Mitchener also be discharged as unfit for service.[103] The outcome is unknown.

In December, 40 privates and 2 sergeants from Boston were ordered to join a battalion due to set sail for the Philippines in January 1903.[104]

On December 22, headquarters sent a ten part directive which required that the Marine Barracks in Boston be divided into companies as follows:

1. Each company shall be composed of (1) First Sergeant, or Gunnery Sergeant, four sergeants, six corporals, one drummer, one trumpeter and 74 privates. 2. In the event that the strength of the command is insufficient to organize a company or if after organizing one or more companies, there would be a surplus, but not enough, a report should be made to headquarters the number and the grade of the surplus or deficiencies.
3. If the command can be organized into more companies than one of such strength, the companies should be preserved intact numerically. When vacancies occur from unavoidable causes, the positions should be filled as soon as possible in order that the companies shall at all times have a full complement.
4. Do not include special and extra duty personnel in the strength of the company or companies.
5. Provide training to the companies as far as facilities will permit in the construction of hasty emplacements, temporary field fortifications, gun emplacements, gun mounts, transportation and mounting guns. Additionally, training should be given in construction and operation of field telephones and telegraph lines as well as search lights, range finders, signal stations, mining and countermining. Lastly, mining, counter-mining, the operation of mines and torpedoes for harbor defense and day and night signaling should also be provided.
6. It was recognized that it may be impracticable to obtain mines, guns and torpedoes for use in practical instruction and the materials for construction of field fortifications, therefore every effort should be made to provide theoretical instruction and whenever possible, practical application should be encouraged.
7. Training in the subject elicited above may render it necessary to modify the routine of instruction and drills and good judgment should prevail.

8. Providing security of information should be stressed.
9. The quartermaster of the Marine Corps will honor your requests for whatever instruments, material and implements that may be necessary to provide the proper training for the company or companies.
10. The commissioned officers of each company will consist of the following: one captain, 1 first lieutenant and 1 second lieutenant.[105]

A furnace in Building 24 had a defective door latch. So workers in that shop had taken to propping up a board against the door to keep it closed until it got fixed. The fire in the belly of the furnace had been banked for the night. In the wee hours of January 16, 1903, the board fell away from the door. The door opened and hot coals spilled out and set the holding board on fire. The sentry on Post 8 noticed this and extinguished the fire.[106]

Transfers to the Far East continued. On January 17, 1903, 42 Marines were transferred to Marine Barracks, Washington, D.C. for duty in the Philippines.[107]

The new desire of the Navy Department to reduce the number of trials by general court-martial gave Colonel Pope an opportunity. General courts-martial produce large numbers of prisoners for Boston. Colonel Pope recommended that Private Frank P. Looke be tried by summary court-martial on a charge of absent without leave. Normally, this would have been a General court-martial offense.[108]

On January 29, 1903, Headquarters forwarded to the Marine Barracks four West Indian Campaign Medals. They were issued for service in the West Indies Theater of the Spanish-American War. These medals were a big deal.

A service member must have performed sea duty in that theater between the dates May 1, 1898, and August 16, 1898. It was a one-time decoration. One couldn't collect several of them and it was rarely awarded. It went obsolete in 1913 when Spain diplomatically requested its discontinued use, as it displays Spain's national colors. Privates Thomas E. Flowers, Harry B. Lamont, Charles E. Bickford and George P. Curtis received this decoration for their participation in the Battle of Manzanillo Harbor in Cuba on August 12, 1898, while attached to the Marine Guard of USS *Newark*.[109] American and Spanish ships blasted away at each other on three separate events that summer in the harbor of Manzanillo.

With Navy Department Letter 5755-6-02, dated 30 June 1902 giving Colonel Pope the out he needed to reduce the prison population, on his desk, on January 30 he submitted a list of prisoners for remission of unexpired portions of sentences; he could let these go. He recommended 34 prisoners for discharge and 7 for restoration to duty.[110] Forty-one general court-martial prisoners were transferred from the eerie USRS *Southery* to the ominous naval prison.[111]

A standard uniform for prisoners had been sent to Boston. Colonel Pope recommended that one be issued to each prisoner when he arrives on board the *Southery*, the way station before space opens at the prison. The uniform could be easily washed while on board the prison ship and in the naval prison as well.[112]

At the turn of the century, recruiting was still a major responsibility for individual barracks. The Marine Corps set up and ran several recruiting posts about the state. A stand out in a negative light was the station at Worcester, MA. Colonel Pope reported to Gen. Heywood at headquarters about the quality of recruits enlisting from there. He complained that quality was very poor and the examining surgeon must have not required the prospects to strip down for a proper physical exam. It was Easy to see that they didn't strip down for the physical when the Worcester recruits were in the Barracks' open bay showers. So General Heywood sent a telegram to Captain R.M. Gibson, the officer in charge of the recruiting station in Worcester, and admonished him to look into the matter. If the doctor was incompetent, then he should get another one. He should endeavor to have all applicants properly examined.[113]

On October 22, the quartermaster of the Marine Corps authorized funding for recruiting offices to be established in Lynn, Salem and Lawrence, MA.[114] Brigadier General Elliott stressed that every effort should be made to fill the Corps to its authorized strength, and he wanted all concerned to use "utmost diligence."[115] By December enlistments were proceeding very well and headquarters was able to remind all those involved that only the best applicants were to be considered, and none under 5'7" in height.[116]

Even though a Navy Department directive approved and eased punishments, civilians were still watching, and noting, waiting for any slip ups, brutal treatment of inmates or leniency. Mrs. Willis Hadley of Winthrop, MA, highlighted that Private Frank P. Looke had been shown a considerable amount of leniency. The offenses for which he was found guilty were typically punished by 1 year confinement and a dishonorable discharge. Looke was only sentenced to one month's confinement and 2 months' loss of pay. Unknown is why she spent the time to write a letter about this case.[117]

Colonel Pope, using Naval directive 5755-666-02, recommended remission of the unexpired sentences for 36 prisoners. His suggestion was that 3 should be restored to duty and 33 prisoners should be discharged.[118]

10. Prison Progress and Changes at the Top

"Please cease writing annoying letters to me and remember that this is not kindergarten."
—Lt. Col. Kelton

Marines returning home from the Far East were finally on the last leg of their journey. En route to the Boston Barracks from New York City, they were on board the passenger steamer *Plymouth*.

On the dark, late-winter night of 19 March 1903, steamer traffic providing coastal transportation service chugged along as usual, keeping to schedule. In those narrow navigable waters, steamers get by on visual sightings of other nautical passersby. This night, the visibility was pea soup. On a night like this, ships could know nothing of each other's existence let alone proximity until they were dangerously close.

Unknown to the Marines on the *Plymouth*, as they were trying to sleep in their much slept in hammocks by so many people, their transportation and hostel was on a collision course with another steamer. Off the coast of Rhode Island in Long Island Sound, the *Plymouth* sighted and maneuvered to avert a collision with *The City of Taunton*. The belated move couldn't spare crushing in of the *Taunton*'s starboard bow. The hole was above the waterline, so it didn't sink. But the bow was where 5 crewmembers were sleeping. The 5 in the forecastle drowned from incoming water.

The crash jolted Marines from sleep below deck and roused them out of bed without clothes or shoes. Upon quick assessment and thinking by their leadership, coupled with their experience at sea, the Marines sprang into action, and were "instrumental in averting a panic." Their sea legs helped calm the less experienced passengers. Out of 550 passengers only one was lost.

This event got the newspapers' attention. The *New York Times* reported the Marines had a "peculiar experience." The Marines' clothing and effects were lost and they had to cut blankets into strips for shoes.

General Heywood read these accounts and wanted to hear what the officer in charge of the troops had to say.[1] On April 6, the General wrote, "The bravery, efficiency and coolness of these men under most trying conditions have been most highly spoken of by the Commanding Officer of the detachment and by many civilians who were present, and it is a source of much gratification to the Major General Commandant, to learn that these Marines, fresh from the vicissitudes incidental to a tour of duty in the Far East, so well exemplified on this occasion the fact that they had learned to meet danger with equanimity and to live up to the best traditions of the Marine Corps." The major general commandant especially wanted to commend the conduct of First Lieutenant William C. Harllee, Quartermaster Sergeant John G. Edwards, First Sergeant Thaddeus P. Shaw, Sergeant Michael Melaney and Corporal Frank E. Abbot. He particularly commented on the bravery and coolness of Corporal Abbot, who remained in a position of special peril and engaged in an effort to save lives until he could escape himself, although with great difficulty. He concluded saying that the men of the detachment had well contributed to the right of the corps to its motto "Semper Fidelis." The letter was read at formation to all members of the Barracks.[2]

On April 1, Sergeant Samuel F. McCauley was directed to proceed to Derby, CT, and take custody of Sergeant Arthur Lahar. Lahar was charged with desertion.[3] Colonel Pope was very disappointed with Sergeant Lahar. He was a brave noncommissioned officer and it confounded him why he would desert. Pope found it appropriate to attach an extract of his military record along with his papers.

In the Philippines, locked in a firefight against insurgents, Sgt. Lahar carried his wounded colleague Sergeant Brian McSwinney from the field near Quinapundan on the island of Samar. Sergeant Lahar was promoted meritoriously on June 18, 1902, for conspicuous courage and fortitude for this effort to save his friend's life (he later died). In a letter of February 1903, the brigadier general commandant wrote to the commanding officer, 1st Brigade of Marines, Naval Station, Cavite, Philippines, and expressed his appreciation for the gallant and commendable conduct of Sergeant Lahar and said he was a credit to himself and to the Marine Corps to which he belonged.[4]

The lack of a proper firing range for going on two years was becoming a chronic problem at the Boston Marine Barracks. Lovell's Island was becoming a forlorn memory. What was on a Barracks commander's plate was getting rights to another firing range. Colonel Pope asked the mayor of Lynn for permission to use the range that the city police utilized for their firearms training. He wanted to make whatever arrangements were possible to use the Lynn range.[5]

When senior officers of the naval service passed away, Marines volunteers were requested for rendering proper honors. In April, Sergeant George Bernard was detailed to report to 1055 Beacon Street in Boston at 2 p.m. on April 10 in the uniform of the day with side arms. That was the residence of the late Rear Admiral R.R. Belknap. Sgt. Bernard's contact person was a naval officer, the son of the deceased, Lieutenant Belknap. Bernard was directed to carry out the orders of Lieutenant Belknap and return as directed.[6] Captain R.M. Gilson, USMC, was also ordered to report to the commandant of the Navy yard for duty at the funeral.[7]

The *Southery* afforded extra rooms for extra prisoners, but Colonel Pope still had to provide men for that detachment too. That cost 35 privates, 1 sergeant and 1 corporal. The prison ship had become a part of shipyard life. It really did help out with any overcrowding of the Charlestown Naval Prison. It was on the books for any future possible rise in prisoner population.[8]

On April 16 Colonel Pope referenced Navy Department Letter 5755-6-02 when he requested remission of 48 prisoners. He recommended that 6 prisoners be restored to duty and 42 prisoners be discharged. This continued and seemed to become the primary method of preventing overcrowding of the naval prison and the *Southery*.[9]

Colonel Pope now tried asking Captain Charles T. Hilliker of the State Armory in Lynn after asking its mayor if the Marines could use their range.[10] Captain Hilliker, not committing on anything, referred Colonel Pope to the chairman of the Board of Public Works of the City of Lynn. So Pope promptly wrote to the chairman and asked to him to estimate the costs of rebuilding the butts (mounds of earth used to stop bullets) at the range in the Wyoma section of Lynn. Maybe Pope wanted to strut deep pockets too. The butts were not in great condition. They were eroding and needed work to make them safe, as the Marines use high-powered rifles. He also wanted to know that the terms of rental would be, and he would agree to pay a proportionate cost of the rebuilding effort.[11]

Working on several shooting range possibilities, Pope didn't hold out the greatest hopes for the range in Lynn. Colonel Pope asked same ranked Colonel James G. White, the inspector general for state rifle practice, for his advice about the Marines' need. His office was in the statehouse in Boston. Never mind the City of Lynn. The State of Massachusetts used a range in Woburn, MA. He made the same offers to help defray costs of improving the butts and other necessary improvements.[12]

Sergeant Conlan had served as a mail orderly for over fifteen years. He was trusted by everyone from postmasters to bank presidents. He was about to retire. Colonel Pope wanted him promoted to gunnery sergeant and retire in that rank as a reward for this long and faithful service.[13] Colonel Pope wrote to his boss, Major General Heywood, on behalf of Sergeant Frank Conlan.

Using the now established custom provided by the naval directive of relieving overcrowding in the naval prison, Colonel Pope recommended remitting the unexpired sentences of 36 prisoners. He recommended that 4 prisoners by restored to duty and 32 prisoners be discharged.[14]

In late May 1903, Colonel Pope learned he would lose access to the *Southery*. It would be moving to Portsmouth, NH. It was to be anchored in the stream of the Piscataqua River at the Portsmouth Navy Yard but would continue to serve as a prison ship.[15]

In June, a Marine had an unusual medical problem. Unusual enough to require placement at an unusual facility. We only know however that Private Ocie E. Batten was transferred to the U.S. General Hospital at Fort Bayard in New Mexico. He was directed to report to the medical officer for treatment.[16]

Every June, the grand marshal of the annual Bunker Hill Day parade made his annual request to the Marine Barracks for participation. In earlier times, other commanders grumbled when this request came in. Times had changed. On June 13, Colonel Pope informed the commandant of the Navy Yard that he would provide the parade 1 officer and a company of 32 Marines from the Marine Barracks. The USS *Massachusetts*, in port at the Navy yard, would also provide 2 officers and 1 company of 32 Marines. And the USS *Atlanta* would provide 1 officer for the parade.[17]

The dreamed of extension of the toilet rooms was finally approved by the quartermaster of the Marine Corps.[18] On June 16, Colonel Pope informed Messrs. Ganey and Burke of 4 Alden Street and Messrs. Huey Bros of 35 Hartford Street, Boston, that they won the bids for the project. He explained to both contractors that they must finish on schedule or he would take appropriate action.[19]

The naval prison now occupied a substantial amount of the Marines' time. An international sized Navy had more sailors, and proportionally more miscreants. So much so that Colonel Pope asked the judge advocate general of the Navy that only prisoners with under a year to serve be imprisoned in the Charlestown facility. From his and his predecessors' experience he felt that those with longer terms were more tempted to escape from the working parties in the yard. He also expressed his opinion that if the *Southery* was anchored in midstream at Portsmouth, it would provide a much more secure facility for prisoners with longer terms to serve than the naval prison in Charlestown.[20]

The practice of remitting unexpired sentences to provide room in the naval prison of general court-martial prisoners continued when Colonel Pope recommended that the sentences of 39 more prisoners be remitted. He suggested that discharges be given to 37 and 2 prisoners be restored to duty.[21] The combined efforts of the Navy Department and those of the naval prison were instrumental in obtaining a slow decline in the prison population at the yard. The July 24 Report showed 102 Navy men and 13 Marines for a total of 115 inmates.[22]

Sentinels spent many long hours on watch—long, often distractionless watches. While on watch, however, sentinels had to not allow people in or out of the yard on occasion. Sometimes people don't like that. And sometimes they tried to do something about it. The sentries were issued clubs as a self-defense weapon just in case this happened.

Like many lifeguards and their whistles, the guards swung the clubs to while away the time. However, a swinging club may conjure up images of arrogance and intimidation. Colonel Pope thought it was a very unsoldierly bearing, swinging these clubs while walking. So he requested 50 frogs, the name for club holsters, from headquarters. The frogs would be attached to the sentinel's belt and would hold the club in a proper manner, a more uniform manner.[23] The body of a Marine from an action in the Philippines was returned to Boston. The Marine Barracks was notified that an Army transport would bring the body of Sergeant Brian McSwinney to the United States. He was the noncommissioned officer that Sergeant Arthur Lahar pulled from battle wounded. McSwinney died of his wounds. He was scheduled to leave the Philippines on the first of September. Sergeant Brian McSwinney was re-interred in the U.S. Naval Hospital Cemetery in Chelsea, MA, with full military honors.[24]

On August 31, Sergeant Frank Conlan, the mail orderly, retired. Major General Heywood did indeed get back to Colonel Pope and promoted Sergeant Conlan to quartermaster sergeant, just in time for retirement.[25]

Stores just outside the Navy yard sold government issued clothing and articles. This was a total violation of federal law.[26] Colonel Pope reported a dealer of second hand clothing to the captain of Boston Police Station 15 in Charlestown. It is unknown why this shopkeeper entered his crosshairs.

More foreign stations required Marines from Boston as the Navy and its commitments enlarged. On October 21, 11 privates were transferred to the Barracks in Washington, D.C., to ship out for duty with the Marine detachment at Tutuilla, Samoa.[27] Again, on October 22, another 30 privates were moved to the Marine Barracks in Brooklyn, NY, for duty in the Philippines.[28]

Colonel Pope honorably turned over command to Lt. Col. A.C. Kelton on November 9, 1903.

Lt. Col. A.C. Kelton

An officer shortage greeted the new commanding officer (we met him before when he was a junior officer). Only two officers were present for duty in Boston, Lt. Col. Kelton told the secretary of the Navy. One of them, Captain Frederick H. Delano, had been detailed as a judge advocate general of a general court-martial trial in session, a temporary duty, but he also had officer of the day rotation, his duties as post treasurer, post exchange officer, and he was the officer in charge of clothing, arms and other logistics. Did he have time to sleep? Kelton wanted Captain Delano at least excused from his duties as judge advocate general so that he could properly attend to his other duties.[29]

The prisoners' report of November 14 showed a drop that could be shared with everybody. This trend was to continue for the rest of the year. It showed 107 sailors and 23 Marines, for a total of 130 men confined.[30]

Dennis H. Finn of Lawrence, MA, desired to secure the early discharge of Private Alfred H. Duckworth. Lt. Col. Kelton informed Dennis H. Finn that the president tied his hands by issuing an order prohibiting discharges of any enlisted man in the naval service before the expiration of his enlistment, except for physical disability, ineptitude or bad character or conduct, so he could not comply with his request for discharge. To keep his hopes up Kelton encouraged Finn that he may have a better chance with the commandant of the Marine Corps.[31]

Overseas duties ballooned after the Spanish-American War. These duties required more Marines from Boston. Private Henry W. Rapp was ordered to Camp Roosevelt on the tiny Culebra Island, seventeen miles east of the Puerto Rican mainland. Pvt. Rapp was transferred in such a hurry that he left his things behind. So Lt. Col. Kelton asked the captain of the USS *Aretusa* to deliver Rapp's personal effects to the Caribbean. The USS *Aretusa* was scheduled to set sail to the Caribbean anyway and could deliver his belongings to the commanding officer of the Marines at the naval station in San Juan, Puerto Rico. Private Rapp was a member of the permanent garrison at Culebra.[32] Its command was located in San Juan.

Private Ralph Mahon repaired other Marines' shoes for spare cash. He did so much work he had to keep a book accounting for money due him from his peers. So when a ditty box was looted, guess whose was targeted. Nine 2-cent stamps were stolen, along with the book from Pvt. Mahon's ditty box. The remainders of the contents were strewn throughout the barracks room. Several witnesses observed Private William H. Bowen sitting on Mahon's box with the box open and holding stamps in his hands and going through the box. To set an example, as thefts had been occurring with increasing frequency, he recommended that Private Bowen be tried by a general court-martial.[33]

Sentinel duty on the third floor of the naval prison might have been a quiet, undemanding detail. Maybe this reality went into the thought process that found Private James McCafferty on November 28 under the influence of intoxicating liquor while at this post. To Lt. Col. Kelton, this was a very grave offense. McCafferty had many years of service and certainly was a very mature Marine,[34] but he went and did something like this.

Advice on food purchases and who to go through was on the mind of the commanding officer of the Marine Barracks in Portsmouth, NH, Major F. J. Moses. He asked Lt. Col. Kelton for his counsel. They knew each other from their junior officer days at the barracks. Kelton provided suggestions for rations and recommended a wholesale dealer to Major Moses. A bill of fare from Boston was enclosed, and he explained that when there were three varieties of meat he alternated the following way: for supper: one week—eggs, one week—hash, and one week—pork chops. He was looking to introduce his men to sausage, scrapple, cod fish cakes and stewed kidneys.

Lt. Col. Kelton did caution, however, that the food requirements at the Charlestown Navy Yard were very different from any other post. There were, after all, the 141 inmates confined in the naval prison that needed to be fed and these rations came from the Barracks. Added to the 106 Marines at the Barracks, 247 mouths needed to be fed. These large numbers enabled Kelton to purchase food wholesale. He criticized his predecessor Colonel Pope, as he thought Pope spent too lavishly and bought large amounts of food. If he continued to follow Colonel Pope's unsustainable feeding program the company fund would run out of money.[35]

The Charlestown Naval Prison facility was approaching obsolescence. A proposed naval prison on Seavey's Island, at the naval shipyard in Portsmouth, NH, was in the works. John F. Watkins of 1745 Eighteenth Street, NW, Washington, awarded the project, requested a substantial amount of information as well as photographs of the naval prison in the yard. Lt. Col. Kelton replied that he did not have clerical staff available at the prison to answer all his questions. It would be better if Watkins sent a representative to gather the data he needed. All Kelton could say to Watkins is that the secretary of the Navy had decided on that location and beyond that he had no further information.[36]

Lt. Col. Kelton's patience was exhausted by the parents of Marines whose behaviors were so poor that it landed them in a naval prison. He reassured Mrs. M. Carwin of 341 Preston Street, Dallas, TX, that her son was well and that he did indeed receive the articles sent to him by her. Her son's release date was May 30, 1904, as long as his good conduct continued. He said her son was actually better taken care of, better fed, better lodged and clothed than a great number of young men his age.

Now he let her have it: "Please cease writing annoying letters to me and remember that this is not kindergarten, and that I have other and more important duties than that of inquiries into the private and personal affairs of several hundred grown-up men, presumably intelligent enough to be responsible for their own actions and find out why they do not write to their mothers, what they received from them, etc."[37]

On Christmas Day, Provisional Company A was formed at the Boston Barracks and Captain George C. Reid was placed in its command. He was now in command of 82 privates, a second lieutenant, a first sergeant, 4 sergeants, 6 corporals, and 1 trumpeter. Company A was to proceed to League Island in Pennsylvania and join with the provisional battalion organizing for overseas duty in Haut Obispo, Panama.[38]

The naval prison now demanded most of Lt. Col. Kelton's attention. Prison issues began to eclipse his attention to the Marine Barracks, his primary responsibility, as problems at the prison became very dangerous. To make matters worse, the lack of reliable electrical power to the prison turned the lights off, often at difficult times. Three times during his watch, he informed Captain Sam G. Lemly, USN, a judge advocate general from the Navy Department, the entire prison blacked out when the lights failed. It was bad luck when there was a disturbance, but it also happened twice when the prisoners were being fed—a routine event that required lighting. If feeding was disrupted by the loss of lights, a prison full of hungry prisoners could become an explosive powder keg that didn't have to happen. At the last power outage, a sobering moment occurred. Five prisoners attempted to create a riot. Fortunately, this time anyway, guards contained the danger.

As a reasonable solution to the problem, Kelton suggested kerosene lamps be made available to provide emergency lighting. Addressing their potential for danger themselves, he assured Capt. Lemly, Washington's point man, that these lamps would be kept under the strict charge of the sergeants, the NCOs on duty, and the kerosene could be stored outside the prison to preclude any likelihood of danger.[39]

The post exchange was a boon to the Marines. For officer and enlisted man alike, the PX, as it was now called, boosted the quality of their lives. In modern terms, it was a convenience store, with quality in-demand merchandise, very centrally located, affordably priced, and tax-free.

But it had warts too. As the Christmas season of 1903 faded into memory and winter darkened and froze, Lt. Col. Kelton went looking for irregularities in the operations and record keeping of the post exchange. Especially the Christmas shopping season records. Kelton had always had an officer shortage. The PX needed them. He used this as a moment of action to try to get more officers. He went public preemptively when he wrote to the commandant of the Navy yard and requested that a board be appointed to determine the extent of irregularities that might exist and place responsibility, to mitigate any further problems, and maybe get some more officers.[40]

The Navy Department continued the program of reducing the prison population under the directive 5755-6-02 of 30 June 1902. On January 22, Lt. Col. Kelton requested remission of unexpired sentences of 10 prisoners, with 5 restored to duty and 5 discharged.[41]

Lt. Col. Kelton could smell when his Marines were up to something. Marine Private G.F. Lawless was bedridden with typhoid fever and quarantined at his mom's house. Margaret Lawless said so. And she said she had a doctor that said it was okay. So Lt. Col. Kelton wrote to Dr. H.S. Flynn of Providence, RI, and asked whether he did indeed give instructions to Margaret Lawless to keep her son indoors for typhoid fever. He also told Dr. Flynn that Private G.F. Lawless was absent without leave and he used the instructions of his doctor, him, as his excuse.[42] Lt. Col. Kelton always thought Private Lawless had very weak character and would resort to any means to cover up his acts.

Instead of sitting at his desk waiting for the mailman, Lt. Col. Kelton followed up with another letter to the chairman of the Lynn public works. He referenced his last letter of August 28, 1903. Kelton reminded the chairman of the Marines' desire to use the target area in the Wyoma area. He had heard nothing from them about the range.

It was likely the chairman was not too thrilled about the thought of federal level troops coming in and out and blasting away with all kinds of noise at a range that probably only got used part time with small arms. Even though his requests may have been going to the circular file in the chairman's office, Kelton requested an answer nonetheless.[43]

Previous commanding officers were able to outfit the naval prison with a chapel furnished with donated items. Right down to the donated organ. This distinguished organ had seen long service. It was time to find a replacement. Lt. Col. Kelton asked the judge advocate general of the Navy if he could replace the organ. Chaplains who celebrated mass at the prison were convinced the organ helped elevate prisoners' souls and made all the difference.[44]

Private Edwin Sawyer couldn't follow rules and regulations enough to stay out of the naval prison. But this prisoner's dad was John E. Sawyer, the postmaster of the Methuen Station in Lawrence, MA. And he asked for special consideration for his son. These requests were another distraction towards the prison and away from the barracks for Lt. Col. Kelton. They happened occasionally and he always cooled when politicians sought personal favoritism for their relatives.

Lt. Col. Kelton told the postmaster in a February 24, 1904, correspondence that his son had been punished for not observing the rules and regulations, period. His release from confinement would be entirely dependent on his conduct and nothing else. Now Kelton spoke his mind. He said he was surprised the postmaster even asked for this very unreasonable request.[45] This was not the first time Colonel Kelton had heard from Sawyer, however.

A letter was forwarded to the Barracks. Postmaster Sawyer had written this letter to Brigadier General Elliott. In this one Sawyer complained that his son Private Edwin L. Sawyer returned from three years in the Philippines but had not yet received a leave of absence. Postmaster Sawyer also complained specifically that his son said he made every effort to secure a leave through his commanding officer, Colonel Kelton. But Kelton wouldn't give him one. And would General Elliott kindly intervene on this matter. General Elliott declined and merely forwarded this letter to the Marine Barracks in Boston.[46]

The West Indies Campaign Medal was awarded to Sergeant Major John Lawler. Sgt. Lawler participated in the Battle of Guantanamo, Cuba, from June 11–13 in 1898. He also was at Manzanillo, Cuba, on August 12, 1898. He was with the 1st Battalion of Marines. He received congratulations from Lt. Col. Kelton.[47]

The days when Uncle Sam paid for the electricity of residents of the shipyard were over. It came from above: the chief of the Bureau of Yards and Docks of the Navy yard. The chief formally announced to the commandant of the Charlestown Navy Yard that the cost of all lights furnished to quarters must now be charged to the occupants. The current would be measured by meters and charged at the same rate as the officers living at the Marine Barracks. Marine officers were already paying for the electricity used in their quarters; now anybody else living on the shipyard had to as well. The meters were installed in all quarters and apartments and were to be read on a monthly basis and billed accordingly.[48]

When recruiting offices in downtown Boston were closed, any recruiting continued at the Barracks. Recruits need to be medically examined, however. There were no specified medical personnel for this purpose. So the shipyard's medical people were asked to perform this duty. Medical Inspector E.Z. Derr of the Navy yard objected to examining any men for enlistment unless he was duly directed by his boss, the surgeon general or the commandant of the Navy Yard. So Kelton wrote to the commandant of the Navy yard and requested that Derr be directed to examine all men who may be presented to him for enlistment in the Marine Corps.[49]

Sailors sometimes can go ashore at the yard, but were not always allowed to leave the yard. Routine gate duty was sometimes as much about keeping sailors in as it was about keeping unauthorized people out. The torpedo boat destroyer *Hull* was docked at the shipyard. By 1904 these destroyers were fast, heavily armed and large. The term was shortened to "destroyer" by World War I. A sailor from the crew made three attempts to get out of the yard through the main gate. He tried representing himself as a yard workman. When those attempts failed he tried to leave through the ropewalk gate. There he was finally apprehended and arrested. He was returned to the ship under guard on October 26.[50]

Captain Reid took over for Lt. Col. Kelton.

The unit was still looking for a suitable place for rifle practice. Overtures to the Lynn range's management received a cool reception. There was another one. Wakefield had a range. The Bay State Military Rifle Range was located there and controlled by the 1st Corps of Cadets of the Massachusetts Volunteer Militia.[51] So Captain Reid wrote to its commander, Captain John A. Blanchard, and requested use of their range.

A proper range facility was now badly needed. For Corporal James Hall it was urgent. Captain Reid specifically requested to have Corporal Hall complete a 300-yard rapid-fire course so that he could qualify as a Marine Corps sharpshooter. Could he be shoe horned in? This apparently did not happen, as on November 28, Captain Reid sent Corporal Hall to Newport, RI, to complete the rifle range work there, in a different state, and qualify as a sharpshooter.[52]

In late November, more West Indies Campaign Medals were awarded. Private James Duncan, James McCaffrey and Sergeant George Reynolds all received the medal for their participation in the Battle of Guantanamo Bay in Cuba during June 11–13, 1898, and for their role in the Battle of Manzanillo on August 12, 1898. They were with the First Battalion of Marines, of course.[53]

Main gate sentinels also had to watch out for pilferage from the Navy Yard. Even paint brushes. On November 21, an employee, Fred Treffethen of the Services and Agencies Department, Building 34, attempted to carry out a whitewash brush through the main gate. The sergeant of the guard spied the item concealed under his overalls and grabbed him.[54]

Arriving ships brought work to the shipyard and liberty bound sailors. They also brought prisoners bound for the naval prison. The sight of some of them emerging from the bowels of an incoming ship could be horrifying. Landsman J.J. Brady, USN, a general court-martial prisoner from the USS *Missouri*, arrived "in most filthy condition." His possessions included only one old set of blue uniforms. He had no socks or underclothing. He also possessed a bad case of gonorrhea and had not bathed in weeks. Upon arrival at the naval prison he was given a bath, and the water turned "literally black." Even after a thorough cleaning of his body, there still was a very offensive odor in his cell for some time afterwards.[55]

Corporal Henry Wesley succumbed to meningitis at the Chelsea Naval Hospital on November 26. Captain Reid reported to his next of kin, Mrs. J.S. Groom of 466 West Broad Street, Savannah, GA, that he was buried with full military honors at the naval hospital cemetery. Corporal Wesley's personal effects would be sent to her if she desired.[56]

Private Gilbert Weston was on guard duty at Post 7 on November 29 between the darkening hours of 4 and 5 p.m. A master shipfitter approached Weston and asked him to arrest two civilians. The shipfitter was accusing these two fellas of stealing copper. Private Weston duly arrested one of the guys. He then proceeded to turn him over to Private Hart. Pvt. Hart was from the Marine guard of the USS *Missouri*. He too was on guard duty, but he was guarding the dock to which his vessel was moored. Private Weston requested that Private Hart hold the man while he went to arrest the other one. Private Weston went back and arrested the second man. But when he returned he found that Private Hart had allowed the first one to escape. Private Hart replied in a very indignant manner that he had no order to arrest people in the yard. Hart's jurisdiction was the dock where his ship was moored.

Captain Reid sought clarification from the commandant of the shipyard. The clarification came down: although Private Hart may not have had specific orders to apprehend individuals in the vicinity of his post, his general orders did. Under those circumstances, he should have held the prisoner temporarily entrusted to him and thus lend aid to the sentinel on an adjoining post to protect government property.[57]

Junior Officers in Charge

Provisional Company C formed in Boston. Ninety-six Marines were shipping out for duty in Panama. Captain Reid too. Marines were heading to where the action was. But it caused some very severe personnel shortages. Captain Hatch, now in charge of the Barracks, explained to the commandant of the Navy Yard that he could not man posts 2, 6 and 10 without replacements because of the severe manpower shortage.[58]

The Barracks tried to purchase their stores and supplies from local providers. This included coal. Good coal should burn to a nice white ash. The coal the Barracks was getting, however, produced too much ash and not enough heat. The deliveries even contained a lot of sand. Sand acted as a flux and formed so many clinkers that the Barracks fireman was kept busy cleaning the fire in addition to the normal routine of raking out ashes. He wrote to Wellington-Wild Coal Company on 7 Central Street in Boston. Hatch complained about the quality of coal that the company was supplying to the Barracks. He said the coal was inferior and did not conform to the standard called for by terms of the contract. The contract required that white ash coal must be first class merchantable quality of Shenandoah or Lee or other equally good quality.

This was not the first time he complained. A previous complaint was not honored, since the last lot delivered was the worst of all. And the coal they went through the previous winter was simply alarming.[59]

Naval prisoners were sent home with little more than the clothes on their backs when they were discharged. James Moynahan of 839 Dix Avenue, Detroit, Michigan, wanted clothing he felt should have been given to him upon release. Captain Hatch responded by quoting Navy yard regulations. These required prisoners to be "discharged without pay, who have no clothing in which to appear in public with decency are furnished with a suit by the Paymaster, USRS *Wabash*." He added that he (Moynahan) did indeed have a suit to wear upon release so it was not necessary to issue him another one.[60]

A "Welcome Home" telegram arrived and congratulated the Marines. It came from Mrs. A. Hurlbut of Holland Patent, NJ. Captain Hatch was so moved he wrote a thank you letter to Mrs. Hurlbut. He told her that it was very nice gesture and that his Marines now referred to her as "Mother Hurlbut" and that the Marines from Boston on duty around the world appreciated her efforts on their behalf.[61]

Fifty-six men enjoyed coming back to the states after a tour of duty in the Philippines. This also happened to improve manpower situation. With all the new fresh men, Captain Hatch was able to re-establish sentinels on posts 2, 6 and 10.[62]

Officers' spouses could join their husbands on some overseas assignments. Captain G.C. Reid's wife planned to join him in Panama. Captain Hatch arranged for the Panama Steamship Company to qualify her for naval rates for her passage January 7, 1905. The cost of her transportation would be paid from Captain Reid's personal accounts.[63]

On January 14, 1905, three privates from the Barracks received unusual orders. They were transferred to the U.S. Naval Home, Philadelphia, PA, and ordered to report to the governor of the home for duty.[64]

The next of kin of the deceased Private Wessell wrote to the Barracks and inquired about his personal effects they had received. They complained that his effects were very scanty. That Marine life may be hard to understand for many people, Captain Little wrote. He gently explained to them that a Marine cannot be expected to have an extensive wardrobe, as the space allotted to him for keeping his clothing and personal items was necessarily very small since they had to be ready to ship out on short notice.[65]

In the dead of the winter of 1905, Colonel Kelton returned to command. The cold climate of Boston was not especially amenable to the Marine tradition of close order drills. So he asked the commandant of the Navy yard on January 20 for use of Buildings 114 and 103 for 2 hours each day for close order drill during the cold winter months.[66]

A dishwashing machine in the mess hall would not only reduce daily labor requirements, it would also be more sanitary. Colonel Kelton wrote to the Insinger Company, Stanton Avenue, Wagner Junction, in Philadelphia, PA, about installing a dishwasher in the mess facilities. He requested information on prices and whether the government received a discount, and he asked for them to send an agent to help them determine the appropriate size, location and other pertinent factors.[67]

Prisoner chasing—escorting prisoners to their incarcerations—can be good duty. It is a break from routine and takes the chasers to new and interesting places. Or it can lead to opportunities for trouble. Private W.F. Decoma, a prisoner chaser from the Marine Barracks in Brooklyn, NY, had escorted a prisoner to the naval prison in Boston. While he was enjoying a liberty in Boston, he got into trouble, was arrested and sent to Deer Island for 8 days confinement himself. The chief of police of Boston notified Colonel Kelton of this Marine and that it would cost $5 to have him released. He wasn't going to pay so Colonel Kelton wrote to the commanding officer, Marine Barracks, Brooklyn, NY, and told him to send him $5 and he would make arrangements for Private Decoma's release.[68]

Sergeant Major John L. Lawler was designated to lead 20 Marines sent to the Marine Barracks in Brooklyn, NY, to ship out for overseas duty on January 21.[69]

Plans for the replacement of the naval prison in the Charlestown Navy Yard were nearing fruition. Colonel Kelton probably giddily received blueprints of the proposed facility planned for Portsmouth, NH. The Bureau of Yards and Docks, at the behest of the judge advocate general of the Navy Department, wanted his input. They all knew of his intimate experience as commanding officer of the naval prison in Boston.[70]

Lt. Col. Kelton held in his hands several letters from the British consulate general in New York. Private J.P. Saxon had earlier asked for and received these letters from the British consulate. These letters verified his service with the Prince of Wales Light Horse.

A few Marines served with other military units around the world. Private J.P. Saxon had served on horseback with the Prince of Wales Light Horse, an Australian Cavalry regiment formed in 1848. Men needed to know how to ride a horse really well, and shoot small arms from the saddle, in full gallop. At the time, riding horses into battle was as prestigious as flying fighter jets. Pvt. Saxon was in the Prince of Wales Light Horse and rode in the Boer War. He was awarded medals and three clasps for his service in South Africa.[71]

The Boer Wars

In the 1830's the Boers were Dutch-speaking farmers in South Africa. They chaffed at subjection to British rule. So they migrated north and crossed the Vaal River to the Transvaal. Fertile lands were the draw to the Transvaal region. So was independence from British rule. However, Britain still claimed sovereignty in the Transvaal too. Tensions escalated.

In 1881, what was to become known as the First Boer War commenced when British troops garrisoned (based) in the Transvaal suffered surprising defeats by the Boers. Humiliating as it was for the foremost great power of the world at the time, the British government was in no mood for an expanded war, so it allowed local self-government, but under British suzerainty. That meant external affairs would require ratification by the crown.

This arrangement worked for five years until 1886, when an Australian discovered gold. Suddenly prospectors, miners, and settlers poured into the Transvaal from all over the world. The city of Johannesburg sprang up as a boom town over night. In another historical pattern, these newcomers were denied citizenship. This time by the Boer government. Tensions in the late '90's grew once again, enough to garner British attention. Additional forces were dispatched to South Africa.

On 10 October 1899 the British government received an ultimatum from the Boer government demanding that the additional troops be withdrawn from the Cape and Natal. After the deadline passed, Boer forces laid siege to the key towns of Mafeking, Kimberley and Ladysmith. British attempts to relieve these townships were failing in damaging defeats. It was here defensive trench warfare, made infamous in World War I, was invented by the Boers. This event defined and established the supremacy of the defensive position, engendering the Great War stalemate and slaughter to come.

During this difficult phase of the war for the British, at the battle of Coloenso, British forces suffered yet another defeat even though the Australian Light Horse and Pvt. Saxon participated. Further reinforcements arrived on Valentine's Day and enabled effective counteroffenses. Kimberley was relieved the next day with the help of the Australian Light Horse. A new front opened up in the north Eastern Cape. Australian Light Horse troops were placed there. They engaged the Boers at Arundel.

The vicissitudes of the Second Boer War eventually led to the last formal set piece battle of the war, the capture of the capital, Pretoria. British observers thought the war was over; however a guerrilla war soon commenced. A modern example might be the American war in 2000s Iraq. After a formal three-week fight and "mission accomplished" established, the "real war" began. The Boers eventually took to the mountains. It became a guerrilla war of attrition. The British needed to find a way to deny them movement.

In the final days of the war British offenses were more successful. Miles of barbed wire (made infamous in World War I) and block houses (reinforced concrete defensive positions also used widely in World War I) parceled up the veldt, restricting Boer maneuvering. Useful intelligence from natives increasingly hostile to the Boers gave the British a decisive advantage. Australian Light Horse units were frequently used in these attacks. The Light Horse spearheaded offensives in April 1902.

The Second Boer War marked the heyday of light horse cavalry units. And Pvt. Saxon was there. Eventually effective use of water-cooled modern machine guns during World War I rendered horse cavalry obsolete. Australia provided the largest number of troops for the Boer war. Since its climate resembled South Africa, Australians acclimated more quickly than British troops from England.

The terms of the peace were the same as before the war: self-government under British suzerainty.

11. The Post Exchange Investigation; Wood's Command

The letter was impertinent, as it was unrestrained in its lack of good taste and quite disrespectful as well.

On February 8, Private Edward Millican was awarded the West Indies Campaign Medal. He sailed aboard the USS *Harvard* in the Battle of Santiago, Cuba, on July 3, 1898.[1]

On February 11, Private Marshall T. Naylor died at the Chelsea Naval Hospital. His next of kin were notified and were informed that he was buried in the naval hospital cemetery with full military honors.[2]

The usual means of transporting Marines to posts in New York and points south was by way of passenger steamers. The ships sailed out of Boston and the line normally used was the Merchants and Miners Transportation Company. Its service had been found to be satisfactory.

In September 1904, Sergeant R.S. Nau was assigned to escort a prisoner to Port Royal, SC. He was provided as usual transportation by a Merchants and Miners passenger steamer to Savannah, Georgia. This time, however, he complained about the accommodations provided aboard the steamer. He found the steerage accommodations grossly unsatisfactory, to say the least.

Even headquarters got involved and instructed the recently promoted Colonel Kelton to inspect the ships of that line. The appointed inspecting officer was to determine the suitability of steerage accommodations on these ships for noncommissioned officers and privates of the Marine Corps. He was to pay particular attention to the cleanliness of the ships, condition of the bunks, and the quality of the food.[3] The report came back. Ouch. On February 9, Colonel Kelton submitted his findings to Headquarters. He inspected two of the steamers and examined the plans of the other three ships in the fleet running between Boston and Norfolk. He also interviewed officers and enlisted men that had traveled on the steamers. His report included the following:

1. The ships were not constructed for the purpose of carrying steerage or second class passengers.
2. Four of the steamers only had two rooms with six bunks each. The *Ontario* had three rooms but stuffed with 18 bunks.
3. The rooms were all located well forward of the main deck.
4. Within twelve feet of these rooms were located three water closets for the officers and the crew. A steam winch was within six feet of the rooms, leaving very little space to move about. The breathing atmosphere was anything but agreeable. The

bunks were provided with a blanket. But this blanket did not get laundered even after it had seen service for a long time with a great many people. The bunks were not inviting and suggested the presence of vermin.
6. The were no urinals, closets or lavatories for the steerage passengers.
7. The was no place for steerage passengers to smoke or rest outside of their rooms during the day.
8. The steerage passengers ate in the officers' mess room and had the same bill of fare, provided there was food left when their turn came. At 7:00 a.m., breakfast was served to the first relay of ships' officers. At 7:45, the second relay was served. At 8:30, the first relay of the steerage was permitted to have their meal. But the second party of steerage waited up to three-quarters of an hour for their meal. The food is first placed out fresh for the officers. Then that same food, what was left of it, stayed out for all the other steerage passengers and subsequently became rather cold and fly covered, picked over and otherwise not too palatable. The same conditions persist for all other meals.
9. A steward and a ticket agent both commented that the ships were not constructed for the comfort of enlisted men of the Marine Corps or Navy.
10. Colonel Kelton extended that he would much rather take a government transport, which takes much longer than these steamers. He concluded that the experience of a passenger with steerage accommodations was not a good one.
11. The steerage accommodations were open to all comers: African, Mongolian, Latin or Anglo-Saxon as well as both sexes, so that many objectionable combinations existed to all involved, according to very early 20th century mores and customs. This could cause great discomfort to those who were clean and well ordered, as were the enlisted men of the Navy and Marine Corps.
12. It was the opinion of the inspector that the steerage accommodations of the steamers leaving Boston were unclean, the rooms are poorly located and poorly ventilated. Furthermore, the system of food service according to the regulations of the company is unsatisfactory at best and the food under the conditions was unpalatable.[4]

It was a scathing report indeed. Maybe steamers only look romantic from the dock.

Several years passed with no solution for a rifle range. On February 15, Colonel Kelton had to report to Brigadier General Elliott that the Boston Marine Barracks were not able to conduct any rifle practice for the whole year of 1904, because of the non-availability of a proper rifle range.[5]

Appropriations problems caused cancellation of the installation of the electric dishwasher in the Barracks mess hall. The installation of the general steam cooking equipment for the kitchen used all the funds designated for those improvements and Kelton had to cancel the dishwasher.[6] He later wrote to Headquarters Marine Corps and explained that the Company Fund had reached $5,026 through profits from the post exchange and wise budgeting. He did ask for permission to expend $835 from the Company Fund for the purchase of a dishwasher ($240), a 40 gallon coffee urn ($135), one 69-gallon steam kettle ($125), two 45-gallon vegetable steamers ($120), and one 5-horse power upright tubular boiler for summer use ($100). He further indicated that he felt that it would be a great benefit to the troops and a proper use of the funds. Brigadier General Elliott approved the acquisition.[7]

Headquarters was cognizant of the successful operation of the post exchange of the Marine Barracks in Boston. It was to be held up as a model and its experience incorporated into new post exchange regulations imposed throughout the Army and the Navy. These were very considerable recognitions worthy of great pride.

The commandant of the Marine Corps tasked the adjutant and inspector to adapt the post exchange regulations of the U.S. Army for the Marine Corps post exchange system. These new regulations were to be published as the new regulation for the approval of the secretary of the Navy. Colonel Rauchiemer, the adjutant and inspector, asked Colonel Kelton for the benefit of his experience and advice with the post exchange in Boston and he enclosed a draft of the proposed regulations. He wanted Colonel Kelton to review the document and make recommendations as to best method of operation of the post exchanges.[8]

Colonel Kelton enforced a policy of very strict accounting for funds of any kind. He called Captain George C. Reid out to headquarters as neglectful and careless in accounting for funds in connection with the prisoners' accounts at the naval prison. Captain Reid was the acting commanding officer while Colonel Kelton was absent from the post on leave. The amount of money involved was $8.57.[9] The Barracks received $8.57 on March 24 from Captain Reid and the account was settled.[10] Captain Reid was subsequently transferred to the Panama Canal Zone.

Colonel Kelton was very interested in the proposed naval prison planned for Portsmouth. He wanted them to get it right. His prison always had that ad hoc feel. Colonel Kelton asked the judge advocate general (JAG) of the Navy Department if he could pay a visit to the construction site and go over plans for the Portsmouth Naval Prison. He seemed determined to examine the interior arrangements of cells, prison corridors, door levers and other aspects that concerned him from his experiences.[11]

First Lieutenant John A. Hughes was to command 50 Marines for further duty beyond the seas via the Marine Barracks in Norfolk, VA.[12] Depletion of Barracks personnel was part and parcel of barracks life and planning.

On April 18, Colonel Kelton wrote an "unofficial" letter to Captain S.W.B. Diehl, USN, after Kelton made his tour of the new construction site for the naval prison in Portsmouth, NH. He told Captain Diehl that he did not want to go through official channels, considering his inspection was unofficial after all. The JAG's reply or silence would influence him as to future correspondence on the subject. He also intimated that he was available for whatever advice may be needed for the successful completion of the naval prison at Portsmouth.[13]

On 11 May 12:15 a.m. Private Martin Mickken, the sentry at the Ropewalk Gate (Post 4), had a man approach his gate he believed to be under the influence. He said his name was Thomas Joyce and that he was a fireman at the yard. The sentry sent him away.

Later that early dark morning, probably about 3 a.m. the fireman arriving for his shift at Building 40 came back to Post 4. He reported a drunken man was in the building, asleep in the office. The sergeant of the guard checked in on Building 40. He found Thomas Joyce. Drunk. And asleep in the office. A flask of whiskey was by his side. The sergeant removed him from the yard again.

It turned out that Thomas Joyce was supposed to be on his watch from 3 to 11 p.m. that night. He then had to continue on with the 11 p.m. to 3 a.m. watch into May 11 for a twelve hour shift. However, Joyce was recorded to have been outside the yard at 12:15 a.m. Seems that Joyce, after his regular shift ended, left the yard to go get some whiskey. He was trying to get back to work when he was stopped at Gate 4. He somehow got back onto the yard and back to his post. When 3 a.m. arrived, Thomas Joyce's relief found him in an unflattering state. This was duly reported and recorded for all time.[14]

The quartermaster of the Marine Corps had appropriated $2,500 to install updated electrical lighting for the Barracks. Colonel Kelton requested materials from Captain H.T. Harris of the Bureau of Supplies and Accounts in the Navy Department.[15]

Colonel Kelton was by now probably very sensitive to personnel levels, as his truly overriding task was to provide security for the naval prison. He pleaded for headquarters not to task Boston for any more transfers until at least there were sufficient numbers of long-term men available. Long term simply means that these men had a lot of time to serve before they were eligible to muster out. Most of his "long termers" had been sent away. His compromise was that he would like to have at least 25 of the recruits coming in that month of June, and he pledged he could whip them into shape by the end of July. He made do by staffing his prison detachment with short-timers due to reenlist for prison duty in Boston and Portsmouth, NH.[16]

It sounded like the post exchange (PX) was a model to be held up for all to see. However, the PX at the Barracks did not always operate in a smooth and efficient fashion. Errors in post exchange accounts were reported and recorded by Captain L. McLittle. First Lieutenant J.A. Hughes and Second Lieutenant J.H. White were called in to get to the bottom of all this reported inefficiency. The lieutenants were to report to the commanding officer (Kelton) with proper recommendations.[17]

Money was left over from the electrical improvements. This was a rare opportunity for the barracks to provide something to the Marines which could improve their lives. So Colonel Kelton requested to purchase 11 electric "smoothing irons" at a cost of $15 each. These were for the use of the Marines so they could iron their uniforms and maintain a proper military appearance.[18]

In the early 1900's, the Barracks were authorized to use enlisted men on additional duties such as painting and carpentry. They were also tasked to repair and maintain the facilities. The Marine Corps correspondingly authorized an additional per diem pay of 50 cents for those assigned these additional duties. Headquarters could only make each assignment for up to three months and these were subject to approval.[19]

Colonel Kelton complained to headquarters about his continual shortage of men. With the routine ebb and flow of Marines, a tendency developed to keep the men with bad habits and to transfer the best men on orders.[20] After filling orders for personnel for ships and other stations, he was left behind with liberty-breakers, drunks, and men otherwise deemed unfit for responsible duty. On 17 July he had to close down one of the public entrances of the yard. He didn't have proper staffing. Headquarters should stop assessing Boston for other posts, he thought.[21]

Colonel Kelton's records indicated he had his preferences about officers. When Captain McLittle was transferred to recruiting duty, he requested a replacement. He said that he did not want Captain Dutton. He would, however, take Captain Muir as a replacement.[22]

A new barracks was going up in Portsmouth, NH, to house the Marines who would be guarding the new prison there. Brig. Gen. Elliott thought the judge advocate general of the Navy Department opined that the quartermaster should have the appropriation for the construction of the building, soon.[23]

In mid August another board was appointed to investigate the condition of the post exchange. Second Lieutenant J.H. White was at it again and now Second Lieutenant E.P. Moses was assigned the inquiry. Colonel Kelton wanted the noticeable carelessness about accounts of the post exchange addressed. He wanted the facts set forth as to how the errors occurred and methods to avoid such errors in the future.[24]

An addition to the building known as the "Officer of the Day Building" was approved and $1,600 was provided for the project. Colonel Kelton wrote to the contractors Starbird and Johnson of 292 Main Street, Charlestown and approved their bid for the job.[25]

On August 15, 1905, the investigation of the post exchange was completed. It formally revealed the gross mistakes and irregularities were due to carelessness. Seizing the opportunity, Colonel Kelton opined to Brigadier General Elliott it was essential that a competent exchange steward be assigned to the Boston. His suggestion: First Sergeant Lawrence Lawson. He should be transferred to Boston from his present station at Marine Barracks, Norfolk, VA. Colonel Kelton said that he had written to Colonel Waller and he agreed to the transfer. After all this transfer was worth money. Lawson came with a resume. Lawson ran a successful post exchange at the Marine Barracks in Newport, RI.[26]

Regulations were due for an upgrade. Brigadier General Elliott informed Colonel Kelton a board was appointed in Washington to draft official government regulations subject to the approval of the secretary of the Navy. General Elliott expected the regulations pertaining to the Marine Corps to be complete, explicit, and have bearing upon the administration of the corps. So Colonel Kelton was welcomed to suggest anything appropriate that he would see fit to submit for consideration by this board.[27] This was his big, and last, chance to have an impact on how the corps would be administrated for years to come.

The investigation into the post exchange (PX) financial irregularities started to bruise some egos. Words were exchanged between officers involved in the investigation and the officers who ran the PX.

There were two investigations into the PX matter. The first team sent in to get to the bottom of it was Lieutenants White and Hughes. After a period, a second team, Lieutenants White and Moses, was sent in to try again. Hughes was changed out for Moses. Why? Would these correspondences shed light on that?

Hughes received a letter from 2nd Lt. Maurice Campbell, the PX officer under investigation. Communications between junior officers can be unabashed. This one was found in the opinion of Lt. Hughes as quite unabashed indeed. So much so, Hughes wrote to Brigadier General Elliott and told him about this letter. Hughes claimed that the letter was impertinent, as it was unrestrained in its lack of good taste and quite disrespectful as well. This letter referred to Hughes' report describing the collection of PX monies by post exchange officer Campbell.

Seems Hughes and Campbell didn't get along. Campbell did not find Hughes' report very flattering. Campbell subsequently had to correspond with headquarters and defend his accounting practices. HQ deemed Campbell's work satisfactory. Leadership decided that Campbell, a young beginning officer, should just take the whole thing in as a learning experience. In that manner, Colonel Kelton reminded 2nd Lieutenant Campbell that it was his responsibility as post exchange officer to keep proper accounts and management of the collection of monies. Finally, 2nd Lt. Campbell was scolded about the unprofessional language used by him in communication to Lieutenant Hughes and was told it shouldn't happen in correspondence with another officer.[28]

Colonel Wood

Colonel Thomas N. Wood assumed command on 12 March 1906.

Several months later, the Union Bureau of News reported that the Marines of the Marine Barracks were forced to live in tents on the parade field. Right in the middle of the city of Boston on June 23, 1906. Lieutenant Kincade was aghast. The newspapers were telling the wrong story. They were trying to make the Marine Barracks look bad. And that could affect recruiting.

To better enjoy this, we must bring ourselves into contemporary times. The modern era of permanently built brick buildings and housing was in place in 1906. It was in the midst of what was to become known as the Edwardian Era, made visual and accessible by the movie *Titanic*.

Queen Victoria had passed after a long, influential, and successful reign. The heir to the throne was the long in waiting, already in his fifties, globetrotting and immensely popular, Victoria's favorite son Edward. It was an era that saw the height of art, fashion, commerce, diplomacy, and architecture. Some of the finest buildings in any city, town main street, and even rural America were built then. A substantial period of peace permitted this flowering. Beautiful new and sturdy buildings were everywhere, and here were the Marines, hovelling in tents like hobos.

In this light, First Lieutenant Kincade replied to the Union Bureau of News that annually the interior of the barracks was thoroughly cleaned and repainted. Three hospital tents were set up on the parade grounds. These were only temporary quarters for men to stay while their section of the barracks was being painted. It was after all, impractical to house all men of the Barracks in the tents.[29]

It was the Fourth of July, a traditional day of parades. The Marines were always ready to march in an Independence Day parade. Usually they are lots of fun. Sometimes they are not.

"Don't rain on my parade" as the saying goes, this time it did. The Marines who were marching left the Navy yard at 6:40 a.m. and arrived in East Boston at approximately 6:50 a.m. The parade was scheduled to begin at 7 a.m. However, it did not start until 9 a.m. because it was raining. During that two hour delay the Marines had to stand in a drizzling rain without any shelter other than an arcade exposed on both sides. No one on the parade committee took any steps to provide them with a proper shelter. The committee also took almost forty minutes to decide whether the parade should take place.[30]

Major A.S. McLemore, assistant adjutant and inspector of the Marine Corps, inspected the Marine Barracks in July. His report came back August 22. The following discrepancies were noted:

1. All post exchange books were carelessly kept.
2. Post exchange officer made a practice of cashing personal checks for officers and presented these as cash on hand of approximately $400 of such checks. But some officers had left the post in debt to the post exchange and the commanding officer had not been properly notified of this.
3. Two privates were detailed as house orderlies, one of whom was the chauffer for the commanding officer and the other was an attendant for the junior officers' mess.
4. Knapsacks were not properly unslung and presented for inspection.
5. The color guard took an incorrect position when passing in review.

It was also noted that the junior officers' quarters required painting. The awning and the courtyard in the captain's quarters should be repaired.[31]

Married noncommissioned officers (NCOs) had virtually no housing for their wives and families at the barracks. It was necessary to place these NCOs in housing outside the Navy yard. The quarters were provided at the expense of the federal government.

The noncommissioned officers were also provided stove coal to heat their apartments. On September 20, the post quartermaster, Captain F.L. Boadman, ordered from C.W. York Company, located on 120 Border Street in East Boston, 5 tons of white ash stove coal to be delivered to the quarters of Quartermaster Sergeant Herman R. Tesch, 51 School Street, Charlestown, Quartermaster Sergeant George Kneller, 101 Leverett Street, Boston, and Quartermaster Sergeant Norman Johnston, 22 Monument Square, Charlestown.[32]

The November 19, 1906, naval prison report indicated a total population of 153 prisoners.[33] Some prisoners rise to the top of infamous recognition. General court-martial prisoner Private Oscar V. Fisk was a poster child for unruly and incorrigible prisoners everywhere who were very disruptive. He cursed and shrieked at all hours of the day and night. Even though he was kept in double irons, he was still assaultive and abusive to the guards. Colonel Wood requested that Private Fisk be transferred to the state prison at Wethersfield, CT, or anywhere else, just out of there. He explained to the commandant of the Navy yard that Private Fisk was an incorrigible prisoner and that he had wrecked his cell and assaulted both prisoners and members of the guard. He asserted that Private Fisk should be confined in an atmosphere where he could be properly restrained, as he was "a most objectionable character."[34]

Sentinels needed to maintain the utmost vigilance at all times while on duty, as they must be able to discern regular activity from odd, abnormal occurrences. May 8 at 7:35 p.m. Private Herbert E. Holt while on sentinel duty observed a shore boat leave from the end of the pier where the USS *New York* was tied. Four men were in the boat. Private Holt hailed them down. But the occupants of the boat gave a foul response to the sentinel's challenge. A quantity of scrap iron estimated to weigh about 300 pounds was found in the area where the boat departed from the pier. A shipkeeper aboard the USS *Detroit* also reported that he had observed the same incident.[35]

Private Fisk, the unruly prisoner, was still causing notable amounts of disruption. Colonel Wood wrote to the commandant of the Navy yard and reported that in his opinion Private Fisk may be insane and should be transferred to the Hospital for the Insane.[36]

When Marines completed their tour of duty in Boston, often they choose to remain in the area and seek employment. Thomas E. Flowers, a former member of the Marine Barracks, applied for a position as a Metropolitan Park policemen. With the civil service exam behind him, he placed number 12 on the list. Flowers was the chief clerk at the Barracks. Colonel Wood wrote a letter of recommendation for him stating that he had performed very well and commended him to be a very competent and reliable man. Also noted in the letter: Flowers had served with the detachment of Marines who protected the American Legation at Peking, China, during the Boxer Rebellion of 1900.[37]

Usually it is privates who endure discipline. On rare occasions it became necessary to discipline officers. Colonel Wood confined 2nd Lt. Emile P. Moses, the same E. P. Moses from the post exchange episode, to the limits of the Navy yard for five days. He was found to have neglected his duties as officer of the day, for failing to comply with paragraph 4, Article 159 of the U.S. Navy Regulations, the expected behavior for when colors were hoisted at sunrise on May 21.

When the flag is raised or lowered every day, the whole Navy yard is expected to stop in its tracks until the observance has run. Those not in uniform must stand at attention. But those in uniform during these solemn rituals must stand at attention and salute. Lt. Moses must have been seen disregarding this daily ceremony. That is easy to do went the whole world stops. And an officer must be punished same as everybody else; everybody's watching.[38]

The telephone at the Main Gate guardhouse could make outside calls. And it became misused. The trolley accident years earlier was the last recorded legitimate reason to call outside the yard. Colonel Wood replaced this telephone line with one connected to Navy yard telephones only. Any information to be relayed outside of the yard could be done through the Marine Barracks telephone.[39]

Measles broke out in the naval prison. No new prisoners could be taken in until it was brought under control. The medical officer was sent in to inspect the sanitary conditions of the prison. He was to report back on when it was safe to take in new prisoners. The outbreak subsided by the end of May. So much so, that the medical officer deemed it safe enough to accept new prisoners.[40]

On a late spring morning in early June at 11:35 a.m. a horse drawn Boston Ice Company wagon was trotting through the Main Gate. One of the horses shied and the rear end of the wagon collided with the gate and tore away a portion of the woodwork on the right side of the entrance. An investigation cleared driver John Mooney of any fault.[41]

Brigadier General Elliott would be in Boston in June for inspection of the men and facilities at the Marine Barracks.[42]

Colonel Wood was concerned about personnel shortages, as he had a very serious naval prison to run as well as the usual sentry duties to fill. So he asked Brigadier General Elliott not to order any more additional transfers to ships or other stations from the assets of the Boston unit. He claimed that he was barely able to detail a relief guard for duty in the Navy yard and the naval prison.[43]

General Elliott saw the light. He agreed with Col. Wood and stated that until strengths of the Marine Barracks were increased, he would not assess any transfers except those absolutely necessary.[44] Not routine ones, but if war was imminent.

Wayward horse drawn wagons and the Main Gate again: this time it was more dangerous. Early evening July 1 at 6:40 p.m. a double team attached to P. O'Riordan's wagon broke away from the driver. The horses ran up Wapping Street at a full gallop, heading straight for the Main Gate. The steeds barreled through, and collided with and carried away a period streetlight right next to the sentinel booth. The area had become an unsafe place. A future means of transportation was rapidly developing; the motorcar was touted as a safer mode of travel.[45]

The Barracks had no real office space. An officer who had much experience as the officer of the day, might be well aware of this glaring defect. The germination of the plan to build a new administration began in July 2. Lt. E.P. Moses requested that the commanding officer of the Marine Barracks appoint a board to determine the feasibility of erecting a building on the east end of the parade ground. It could replace the building that had been used as an office for the officer of the day. His proposal was that the new structure be used as offices for the post quartermaster, for the use of boards and for court-martial hearings, prison matters, just real office space.[46]

Corporal Quinn was found dead at Guantanamo Bay. An investigation indicated he was murdered. A murderer therefore had to be found. The investigation revealed enough evidence to accuse and hold Private Edward F. Lang for the murder of Corporal Quinn. He was shipped to Boston and held in the naval prison to await his trial.

Pvt. Lang's life was on the line with the opening gavel of his trial. Prosecutors presented their case against Pvt. Lang. The overall evidence swayed the decision. Guilty. Private Lang's future would be life imprisonment at the federal penitentiary at Atlanta, GA.[47]

Rifle range problems continued to plague Barracks commanders; now it was Wood's turn. He sent Captain Thomas F. Lyons to Woburn, MA, to meet with Captain John M. Portal of the Bay State Military Rifle Association to seek arrangements for the Marines to use their range.[48]

This was huge. For the first time since Lovell's Island in the Boston Harbor rifle range many years prior, the reality of having access to a real rifle range made it necessary for the post quartermaster to make arrangements for transportation. Lt. Moses asked the passenger agent of the Boston and Northern Street Railroad Company in September 1907 to charter a trolley car for the Marines to get to Wakefield and back. This would be on a daily basis for two weeks at a time. Requested departure was 7 a.m. and return from Wakefield at 5 p.m.[49]

During that summer, personnel strengths dwindled so much that Colonel Wood had to close two gates at the Navy yard. He let headquarters know this. He only had 193 Marines available for duty. But 17 were in the hospital, 3 were awaiting discharge, 4 confined and 3 absent without leave. That left 166 men to work with for ships deployments, guard duty and the prison. The heavy burden of staffing the naval prison was not to be overlooked. Guards were critical for the safety of 210 prisoners. He reminded headquarters that Boston and Mare Island, CA, one on each coast, were the only Barracks in the whole corps that supported naval prisons. The rest don't. So Boston and Mare Island ought to be staffed appropriately.[50]

The Marines finally had permission for a place to practice weapons firing after five long years. Colonel Wood asked headquarters to make arrangements to secure the firing ranges in Wakefield for the Marines.[51] His efforts were successful.

Captain Thomas F. Lyons became the officer in charge of firing detail at Wakefield. The first shots rang out on September 28, 1907.[52] After such a years-long search for a proper place to train, the years-long search inadvertently understated the need for ammunition. They ran out of bullets. Firing was suspended, the colonel had to report to headquarters. Wood had to borrow ammunition in the first place from each ship present in the Navy yard.[53] In his defense, he did say he made his ammunition requisition with proper lead time, but he never received his order. This is why he had to borrow from the ships.

General Elliott requested 22 privates from the Barracks in Boston to ship out to Camp Elliott on the Isthmus of Panama. Instructions were provided that men packing their duffel bags should include as many baseball players and musicians as possible. Camp Elliott was very isolated with few amusements. The musicians were to be a part of the newly formed volunteer musical group.[54]

Headquarters (HQ) began assembling men for the prison guard at Portsmouth, NH. HQ wanted men with experience and proven reliability. HQ wanted to know how many men in Boston may be available for this duty. Volunteers were preferred and assured that this would be permanent duty, entirely dependent upon the good conduct of the applicants.[55] Volunteers would be free from the uncertainty of shipping out at any time, and would be able to build a life.

By February the naval prison population was exploding. Colonel Wood was in askance about how to keep a 150 bed prison safe bulging at the seams with 220 inmates. The Barracks had 223 Marines when Col. Wood arrived until May 1906, when emergency transfers to the Canal Zone decreased the strength to 151. That's 69 more prisoners than Marines. In February, the strength rose to 177 but 11 of them were green recruits. He preferred not to give these "men with experience and proven reliability" away to Portsmouth. Indeed, Col. Wood requested that Boston be exempted from the transfer of any prison guards for the proposed naval prison at Portsmouth, NH.[56] Staffing of the naval prison was straining the Barracks almost to the breaking point. But light was at the end of the tunnel.

In February 1908, the *Boston Globe* printed "Scales Wall of Navy Yard." M.D. Charles claimed he was a naval prisoner who escaped from the Charlestown Naval Prison. Colonel Wood was thunderstruck. Nobody escaped from his prison. He shot back at the *Globe* that all prisoners were accounted for. He was bewildered as to how the newspaper could even print such erroneous information. No prisoner had escaped. There in fact was no prisoner by the name of M.D. Charles ever confined at the prison. The article dishonored the vigilance of the men under his command. He asserted that no one from the *Boston Globe* ever consulted with anyone at the Marine Barracks and grossly misled the public.[57]

Headquarters wanted to know all about the guard duties. They really wanted to know just how a naval prison functions so they could fully understand how to staff them. Colonel Wood outlined this breakdown of Yard wide guard responsibilities. The posts in existence were:

1. patrol along the waterfront
2. an orderly post at gate 4,
3. an orderly post at gate 5,
4. a sentry post at gate 3,
5. an orderly post in rear of Commandant's Gate
6. four interior posts in the naval prison.

Colonel Wood offered his insight, warts and all, on these guard posts. He thought patrol along the waterfront was inadequate. There should be four regular sentry posts. The Main Gate should include one sergeant and three corporals. The Barracks guard should include one sergeant, three corporals and 6 privates and should maintain the patrols along the waterfront and the post at gate 3. The interior guard of the prison consists of one sergeant, three corporals and 12 privates and provides for a guard for each corridor except the lower floor. Because of the unavailability of personnel, gate 2 was closed. In order to furnish the three additional posts suggested for the waterfront, re-establish gate 2, and relieve the privates now performing duty at gate 5, it would require 104 more men (9 sergeants, 15 corporals, 80 privates).[58]

The Boston Marine Barracks finally had access to a firing range but now they needed to keep it accessible. Other Marine Barracks all over the world had decent practice ranges. Not Boston. It was one of the Boston Marine Barracks' more glaring weaknesses. Colonel Wood was anxious for Headquarters' authority to utilize the Bay State Military Rifle Association range in Wakefield for the coming months of May and June. These were the best months for when the Marines could have unlimited use of the range. Back when he first assumed command, the men had no place for even gallery practice. Since he has been in command he found an unused building in the yard for that purpose and the men began using that on a regular basis.[59]

The naval prison population, already far beyond what was believed possible, had ballooned to 236 prisoners. With this reality, Colonel Wood asked headquarters for another duty officer.[60] This factual prison overpopulation required another duty officer, period.

All three major religious faiths now provided services at the naval prison. Colonel Wood asked Rabbi Nathan Blechman, the secretary of the Passover Society located on 36 Gaston

Street in Roxbury, if he might be able to provide Passover services for the Jewish prisoners. The rabbi agreed with Col. Wood that the Jewish prisoners should be able to observe the April 1908 Passover appropriately, coming up in a few weeks. Rabbi Blechman would make the effort to accommodate the request.[61]

Captain Charles G. Carpenter received orders from headquarters May 29, 1908 directing him to now report to the commandant of the Navy yard for duty as the officer in charge of the naval prison. Carpenter was switching bosses. He was now in charge of the prison. The correctional facility was no longer Wood's responsibility. Headquarters outlined what he would do:

1. Immediately after "guard-mounting" each day (the mustering of prison guards) at the Barracks, those reporting to duty for this detail for the next shift of prison guard duty would be marched to the prison by the noncommissioned officer in charge. They would then report to Captain Carpenter for duty.
2. This detachment would be under Captain Carpenter's command until relieved by the detail on the succeeding day. This meant they went back under Colonel Wood's responsibility after their shift is up.
3. Captain Carpenter would report to the commandant of the yard for matters of maintenance, cleanliness, efficiency of the prison, security, and discipline of the prisoners.
4. Captain Carpenter would report any misconduct or inefficiency of those performing prison guard duty to the commanding officer of the Marine Barracks. These Marines were still under his command. It is he who would take the responsibility for their discipline.[62]

The proposed administration building was close to becoming a reality. Colonel Wood contacted Messrs. Bruse, Price and DeSibour of 527 Fifth Avenue, NY, in June and expressed his desires of what he would like for the building scheduled to be numbered 136.[63]

Ninety-seven Marines were ordered to the Isthmus of Panama in June 1908. Colonel Wood was beside himself. They really don't realize he has a dangerous prison to keep safe, do they? He previously asked headquarters not to do this. Headquarters said they said they would not unless absolutely necessary. But they did it anyway.

For starters, he told the Commandant of the Navy Yard if they do that then first of all, he would have to close down gate 2.[64] Now the kicker. Col. Wood complained that in order to provide the 97 Marines, he would have to entirely relieve the whole prison guard. Remaining to keep a lid on the facility was the prison sergeant, assistant prison sergeant, and civilian sergeant in charge of the local police. Three guys to cover over 200 prisoners.[65] If this is what they wanted then he would need the naval hospital in Chelsea to release as many Marine convalescents as was possible and return them to the Marine Barracks for duty.[66] Men in wheelchairs and on crutches would have to guard very scary people.

The auditor of the Navy Department directed a favorable change, they thought, as far as the Barracks were concerned, in the method of accounting for rations for the naval prison. Until July 1908, the navy had recognized the prison for only eighteen years. For those eighteen years the prison population had been subsisting on the general mess of the Marine Barracks. The Barracks company fund was reimbursed for this from the commuted ration funds of the prisoners.

The auditor requested vouchers be submitted for expenditures incurred for the subsistence of the prisoners. Colonel Wood complained to headquarters that it would increase administrative efforts. It would essentially require the Marine Barracks to manage two sets of books for the mess.[67]

The Great Chelsea Fire of April 1908 raged out of control. Smoke and flames could be seen from the Navy yard. Minutes before 1 o'clock in the afternoon, a call for help came into the Boston Marine Barracks. Less than five minutes later, one hundred Marines assembled. Junior Officer Captain Charles S. Hill was hurriedly tasked to command this detachment. Into the fire zone the Marines hastily went. In Chelsea Square, Captain Hill found the chief of police and offered the Marines' services. The chief relayed to the young captain that it was the mayor's desire that the Marines give every assistance to the chief's force and the fire department to help protect and save lives and property.

Men were sent out in squads under noncommissioned officers. Some Marines were to hold back people from the fire zone. Others warned people out of burning buildings. Still others protected property from Congress and Central avenues to Essex and Maverick street. The Marines were sent to where the fire was hottest. The Marines saw to it that people left their houses in time. They removed the sick and disabled. The Marines rose to the occasion.

More Marines were arriving on the scene as they were returning from liberty, officers and noncommissioned officers too.

One squad came around a corner and discovered the post office in danger of going up in flames. All that mail. The Marines sprung into action. They saved the mail from destruction in the blaze. Postal property was protected and guarded.

Grim discoveries were made. Two bodies were found motionless in the smoldering rubble. Four safes lay nearby, vulnerable to looting, also among the ruins. The Marines guarded the bodies and the safes.

Marines were placed at a cordon of posts between Chelsea Square and the incredibly dangerous Standard Oil tanks at Chelsea Creek. They kept guard at these posts awaiting authorities, whenever that could happen. The fire was getting closer. Civilian relief was just getting organized. It would be some time before they could take over for the Marines. So until further notice, the Marines remained in the inferno, surrounded by danger everywhere.

The Marines held their ground in the heat for what seemed like endless hours. Finally, at 2 in the morning, reinforcements arrived, in the form of state troopers.

The detachment finally made it back to the shipyard by 3 a.m. Many had been on duty since 1 p.m. that afternoon. Aside from eight men incapacitated by burns, smoke inhalation, and minor injuries, all others were ready for duty on 13 April 1908, the following morning.[68]

12. Woes at the Gates

"I hit a son-of-a-bitch of a Marine and ran out the gate!"
—Boatswain's mate

Colonel F.L. Denny, quartermaster of the Marine Corps, wrote to Colonel Wood and informed him that the sum of $20,000 had been provided to him from the Naval Appropriation Act of 1909. These monies were for the erection of the administration building, providing offices of the officer of the day, officer in charge of the prison, post quartermaster and room for the meeting of boards and courts and an office for the commanding officer. It would also provide for 10 jail cells and extra space just in case. Colonel Wood was advised that Mr. Rosengarten of the firm Bruce, Price and De Sibour, architects from New York, NY, would visit the Barracks to look over the site for the proposed building. Mr. Rosengarten would be performing levels and taking measurements which would be necessary for preparation of plans.[1]

In August, Colonel Denny requested bid proposals for the administration building to be numbered 136. He directed that the following notice be inserted in the approved newspapers on August 26 and September 2, 1908: "SEALED PROPOSALS, in duplicate will be received at this office until eleven a.m., September 14, 1908, and then be publicly opened, for the completion of the Marine Barracks, Navy Yard, Boston, Mass. Proposal blanks, plans, specification and other information may be obtained from the architects, Bruce Price & de Sibour, 527 Fifth Avenue, New York, the Commanding Officer, Marine Barracks, Navy Yard, Boston, Mass., or from the undersigned, who reserves the right to reject any or all bids or parts thereof, and to waive informalities. F.L. Denny, Colonel, Quartermaster."[2]

Continuous transfers of Marines to other posts and ships frustrated Colonel Wood to no end. He wrote to headquarters and asked them to please hold down transfers from Boston. He absolutely had to maintain present strengths at the naval prison as well as guard posts throughout the Navy yard for which the Barracks were responsible.[3] By the end of August, manpower dropped to 177 Marines. Recently promoted Major C.S. Hill reported to headquarters that there were not enough men to perform sentinel duty. He had to close down two gates. A good level, he recommended, would be 200 Marines. He again requested that Boston be spared from transferring its meager assets.[4]

Many veterans of the Spanish-American War, the Philippines and China were assigned to the Barracks. Major Hill sent a list to headquarters of Marines who had served in those areas and who were entitled to the appropriate campaign badges.[5]

The parents of Private Howard F. Ames insisted that he possessed a gold watch that was not returned to them with his other belongings. Colonel Wood assured his mother, Mrs. J.H. Mitten, that his personal belongings were inventoried when he was transferred to the naval hospital in Chelsea, MA. There was no evidence of the gold watch in question. He sympathized with the late Marine's parents, but there was no way to determine whether he had sold it, given it away or was stolen from him.[6]

Marines available for duty in September dropped to 164. Of those, 13 were hospitalized, 2 were absent without leave and 3 were on authorized leave. Colonel Wood complained that these numbers left him incredibly unable to fulfill his missions. He absolutely needed 6 sergeants, 12 corporals and 30 privates. He again stressed the fact that the Marine Barracks not only had the responsibility of securing the Navy yard, it also had the naval prison, which required more men than he had at that time. Two gates closed down due to lack of staffing and waterfront patrol was curtailed to help properly staff the overcrowded prison.[7]

Men assigned the USRS *Wabash*, the other floating Marine Barracks, were written up for attempting to leave the yard through gates other then the Main Gate. Protocol for entering and exiting the Navy yard were established by the commandant of the Navy yard and enforced by the Marine sentinels. Only specific passes authorized passage through specific gates. The captain of the yard, Captain Herbert Winslow, further specified that only personnel with passes signed by him would be allowed out of the East Gate.[8]

A night out on liberty found two Marines going to the movies at Boston's Star Theater. As the curtains rose and the projector lit up the screen, the national anthem swelled from the speakers. The two Marines rose from their seats at attention as required, as they were in uniform. Those folks behind them couldn't see whatever was on the screen during the national anthem. The ushers ejected the two Marines from the theater.

The story in Boston's newspapers the 9th and 10th of September said that Marines were thrown out of the movie theater for standing at attention for the national anthem. This time the theater got hit with the bad press stick, not the Marines. Colonel Wood was called on the telephone by the Associated Press and invited to comment on the allegations. Colonel Wood could not confirm to them whether the incident occurred or not. He told the reporter from the Associated Press that if the matter were indeed true, he would have spoken to the movie theater people himself and brought this to the attention of higher authorities.

After the second day of newspaper stories, in the evening of September 10, the manager of the Star Theater called Colonel Wood. Col. Wood assured him there was no basis for the charges made against the theater. Colonel Wood could not even ascertain the identity of the Marines involved. He determined that it did not happen.[9]

Although the Navy yard was hooked up to the latest telephone equipment, it was still a fledgling technology. Telephone service required live operators to connect calls. Operation of the central switchboard on the shipyard was the responsibility of the Marines. Before automatic switchboards, people did the switching. But people can be subject to human fallibilities. In September 1908, the Charlestown Exchange of New England Telephone and Telegraph did not answer the Navy yard operator. The Marine operator could hear people talking and music playing at the Charlestown exchange. Colonel Wood thought that the episode was due to gross inattention on the part of the Charlestown Exchange.[10]

Women were not allowed on board Navy ships. Early evening in late September, Waterfront Sentinel Private Levi S. Conant, at Post 2, observed a man and a woman together heading to the *Hannibal*, docked nearby. He challenged them but they did not reply to his challenge. Then the man said he was captain of the *Hannibal*. The man and woman then went aboard the ship. Several hours later at 11 p.m. the couple emerged from the *Hannibal*. After being told he was going to have to report the incident, the man told the sentry that he did not care whether he was reported to a higher authority. The sentry reported the incident to Colonel Wood. Colonel Wood referred the matter to the commandant of the Navy yard. Wood thought that the rules should be followed by all members of the naval service, especially officers.[11]

A story hit the newspapers that a Marine in uniform was excluded from a synagogue in Roxbury. As appropriate, Colonel Wood contacted Rabbi Phineas Israeli of the Congregation Adath Joshua at 19 Intervale Street in Roxbury on October 9 to see what the real story was. After all, over and over again the newspapers had published spurious stories before. Colonel Wood explained to Rabbi Israeli that a contradiction from him in regards to the incident would have more credence if the same came from the marine commanding officer. In other words, the rabbi tried to refute the story but Colonel Wood thought that if he could refute the story instead, it would have more credence. Colonel Wood advised Rabbi Israeli to furnish the Associated Press with Wood's version of the occurrence and request that it be given full publicity.[12]

When vehicles of any type entered through the Main Gate, they did not always approach at a safe speed. A naval hospital ambulance approached the gate at a high rate of speed. The sentinel cautioned the driver to slow down, which he did, however, Hospital Apprentice Miller in the front seat turned to Private Carroll and hollered "bullshit!"[13] We are left wondering whether the ambulance was in a hurry to an emergency.

Private Fitzgerald had syphilis and the strong odor from the sores on his body was very disturbing to the other Marines. Other men would not sit with Fitzgerald in the mess hall nor would they utilize washbasins after he had used them. Colonel Wood explained to Surgeon John M. Edgar that there was not enough space in the building to segregate Pvt. Fitzgerald. What could they do to allay any fears?[14]

In October 1908 Private William I. Benson[15] and Sergeant Daniel King[16] passed away at the naval hospital in Chelsea. The officers at the Barracks were required to inventory their personal effects and make the necessary notifications.

Colonel Wood appreciated transfers to Boston. He did receive a corporal and 21 privates from the Marine Barracks in New York. But every last private was a recruit. It takes time to properly train recruits to be useful and ready. Otherwise they are just warm bodies on paper.[17]

November 9 at 11:30 a.m. Main Gate sentinel Private Robert Day stopped a horse drawn ambulance buggy and would not permit it to leave the navy yard. He found pipefittings and boxes inside the buggy on the floor. The occupants did not possess a pass for these items. They weren't supposed to have them.

Forty minutes later at 12:10 p.m. the same ambulance buggy was eastbound on Chelsea Street heading towards the bridge to take it back to the naval hospital. As they were passing the Commandant's Gate (#4), they thumbed their noses at the Marine orderly providing security at that gate. They yelled out insults and made noises at him. All the sentry got on them was that the person who was driving wore an Navy enlisted man's uniform.[18] They did, after all, work for the naval hospital.

A November 1908 roll call listed six officers assigned to the Barracks: Colonel T.N. Wood, Major C.S. Hill, Captain A.S. Williams, Capt J.T. Buttrick, First Lieutenant J.F. Dyer, and First Lieutenant E. P. Moses.[19]

The new telephone system in the yard still had bugs to work out. Colonel Wood was frustrated that he couldn't use his pricey new telephone system. He let the yard electrician, Mr. Low, know that he had great difficulty simply talking to another person in the yard. He was totally unable to contact the other person. He was so incensed that he wanted facts.[20] He wanted to determine whether blame and action should follow, maybe roll some heads.

Marines operated the telephone switchboard for the yard. A detail of six enlisted men maintained the switchboard at the central telephone office twenty-four hours a day. That's 2 per eight-hour shift in 24-hour rotation. These bodies to fill these duties came from the guard. Colonel Wood asked the commandant of the Navy yard to consider the newer technology of the Strongberger automatic telephone system. An upgrade was long overdue and badly needed for the yard's telephone service. Many communities in the area eliminated the need for operators by installing the Strongberger system.[21] That would be a big help for the barracks with its personnel strains stemming from prison needs.

Private John H. Hogan, on watch as corporal of the guard at the Main Gate, noticed an unusual light coming from Building 5 on November 16, 1908. He went to have a look. Private Hogan burst the door open to the building. Inside he found a fire in a box filled with refuse paper in the passageway adjacent to the band room. He dragged the box out to the street and extinguished the fire. A bad fire in Building 5 was averted because of the watchful eye of Private Hogan. He was commended by the Marine Barracks commanding officer. Private Hogan had prevented a larger and more serious fire by his alertness and quick action.[22]

The Marines at the Navy Yard found it very difficult to find proper tailor services. To this end Colonel Wood requested permission to hire a civilian tailor. He wanted to use the same method of checking the pay of the users as the post exchange.[23] The Marine Barracks detailed Private Harry C. Orfant as the post barber.

The Barracks found a better way for Marines to pay for services. It would no longer be necessary to check the pay of the users; the Barracks would now use a method of direct payment.[24] Men could now use cash to buy their cigarettes and chewing gum.

Private Henry J. Cudder was transferred from Annapolis, MD, to Portsmouth, NH. While waiting to board the boat in New York for passage via the Fall River Line, he was detailed by the sergeant in charge to get some liquor. Subsequently Private Cudder missed his boat. He made his own arrangements to board another steamer bound for Boston. Colonel Wood, sympathetic to Private Cudder's plight, went to bat for him. He asked the commander of the Marine Barracks in Portsmouth to see if it was true what Private Cudder had claimed. If so then he should not be checked in pay for transportation, as it was not his fault.[25]

The Marine Corps was a small world. The officers knew who the troublemakers were and where they were located. When Sergeant Calvin T. Matthews came to the Marine Barracks from duty in Cuba, Colonel Wood recoiled. Not happy at all about this transfer, he asked headquarters to transfer him to another post. Colonel Wood was convinced he would cause trouble in Boston because of his demonstrated tendency to criticize others in the chain of command by the use of rude and offensive language. If he were to remain in Boston, Sergeant Matthews would become a discipline problem.[26]

Private William Franklin joined the Barracks after duty in Cuba in February 1909. On February 16, headquarters notified Colonel Wood that Franklin was probably addicted to cocaine. Colonel Wood was instructed to observe him very carefully and report whether he should be retained in the service.[27]

Headquarters listened and finally provided Colonel Wood with plenty of men. Colonel Wood's complaint now was that with 237 enlisted men he was hard pressed to house them. He could not further augment the guard at the naval prison, as it would create severe overcrowding in the living quarters if anymore men were assigned to Boston.[28]

Public Charities of New York wanted Sergeant James Julian to provide support for his mother, Mary Conway. She was a public charge. Sergeant Julian declined to provide any support whatsoever to her. Colonel Wood replied to the superintendent of Public Charities that she had abandoned Julian at the age of four and never had anymore to do with him. He was raised in an orphanage.[29] That was why he felt he shouldn't have to pay for someone who was not really his mother.

In early March two young girls, fifteen years of age, were allowed into the guardhouse at the Main Gate. One of the young girls was alleged to have had illicit relations with Sergeant Homer C. Whiting. A review of the guard revealed that indeed Sergeant Whiting was on duty at that time on January 31, 1909. Mrs. A.B. Montgomery of the Massachusetts Society of the Prevention of Cruelty to Children got involved. Montgomery brought the two young girls to Colonel Wood's office. But the girls would not identify Sergeant Whiting or any of the others present. Colonel Wood still believed the incident did occur and he would take appropriate action.[30] What are young girls doing around a shipyard gate? More on that later.

In March, Colonel Wood convened a board to enumerate the responsibilities of the telephone operators. The board convened because unauthorized telephone calls occurred while the enlisted Marine operators were on duty at the switchboard.[31]

The navy yard used brass number checks as its means of accounting for the presence of civilian workers in the Navy yard. The worker picked up his brass check (a round brass medal about the size of a coin with a number stamped on it) at the gates when he reported in for work and returned it when he finished his shift. Some confusion occurred when surges of workers arrived at the gate and did not deposit their checks in the proper boxes. On the whole there was usually no difficulty managing the brass checks.[32]

The Barracks had telephones, but not for private use. Colonel Wood wanted one for his private use and was willing to pay for it. He asked the commandant of the Navy yard for permission to install a private telephone in his quarters at his expense. The only telephone with a line to the outside was located in his office. It was impractical for members of his family, his wife in particular, to go to his office to make telephone calls.[33]

Automobiles increased in number and went from a curiosity to a new reality. They brought new problems to the Navy yard, and as we have seen, new technologies usually have. Colonel Wood asked naval constructor Elliot Snow to install a light chain at the Main Gate to deter motor vehicles from entering or departing without slowing down. The chain would be raised and lowered by the corporal of the guard.[34]

Attack of the Children

The Boston Naval Ship Yard was under siege. Plentiful and increasing: children, "playing" or loitering by the Main Gate every day, like it was their sole entertainment. There was no playground by the gate nor were the children playing street sports. Daily, daily, daily, all day, every day. And it wasn't always charming.

These children knew their boundaries. They knew the Marines couldn't do anything to them or about their behavior or presence or anything. The children pushed the bounds of many envelopes. Cherubs as young as six years to as old as twenty menaced the Main Gate, with their knowledge of boundaries and this knowledge got nuanced.

Children climbed on the gates until they were actively shoed away. Older kids egged on the younger children to try and steal from incoming and outgoing regular shipyard delivery wagon street traffic.

If they weren't getting into things, they annoyed anyone "fun" with open foul language. That may have been the soundtrack to many shipyard workers' daily transverse through the Main Gate: children swearing like sailors. The younger children, ever more pliable, were convinced by their "elders" to lift the skirts of women commuting in and out of the Main Gate. All this activity was outside the jurisdiction of the Navy yard.

Open drinking of alcohol by the "children" occurred regularly. Guess where they threw the bottles when they were done with them. These missiles were a daily reality. The sentinels might as well be in a war zone when they were on guard duty. Stones and bottles. They hurt. And then there were the girls.

Just before dark, girls from the ages of 12 to 20 turned foul language on its ear. They engaged not just in foul language, but also foul gestures and unseemly behaviors not possible for boys. They not only used their femaleness in their derogatory remarks towards the guards, they even grabbed them, yes grabbed them.

And then there were the prostitution attempts. Men leaving the shipyard for long awaited liberty were immediately solicited by the older girls right after they exited the Main Gate. The girls would invite the men to trysts in local alleyways. There was also a house on the corner of Wapping and Water Streets that offered easements.

Beyond the youngsters, Marines and sailors leaving the shipyard for liberty, although it may have been sporadic, were occasionally assaulted by adults. Outside the gates of the yard, it was tough.

Children can be befuddling. They do not think like adults. Treating children like adults, in the movies anyway, amounts to endless humor. Well, disperse them then. But they are children. They will come right back.

Well, any names boil up from all this activity? Four girls, age from 15 to 17 years old. The name Lucy Carter was recorded for all time. Another known as "Chelsea Re" surfaced. A girl known as Esther and another named Mary were recorded in these letters.[35]

The Navy yard approved Colonel Wood's request for a private telephone in his quarters. He accordingly put in his order to the New England Telephone and Telegraph Company on April 8.[36]

Rifle target training was once again going to be an important part of the Barracks. Accordingly, Colonel Wood suggested using the Wakefield site in May and June to not conflict with the operator's seasonal use of the range. In return for off-season use, the Marine Barracks desired continuous access for those weeks.[37]

About Patriot's Day, April 20, 1909, Major General Elliott told Colonel Wood he would like to locate a camp near the rifle range for the Marines to stay while training in Wakefield. There was no real hotel space in Wakefield in 1909. Or modern roads. Or reliable trucks or buses. Trains were the best transportation. Railroads were quite comprehensive in the 1900s. Indeed, they were enjoying their heyday.

The camp would provide officers and enlisted men alike the opportunity to qualify with the rifle. The first rotation to the Wakefield camp, now known as Camp Curtis Guild, would be a detachment of 25 men. Captain Charles H. Lyman was designated commanding officer of the camp. He was sent ahead to set up the camp in time to receive detachments for shooting season. Wood would be anxiously awaiting Lyman's "bring 'em in" word. Men would enjoy, or hate, one to two weeks of camping out away from the city in the countryside during the finest months of the year.[38] Men transferred to the camp would still be on the muster rolls of the Barracks. For the accounting of rations and quarters (food and shelter), they were shown as transferred. For years, the barracks had nowhere to practice firearms. Until now. This was a milestone to have a place to train once again for the first time since Lovell's Island.

The investigation into the main gate incident of January 31, 1909, involving two local teenage girls and a sentry was well underway. On April 13, the United States commissioner in Boston indicted Sergeant Homert C. Whiting for the alleged offense. The United States commissioner had requested the presence of Corporal Ward Lewis, Michael Murray and Edward L. Melvin as witnesses to the offense.[39]

The investigation concluded April 29. The charge of statutory rape involving Sergeant Homer S. Whiting was dismissed by the United States commissioner. Sergeant Whiting was found in violation of regulations, however, by allowing unauthorized persons into the authorized personnel only area at the Main Gate.[40] Perhaps these girls were some of the young gate "hangers on" whom Whiting befriended, and he just showed them where they could hang up their jackets, eat their sandwiches, and smoke. Or for the girls, maybe turning in their Johns was bad for business and would perhaps spook the rest of these girls' friends trying to sell tricks to shipyard men.

Personnel drawdowns created problems so much so that Colonel Wood asked headquarters for 20 privates. His outstanding reason was that the naval prison required, on a daily basis, one first sergeant, three sergeants, three corporals and 34 privates. That's the first sergeant during "duty hours" or "day shift," then a sergeant and a corporal each for 2nd shift and graveyard shift, 12 privates for day shift and 11 each for 2nd and 3rd shifts. He expected more men to

Early century mustering.

be sent away on ship's detachments to overseas duty.[41] We have heard about it. But when does that new Portsmouth naval prison open for beds?

Private John Mannion received orders for duty overseas, not unusual for a Marine billeted at the barracks. Pvt. Mannion made very good friends with a member of Father Kelly's parish. While stationed at the barracks, many Marines make friends. Their friendships can cross into many different cultures. So Father Kelly of St. Mary's Church in Newton, perhaps not fully cognizant of how transfers work, requested that Private Mannion be relieved from the overseas draft so he could marry one his parishioners. Colonel Wood impatiently had Father Kelly execute the marriage ceremony right away. He reminded the priest that marriage to a Marine involves frequent absences from home, period.[42]

On April 27, 1909, a permanent Marine guard for the naval prison was established, per order of Navy Department Letter 12494-63-C. The Navy Department now considered the naval prison a priority to be staffed appropriately. Captain Charles S. Hatch assumed command. His men would be carried on the rolls of the Marine Barracks for quarters and rations only. He recommended to Captain B.H. Campbell, the judge advocate general of the Navy Department, the following staff levels for the prison: 2 officers, 1 First Sergeant, 2 sergeants (overseers), 3 sergeants (for duty), 10 corporals (for duty), 1 corporal (outside worker parties) and 78 privates. His prison should be run in the same fashion as the naval prison in Portsmouth.[43]

On 10 May, Colonel Wood learned headquarters had ordered the following transfers from other Marine posts up and down the Eastern Seaboard to the Marine Barracks in Boston for the purpose of guard duty at the naval prison. Marine Barracks at the Naval Academy in Annapolis, MD, gave up 4 sergeants, 5 corporals and 10 privates. Marine Officers' School in Port Royal, SC, was assessed 2 corporals. The Marine Barracks at the Navy Yard in Philadelphia, PA, was directed to send 2 sergeants, 10 corporals and 20 privates. Norfolk Navy Yard's Barracks was ordered to transfer 3 sergeants, 4 corporals and 10 privates. And the Barracks at the Navy Yard in New York City was detailed to send 1 sergeant and 10 privates.

Colonel Wood was instructed these men were meant exclusively for the prison. The naval prison was to be organized as a separate company with its own commanding officer. It was his responsibility to drill and exercise his men. He would have general charge of the men. His boss was the commander of the Marine Barracks. No more changes would take place. Colonel Wood was cautioned that after the prison guard was established, no changes would be made relating to strength or personnel except in the case of an emergency or for cause. Any changes would be immediately reported to headquarters with appropriate reasons.[44]

On June 22 Colonel Wood convened a board. It was tasked to determine the practicality of wearing white uniforms in preference to khaki uniforms during the summer season. Major A.W. Catlin was tasked as the senior member. Junior officers Captain H.J. Hirshinger and First Lieutenants H.O. Smith and C.S. Owen filled out the board.[45]

The results of the seasonal uniform board meeting became known. What to wear for uniforms during warm weather was considered. After a thorough investigation and considering the lack of laundry facilities and the extra expense for enlisted men involving the wearing of a white uniform, the board unanimously recommended that khaki be worn in preference to the white uniform during the warm weather.[46]

Another board convened by Colonel Wood was given the task of improving the enlisted mess (their food service). The board consisted of Quartermaster Sergeant M.J. Grealy and Sergeants Laurence F. Corbett, Harvey L. Glidden and Robert E. Connor. The board's report considered the food served satisfactory. They were not able to make any recommendations for changes at that time. They did, however, advocate for more fresh vegetables be used in preference to canned, whenever it was possible to do so.[47]

With the staffing of the naval prison officially resolved, the barracks continued to be short on men nonetheless. The letter of May 7, 1909, from the commandant of the Marine Corps did indeed authorize increased strengths at the naval prison and placed guards there on a permanent basis. The Barracks could not draw on these Marines assigned to the naval prison for navy yard duties. It seems headquarters solved its staffing problem of the prison, but not for Colonel Wood. Colonel Wood explained his needs to the major general commandant. Now he had men on his muster rolls he couldn't touch, but the assignments continued. CMC [Commandant of the Marine Corps] Letter #10836 directed the assignment of 13 more enlisted men for the permanent detachment at the naval powder depot in Hingham.[48]

On July 17, 1909, First Lieutenant H.O. Smith, the post quartermaster, went and saw the facilities of the naval magazine in Hingham. The building assigned to house the Marines was a two-story frame dwelling in good repair. It was located on a slight elevation with ample room for the complement of 14 men. The building was equipped with a new latrine and a washroom. It was also had a cooking range.[49] The guard for the U.S. Naval Magazine at Hingham was established on July 19, 1909.[50]

Again, on August 11, Colonel Wood wrote to headquarters. He quoted CMC Letter #6520 of May 4, 1909, which established a permanent naval prison guard of 94 Marines. Given this reality he reported his strength on August 11 as 24 sergeants, 37 corporals and 220 privates. He requested augmentation of the Barracks by 4 more sergeants, 6 corporals and 76 privates[51] for a total of 28 sergeants, 43 corporals and 296 privates.

Private Oscar J. Field was listed as a deserter. To Colonel Wood, however, this did not make sense. He did not believe Pvt. Field was a deserter. He did not fit the typical profile of a deserter. First of all, Private Field had only nine more months left on his enlistment. His conduct record was very good and he did have considerable deposits with the paymaster. So Colonel Wood asked the chief of police in Boston to look for Private Field in area hospitals, as he may have met with an accident or some other misadventure.[52]

Planning for the new administration building for the Barracks was uneven. Lieutenant H.O. Smith duly reported to the quartermaster of the Marine Corps on July 24 on the progress of the E.M. Leach Company.[53]

A month later in late August, Colonel Wood told the quartermaster of the Marine Corps that the original plans for the building had no provision for cells. So he had the plans revised for ten cells. But then a later modification deleted these cells. Colonel Wood argued that there was only one cell in the barracks and it was totally inadequate. It was situated in the guardroom without any ventilation. He requested that ten cells be added back to the building plans.[54]

Boston police found Pvt. Field several days after they were notified of his disappearance. He was in the can at the Charles Street Jail. Turns out he was arrested in Division One on August 7. He was being held on a charge of committing an unnatural act with another person.[55]

The Marine Camp for Rifle Instruction in Wakefield wasn't a paradise of firearms training everybody had hoped. Disciplinary problems occurred in Wakefield too. Captain C.H. Lyman's offense report to Colonel Wood listed two violations: Corporal John C. Wilson was found guilty of unmilitary conduct on the streets of Wakefield and was given five days arrest in his tent, and Private George H. Lake was found guilty of unmilitary conduct on the streets of Wakefield and accordingly was restricted to camp.[56]

Major Albertus W. Catlin received orders to become the post quartermaster at Boston's Marine Barracks.

Years prior, Catlin was a senior officer on board the USS *Maine* during the explosion heard around the world launching the Spanish-American War. He was in his stateroom (bedroom) writing a letter home when an explosion occurred. Fortunately, he was not harmed.

Major Catlin arrived in Boston in September 1909. He needed to make proper arrangements for his horse, his personal property, and for the horse's uses. Major Catlin was a mounted officer. The horse was part of his uniform. He made a request to the post quartermaster to provide forage for his horse.[57] On September 4, he requested approval for utilizing a farrier to shoe his horse for the period of 8-16-09 to 6-10-10 at a cost of 50 cents per shoe.[58] He also made a request for stabling his horse for the period 8-16-09 to 6-10-10 at a cost of $12.50 per month.[59]

Major Catlin went on to have an interesting career. He commanded the Provisional 3d Regiment when it landed at Vera Cruz in 1914. During the Great War, as a colonel, he commanded the 6th Marines in France in 1917. At the Battle of Belleau Wood he was wounded, a bullet shot through his right lung. He recovered.

It was a beginning of a new day September 10 1909 when the safe was opened in the presence of Major A.W. Catlin, as it was the normal start of a business day routine. This is customary and sanctioned by regulations that the cash from sales are turned in to the post exchange officer the following morning. When they opened the safe, they found only $4.50 in nickels and dimes. The day prior started with cash on hand of $12.25. Sales for that day were $40.95, totaling $53.20. That's $48.70 missing. Cash was absent so they looked to see if any inventory was missing too. Yes, $11.75 of stock was gone. That's $60.45 unaccounted for.

The first individual to check out would be the one who had the key to the safe last. That would be salesman, Private Jewell. The key is usually in the custody of the steward, Sergeant Harvey Glidden. This time, however, Sergeant Glidden went on liberty (off duty) about 7 o'clock that evening. He turned over the key to Private Jewell so that the cash sales could be placed in the safe. The shortage was discovered after Private Ernest E. Jewell, salesman in the post exchange, went absent without leave.

The Post Exchange Council set out to investigate this deficiency of funds. The board found Private Jewell took the cash from the safe. Any breaches in protocol that may have made conditions favorable for this pilfering were looked into. Post exchange officer, First Lieutenant Harry O. Smith, the report found, had taken all due and reasonable precautions. A new combination safe of approved design was to be purchased. Only the post exchange steward was to have the combination. They also advocated that the cash sales for the day be removed from the cash register at some time in the evening by the steward and placed in the safe, leaving only a necessary amount of change available for the clerks. The board also recommended that the post exchange officer be authorized to drop from his books the cash and stock as "lost by theft." The members of the council included Major A.W. Catlin, Captain H.J. Hirshinger and First Lieutenant Frederic Kensel.[60]

Shooting season closed and the camp had to shut down. Captain Lyman closed the Marine Camp for Rifle Instruction as per order #13152.[61]

The Boston Marine Barracks accrued much training data during their "spring training." Captain Lyman juxtaposed Boston's scores against Portsmouth and the guys from Portsmouth's prison, the detachments from the floating barracks and the floating prison at the Navy yard, and detachments from three ships at the yard at the time. This data he reported to the adjutant and inspector at Headquarters. This was his list of percentage of shooters achieving merit.

1. Marine Barracks, Boston, 76.3 percent
2. Marine Detachment, Naval Prison, Portsmouth, 64 percent
3. Marine Barracks, Portsmouth, 63.3 percent
4. USRS Wabash, 61.4 percent
5. Marine Detachment, USS *Southery,* 55 percent
6. Marine Barracks, Newport, 52.6 percent
7. Marine Detachment, USS *Missouri,* 52.2 percent
8. Marine Detachment, USS *New Jersey,* 49.6 percent
9. Marine Detachment, USS *Wisconsin,* 43.6 percent

Notice whose scores made the top of the list.[62]

Spring training was receding into the past. Many spent the summer talking and thinking about the scores. When summer ended, the heat broke and concerns about the scores came out. By October 27, 1909, Captain Lyman had to report to Colonel Wood about possible cheating on rifle scores at the Wakefield range. Private Levasco Wardee's name came up. Private Wardee was assigned as a "marker in the butts" during record firing on the range. He kept score.

Private Wardee ended up admitting that much of the marking was not honest. What was his motive for the false values? He was helping the men who were shooting. But Captain Lyman could not take any disciplinary action since his camp was shutting down for the season. He asked Colonel Wood if he could take appropriate action instead.[63]

On October 28, 1909, a Marine standing sentry duty at gate 4 was punched in the mouth. The puncher then ran towards Bunker Hill Street. About the same time, First Sergeant Jackson left the Barracks on liberty. He observed a "blue jacket" (slang for sailor) running rapidly from gate 4 in the direction of Bunker Hill Street, but thought nothing of it. Later, while he was on the train platform of the brand new elevated railway at Haymarket Square, four blue jackets passed by him. Jackson overhead one of them boast, "I hit a son-of-a-bitch of a Marine in the mouth and ran out the gate!" His interest was piqued. He was "on the case." Jackson followed this blue jacket until he entered a saloon. He overhead the same remark again. He got close enough to distinguish his rank as a boatswain mate 2d class. And Jackson recognized him as the guy who ran from gate 4.[64]

13. *Samar*

*"This tablet is erected to the memory of the ten Marines
who died in the Island of Samar, P.I., January 13, 1902."*
—Inscription

A memorial tablet was to be mounted by the doorway of the new administration building, now designated Building 136. The Veteran Marine Association insisted the tablet be installed in memory of members of the Marine Corps who suffered slow deaths under horrible conditions in January 1902 on the Island of Samar in the Philippines.

The inscription read:

> This tablet is erected to the memory of the ten Marines who died in the Island of Samar, P.I., January 13, 1902. Privates Thomas BrettPatrick Connell George Foster James Woods Joseph Basoni Morgan Bassert Timothy MurrayFrank Brown Eugene SanjuleArchibald Bailey They died while serving for their country and flag. They were faithful and fearless. Erected by the officers and men of the Samar expedition.

During the years 1908 to 1909, a small building (Building 30) was removed to make way for the new Marine Barracks Administration Building 136.[1]

Colonel Wood was so concerned about the dwindling strengths of the Barracks that he wrote a personal letter to Major Louis Magill, the assistant adjutant and inspector at headquarters. He personally asked if an entire company of a Panama Battalion completing a tour could be transferred to the Boston. He acknowledged his authorized strength of 367 men. But that included the untouchable 94 men assigned to the naval prison. They could not be assigned duties outside of those involving the prison. His strength was woefully short and he had great difficulty carrying out the security responsibilities of the Marine Barracks.[2]

Corporal Peter F. Frederick took the civil service exam for an assistant light house keeper. He passed the exam. The Light Keeper Service then offered him a position paying $42.50 per month and quarters with a fuel allowance for his family. It was a good job. But he still had his service commitment. So Corporal Frederick wrote to the commandant of the Marine Corps and requested early discharge so he could take the position. With Colonel Wood seemingly chronically strapped for men, he just might have said no. However, Colonel Wood couldn't punish a good man. So he wrote in his letter of recommendation that Corporal Frederick had undertaken his duties at the Marine Barracks with the utmost professionalism, and he recommended that his request for early discharge be granted. The commandant of the Marine Corps approved the request and Corporal Frederick left the Marine Corps and entered the Light House Service.[3]

On Christmas Eve 1909, Major Catlin announced that the contractor constructing the new administration building would turn over the structure to the Marine Barracks on December 28, 1909.[4] That was just four days away.

Colonel Denny, the quartermaster of the Marine Corps, responded to Colonel Wood's concern regarding personnel strengths. He acknowledged the troop strength of the Barracks had been reduced in order to organize an expeditionary force for special duty in a South Atlantic Station. Without anything else to give Colonel Wood, Colonel Denny requested he take advantage of fewer personnel by reducing consumption of coal and wood during heating season.[5] Very funny.

In early January 1910, a young second lieutenant with a very famous name reported for duty. Second Lieutenant John Quincy Adams requested assignment to quarters. Famous name or not, Lt. Col. Prince, the assistant quartermaster of the Marine Corps, replied that no quarters were available. Where was he to stay? The lime shed was long gone, the stables were no longer an option and tents got written up in the newspapers. Second Lt. John Quincy Adams was entitled to commutation of quarters for the authorized number of rooms and should submit the proper vouchers to quartermaster of the Marine Corps.[6] In other words, he was entitled to local housing paid for by the Marine Corps.

The new administration building was complete and ready for occupation. But buildings are empty without furniture. So the quartermaster of the Marine Corps approved the bid of Paine Furniture Company to provide furnishings for the building.[7]

Private Wharter was assigned to duty as the orderly of the commandant of the Navy yard. The commandant of the Navy yard resides in the great house to the west of the Barracks. On April 3, he deserted. An inspection of what personal belongings he left behind revealed he had disposed of everything. He possibly stole $30 from the library in the commandant's quarters.

An investigation found records revealing his mother lived in Melrose, MA. The Melrose Police were notified and they subsequently picked him up at his mother's house. When he was arrested he was attired in brand new clothing. The Melrose Police knew him and reported he had a bad reputation and was a convicted burglar. He was also suspected to be a deserter from D Company, 3rd Field Artillery, U.S. Army.[8]

The Wakefield camp was coming back to life this year. The quartermaster of the Marine Corps on April 28, 1910, forwarded a large shipment of supplies to the Marine Corps Camp of Rifle Instruction in Reading, MA, the long awaited weapons training area for the Marines of the Barracks. Men of the corps could train here and be now be ready for anything events sent America's way. Ships' detachments when docked in the Navy yard would send their men there to train as well.[9] On the same day 11 men were transferred for duty at the rifle range camp.[10]

The personnel in the naval prison were to be maintained as a separate detachment from the Marine Barracks. This was a considerable change. The naval prison now had its own commanding officer. When assessments for men were made to provide for a ship's detachment, the men could not be drawn from the assets of the naval prison. It was no longer an additional responsibility for the commanding officer of the Marine Barracks. For years and years, many commanding officers of the Barracks considered the prison too much of a drain on their attention. But solutions can create new problems, or exacerbate existing ones.

Headquarters basically gave Wood some more men, and then forbade his use of these men. The same rotation schedules of ships' detachments were kept up and his shipyard responsibilities remained unchanged, to be filled with fewer men. This chagrined Colonel Wood to no end. He constantly complained to his command that his assets were being depleted to the extent that it was difficult to properly safeguard the Navy yard.[11]

Officers were expected to know how to ride a horse. A requirement of their annual physical tests is that they ride a horse as an exhibition of their ability to ride. Recall Major Catlin and his horse. There were no stables in the Navy yard. Colonel Wood didn't own a horse. He had to rent a horse for this test. Since the Marines required this test, maybe the Marines might help out with the rental fees. But his requested reimbursement for the horse rental of $15 was disallowed by the comptroller of the treasury. Colonel Wood wrote to the comptroller and protested the action.[12]

The sentinels of the Navy yard had their hands full controlling entry and exit of individuals, watching for fires and unusual activities, and they were also required to enforce the no smoking regulations prescribed by the commandant of the Navy yard. Enforcing the rules ruffled feathers. Sergeant John O'Loughlin stopped workman C. McClure, check number 3593, as he entered Gate 4 with a cigar in his hand. Sergeant O'Loughlin told him to throw his cigar away; he wouldn't and continued to hold the cigar in his hands. Sergeant O'Loughlin followed McClure and removed the cigar from him. Sergeant O'Louhglin then returned to his post.[13]

The officers of the Barracks and their ladies were invited to dances and other social gatherings hosted by the officers of Fort Banks and Fort Warren and other forts in Boston Harbor, making for a lively social life. The Navy yard provided the use of the yard tug to transport the officers and their ladies to the forts in the harbor.[14]

A fire alarm sounded in the yard. The officer in charge, 2nd Lieutenant Sidney N. Raynor, according to those present, failed in all respects to carry out Navy yard fire protocol. Colonel Wood, considering Raynor's youth and inexperience, and the fact that he did not have quarters on base, did not want to restrict him. But May 13, Colonel Wood chastised 2nd Lt. Raynor for neglect of duty and the incident would be included in his next report of fitness.[15]

Headquarters set forth the procedures for sending groups of Marines to the newly established rifle instruction camp in Wakefield. Men from the Marine Barracks, naval prison, the floating barracks, the floating prison and Marine detachments from ships in the Charlestown Navy Yard would complete a 2 to 3 week course. Marines were to bring their heavy marching packs without weapons.[16]

The Marine Barracks at one time used the naval prison as a brig for recalcitrant Marines. But now that the naval prison was its own entity, self-administered in matters of subsistence of prisoners and guards, Colonel Wood wanted the quartermaster of the Marine Corps to install the cells in Building 136 with due dispatch. He did not want to use the cells at the naval prison for minor infractions and short time confinements.[17]

When men were honorably discharged from the Marines and left the Barracks for civilian endeavors, many settled in places quite distant from Boston. Sarsfield Williamson applied for employment as a guard at the Minnesota State Prison. So Colonel Wood wrote a letter of recommendation for him. During Williamson's time at the Barracks, he staffed the central telephone switchboard as an operator, another Marine Barracks responsibility. They don't just let knuckleheads be telephone operators. He was highly recommended for the job by his former commanding officer.[18] Serving at the Barracks could be good for your resume.

Colonel Wood kept on reminding Major General Elliott that constant drawdowns for ships and other posts were crippling his command.[19] This time so much so he invited the commandant of the Navy Yard to pay attention to these excessive reductions in strength, as it affected entry and exit into his Navy yard. Colonel Wood said he could not maintain some security posts and he would have to permanently discontinue Gate 3, the Marine Barracks' own entrance. This gate was used by the commanding officer's family and the local mailman. Colonel Wood really hoped that this serious situation would receive the commandant of the Navy yard's utmost attention.[20]

These personnel drains on the Barracks began to cause permanent changes to shipyard gates. Some gates were closed forever and forgotten. The surviving gates became the modern gates used today. Gate 3 closed and never reopened. It can be seen today as one walks Chelsea Street outside the yard along the dark, old, ivy covered, cut stone wall behind the Barracks. Between two granite pillar stones hangs a wrought iron gate interrupting the sameness. Augmented with chain link and plywood, shuttered for all time, is the Barracks commanding officer's own gate.

On Sundays, to have accountability for visitors to the Navy Yard, visitors were given passes. These were different people than the workweek shipyard employees. They came to visit those who actually lived on the Navy yard.

A shipyard is not where many would call home. Yet the officers of the Barracks lived right there with their families and children. Not to mention the commandant of the Navy yard and his family, who lived quite comfortably in a red brick mansion on a spread of landscaped greenery with in the shipyard itself. To the southwest of the commandant's cottage over a half dozen naval officers and their wives and children lived cheek-by-jowel in brick townhouses situated between the Main Gate and Gate 2. These families had visitors on Sundays.

Colonel Wood wanted the pass practice discontinued. Preparing and issuing tickets created extreme congestion at the Main Gate. It took some time to write the required information on the passes.

The previous Sunday illustrated the issue. The main gate used up its tickets and had to get tickets from another gate, which were of a different color and caused confusion.

The use of the tickets emanated from a former manager of the Manufacturing Department. He used it to distinguish visitors from workmen. Colonel Wood thought the practice was not really necessary since there were few workmen at the yard on Sundays.[21]

Men leaving on liberty had to use the Main Gate before exiting the yard. That is where the liberty list was. But naval prison guards leaving on liberty could use Gate 4. And Gate 4 was not staffed for this kind traffic. This gate was normally closed except for the entrance or exit of authorized persons. Recall the staffing problems. And then comes "Bell Ring." At the beginning of each workday thousands of shipyard workmen passed through needing their brass checks. The end of the day "Bell Ring" these thousands passed through the gates and need their brass checks turned in. Congestion occurred when the Gate 4 sentinel was checking the liberty list. An officer explained it took time for the sentinel to answer the bell, since the guard was busy scrutinizing the liberty list. Colonel Wood could now only suggest that naval prison personnel use the Main Gate, as it was better suited for liberty checks.[22]

A couple of guys beat up Marine Private Alexander C. Fraser. The story hit the papers. The *Boston Herald* and the *Boston Transcript* on June 9 reported the police claimed the assailants were Marines. Private Fraser did not agree. He knew who beat him up and they were not Marines. Pvt. Fraser said he was attacked by a number of civilians. Colonel Wood wrote a letter to both newspapers refuting the facts of the report and chastised them for making such a report without proper verification. He explained that there were a number of lawless characters in that particular area, involved in assaults of that nature.[23] Lost to the record was where this area civilized members of society needed to avoid was.

Colonel Wood's pay was debited for the cost of the hiring of the horse he used for his physical. He protested to the comptroller of the treasury.[24]

By June 1910 rifle instruction at the Wakefield location was becoming a welcome routine for Marines at the Marine Barracks. Colonel Wood directed its commander that data on men at the camp be forwarded no later than the 28th of each month to be available for entry on the muster roll.[25]

With staffing relief not seeming so imminent, Colonel Wood sought other means to bring respite. The first target was the requirement for sentries to check civilian employees in and out the yard. He wanted the sentinels relieved from this burden of acting as timekeepers by checking employees in and out of the yard, and issuing visitors' passes. The requirement interfered with their regular duties and diverted their attention from observance of the gates. He submitted the chore impaired the efficiency of the orderly.[26]

The post exchange (PX) books from four years ago for the period of March 1, 1906, to September 1, 1906, gained headquarters' attention; they wanted them. But the PX books weren't around. The Barracks had to find them. Fortunately they were able to locate them. It turned out that the Marine Corps inspector took them August 1906. He was going to report on the involved and confused character in which he found the books of the PX officer, First Lieutenant G.M. Kincade.[27] He didn't return them until now.

Someone stole Private Willis Reed's olive drab flannel shirt. An investigation commenced. The report determined that a theft had occurred. There were no shortage of witnesses that believed Private Harry Clark took it. The Marine Barracks punished severely those who stole from other Marines. Colonel Wood recommended that Private Clark be tried by general court-martial.[28] If convicted, he could end up at the notorious naval prison. All for an olive drab flannel shirt.

On July 11, 1910, Colonel Laucheimer, adjutant and inspector of the Marine Corps wrote to Colonel Wood and directed the transfer of 1 corporal and 5 privates to the USS *Dolphin* at Gloucester, MA.[29] This wasn't just any transfer.

The USS *Dolphin* was the flagship of the Atlantic fleet. Men considered for duty aboard it were especially select, of neat and soldierly appearance, and with experience at sea. Very special care was taken in selecting the corporal. He would become the orderly for the secretary of the Navy, who at the time was William Henry Moody from Massachusetts, whenever he was aboard the USS *Dolphin*. An orderly from the Boston Marine Barracks in Massachusetts would be an appropriate selection. What a sweet detail.

From 1899 until World War I, the USS *Dolphin* served as the special dispatch ship for the secretary of the Navy. It was basically his yacht. Often the president and other important officials and diplomats came along as guests of the secretary. It was beautiful, white, with a boiler and a prominent central smoke stack, modern yet with three masts for sails. Smoke stacks were as much status symbols then as a "Hemi" in sport utility trucks are today. It was armed with seven guns, the *Dolphin*'s version of an officer's side arm.

The first captain of the USS *Dolphin* when it launched in 1884 was Captain Dewey. It was the first Navy ship to fly the flag of the president of the United States, during the Chester A. Arthur Administration. It was his presidential yacht. It once carried peace plenipotentiaries from New York to Portsmouth, New Hampshire, to negotiate the settlement of the Russo-Japanese War. The first song broadcast over wireless was sung from its deck in 1907, peacefully demonstrating its modern communications capabilities.

When Franklin D. Roosevelt was assistant secretary of the Navy in 1913, he often transported his family aboard. He began lifelong friendships with its officers, captain and future Fleet Admiral William Leahy, and Richard Byrd. Byrd was a dashing pioneering aviator and explorer who eventually became the first to fly an airplane to the South Pole. This was another peaceful demonstration of useful technology, not unlike shooting rockets at the moon. The USS *Dolphin* was overhauled in 1920 at the Charlestown Navy Yard.

The sentinel boxes at Gate #4 and Gate #5 were in deplorable condition. Floors were in terrible shape. The boxes were built to require people passing through the gate to walk over the floors of the boxes. Colonel Wood wanted them remodeled and placed in an area where the sentinel could be sheltered and could observe the passage way and not have all that traffic passing though the boxes.[30]

Private Thomas Delaney needed to be hospitalized for surgery. The problem was that he was a central telephone switchboard operator. Not everybody could do this. This was a highly specialized skill; men had to be highly qualified. Colonel Wood had no one to replace him when he went under the knife. Except one, but he was at the Marine Corps Camp for Rifle Instruction in Wakefield and would not be available for a week. The surgery was necessary but not life threatening, so Colonel Wood asked that his admission be delayed for a week.[31]

Baseball just became America's favorite pastime. The commander of the USRS *Wabash*, the floating Marine Barracks, requested two specific Marines be transferred to his vessel. Colonel Wood probably rolled his eyes at this "pathetic" letter. He was not at all agreeable to transferring these two specific men. First of all, they had just finished their tour of sea duty and deserved to have their land legs back. He suspected the real motivation for this request was that they were excellent baseball players, and the commander wanted them for his team. The Marine Barracks needed them for their team instead.[32]

Colonel Wood appealed again to the comptroller of the treasury for reimbursement of $15 for the hired horse required by his annual physical.[33] He felt their thinking needed to change with the times and not assume modern officers have horses, especially if they serve sea duty. The policy probably dated back to the 19th century when landed gentry style officers just happened to own horses.

A routine day at the medical officer's office was unfolding to everyone's comfort. The usual patients to be seen were slowly gathering. A Marine was in the waiting room for a possible illness he felt he was suffering, as was protocol. But after an examination, the medical officer's professional opinion was piqued. His suspicion of Pvt. Henry Priviater's potentially bogus symptoms prompted an investigation.

The investigation's findings came back. It determined Pvt. Priviater wanted out of the service to seek employment with the White Star Steamship Company. He would make a much greater salary with them than he was presently receiving. Marines do gain valuable skills as Marines, but an example had to be set for anyone trying to skip the rest of their hitch for better pay. They should patiently wait until their enlistment is up and not jump the gun. Colonel Wood recommended he be tried by general court-martial for malingering.[34] He could end up at that ripe naval prison two blocks away.

Regulations required field musicians to practice various trumpet drills and they had to do it every day. Their practice area had been near Building 109 (Coal Power Plant Building). All well and good, all this trumpet drill was away from residential areas, except when vessels were docked at the pier discharging coal, fueling the plant. The musicians were chased away by a warrant officer. The warrant officer said they were disturbing the workmen in the area.

Colonel Wood, looking out for his men, requested from the commandant of the Navy yard a suitable place for the field musicians to practice.[35]

Death in the Jungle

Major Albertus W. Catlin was appointed to set up the ceremonies for the unveiling of the tablet in memory of Marines who died during the Samar, Philippines, insurrection.[36]

Samar is a large island south of Manila in the Philippine Archipelago. Manila hemp grew in large quantities there. This hemp was desired at the time by the United States. Repressive treatment by the United States drove the villagers on Sept 28, 1901, to rise up and kill 36 men of the U.S. Army's Company C during evening mess, including all of its commissioned officers. The atrocity hit just when it was thought Filipino resistance had collapsed. This event shocked the U.S. public. Newspapers equated it the worst massacre since George Armstrong Custer's last stand at Little Big Horn.

General Jacob Smith was appointed to tend to the matter. He ordered a scorched earth policy, and was quoted "kill and burn" and "Samar must be made a Howling Wilderness." He became known as "Howling Wilderness Smith." The order was countermanded, however. He subsequently ordered the killing of all persons capable of bearing arms. All ages right down to ten years old. Starvation was used as a weapon, as was the burning of villages, and the forced relocation of villages: images eerily reminiscent of America's experience in Vietnam.

Marines from Cavite City Navy Yard, often staffed by Marines from the Boston Marine Barracks, were deployed to Samar. The entire southern region of Samar was the responsibility of the Marines who were sent in almost daily on search and destroy missions to pacify the countryside. This harassment drove the insurgents back to their fortified defenses on the Sohoton Cliffs on the banks of the Sohoton River.

In November three columns of Marines set out to attack this stronghold, reported to be impregnable. Filipinos had set up these defenses to be used against the Spaniards years earlier. This was where they would make their last stand. But the Spaniards never saw them. Neither had any other Westerners, until the Marines laid their eyes on these prepared cliffs.

Two columns marched along the banks of the river while the third went up the river by boat. The plan was for the three to attack on 16 November. The next day Marines marching along the riverbank came upon a number of bamboo guns. Placed to defend the riverside trail, one had a lit fuse burning. Corporal Harry Glen ran to pull out the fuse.

If the gun went off it would have alerted the defenders. The Marines attacked with complete surprise. The enemy was routed and fell back to the cliffs. Running with their momentum, the Marines crossed the river and assaulted the cliff defenses.

To reach the enemy's position, they had to climb up 200 feet of sharp volcanic rock rising sheer from the river, shot through with caves. They gained access by bamboo ladders and narrow ledges with bamboo handrails. Tons of rocks were suspended in cages by vine cables, ready to drop on invaders below. But the defenders couldn't use these rocks on the Marines. Decorated war hero Gunnery Sergeant John H. Quick's heavy cover fire with his Colt machine gun (the first machine gun adapted by the U.S. military; air-cooled and gas, operated, it could fire 450 rounds per minute) prevented their use by blasting the cliffs with a lot of bullets. The insurgents were driven from their positions.

The third column's boats were to be Johnny-come-latelys. But that turned out to be a good thing. Had they arrived before they defenders were removed, they would have been pulverized. With rations exhausted and Marines' shoes ripped to shreds by the rock, many were barefoot; further pursuit wasn't going to happen.

The cliff and hanging rocks defenses they had just overcome took years and years to prepare. No western troops had ever gotten that close before. The jungle redoubt was constructed to be the (insurgents') local peoples' final stand against the Spaniards. After all that, no Marines were killed in the attack.

After Samar was "pacified" the Marines started their "March across Samar" from Lanang, 28 December 1901. Their reason to the world as to why they were scouting out an inland route across this new American possession was to find a suitable telegraph route to link America's future ports on Samar.

The explorers plied inland by boat up the Lanang River. It wasn't long into the journey when they hit rapids. Forced to encounter the rest of the journey on foot, the men rose to occasion. They needed to. The swollen river, an advantage for the boats, now had to be crossed and re-crossed by the men physically. Not only dangerous, it was leaving the Marines wet and taxed. This wasn't part of the plan. The sojourn was taking longer than the plan on paper. Rations were reduced. And reduced again. As the Marines crested the mountainous spine of Samar, their feet were bleeding. Sickness emerged. Food was running out. Their clothes were rags, and they were lost.

A decision among the officers was to send Major Waller and 13 Marines in the best condition to get help. Captain Porter and the main body were to follow Waller's trail slowly. As the advance column pressed forth, they sent word back to the main body to follow the advance column's trial to a clearing, with plenty to eat—sweet potatoes, bananas, and coconuts—and rest there. But this word never made it back to the main column. A native sent with the message returned, saying that there were so many insurgents out there in the jungle he was afraid.

On January 4, Waller's men rushed a thatched hut and captured a man and a boy. They ended up knowing the way to the old Spanish trail to Basey, where the relief party for the expedition was located. By their guidance, the Marines found their way to the camp established to await their arrival. Waller's men made it home. But what about Captain Porter's men?

The very next day a relief party of fresh men and Major Waller left the Basey camp and set out to find Captain Porter and his men. After nine days of searching and the discouragement of finding former campsites, places they expected to rest, under many feet of floodwaters, the relief party broke down and returned to Basey.

Meanwhile, Captain Porter's men were languishing. Porter decided to turn around and retrace his trail back to Lanang with whoever could go with him. Most of his men, however, lost most of their mobility. Porter left those who couldn't come along with Lt. Williams. He left Williams with orders to follow along as best as his men could.

Captain Porter took seven Marines and six natives with him back to Lanang. With food almost gone and dangerous river crossings high with strong flood waters, Porter nevertheless reached Lanang on January 11. Porter's men were safe. A relief party of fresh men was organized. But they were unable to get going for the flooding rivers.

Left behind and facing starvation, Lt. Williams' men as best they could struck the camp and crept up Porter's trail to Lanang.

By now the condition of some men was so bad, the weakest men were left behind trailside, to die alone in the jungle, slowly. Ten men were left behind to die alone like this.

The survivors endured a man going insane and the porters becoming mutinous. Some with Bolos attacked Lt. Wlliams. Porters were hiding food and living off the jungle while the Marines starved. The relief party eventually launched from Lanang finally reached what was left of Williams' party, and they brought the survivors back to Lanang. Once the Williams party arrived in Lanang, 11 porters were arrested.

Waller eventually ordered the mutinous porters summarily executed without trial. They were to be shot. Eleven Filipinos were executed for their role in the mutiny. Ten Marines died slowly and alone in the jungle.[37] These are the 10 Marines on the tablet.

14. Ebb and Flow of Peacetime

"Until further orders, liberty is stopped for all enlisted men from the barracks."
—Lt. Col. Moses

Master ship fitter Outside was finding shipyard worker Hugh McCrossin insubordinate and abusive. McCrossin used very foul language. The master ship fitter requested Marines to help him eject this unpleasant man from the yard.[1] Whenever a problem occurred in the yard, they sent for the Marines.

Liberty rules changed in early September. The liberty list now authorized Marines time off until 0700 hours. Men who behaved stayed on the list. Those who misbehaved on liberty had their names removed from the list. The liberty could not interfere with duties at the post. There were three sergeants, one corporal and 16 privates on the initial list.[2]

A rifle competition between posts was scheduled at the Wakefield Camp in September. The Barracks was directed to assign a second lieutenant as range officer for the competition.[3]

The Mystic Ball Park was located across Chelsea Street from Gate 5. It was where many young boys played baseball. So it was bound to happen. In mid September, a baseball broke a window in Building 79. The sentinel at Gate 5 retrieved the ball and held it until the boys paid 10 cents to cover the damage to the window. He got it. The 10 cents was forwarded to the commandant of the Navy yard.[4]

Colonel Wood wrote a letter of certification of service for Joseph F. Scott. A certification of service letter is like a letter of reference. He confirmed that Scott served in the Marine Corps from August 11, 1888, to May 7, 1901. He had served under Colonel Wood's command before back in September 1890. Scott was a veteran of the Philippines and the Boxer Rebellion. He was also in the Spanish-American War. Scott was awarded the Medal of Honor for gallantry while under fire cutting the cables off the coast of Cienfuegos in Cuba on May 11, 1898, as a member of the Marine Detachment aboard the USS *Nashville*.[5]

At 6:45 a.m. on May 11, 1898, back during the war, the USS *Nashville* and the USS *Marblehead* opened fire on a telegraph cable house. The ships then dispatched boats of men to cut the cables. Surprise was lost when a Spanish cavalryman on land discovered them and rode off to get help. Three cables needed to be cut. The first one was relatively easy, but the second one was caught on coral and Spanish forces were converging. With effort they got the second one cut but the third smaller one remained as the Spanish main force arrived to repel what they thought was a full scale invasion. Scott was there.

Major Albertus W. Catlin's horse was moving to Philadelphia. An enlisted man was directed to accompany the horse on the trip to Philadelphia.[6]

The rifle camp at Wakefield closed for the year as September 1910 came to an end. One quartermaster sergeant, 2 sergeants, 1 corporal and 14 privates were transferred to various posts and stations.[7]

In October 1910 a general court-martial prisoner escaped from the naval prison. He somehow gained possession of a uniform and a pistol. Egress through the Navy yard is easy when you are in uniform and know how to wear it. The escapee approached the orderly at Gate 2. The orderly, unaware the man in a sentinel uniform was an escaped prisoner, suddenly had a pistol in his face. "Open that gate as quick as Christ will let you," Private Ernest Strauss submitted the individual said to him during the investigation. But since he was armed with only a club, he allowed the person to leave the yard. He claimed that it was sometime later he learned the person was an escaped prisoner.[8]

Private Daley stated that on September 13, 1910, he was confined in the naval prison for "returning from liberty under the influence of intoxicating liquor." Okay, but at his court-martial, he claimed the medical officer testified Daley was sober and fit for duty prior to confinement. He was given summary court-martial and was thrown into solitary confinement for 14 days. He was also reduced from first to fourth conduct class, which required him to do extra hours of duty. After all this, on September 30, Private P.J. Daley wrote to the major general commandant. He added the commanding officer of the Marine Barracks had declined to forward his protestations. He further stated that Colonel Wood refused to redress the perceived wrongs and Private Daley wanted a transfer to Marine Barracks in New York.[9] Unknown is why Colonel Wood "threw the book" at Pvt. Daley.

On November 8, a detachment consisting of Sergeant George H. Barrett and 8 privates was sent for duty at the naval magazine in Hingham, MA.[10]

First Lieutenant A. Stokes received orders to ship out within thirty days. The trouble was, he was training 74 recruits who were not ready for duty. These recruits amounted to approximately 35 percent of the total strength of the Barracks.[11] Captain Wadleigh advised Major General Elliott there were only three officers available for officer of the day duty and the loss of one would seriously increase the workload of the others.

Captain Wadleigh sent recommendations for the promotions of Privates George P. Tielsch and Joseph W. Coggin to headquarters for approval. The promotions were denied. The letter, CMC #6978, stated they were not eligible because they committed a number of offenses. Captain Wadleigh was in askance as to whether any regulation existed spelling out the number and gravity of offenses which would disqualify a man for promotion. If one did indeed exist, it would prevent many privates with several months of clear records from detailing as acting corporals, even though these improved records indicated an intention to become a candidate for promotion. Men possessing zeal, intelligence, and soldierly appearance, who would certainly make solid noncommissioned officers, could be denied promotion. If offenses were done through inexperience and immaturity early in their enlistments, consequently they must, if they were detailed as acting corporals, return to duty as privates. This reduced the candidate pool for corporal. The billets would still be there but, this ruled out some very qualified men. This scrutiny would be fine if there was stiff competition for these slots. But there was a shortage of candidates. Perhaps a Marine's record built up at another post, but while he has served at the Barracks, his service was exemplary. Captain Wadleigh explained that a ruling was needed since Corporal H.P. Bobb was promoted and he showed a summary court-martial and twelve minor offenses. Private Coggin had one deck court and thirteen minor offenses, and Private Tielsch had one deck court and ten minor offenses.[12]

Private Peter F. Brown signed up for recruitment into the Marine Corps at the office in

Nashua, NH. The sergeant in charge asked for his watch as security for his transfer to Boston for his pre-enlistment medical exam. Perhaps not thinking this was unusual, Brown handed it over. Pvt. Brown apparently had enough of a relationship with the sergeant that he was with him on the Saturday night, 26 November 1910, before he departed Nashua. The sergeant got into a drunken fight with a third party. Pvt. Brown removed the watch from the sergeant to prevent its damage. The Monday after, November 28, the sergeant asked for the watch and got it back. At the railroad station, prior to leaving for Boston, Private Brown asked for his watch back. The sergeant said he would mail it to him. After being in Boston a few days, as of December 1, he still had not received the watch. Pvt. Brown reported the matter to Captain Wadleigh. Captain Wadleigh reported the matter to the officer in charge of recruiting in Boston.[13] Within several days after the intercession of the officer in charge of recruiting, the watch was returned to Private Brown.[14]

Remember Private Daley? He was the private who wrote to the commandant of the Marine Corps (CMC) about his unfair treatment by Colonel Wood. Captain Wadleigh, perhaps possessing more of the big picture than Pvt. Daley, wrote to headquarters in response. Wadleigh recommended that Private Patrick J. Daley be discharged as undesirable. This, after all, would be in compliance with the endorsement of CMC Letter #26059 of October 26, 1910.

Headquarters replied that Private Daley should be carefully observed. If he didn't measure up, then he should be discharged. Since the receipt of the October 26 communiqué from Washington, he had twice returned from liberty intoxicated and unfit for duty. His consequence was two weeks' restriction. On December 6, he reported for duty drunk and unfit, this time, however, he was a supernumerary (additional member) of the guard. Private Daley was confined awaiting disposition from Washington.[15]

Recalling Private Ernest A. Jewell: he deserted and went absent without leave September 9, 1909, after running away with the PX's cash and inventory. He surrendered to the Marine Barracks. An investigation convening September 10, 1909, found Private Jewell responsible for the loss of $48.70 from the safe. On November 3, 1909, Private Jewell's mother appeared at the post and turned over $48.70 to Captain Wadleigh. She submitted the sum as restitution for the amount her son had embezzled. Unknown is whether it was the embezzled money, or from her savings. Colonel Wood noticed Private Jewell was very well dressed, maybe in his Sunday best, when he surrendered.[16]

Colonel Wood, having some rare spare time, sorted through some of the belongings of his late father. His father, Chief William W. Wood, was an engineer in the old wood and rope U.S. Navy. He died almost thirty years prior back in 1882.

To Wood's wonderment, he found a piece of small cloth. After he looked into it, the cloth turned out to be a four by nine inch crape that had come from the catafalque (the scaffolding around a casket) from the funeral of the late President Abraham Lincoln. Upon this revelation, Wood wrote to the curator of the National Museum in Washington, D.C. He offered it as a gift to be placed among the relics of the museum. Look for it at the museum.[17]

Colonel Wood asked headquarters to reconsider the promotion of Privates Joseph W. Coggin and George P. Tielsch. There were 5 slots available. Only 15 corporals occupied 20 positions. The Barracks needed these slots filled. He opined that Privates Coggin and Tielsch were the best-qualified men for promotion.[18]

The iconic uniform of the Marines during the Edwardian era differed between shore duty and sea duty. This came to light with a commandant of the Navy yard who was wistful of his sea duty days. Possibly for a Christmas party, on December 13, the commandant asked for a field music unit detailed for duty in full dress uniform, at his quarters, the mansion next door. Colonel Wood responded that Special Order 58 tied his hands. It provided full dress uniforms for men only assigned to service afloat. He recommended that the field music unit could wear clean blue undress uniforms.[19]

On December 1910 the commandant of the Navy yard asked for a breakdown of the Marine Barracks' use of its Marines as it affected the security of his Navy yard. Colonel Wood had 178 privates at his disposal. Of those, 45 were green recruits, 5 were acting corporals, 11 were sick, 9 were confined, and 2 were absent without leave. There were also 32 orderlies. The commanding officer's house had an orderly, the junior officers' house had one, commanding officer's office was also staffed with an orderly, there was a general court-martial orderly, mail orderly, 6 telephone orderlies, and 5 orderlies at gate numbers 2, 4, 5 and 10. There were also 25 men involved in special details. They were the bakers, clerks, cooks, mechanics and other essential positions imperative for the proper administration of the command.

This communication was in respond to the prison commander's request for men. Colonel Wood tutored the commander of the naval prison to select men by inspecting their records personally, and suggested that maybe he should look at other posts and stations to fill the requirements of the naval prison.[20]

After all that, January 1911, twelve privates were transferred to the naval prison. The commander of the naval prison made his selections based on Colonel Wood's recommendations.[21]

Nothing but the latest information technology was good enough for the Marine Barracks. The adding machine used in the Barracks required repair. A letter was written to Mechanical Accountant Company, 17 Warren Street, Providence, RI, for this service.[22]

Colonel Wood officially informed the commandant of the Navy yard that certain lights in front of the Barracks were out and the lighting along the waterfront was out too. It was very dark along the waterfront. The Officer of the Day tried to get a hold of anyone at the Power Plant Valentine's Day 1911 starting at 9:20 p.m. He finally got somebody on line by 9:45 p.m. 25 minutes later.[23]

Private James M. McKean began to not seem to be who he said he was. Enlisting in the Marine Corps gave a few, for various motives, a chance to change their names. Many Marines were discovered to have enlisted under an alias. One such person was Private James M. McKean. The investigation found he enlisted several times before under the aliases Joseph M. Shea and Harry J. Edwards. He was also a coal passer in the Navy. For this deception, he received a stay at the brand new naval prison in Portsmouth, NH. He was convicted of fraudulent enlistment and was awarded a general court-martial.[24] It was not okay to have enlisted under a false name.

Placing Marines in the naval prison at the yard for minor offenses on a short-term basis was not practical. It was like going to the Mall of America for a pack of gum. Colonel Wood needed some cells put in the new administration building. He asked Major General Biddle for prompt installation of new cells in Building 136. All he had was one poorly ventilated cell located in the guardroom.[25]

Captain D. Hull was the aide de camp for the commandant of the Marine Corps. For the 21st Century mind, an aide to camp is an adjutant, or a personal assistant. Usually they are cherry picked top men. On March 20, Captain Hull forwarded a letter to all commanding officers quoting the secretary of the Navy. It concerned the recent organization of expeditionary forces for tropical duty: "In view of the efficient and rapid mobilization of the provisional regiment of Marines recently dispatched to Guantanamo and San Diego, all detachments having been embarked on the transports in a shorter time than had been anticipated, the department takes pleasure in congratulating the Marine Corps in having maintained its past record for readiness for service."[26] The Marine Corps was doing a few things right.

Private Fred Langille wanted a discharge, he said, in order to provide better for his wife and child. He, however, was estranged to them. If he could provide the documentation, his request to be discharged might have been granted. But he could not. His request was not granted. April 24, Major General William P. Biddle told Colonel Wood he received a letter from an attorney in Lynn, MA, representing Langille's wife. It stated Pvt. Langille not been contributing any support whatsoever. Colonel Wood subsequently admonished Langille about his responsibility to provide proper support for his family. Colonel Wood acknowledged he only could appeal to his sense of responsibility; he did not have the authority to order him to do it.[27]

Headquarters asked Colonel Wood why he did not participate in the physical tests required for the quarter ending October 31. Colonel Wood explained that he awoke on October 10, 1910, having great difficulty with his vision. He described it as "extremely dull." He duly reported to the medical officer to be checked out. The senior medical officer advised him not to take physical test at that time.[28] Colonel Wood took the senior medical officer's professional advice.

In early April 1911 Colonel Wood was in the mood to enlighten headquarters about his chronic shortage of men. He had available for duty 4 sergeants, 13 corporals and 22 privates. He could only maintain three posts. One covered the entire waterfront. Another was a yard patrol during the day and still another covered the payoffice after working hours. Orderlies guarded the five other gates after the Main Gate. Each day's requirement was 2 sergeants, 6 corporals and 9 privates. Any more transfers would deeply hurt the Barracks.[29] The following day, Colonel Wood, perhaps knowing which gate he could close, requested from the commandant of the Navy yard to discontinue the orderly post at Gate 2.[30]

After distinguished service as the Marine Barracks commander for so long, Colonel Wood felt that it was time to retire. Summer was coming up too. On April 25, 1911, Colonel Wood wrote to Major General Biddle and requested to be placed on the retired list.[31] A month later, on 25 May 1911, Colonel Wood was placed on the retirement list.[32] The search commenced for a new commanding officer of the Marine Barracks.

Major Moses Is Back

The next day, May 26, 1911, First Lieutenant J.R. Henley from the officer of the day rotation was placed as acting commanding officer until the arrival of the next commander. Major Laurence H. Moses assumed command on June 7, 1911.

Major Moses' first issue faced as a commander, a problem that seemed to pester each and every Commander of the Barracks for a hundred years, was the lack of personnel to properly staff postings. Major Moses came up with something innovative. He was able to get headquarters to commit to a fixed strength of 201 men for the Barracks.[33]

Major Moses reported on the organization of his command to headquarters in compliance with the 5 July 1911 CMC #6570 letter. Captain John W. Wadleigh with Second Lieutenant Harry L. Smith as his co-commander headed up Company D. One gunnery sergeant, then 4 sergeants, and then 9 corporals, was the traditional structure to lead 45 privates. The field musicians were 1 drummer and 1 trumpeter for a total of 63 men.

Why bother with field musicians? Before practical radios, commanders used a particular tune on the trumpet or a drum cadence to command troops in the field of battle. By 1911, field music was imbedded into soldiery for at least two thousand years. It had always been that way. Well into the dawn of the 20th century, even though radio communication was right around the corner, it was the primary method of field communication. Until the greatest war in history, just a few years away, changed everything.

The full Barracks detachment census consisted of Major Laurence H. Moses, commanding officer, Captain Thomas Holcomb, Jr., Captain Douglas C. McDougal, First Lieutenants John R. Henley, Ralph S. Keyser, Edmund A. Osterman, and Littleton W.T. Waller, Jr., and Second Lieutenants Sidney Raynor and Charles G. Sinclair. The enlisted men were 5 quartermaster sergeants, 1 first sergeant, 18 sergeants, 24 corporals, 1 trumpeter and 101 privates for a total of 162.[34] This report was in compliance with the July 5, 1911, CMC #6570 letter.

The Navy yard had always been a tourist attraction. With motorized vehicles proliferating as one of the most ubiquitous technologies of the age, this tendency became more acute, manifesting itself in the increased traffic of sightseeing buses. Major Moses reported this to the commandant of the Navy yard. He listed the sightseeing companies bringing tourists to the yard: Tourist Auto Company, 40 Hancock Street, Boston; Sightseeing Auto Company, 14 Park Square, Boston; Pilgrim Auto Company, Hamilton Place, Boston; Puritan Auto Company, Hamilton Place, Boston; and Colonial Auto Company, 14 Park Square, Boston.

Major Moses, having been in the officer of the day rotation at the Barracks before, had precise ideas on how to administer the operations of the Marine Barracks. Another challenge facing the new commanding officer was the new post exchange (PX).

The PX was a relatively new concept, and it was likely many pined for the old way, the usual initial resistance to change. Everybody was still getting used to the post exchange (PX) system, even though memories of the previous sutler system had already receded well into the past. These tendencies created the problems accounting for items in stock and cash on hand. Fortunately, Moses had considerable experience with post exchanges and knew how to run one. Accordingly, he compiled a thorough report on improvement of the administration of the post exchange.[35]

A Marine served for 29 years as a private and was ready to retire in October 1911. Major Moses, showing compassion for the private, contacted Captain Fay at headquarters. He asked if Captain Fay could intercede on the private's behalf along with Major General Biddle to promote this old and faithful Marine. Moses wanted him promoted to corporal or sergeant prior to his retirement. Moses did volunteer that this Marine was old and feeble and would not be of much use to the post. He was curious how the major general commandant would view the promotion of the mature Marine.[36]

The Marine Corps classified its Marine Barracks all over the world as one, two, three or four company posts, depending on their sizes. Major Moses inquired how headquarters would classify the Marine Barracks in Boston. While he was at it, in the same letter he asked whether the post council was authorized to pay per diem to the baker and if this came from the baker fund. The chief baker received 60 cents a day pay diem and his assistant received 45 cents a day from the bakery fund.[37]

Sergeant Hingle was a talented and inventive guy. He constructed a scheme for an expert rifleman's course for use in the shooting gallery. It must have been pretty good. Newport, RI, wanted one and had it installed at their Marine Barracks. Major Moses explained to Captain Fay at headquarters that another device had also been shipped to Port Royal, SC, for use.

Moses wanted to make sure Sergeant Hingle got proper credit for his scheme. He even gave it the name the "Hingle Gallery Device."[38]

There were still insufficient cells for use for short-term confinement. Major Moses asked Colonel McCawley, the quartermaster of the Marine Corps, to recall the visit he had with him and when he was assured an arrangement had been made for cells in the new administration building. Moses emphasized that the cell space was badly needed.[39]

The post council had approved the chief baker and his assistant's extra pay. First Lieutenant Edward A. Osterman and Second Lieutenant Leander A. Clapp comprised the post council, which had reviewed the recommendation for extra pay in June 1911.[40]

Horrible family news descended upon one Pvt. Walter A. Lacross. So bad that he just picked up and took off; he deserted. After a decent interval, he returned from desertion. Major Moses, knowing that the Marines who desert usually stay gone, or they return in chains, not hat in hand, was intrigued as to why Pvt. Lacross went AWOL like this. It turns out he made way for his hometown of Worcester where his parents lived. He learned they both recently died from tuberculosis. To compound matter further, Private Lacross's two sisters were also hospitalized with tuberculosis. His whole family was stricken with this dreadful disease. All these facts were verified by the Lacross family physician, Dr. Overlook. Lacross's sisters were probably minors. Major Moses recommended that Private Lacross be discharged as expeditiously as possible to care for the youngsters.[41]

This year's inter-postal rifle marksmanship match, an annual national competition, was held at Camp Perry in Ohio. Camp Perry is a little down shore of Toledo, a nice location on the coast of Lake Erie. The detachment heading there in early August consisted of First Sergeant Victor H. Czegka as the noncommissioned officer (NCO) in charge of 7 sergeants, 8 corporals and 25 privates. They were assigned to duty as markers.[42] They were to keep score.

Also in early August 1911, the commandant of the Navy yard appointed and convened a board on the protection of the Navy yard. The board was to study and offer recommendations for its safeguarding. Maybe after numerous and ongoing concerns from Marines Barracks commanding officers about the staffing of the established guard points on the yard, he took it upon himself to study the matter with his own resources.

After all the data was collected and compiled, the recommendations of the Board followed. Sentries should be maintained on a twenty-four hour basis at the Main Gate and also Gates 2, 3, 4 and 5. The waterfront's Post 6 should be manned from 0900 to 1600 hours (9 a.m. to 4 p.m. local), basically the duty hours of "day shift." This post should extend along the waterfront from Lincoln Avenue to the southern end of Pier No. 1. Then from 1600 to 0900 hours (4 p.m. to 9 a.m. the following day), the sentry would patrol a larger area, from the pay office, along Lincoln Avenue to the southern hydrant on the west side of coal and back again. Post 7 should extend from there, the southern hydrant on the west side of dry-dock 2, proceeding south to the sea entrance of the dry-dock and then along the waterfront east to Pier 5. Post 8 would extend from Pier 5 and run along Dock Street to Pier 9. Post 1 sentries should guard prisoners at the Marine Barracks' cells in the Administration Building on an as needed basis. Orderlies should report to duty at the residence and the office of the commandant of the Navy yard. They will also report to the general court-martial room and to the commanding officer of the Marine Barracks. A noncommissioned officer should patrol all buildings in the yard immediately after the day's working hours to ensure that all doors and windows are properly secured and to make sure nothing was left on, or left burning. When more Marines became available, a post would be established to patrol buildings east of 7th Street from 1700 to 0700,

5 p.m. to 7 a.m. The board also recommended that a suitable iron fence be provided to secure the space behind the northeast end of the ropewalk to Gate 4. The board recommended additional lighting along the waterfront between Piers 2 and 7.[43]

Having already experienced the utility of telephone communications throughout the yard, Major Moses requested that a telephone be installed in the office of the sergeant major of the Barracks. That the sergeant major administered all facets of Barracks operations was beyond dispute. With telephone service becoming more ubiquitous, the cost of telephones was inching down; the time had come for this busy office to have telephone service.[44] Life blissfully without telephones was still within living memory of quite a few people. Many living in modern times couldn't imagine life without phones, but these folks could.

In mid August 1911, headquarters directed each of the Marine Barracks throughout the United States to compile a list. On this list were to be named qualified Marines with good records and plenty of time left on their enlistments. Sounds like green Marines would fill the bill, just starting their careers, fresh from training and little time to affect their records. The Navy was setting up a U.S. Naval Disciplinary Barracks in Port Royal, SC, to be staffed by Marines. Accordingly, a proper list of eligible Marines was forwarded to Headquarters Marine Corps.[45]

Back in 1883 (from 1911's point of view), the federal government began buying up land on nearby Parris Island for a naval station. The station opened in 1889 but was mothballed by the turn of the century.

Probably because it was surplus land, in 1909 the Navy allowed the Marines to establish an officers' school there. A few years later, the Marines decided to open a recruiting depot in Port Royal in June 1911, under the Marine Officers' School command. At about the same time, the Navy Department decided to open a disciplinary barracks (prison) at the recruiting depot instead. On August 22 the recruiting depot became the Naval Disciplinary Barracks. The Navy ran the facility but the Marines staffed it. It was a mutually beneficial relationship: the Navy acquired experienced Marines and the naval paymaster paid for them, not the Marines.

Only several years later, as the numbers of naval prisoners decreased and the need for the facility declined, the Navy turned the property back over to the Marines for a recruiting depot. A Marine Barracks at Port Royal was established and began its duties. A great war also established itself in Europe and the most general recruitment since the Civil War unfolded. From November 1915 to modern times, the former naval station's primary mission was to train recruits. Training recruits for the Marines became centralized to there. No longer were they trained at their local barracks. The depot transformed the role of Marine Barracks across the land. The Marines started to become more recognizable to the modern mind. Any Marine knows the place as Parris Island: where Marines go for boot camp.

The naval prison at the navy yard enjoyed the Naval Disciplinary Barracks Company. In September 1911, six prisoners were transferred from the naval prison in Boston to the Naval Disciplinary Barracks in Port Royal.[46] Four days later seven more were sent along.[47]

The detachment at the naval magazine in Hingham, MA, was gaining more permanence. Major Moses recommended Sergeant Arthur E. Lee to Major General Biddle as qualified to be the noncommissioned officer in charge of the Hingham magazine and recommended his assignment.[48]

Corporal Edward Melvin was tried and convicted of murder in the second degree. He was sentenced to life imprisonment. On September 25, 1911, this story hit the newspapers. Major Moses asked the Clerk of the Superior Courts in Pemberton Square in Boston for an official notice of the courts' action. He needed these papers in order to prepare the proper documents to discharge Corporal Melvin from the service.[49] When he received them September 30, a letter was forwarded to headquarters with a copy of the court order and requested that Corporal Melvin receive with an undesirable discharge from the Marine Corps.[50]

October 1911, now Lieutenant Colonel Moses issued the following order: "Until further orders, liberty is stopped for all enlisted men from the barracks, by order of the medical officer. Men are warned that breaking quarantine is a very serious offense and is liable to subject the offender to trial by court-martial."[51] That could require a possible stint in the infamous and still open naval prison.

Two nine-year-old boys were strolling up their neighborhood, Chelsea Street, probably on their way to play, a stone toss north of Gate 2. On November 12 Private John Finley, while on duty as Gate 2 sentinel, allegedly beckoned them over to his guardhouse. Pvt. Finley allowed one boy to enter the guardhouse and then closed the Gate 2 gate. He sent the other lad off for a newspaper.

All this piqued the curiosity of a Charlestown women watching from the second story of a nearby building outside the yard. She sent a 14-year-old boy out to the gate to check it out, as he most likely played in that area and probably knew the boy. The teenager went out and approached the closed Gate 2. He had to ring the bell several times. It took the third ring for the gate to open. The middle schooler asked Pvt. Finley to let his friend go. Finley shooed the nine-year-old boy away.

Later, the boy said that Finley told him to stand in the corner while Finley opened his fly and reached over to open the boy's trousers. The boy said Finley took him by the neck and pushed him around. When the bell started ringing, Finley stopped and handed the boy a magazine and sat him on a stool. After the boy was released, he told the story to the lady who had observed the initial contact. The women told him to report it to the police.

Officer Michael J. Fealy of Station 15 came to the Marine Barracks to investigate the call. Lt. Col. Moses questioned the boys about the incident. And then Private Finley was summoned to his office. Other Marines were questioned as well. After all this, they were not able to make a positive identification.

The following day the 14-year-old boy was invited to Moses' office. Oddly, he was also unable to provide a positive identification.

The woman involved in all this did not want to get involved in any of it. Indeed she wanted her name to be kept out of the whole affair. Meanwhile, the affected boy pointed out the corner in the guardhouse where he had been told to stand. Both boys said the Marine in question had a brown mustache. Private Finley had a brown mustache. Lt. Col. Moses felt the incident did indeed take place as alleged. So much so, he recommended Private Finley be tried by general court-martial.[52] If convicted, he could go to the dreadful naval prison a block away. Lt. Col. Moses wrote to Major General Biddle about the avoidance of a very scandalous situation if he let the witnesses' testimony carry the day.

Gunnery Sergeant Daniel Daly received orders November 14, 1911, to report to the Marine detachment at the naval prison in Portsmouth, NH. He was in the midst of a most distinguished career as a Marine. He was one of seven Marines to have received the Medal of Honor. Twice. Of these Marines, only General Smedley Butler could pull it off. Daly won them in two separate actions. He was offered officer's commissions twice. He said he would rather be "an outstanding sergeant than just another officer."

In Peking, China, during the Boxer Rebellion of 1900, he held an advance post along the wall facing west toward the Chien Men gate. Alone.[53] But he had with him his trusty machine gun. He defended his position from repeated attacks and single-handedly took out 200 Boxers. He won a Medal of Honor for this.

Fifteen years later, after his tour at the Portsmouth Naval Prison, he distinguished himself again in Haiti. In 1915 he was a member of a patrol crossing a river in a deep ravine in darkness. The detachment was then ambushed by 400 irregulars hidden in the bush. The animal carrying the only machine gun of the patrol was killed in midstream. Gunnery Sergeant Daly, responsible for the gun, went back into the night-lit river and got it. He earned a second Medal of Honor for this action.[54] The Marines fought their way out and held their ground until morning from a defensible position, thanks to this gun.[55]

Fast forward to the Great War. Gunnery Sergeant Daly on 5 June 1918 at Lucy-le-Bocage extinguished a fire at an ammunition dump, very dangerous. Two days later, under heavy bombardment, perhaps preparing to be attacked, Daly visited all of his gun crews over a wide area and kept up the morale of his men. Three days later, he attacked an enemy machine gun emplacement alone and captured it with nothing but hand grenades and his automatic pistol. Later that day, he brought in wounded under fire. Then, in the battle of Belleau Wood, the famous World War I correspondent Floyd Gibbons reported to the world he heard him yell to his platoon during an attack, "Come on, you sons of bitches! Do you want to live forever?!"[56] The words live on. A new generation experienced the inspiring words in the 2012 video game Call of Duty: Black Ops 2. The intro to the last level asks the player, "Come on Bitch you wanna live forever?"

Lt. Col. Henry C. Haines, the assistant adjutant and inspector, inspected the Barracks. The results were not too flattering. Twenty-one members of the command were wearing civilian shoes during his inspection. This resulted in the major general commandant directing that steps be taken to ensure that all men wear regular issue shoes, unless there was a reason approved by the medical officer.[25]

On August 24, the secretary of the Navy issued a directive to the Major General Commandant. This crossed the Navy-Marines line. Enlisted men of the Marine Corps serving General Courts martial sentences involving the loss of allowances, were directed to be transferred from both the naval prison in Charlestown and the facility in Portsmouth, NH, to the U.S. Naval Disciplinary Barracks in Port Royal, SC. The secretary of the Navy also directed that loss of allowances be remitted in order for the men to have clothing issued to them.[58]

During the next two years following this secretary of the Navy directive, 53 Marine and 60 Navy personnel serving sentences of general courts-martial were transferred from the naval prison in the Charlestown to the U.S. Naval Disciplinary Barracks at Port Royal, SC.[59]

The Barracks possessed a motorboat named *Samar*. It was the property of the post exchange and was used for recreational purposes by the members of the command. The Navy yard officials were very generous and cooperative and provided storage of the boat in a shed during the winter months and hoisted the boat in and out of the water whenever it was required. The Marines were very appreciative of the efforts of the Navy yard.[60]

The junior officers' quarters had been languishing in poor condition for years, and it had become necessary to provide the junior officers with commutation of quarters payments to enable them to live in the civilian community since there were no suitable quarters available for them at the Barracks. This included both married and single officers.

The discussions on plans to renovate the east end of the Barracks lasted a least a year. Several plans were proposed. All of the schemes essentially provided for four sets of flats interchangeable for single officers or married officers. The major concern was the amount of space that would have to be added to the front of the east end of the building. The commandant of the Navy yard objected to the initial plans since he thought that too much was added to the front of the east end.[61]

This was finally resolved and everyone concerned agreed on scheme 2, which provided for an apartment on each floor consisting of a chamber (12 feet by 13 feet), two bedrooms (10 by 13), a living room (14 by 17), a dining room (16 by 16), a kitchen (11½ by 14), a bathroom (7 by 8½), a maid's room with separate bathroom (9 by 11½), a pantry, a butler's pantry and a trunk room.[62]

On May 29, 1914, R.E. Bakenhus, the yard civil engineer, wrote to the commandant of the Marine corps and requested $14,500 for alterations to the east end of the building to provide quarters for the junior officers.[63]

15. Shipshape Under Major Hall

*"The ancient, inadequate and dilapidated Marine Barracks
need but a word and that is condemnation"*
—Annual Report of the Medical Officer of the Yard for 1914

On January 5, 1915, Major Newt B. Hall assumed command of the Marine Barracks. Fifteen years prior, he had distinguished himself during the Boxer Rebellion in May 1900. He was second in command when he joined up his 26 Marines from the USS *Newark* with those of Captain John Myers. The combined detachments commandeered a tug to haul supplies the forty miles up the river to Tientsin. Captain Hall led his forces from the legation compound and cleared the street at bayonet point. He later took over command after Captain Myers' leg became badly infected.[1]

On January 25, 1915, the commandant of the Charlestown Navy Yard recommended to the major general commandant that the Marine Corps should seriously consider tearing down the present Marine Barracks and erecting new facilities. Admiral W.R. Rush quoted paragraph 7 of the Annual Report of the Medical Officer of the Yard for 1914 as follows:

> Marine Barracks. The ancient, inadequate and dilapidated Marine Barracks need but a word and that is condemnation. Every Annual Sanitary Report of which there is any record in this office contains pages devoted to enumerating the many defects of the place and pointing out how unsanitary it is and how impossible of betterment except by complete demolition. There is nothing I can add to what has already been said except that all these conditions have grown steadily worse as time has gone on, and that today the building is absolutely unfit for habitation as a barracks. The only reason I can see why disease has not flourished there, as the lower animal life has, is because it has never been successfully introduced, but if an epidemic should ever start, nothing but fire and a kind Providence would ever eradicate it. It is quite plain to me that every man who is forced to live in this building must suffer to a greater or less extent in his general vitality and energy.[2]

It had been a long time since the lime shed days when this building was the Boston Marines' comfortable new home.

Three days later, Major General Barnett wrote to Admiral Rush and acknowledged receipt of the January 25 letter. General Barnett also said he forwarded a copy of the report of the conditions of the Barracks to the secretary of the Navy. He added that the dilapidated and unsanitary condition of the Barracks had been the subject of repeated reports, with no movement. Barnett hoped that sufficient appropriations for a new building could be made in the near future. He deeply regretted that nothing more definite could be done at the time.[3]

Improvements were in progress at the Barracks nonetheless. On February 13, 1915, R.E. Bakenhus, the yard civil engineer, asked the commandant of the Navy yard that the project to renovate the east end of the Barracks be expedited. The property was sitting there lying idle and in its present condition was of no service whatsoever. The officers that should be occupying the quarters are paid a commutation of quarters allowance and must live off base.[4]

Months later, June 11, the improvements to the junior officers' quarters had been approved by the Bureau of Yards and Docks. The bureau also approved that the yard civil engineer could do the work with his people and equipment.[5] On September 1, Major General Barnett approved the remodeling project and authorized $13,500 of the Bureau of Supplies' inventory for the project. The cost would be charged to maintenance under the Quartermaster Department of the Marine Corps in 1916.[6]

On August 15, 1915, Major Hall turned over command of the Barracks and shipped out for duty in the Caribbean. It had been the sea of pirates, hostiles, commerce, and maneuvering by powers from outside the Western Hemisphere for hundreds of years. Major Hall's ship was not steaming towards Haiti, but to the other side of Hispanola, the Dominican Republic.

In May 1916, the United States was at "peace," when it came to the Great War. Marines were already on the other side of the island in Haiti. In May, 375 Marines and 225 sailors amphibiously (waterborne) assaulted the ancient walled city of Santo Domingo, the oldest city in the New World.[7] The city was taken and the United States began its occupation of the Dominican Republic. The Dominican Republics' political instability aroused North American attention. It was enough to consider, and follow though on, intervention. Europe was in the midst of a Great War with no end in sight. The American Army crossed the border into Mexico. And now Marines swarmed over the whole island. War was the way of the world in 1916.

The renovations at the junior officers' quarters uncovered previously unknown problems. No "as-built" drawings existed for any of the many modifications made over the years. In places where a curtain wall (merely creating rooms) was indicated, the wall turned out to be a bearing wall (supporting the building structure) instead, and thus required changes to the plans. Chimney work should have been and could have been included in the plans but weren't. The project was eventually accomplished.[8]

Back home at the yard in May 1916—while other Marines were amphibiously assaulting ancient walled cities, while General John J. Pershing and his men were penetrating Mexico ever deeper in search of Pancho Villa, while the Battle at Verdun had been killing and destroying hundreds of thousands of French and German men for months, while British volunteers were gathering for an offensive at the Somme River, while Allied maneuvers in the Middle East were occurring which would ultimately finish off the ancient Ottoman Empire and shape the modern Middle East—the shipyard commander asked for the Barracks to send Marines to report to the master joiner in Building 36. He wanted them to pick a piece of scroll work which would be suitable for use at the Barracks as part of a coat of arms. The coat of arms would be displayed in a prominent part of the building.[9]

The beginning of hostilities in Europe in 1914 had little impact on the tempo of activity at the Charlestown facility until the latter part of 1916.[10] Although a peacetime quality lingered over repair activities in the yard, the war and its possible effect on the Navy Yard was on everyone's mind.[11] While the yard slowly began to prepare for war, it had picked up a role in the enforcement of United States neutrality. The number of passenger and merchant ships flying the flags of the Central Powers created a need to actively defend America's neutrality.[12] The geographical locale of Boston as a major seaport made it one of the choices. The shipyard commandant also had authority as the commandant of the First Naval District. This sealed the deal for the Navy yard to begin to perform quasi-military assignments.

Once American participation in the European war became a real and imminent possibility, changes occurred in the Navy yard. A real gate pass system began as an effort to control entry into the yard in February 1917. Previously, except for the prohibition of visitors during the Spanish-American War, there was no formal pass system used on a permanent basis.[13] A wall was built around the Navy yard and Marines manned the gates. It took entry into a very major war indeed to begin a permanent pass system. A gate pass procedure existed for a very brief period in 1909,[14] as mentioned earlier. When the war in Europe began, there was no system of passes available to provide identification of yard workers. By December 1914, as a precaution against thefts of government property, the commandant of the Navy yard instructed his staff to develop a manageable system of badges.[15]

Instructions issued in 1916 directed Marine sentries to prevent entry into the yard certain categories of people deemed undesirable: "women of questionable character" and "Italian laborers." No packages or bundles could be brought out of the yard without authorization. The exceptions included officers, members of their families, and their servants or orderlies.[16]

February 1, 1917, a credible gate pass system began. Various groups, laborers, sailors, Marines, authorized civilians, military dependants, depending on their status, were issued passes of different colors. All persons that entered the Navy yard were required to possess a pass.[17]

A small fire occurred in the junior officers' quarters occupied by First Lieutenant John Quincy Adams. First Lieutenant Adams' report to Lt. Col. Hall about the incident said:

> 1. At 6.10 p.m. March 8, 1917, Martin J. Johnson, Engine No. 37 (Fire Boat), and D. Condon, Ladder No. 1, of the city fire department, who were on Chelsea Street opposite No. 4 gate, discovered a fire burning in the kitchen window of my quarters. The above named men turned in the alarm for the city fire department from box No. 427, on Chelsea Street, and then proceeded to the scene of the fire and extinguished same with two small, hand fire extinguishers. 2. The fire was caused by my wife who emptied an ash tray into a waste paper basket, she not realizing that there was a smoldering cigarette stump burning in the tray. The damage was insignificant as the paint on the window sill was scorched. The fact that fire did not gain headway there from was due to prompt action taken by Martin J. Johnson and D. Condon, who were off duty at the time and on the way to their homes.[18]

Mr. O.A. Thayer had shown interest to bid on the contract to rebuild the Marine Barracks. On April 25, 1918, Ensign M. Griswold, U.S. Naval Reserve Force, responded. Back in 1913, the proposal was the subject of considerable correspondence between the Navy yard, Headquarters Marine Corps, the Bureau of Yards and Docks and the secretary of the Navy. Ensign Griswold informed Thayer that the secretary of the Navy had shown no interest at this time (1918) to rebuild the Marine Barracks.[19]

During World War I, the Navy yard employed approximately ten thousand workers, who labored on 450 different vessels. The Navy yard essentially performed such a volume of work this period that it was unmatched in the previous century of its existence. Many shops in the yard began to work around the clock, seven days a week.[20] This was when the Navy yard acquired the South Boston Annex, during the World War. This provided the Navy with the largest drydock in the world. There was with little else there in South Boston other than a pump house and two piers. The recently gained facilities now needed Marine guards assigned to the South Boston Annex.[21]

The peace of the 1920's saw a contraction in the number of civilian employees in the yard. By the end of 1920, 5,865 workers staffed the offices and shops around the yard. Ten years later, this dropped to 1,687 employees. Activities connected with World War I lingered into the early 1920's but continued to decline. The yard's return to a peacetime footing was accomplished through layoffs.[22]

Colonel George Van Orden became the Marine Barracks' commanding officer on July 2, 1920. He had distinguished himself in 1915, when he was the commander of an improvised battalion of sailors and two companies of fleet Marines from the armored cruiser USS *Washington*. They landed at Port-au-Prince, the lawless anarchic capital of Haiti. Disorganized sniper fire made the mission dangerous. But Orden's men persevered and restored order to its streets so its citizens could feel safe enough to resume commerce, and their daily lives.[23]

On January 27, 1921, Colonel Van Orden received the report of the inspection by Colonel L.J Magill, assistant adjutant and inspector, Headquarters Marine Corps. The report was very gratifying.

Rear Admiral S.S. Robison, commandant of the Navy yard, commended the Marines for their fine showing. The inspection report noted that the cells in the Administration Building were not being utilized. They were using instead the cells in the old naval prison (Building 38). The Marines referred to it as the Navy Brig. Marines from the Barracks again manned the brig.[24] The naval prison had been closed and the last of its prisoners had been transferred to the new Naval Prison in Portsmouth, N.H.

The archaic heating system in the Barracks was causing major problems. The best solution was to tie into the yard stream supply and remove the old coal fired furnaces. Major H.O.

November 1, 1930, the Barracks and the administration building are pictured with the Mustering Building, which still stands, in the background.

March 19, 1921, the newly and comprehensively renovated Marine Barracks. It was built in the day before fireproof stairwells were required. Chelsea Street was still there.

September 5, 1923, the commanding officer's deck is enclosed.

Smith, the post quartermaster, wrote the public works officer of the Navy yard to request a connection with steam supply system in the yard.[25]

The old independent heating plant in the Barracks cost too much in repairs and the best long-range plan was to use the yard steam system.[26] On July 5, 1920, the endorsement of Colonel Van Orden gave approval to Major Smith's request for a contract with Bradlee and Chatman Co. of 54 Canal Street in Boston to install the steam line and establish a new heating plant in the Barracks.

The Yard Welfare Laundry operated for years and provided service to the Navy yard and the Marine Barracks as well as the naval ammunition depot at Hingham, and the Boston recruiting officer. Due to a considerable drop in volume of laundry throughout the Navy yard, it was scheduled for closure. The Marines now needed to find another place to do their laundry.[27]

Recreational activities for Barracks personnel were more important than they might seem at first glance. Colonel Van Orden asked the major general commandant that tennis courts be constructed on the southeast corner of the parade ground. The requirements were 50 by 120 feet in size, 5 feet thick with an 8 foot cinder bed.[28] They still stand today ready for volley.

After the connection to the yard steam system was complete, everybody looked around to see what else could be updated. They zeroed in on the aging galley (kitchen) equipment. The old coal boilers were also slated to be taken out. Natural gas came up as the latest in the state of the art of heating, but steam was thought more dependable than the proposed alternate gas installation.[29] On August 26 the steam connection project was completed. Major H.O. Smith, the post quartermaster, approved the payment of $3,500 to Bradlee and Chatment, 54 Canal Street, Boston.[30]

The Barracks were inspected November 15, 1922, by Major Richard B. Creecy, assistant adjutant and inspector from headquarters. The report included the following.

There were present for inspection 7 officers, 18 non-commissioned officers, 2 musicians and 89 privates. The uniform was winter field: field hats, leggings, rifles and belts. Major Creecy's impression was that the command presented an excellent appearance and executed the inspection ceremony in a smart and soldierly manner.

The condition and fit of the clothing was excellent and all articles of clothing were properly marked. Arms and accouterments were in excellent condition and each man had the required articles of clothing and equipment. It was noted that the new style stiff brim field hats, furnished by the depot quartermaster in Philadelphia under the invoice dated July 7, 1922, were unsatisfactory. The size 7⅛ hats corresponded in size to the old style size but the new hats failed to conform to the shape of the men's heads. Their inside shape was more nearly round than oblong.

The guard was properly accounted for. Its members were found to be properly instructed, and their appearance and bearing were excellent. The guard-room and cells were properly arranged and in excellent police. The cells were secure and the facilities for policing prisoners were ample and satisfactory. Public property on charge to the guard was properly accounted for. The guard maintained 6 sentinel posts and 3 orderly posts. The command executed close and extended order drill in a smart and soldierly manner. Signal drill, in wig-wag and semaphore, was executed in a satisfactory manner. A Barracks fire drill was held, in which 8 extinguishers, 12 fire buckets and 2 fire ladders were brought to the scene of the fire within 25 seconds of the sounding of the fire call. The buildings consist of an old brick barracks building and an administration building, also of brick. The buildings were in very good condition and were secure against fire. A note was made that all seats and urinals were in the basement of the barracks building, and it was recommended that a reasonable amount of these toilet facilities be installed in the upper stories of the barracks building. With the exception of the lack of toilet facilities near the squad-rooms, the enlisted men's quarters were conveniently arranged, adequate, comfortable and in excellent sanitary condition. All furniture and fixtures were in very good condition. The sick were cared for in the Navy yard dispensary and the naval hospital in Chelsea. The messing facilities, kitchen and mess hall furniture and equipment were found to be in excellent condition. The food was properly cooked and served and the mess was administered in a highly satisfactory manner. The system of receipt and issue of subsistence stores was efficiently administered. Ample opportunity was afforded to all members of the command to be personally interviewed on the subject of the mess. No complaints were made.

The post library was examined and found to be neatly arranged and properly cared for, with a sufficient number of books to meet the requirements of the post. The post bakery was well arranged, had all the necessary equipment and turned out bread of excellent quality. Its average daily capacity was 150 pounds of bread. There was no post laundry. The post quartermaster had a contract with a civilian laundry company for the laundering of public property, and the enlisted men's work was done at the Navy yard laundry. The accounts of the Company Fund were audited and found to be in excellent condition. All receipts and expenditures were supported by proper vouchers. The post treasurer, First Lieutenant Lucas I. Bruns, U.S. Marine Corps, was in charge of the fund. There were no liabilities. The storerooms for clothing and public property were conveniently arranged, secure against fire and theft, and in excellent police. The grounds, fences, walks, road, trees and shrubbery were in excellent police. The motor transportation assigned to this post consisted of one 1-ton white truck, which was found to be in very good condition. All officers in the command had in their possession the required articles of uniform and equipment and their files of orders and publications were up to date. In compliance with recent memoranda issued by the adjutant and inspector, a thorough inquiry was made into the following matters: sale of ice, use of motor transportation, employment of enlisted men as servants, use of public animals, purchases of fuel, purchase of forage, public property issued on memorandum receipts, preparation of ration returns, and duties of gunnery sergeants. It was found that existing regulations were carefully complied with in these matters. The command was in an excellent state of discipline and the men appeared to be contented and interested in their work, notwithstanding the fact that there had been an average monthly turnover of personnel amounting to about twenty-seven percent. The inspecting officer made a general statement that it was his opinion that this post was in an excellent state of discipline and was administered in such a manner that it carried out its assignments in very efficient manner. The men practiced before Headquarters came. The men were inspected in their squadrooms, with clothing, packs and equipment laid out on the bunks, just like the real thing.

Discrepancies at the post exchange prompted an investigation. The post exchange (PX) was carefully examined and all accounts audited from date of last inspection. The report concluded the PX was efficiently run and met the requirements of Paragraphs 1 and 2, Section 1201 of Exchange Regulations of 1921. Marine Gunnery Sgt. John S. McNulty was the post exchange officer. Cash on hand was counted and verified. The reported shortage in merchandise was thoroughly investigated by the inspecting officer. It was determined that Private First Class Parker H. Holmes and Royal D. Howard, former exchange steward and assistant exchange steward, respectively, misappropriated exchange funds and merchandise totaling $1,034.75. They are awaiting trial by general court-martial for these allegations.

The above mentioned men allegedly ordered merchandise from various dealers without the authority or knowledge of the post exchange officer, sold it to the post exchange, and did not account for the proceeds of the sales. They were also held responsible for shortages in inventories for the months of August and September 1922.

In addition to the disciplinary action, a claim had been made by the bonding company for reimbursement. The commanding officer had taken all possible measures to prevent further unauthorized deliveries of merchandise to the exchange. It was the opinion of the inspecting officer that only by frequent and unexpected inventories could the presence of unauthorized merchandise in the post exchange have been detected. While such inventories might have been made, there appeared to be no particular reason for such action prior to the discovery of irregularities in the stewards' accounts. The inspecting officer, however, suggested to the exchange officer that it would be advisable to make unexpected inventories of merchandise from time to time.[31] There appeared to be no necessity for other disciplinary action in this matter.

Improvements to the washroom, mess hall and galley of the Barracks involved a considerable amount of work. The commandant of the yard notified the Bureau of Yards and Docks of the requirements. The first floor of the wing of the building enclosing the galley had been enlarged by moving the wall outward. The load of the floors above and roof were carried on steel I-beams spanning the galley, toilet and washroom. The design included a waterproof concrete floor to be laid over the present wood flooring. Support was stiffened by two steel I-beams. A column was placed under the center of the existing beam span to provide additional dead load. Careful finishing of the concrete floor and proper reinforcement could obtain the waterproof quality. An investigation of the beams under the wooden part of the galley floor indicated they would not be safe to support the new concrete floor.[32] The project was completed on June 21 at a cost of $4,275.07.[33]

Rear Admiral L.R. De Steiguer of the Bureau of Yards and Docks wrote to the major general commandant and provided an estimate of $80,000 to tear out the interior of the present Barracks and rebuild from the ground up. He indicated that the exterior wall would be used and the two wings would be raised two stories.

But an expenditure of this magnitude would require an appropriation from Congress.[34] The major general commandant in his endorsement stated that while he would prefer to do these extensive repairs, he realized the hopelessness of getting $80,000 from Congress. Plan B would be that the bureau make an estimate of absolutely necessary repairs in order to keep it serviceable and in a satisfactory condition for ten more years. Major General Lejeune hoped that by then, political conditions in the nation would improve to the extent that Congress would look more favorably upon reenacting appropriations for a new Barracks, which had been given in 1913, but cancelled shortly afterwards.[35]

An improvement deemed absolutely necessary involved the electrical rewiring of the whole building. The commandant of the Navy yard desired to use yard people to do the job. There was a considerable amount of dead wiring in the building needing to be removed and the yard forces would do a better job, in his opinion he rendered to his boss, the Bureau of Yards and Docks.[36] The bureau agreed and on June 11, 1924 the chief of the Bureau of Yards and Docks approved the use of yard people. On the books they were to be carried as "continuing" Project No. 9 so it could be carried over into the next fiscal year.[37]

Remember the $80,000 price tag on proper permanent overhaul of the Barracks requiring approval from Congress? They approved it. The work was done. The Barracks stand solid today well into the 21st Century, outlasting its use as a Marine Barracks.[38]

15. *Shipshape Under Major Hill*

In 1941, while the United States was at peace, the Marine Barracks got fireproof stairwells put in and a modern strong reinforced steel and concrete porch. The façade fundamentally changed.

March 6, 1941, progress on the stairwell and porch.

The completed renovation with an early World War II era mustering.

On March 30, 1926, the 301st Company of the Marine Corps Reserve (USMCR) was ordered to Quantico, Virginia, for annual training. This was the first time in six years that it had been involved with training away from the Navy yard. Training had been suspended since the World War.[39] Fast forward over five years later to July 21, 1931. The 301st Company USMCR was being considered for expansion into a battalion. There was concern, however, if suitable armory (secure place to hold weapons) facilities could be found on the Navy yard to accommodate a battalion size unit.[40] The 301st Company, USMCR, had a strength of 2 officers and 60 enlisted in March 1932.[41] The reserve unit was now the 2d Battalion. It was to be located in Building 36 in the Navy yard, the old naval prison building.[42] The unit's annual training duty would be at Portsmouth, New Hampshire, during the period June 16 to 30. The battalion consisted of Battalion Headquarters, 3 officers and 6 enlisted; Company A, 2 officers and 47 enlisted; and Company B, 1 officer and 37 enlisted.[43]

By January 1940, stringent budgetary constraints caused the reduction of Marine Barracks personnel to the extent that civilian guards manned the gates and patrolled the waterfront and the shipyard perimeters.[44]

The Band

The Marine Barracks was not authorized to have a marching band. So in 1944 well into World War II, volunteers formed a marching band. Individual Marines with musical ability and experience from school and church bands made up the ranks. The genius behind the formation of the musical group was an older Marine called to active duty for World War II and assigned to Marine Barracks. Sal was the only name he was known by. From the North End of Boston, Sal had been a member of the Boston Roma Band. Sal scavenged musical instruments from friends, teachers, and any other source available. He interviewed every incoming Marine to determine whether they had the requisite musical skills. The volunteers practiced at the Barracks. When the band matured into a marching unit, they paraded up and down an isolated street near the ropewalk playing music arranged by a friend of Sal's. This friend rearranged the music to accommodate for instruments they did not possess. Commanding Officer Colonel Pierce knew headquarters would not authorize an official marching band. Pierce fortunately had no objection to members of the Barracks forming a band for recreational purposes. After several weeks of practice, the Marine Barracks marching band made its debut at the Armistice Day (Nov. 11, soon to be known as Veterans' Day) parade of 1944. The 24 proud Marines, four across and six rows deep, were met with cheers from the crowds of spectators as they marched down Tremont Street in downtown Boston.

When they reached the reviewing stand, the music stopped. Only the marching feet of the Marines broke the silence. When the color guard reached the reviewing stand, the band struck up the "Marine's Hymn." The cheering crowds went wild. Everyone was unbelievably proud. None more so than Colonel Pierce. He was standing with the dignitaries on the reviewing stand.[45] Perhaps the "bean counters" who wouldn't authorize the marching band know the cost of everything but the value of nothing.

PART IV—TWILIGHT

16. Lt. Col. Yates, the Vietnam Era and Memories Preserved

"Land the landing force."
—Rear Admiral J.C. Wylie.

On 13 July 1969, Col. Edward H. Mackel received command of the Boston Marine Barracks. Mackel's Marine Barracks responsibilities spanned the turn of the decades. An institution tradition bound with over one hundred fifty years of history, this Barracks Mackel inherited at the height of the Vietnam War. Although the war turned a page during this period, it didn't feel like it as the war news droned on and on.

When the Vietnam War became America's commitment in the mid '60's a few years before, the Marine Corps resurrected the practice of notifying the next of kin for Marines killed or wounded in Vietnam. Officers make personal visits to these family members.

On Mackel's watch the war went full scale. His junior officers took on the notification responsibility almost full time. They went anywhere throughout the eastern Massachusetts area. All too often these officers visited nice people and delivered sad news face to face in the most humane way the corps could full scale. It was emotionally draining on these men. The work wasn't done there. The Barracks, the junior officers really, assisted the family with funeral arrangements, military honors, pay and insurance claims.

A duty not much more pleasant then notification was delivering deserters to their East Coast stations. As the Vietnam War soured into unpopularity, desertions became dangerously high, particularly by conscripts drafted for the war.

When a Marine went AWOL the pattern was that they would usually return to their hometowns. A unit would simply contact the next of kin and the local police of his home of record.

The local police were usually the ones who found the deserter first. The individual was then turned over to the Barracks for disposition. A determination was made as to whether the Marine would have returned on his own volition or not. If so, he was housed at the Barracks until headquarters issued orders to have him transferred to his unit. If not, he was sent to the naval brig, no longer called a prison, in the Fargo Building in South Boston.

When orders from headquarters were cut, noncommissioned officers from the Barracks escorted the detainee to his assigned unit, usually Camp Lejeune, NC, or Cherry Point, NC. The only duty of these "prison chasers" was to return deserters. Years later the desertion rate was corrected by raising standards of recruitment.

The early 1970's brought on a new decade with an uncertain future. From its beginnings as a sailing ship era shipyard with a perennially useful drydock, everybody around felt that since the Charlestown shipyard had been there for such a long time, everybody expected it to continue repairing ships. There was a war on and business was steady.

The late sixties counterculture hair fashion for men was long and plentiful. Hair lengths had not been seen for a hundred years, since the last sixties (1860's, which also had a war on). By the early '70's longer hair length on men became more mainstream and ubiquitous. This contrasted starkly against the trim Marine appearance. Times they were a-changing.

Although President Richard M. Nixon had begun gradually pulling troops out of Vietnam, the war was on its sixth year and felt endless. In the midst of all this, on 14 October 1971, Col. Mackel completed his command of the Barracks. Ret. Col. Mackel spent his last tour at the Barracks before his retirement. He moved his family to his wife's hometown in Wells, ME.

Restless in retirement, he immediately became active in town, county, and state politics. He was elected twice to the state House of Representatives. After his service to the state he became the chairman of the York Republican Committee. With this network he became involved in the George H. W. Bush presidential campaign in 1980. Subsequently he also served in the Reagan-Bush campaign of 1984. Mackel throttled back from the national campaigns and became vice chairman of the Wells Republican Town Committee for four years. Finally he served two terms as selectman and established a Christmas tree farm before succumbing to cancer.

Lt. Col. John R. Yates assumed command of the Boston Marine Barracks on 15 October 1971. Lt. Col. Yates encountered the same push and pull of any Barracks commander of the previous one hundred sixty years. Troops to dispatch on outgoing vessels, gates to man although the Main Gate (a 24 hour gate), #2 walk in gate (daytime), #4 walk in gate (daytime), and #5 drive through gate (day time) seemed to be manageable. Long gone, however, was the naval prison and its headaches. Also long gone was the floating prison ship the USPS *Southerly* tied up at dock side along with the floating Marine Barracks ship the USRS *Wabash*. Yates met these staffing responsibilities with those bunked in the Boston Marine Barracks. Even the Vietnam War seemed routine and part of the background. Perhaps as other wars did as well at the Boston Naval Ship Yard.

Lt. Col. Yates also went on a casualty assistance call to an eastern Massachusetts area. This call was to the island of Martha's Vineyard, virtually heaven on earth during summer. He and a junior officer flew down by helicopter to deliver papers to the widow of a brigadier general who died of natural causes.

On a crisp fall Sunday afternoon in 1973, Lt. Col. Yates and his family, all packed in a '68 pea green Buick Sports Wagon, were driving home to the Barracks. Lt. Col. Yates and his wife and kids spent their afternoon at the Revere drive-in theater flea market by the rotary of Routes 1 and 1A. Nowadays the location is the multiplex visible from the highway. The Yates family had to thread their way home though the city of Chelsea. The usual way home was closed.

As they approached the Main Gate, the bright blue lights of Boston police cruisers rotated in their all too real way, dominating the scene. Yates halted the family station wagon and got out. He told his wife, Virginia, to go ahead and drive the kids home, he needed to be there.

On the fine Sunday afternoon, a Marine was just outside the Main Gate off duty working on his car. This car was a loud early seventies muscle car that let the neighborhood know of its power and robust exhaust. Nearby, maybe 100 feet away, was a bar with a nefarious reputation. Throughout the whole city of Boston, there were only two bars labeled out of bounds for all military and naval personnel. One was in the "Combat Zone." This was the other one.

A man burst out of the bar waving a pipe. Irate about the noise, he smashed the windshield

16. Lt. Col. Yates, the Vietnam Era, and Memories Preserved

of the Marine's car. The young Marine called to the Main Gate sentry to stop him. The crazed pipe swinger came at the sentinel. The guard ordered the man to halt. No results. He fired his pistol in the air. Ineffective. Pipeman continued to move toward the sentry with raised pipe. The sentry fired to wound him. The family of the individual shot by the Marine sentry filed charges against the Marine in Charlestown District Court.

Just as this drama stabilized, smoke was rising across the Mystic River from the City of Chelsea. Only hours before the Yates family had meandered their way through its narrow streets. Flames rose and took on incredible energy. Not just a triple decker on fire but whole city blocks. It grew into the Great Chelsea Fire of 1973. Many from the shipyard could only look on in safety across the Mystic River at the awful glow of orange and pink above the silhouette of dark low buildings shrouded by massive black-brown billowing clouds of smoke rising high beyond the Mystic River Bridge that eerie evening.[1]

The Mystic River Bridge was colossal, modern, vital, a green metal structure rising into a cobalt blue sky when looking up at it from the east end, the land's end of the shipyard. The Tobin Bridge, as it is also called, connects the north shore to Boston and points southbound. It is a primary northbound route out of the city of Boston. Already an inescapable part of the Boston skyline, it was an imposing structure. Southbound drivers on the upper deck, moribund at the tollbooths, at least enjoyed a striking vista of the city of Boston from high up while

Aerial view of the newly completed Mystic River Bridge taking over where Chelsea Street once ran, leaving a barren alleyway between the modern bridge and the shipyard. The all-day shadow of the bridge, however, fell upon Charlestown and not the barracks.

Monthly formations in summer only. Any awards, citations or retirements are acknowledged during these events.

they waited. The great Mystic River Bridge was only across the street (Chelsea Street) from the shipyard.

Early fall 1973, in the morning twilight commute, an overweight truck was barreling though northbound on the lower level of the double decker bridge that crosses the wide and busy Mystic River. This part of the bridge was level with and right behind the commandant's house and the Marine Barracks. A thundering metallic thud, unusual during the early morning commute, aroused Lt. Col. Yates from slumber. He climbed to the upper floor of his quarters to have a look at where the noise came from.

The truck had plowed into a support girder, killing the driver instantly. With the support girder taken out, the southbound upper deck failed. The pavement on the upper deck dipped under surprised commuters. Traffic on top ground to a halt given the immediate danger. A traffic jam of epic proportions ensued. Remarkable is that traffic stopped and did not continue over the unsupported bridge.

The day unfolded and the facts started to set in that this important bridge had indeed been taken out, not just for hours or days, but for months. This was one of the most major disruptions of traffic in Boston for decades, until the Big Dig. An enemy bomber couldn't have taken out this vital bridge more effectively.

Chelsea Street in the early 1970's was a ghost of what it once was. The gigantic bridge had wedged itself in between Charlestown and the ancient ivy covered stone walls of the shipyard. Other than the daily comings and goings of the walking working commuters, Chelsea Street was little but an alleyway with a small bar outside walking Gate 4 providing libations for off duty shipyard workers.

This day Chelsea Street was alive as the center of attention of the New England news media. The day wore on. The scene was so delicate that the body of the driver was still in the truck cabin into the afternoon. School kids were getting out of school. They were converging on the scene as well. Everybody wanted a better look, including local Charlestown kids. The best view for kids was on top of the old stone wall and kids were climbing the best access onto it, in between the commandant's house and the Marine Barrack's commander's quarters.

Unauthorized personnel were climbing the walls, a clear breach of security. Lt. Col. Yates lent his presence to the scene. The local "townie" children got an earful about the sanctity of shipyard security from Lt. Col. Yates, one of his primary duties to maintain.

With the immediate danger alleviated and the new commuting realty sinking in, an unexpected quiet descended upon the area. Weeks turned into months of construction. An office trailer was set up behind the Marine Barracks commander's quarters. The whole ordeal became a lesson contemporaries never forgot.

Most members of the Barracks were unaffected by the loss of the bridge and spent no time in commutes. With no commute and no driving necessary, Barracks personnel enjoyed free time either in the Marine Barracks Officer's Club located underneath the junior officers' quarters or the Enlisted Men's Club located underneath the Administration Building, depending on their rank. Dank, dark, underground, they were nonetheless a place to gather with friends. Ubiquitous cigarette and cigar smoke, its residue, and stale beer smell all permeated completely each setting, betraying their use.

The probable cause hearing for the young sentry involved in the Main Gate shooting was coming up quick. The young sentry needed defense. A reserve Marine lieutenant colonel was called to active duty. The sentry's representation showed up, and happened to be one of Boston's more experienced criminal attorneys. He worked his magic. Nonetheless the hearing proceeded duly.

The final verdict came in: "No probable cause." The young Marine was exonerated. There was more. The person shot was bound over to the grand jury for attempted assault with a deadly weapon, "to wit a steel pipe."

A short walk from the Barracks the building that used to be the naval prison, the post exchange (PX), a library with a bowling alley located right above it, and a movie theater viewing second run movies for 30 cents now occupy its space.

It wasn't all Marines around the Barracks. Wouldn't that be nice? The officers of the Barracks children were a daily and included part of Barracks life. They played everywhere they were allowed to go, and sometimes found where they weren't allowed to go. They often played in the tennis courts. Sometimes they were mistaken for Charlestown locals who might have gotten onto the yard in an unauthorized fashion. They would come and go through the Main Gate either on the gray Navy school bus taking them to school everyday in Brookline or they would walk in and out of the gate to the old City Square elevated T station for the orange line to Boston. Provided, of course, they carried their Military dependent ID card with them when they did this. In the minds of these children, the shipyard was their home and their playground, they were entitled to this.

This even included pets. Lt. Col. Yates' cat Patches called the shipyard his territory. He was often seen strolling about along the ropewalk and entering and exiting as it pleased through Gate 4. The sentinels knew whose cat that was. Patches was often saluted for fun by the alert sentries.[2]

The Vietnam Era Reaches Out to the Barracks

The Boston Marine Barracks, as we have seen, had its roots in the newly minted United States of America way back in the early 1800's. It survived for about 170 years. This is where old meets new. Ancient and stoically steadfast, the Barracks faced modern times and its politics.

Anti-Vietnam War sentiment across the nation reached unprecedented heights as America entered its seventh year in a seemingly unending war in a faraway land. Nineteen seventy-two was an election year. This brought the debate to Main Street. And to Boston. Anti-war demonstrators, consisting of students, rabble rousers, many just desiring to be where the action is (a modern event similar would be the Camp Out on the Green Way, protesting a banking issue in 2011–2012) picketed the Kennedy Building in downtown Boston, complete with their own cameras, on a daily basis.

On 10 May 1972 this energy made its way to the USS *Constitution*. "Visitors" boarded the local and esteemed icon. These visitors were a group of protesters who went below deck and proceeded to the ship's captain's quarters. With bolt cutters knowingly brought on board, (post 9-11 security procedures would have prevented this), they broke the lock to the cabin and entered the captain's quarters. That it was the most comfortable location aboard the USS *Constitution*, a wooden sailing era ship, probably occurred to the occupiers. The youngsters declared that they would live in the quarters until "Nixon ended the war."

Captain John McKinnon, skipper of the USS *Constitution,* responded to this affront up the chain of command to his boss, the commandant of the First Naval District, Rear Admiral J.C. Wylie. Within his authority, Wylie ordered the Marine Barracks to "land the landing force." Get some men down there.

The USS *Constitution* was an active duty naval ship. To violate it was more than just occupying the local chamber of commerce. It was an act just short of war, and was addressed at federal levels. Enter the SAT Team. The Marine Barracks maintained a group of off watch members of the guard to provide emergency assistance whenever circumstances warranted an additional security element or a show of force. The Marines selected for this duty attended training for this capability and eventuality. This time, however, it was real world. The gate alarm glared. Within full view of collaborative television news cameras, newspaper reporters, and friends of the protesters aboard the vessel, the Marines from the SAT Team removed the demonstrators towards the port side (facing the Navy yard) gangway. Amid the vociferous chants from their compatriots, they were placed in a Navy Yard security van. The USS *Constitution* was thoroughly inspected and any damaged was properly recorded.

On Saturday, May 13, 1972, three days later, commissioning ceremonies were underway for a capital ship (capital ships are some of the most important ships of any navy; they generally possess more armor, and fire power than other vessels in the navy) at the navy yard. Even the assistant secretary of defense officiated at the ceremonies. Once again a group of anti-war protesters planned a large confrontation at the navy yard to disrupt the ship commissioning ceremony. As saluting batteries of cannons fired in honor of the assistant secretary of defense that morning, individuals dressed as Vietnamese peasants, calling themselves "guerrilla theater," were creating a scene at the Main Gate. Each time a cannon fired, they smeared ketchup on each other, simulating wounds from similar cannonade in Vietnam. Much to the amusement of the navy yard children watching nearby, they rolled around on the ground on Water Street near the Main Gate. Reliable intelligence was availed upon the Marine Barracks about protester plans to add drama to the commissioning ceremonies that weekend. Executive Officer Major

Smith Sweeney was able to draw up a very effective plan of action to protect the Navy yard. One navy yard fire truck was positioned in front of Building 5 (the officers' club near the Main Gate) with its hoses ready to spray water at any trespassers improperly entering at the Main Gate, if necessary. Another yard fire truck was placed adjacent to Building 79, instructed to do the same at Gate 5. The yard tug was assigned the mission of patrolling the waterfront and took up a position by the USS *Constitution*. The yard tug trained its water cannon on the starboard gangway (facing towards the sea) to prevent any unauthorized persons from boarding the ship by water. A Marine in dress blues stood as usual on watch at each gate. But there was also a contingent of Marines in full battle dress, located close by as a show of force at each gate toward any potential trespassers. At 0800 on 13 May 1972, Sweeny's shipyard civil disturbance plan was executed. This placed the commanding officer of the Marine Barracks, Lt. Col. Yates, in command of shipyard protection and protection forces. These also included sailors from ships tied up in the yard as well. These sailors were assembled at the Marine Barracks for use if necessary. The Boston police provided the Tactical Police Force (TPF) to patrol the areas outside the navy yard. The Boston police had some experience with this very group of protesters. They have been monitoring and assessing the group's activities for weeks and indeed sustained some casualties from this experience. Several thousand individuals in a protesting mob associated with this activity marched up Chelsea Street chanting anti-war slogans and carrying anti-war signs, with the ground level Mystic River Bridge as a background. They were "marching" to an athletic field in Charlestown to attend a rock concert. A stage was set up and ready to go near the Charlestown affordable housing units (the "projects") across the way from Gate 5, the back gate. The music was interlaced with anti-war messages from selected speakers educating and edifying the assembled and sympathetic crowds. In spite of all this, the capital ship was commissioned, and there was no attempt by any trespassers to forcibly enter the yard. This became a testament to the soundness of Sweeny's security plan. After the rock music silenced, and the opinions of the outspoken speakers passed forth, the Tactical Police Force escorted any straggling, unruly throngs to the Cambridge line. Remainders of the group proceeded to the less secure Harvard Square, where they caused considerable property damage.

The presidential election year of 1972 was unfolding. It became as race between the incumbent President Nixon and George McGovern. This was the left's chance to remove this "hawkish" war president. Massachusetts was behind McGovern all the way.

All the while, under the radar, Nixon sent his man Henry Kissinger to negotiate a peace deal with North Vietnam. Nixon was well aware that events in Vietnam were often influenced by Russia and China. He arranged to meet with their leaders in 1972.

It is likely that any American leader, whether left or right leaning, could have walked away with the same "bag of goodies" from these leaders. Nixon, however, given his anticommunist resume, was able to appear to be driving a "hard bargain" with the communists whereas a left leaning Democrat might have ended up looking like they were appeasing the communists. Kissinger achieved a peace with North Vietnam that ended up lasting. Talk of bringing home the prisoners of war, many languishing for years in captivity, became realistic. Just in time for the election in November 1972.

Richard M. Nixon won his second term in the White House in a landslide by carrying 49 out of 50 states. A record. The one state that he did not carry: Massachusetts. Seemingly as his first act of his second term as president, Nixon signed documents closing the Boston Naval Ship Yard and along with it, the Boston Marine Barracks. Many were stunned. After one hundred and sixty years, was it really all over?

Lt. Col. Yates merely expected to be one in a continuous line of Barracks commanders. He didn't expect to be the last. His last duties as commander were to wrap things up, shut things down, and transfer all remaining personnel.

Boston's news media converged on the parade grounds for the formal closing ceremonies. Yates was quoted on the local TV news that the closing was "very sad...."

On 30 June 1974, Lt. Col. Yates completes his command of the Boston Marine Barracks, the last commander to do so. His final log entry was written from his civilian home in Topsfield, Massachusetts.

The Shipyard in the Twenty-First Century

People come for the USS *Constitution*. People stay for the waterfront condominiums overlooking the watery foreground to the Boston skyline spreading out and pointing to the sky, all framed by different periods of industrial architecture still existing at the Boston Naval Shipyard. The striking and reassuring impression one gets when walking the quiet streets of the Charlestown Navy Yard is that it essentially stands as it did back in 1974, its last days of a long and venerable career.

A section stands protected as a national park, while along the waterfront live many people who enjoy the amenities of a world-class city but want to live across the water from it. These units face south, the sunniest, wateriest direction. A few small city blocks inland, office space fills old historic and sturdy structures. New glass, steel, and concrete buildings occupy previously open areas. Their juxtaposition marks time as only architecture can. These round out the third part of the shipyard's retirement. As one walks to the end of a pier jutting out into the Boston Harbor, one is struck by all the water, all the sky and all the sun (weather permitting), right there in the city. Only other intrepid people are out there with you at land's end.

The Freedom Trail takes many to the resident tall ship. And then it takes them up a hill to the foundations of the Bunker Hill Monument. Left behind are the quiet, ageless streets of the shipyard, and the Boston Marine Barracks.

The Barracks stand as they did since the last major overhaul during the World War I era. And as they did in 1974, when the Marine Corps no longer transferred Marines in and out of them.

The Administration Building has since been knocked down to make way for the expansion of Gate 4. Back when this was an active shipyard, Gate 4 was a walkthrough gate for shipyard workers from Charlestown living just outside the yard walls. Now it is one of the two ways in for autos and trucks and foot traffic too. Gate 5 is the other drive-in gate. No Marine sentinels hold watch at these gates anymore. The Main Gate is now restricted to foot traffic only, standing as a museum piece of its heyday as the Main Gate into the yard. Gate 4 and the Main Gate have traded places.

The last officers moved on but left their names on the officer's wings where they once lived. The commanding officer's name, Lt. Col. Yates, was moved sometime in the 1980's to the junior officers' east wing. Enlisted men billeted here are long gone, with barely a trace. The structure stands, silent and unknowable.

The Marine Barracks' "pre-modern" history, that is the pre–World War II age, reflects life in America before modern highways, television, and televised history. It was the time before America began carrying the weight of the world on its shoulders. The Golden Age, when

America was showing the world how much potential she had, how great she could be, how hopeful she was. The world was convinced by the outcome of World War II. America then acquired the adult responsibilities of preventing a third world war in the midst of an unbelievably frightening nuclear arms race after having pulled the trigger on this horrific destruction technology first. Letters from the sunny days of young America, with its tall ships and Great White Navies, portray a comfortable life and yet never dreaming of electricity or indoor plumbing. How infuriating these new technologies were when introduced to the Barracks. Either written by hand or by a basic typewriter, these letters all lay safe and sequestered in archives, just as the letter writers had intended, but unread and forgotten.

That is, until Ret. Lt. Col. Yates made the trek to seek out these archived letters.

It was like finding a small chest full of letters from when your grandmother was a young woman. How they unexpectedly flesh out the youthful days of her life, how they even draw out moods, thoughts and even the weather. And the drama. The Marines and their dependents, their moods, their thoughts, their weather, and their drama were left behind written down and eventually discovered and brought back to life by Retired Lt. Col. Yates.

Appendix:
List of Commanding Officers

During the early days of the Marine Barracks, Boston, the commanding officers of the Marine detachments of the various ships laid up or outfitted at the Boston Navy Yard were assigned temporarily as commanding officer of the Marine Barracks, Boston.

OFFICE ASSISTANT SECRETARY,
WASHINGTON.

September 17, 1897.

Sir:

The Department directs that to further test the system of post exchange as it exists by law in the Army, you will authorize the Commanding Officer, Marine Barracks, Boston, Massachusetts, to establish a post exchange at that post, to be conducted in all respects in accordance with the laws, regulations and rules governing the conduct of post exchanges in the United States Army, so far as practicable. A competent officer will be detailed as officer in charge, who will report monthly, in detail, to his commanding officer, the operations of the canteen and its results, whether beneficial or otherwise, to the enlisted men of the command, and with such remarks as he may have to make in regard thereto; such reports to be forwarded without delay to the Colonel Commandant of the Marine Corps by the commanding officer, with such remarks as he may desire to make as to the advantages and disadvantages, and the practicability of continuing the system at that post. At the end of six months such reports to be forwarded to the Secretary of the Navy by the Colonel Commandant, with such remarks and recommendations as he may desire to make.

Very respectfully,

T. Roosevelt
Acting Secretary.

The Colonel Commandant,
U.S. Marine Corps.

1st Lt. Henry Caldwell, May 1802–June 1803
1st Lt. Robert Greenleaf, June 1803–November 1803
1st Lt. Newton Keene, December 1803–November 1805
1st Lt. Robert Greenleaf, December 1805–February 1807
1st Lt. Henry Caldwell, March 1807–June 1809
Capt. James Thompson, June 1809–December 1810
1st Lt. John Brooks, Jr., December 1810–December 1811
Capt. Henry Caldwell, December 1811–March 1812
1st Lt. Charles L. Hanna, March 1812–July 1812
Sgt. McKim, 1 July 1812–21 July 1812
1st Lt. James Broom, 22 July 1812–7 September 1812
Capt. Archibald Henderson, 8 September 1812–November 1812
1st Lt. Robert Mosby, November 1812–January 1813
Capt. Archibald Henderson, 9 January 1813–8 September 1813
Capt. William Anderson, 9 September 1813–27 August 1815
Capt. R.D. Wainwright, 28 August 1815–October 1822
1st Lt. George Cooper, November 1822–December 1822
Lt. Col. R.D. Wainwright, January 1823–November 1829
1st Lt. Thomas L. English, December 1829
1st Lt. Thomas T.C. Watkins, January 1830–February 1830
Lt. Col. R.D. Wainwright, March 1830–12 July 1830
Capt. W.H. Freeman, 13 July 1830–January 1836
Capt. Thomas L. English, February 1836
Lt. Col. W.H. Freeman, March 1836
Capt. Thomas L. English, April 1836–May 1836
1st Lt. F.B. McNeil, June 1836
Sgt. E.C. Young, July 1836
1st Lt. Richard Douglas, October 1836–December 1836
Capt. Thomas L. English, January 1837–March 1837
Capt. Ward Marston, April 1837–August 1838
Lt. Col. W.H. Freeman, September 1838–October 1842
Lt. Col. Samuel E. Watson, November 1842–May 1847
1st Lt. B.E. Brooke, 27 May 1847–10 December 1847
Capt. N.S. Waldron, 11 December 1847–14 April 1848
Capt. A.N. Brevort, 15 April 1848–8 May 1848
Capt. Thomas L. English, 9 May 1848–1 November 1853
Lt. Col. F. Dulany, 2 November 1853–27 September 1862
Lt. Col. John G. Reynolds, 28 September 1862–August 1863
Capt. George Butler, September 1863–February 1864
Lt. Col. Ward Marston, March 1864–December 1864
Capt. J. Schererhern, 15 December 1864–23 April 1865
Maj. C.G. McCawley, 24 April 1865–20 April 1868
Captain J.G. Baker, 21 April 1868–7 May 1868
Lt. Col. C.G. McCawley, 8 May 1868–1 August 1871
Lt. Col. James Jones, 2 August 1871–17 January 1872
Captain P.C. Pope, 22 April 1874–23 May 1874
Lt. Col. James Jones, 24 May 1874–28 December 1874
Capt. P.C. Pope, 29 December 1874–4 February 1875
Lt. Col. James Jones, 5 February 1875–6 April 1880
Capt. William Wallace, 7 April 1880–15 May 1880
Lt. Col. Clement D. Hebb, 16 May 1880–20 June 1880
Capt. William Wallace, 21 June 1880–5 July 1880
Lt. Col. Clement D. Hebb, 6 July 1880–24 October 1880
Capt. William Wallace, 25 October 1880–20 November 1880
Lt. Col. Clement D. Hebb, 21 November 1880–1 February 1885
Lt. Col. J.L. Broome, 2 February 1885–8 March 1888

Maj. George P. Houston, 9 March 1888–6 November 1889

Lt. Col. George P. Houston, 7 November 1889–28 February 1890

Col. Clement D. Webb, 1 March 1890–9 September 1890

Capt. Louis E. Fagan, 10 September 1890–12 February 1891

Col. Clement D. Hebb, 13 February 1891–9 July 1892

Maj. Percival C. Pope, 10 July 1892–15 December 1893

Capt. Francis Harrington, 16 December 1893–14 January 1894

Maj. Robert L. Meade, 15 January 1894–20 December 1897

Capt. Allan C. Kelton, 21 December 1897–25 March 1898

Maj. Percival C. Pope, 26 March 1898–22 April 1898

Capt. Richard Wallach, 23 April 1898–9 September 1898

Lt. Col. Percival C. Pope, 10 September 1898–26 March 1899

Capt. Allan C. Kelton, 27 March 1898–16 April 1899

1st Lt. Lawrence H. Moses, 17 April 1899–15 May 1899

Lt. Col. H. Clay Cochrane, 16 May 1899–11 January 1900

Col. H. Clay Cochrane, 12 January 1900–3 August 1900

Col. Percival C. Pope, 4 August 1900–28 September 1902

Capt. Charles Long, 29 September 1902–15 January 1903

Col. Percival C. Pope, 16 January 1903–7 November 1903

Lt. Col. Allen C. Kelton, 8 November 1903–31 October 1904

Capt. G.N. Reid, 1 November 1904–13 December 1904

Capt. Charles S. Hatch, 14 December 1904–7 January 1905

Col. Allen C. Kelton, 8 January 1905–21 May 1905

Capt. L. McLittle, 22 May 1905–6 June 1905

Col. Allen C. Kelton, 7 June 1905–11 March 1906

Col. Thomas N. Wood, 12 March 1906–18 October 1910

Capt. J.W. Wadleigh, 19 October 1910–9 December 1910

Col. Thomas N. Wood, 10 December 1910–25 May 1911

1st Lt. J.R. Henley, 26 May 1911–6 June 1911

Maj. Laurence H. Moses, 7 June 1911–13 October 1911

Lt. Col. Laurence H. Moses, 14 October 1911–19 March 1912

Lt. Col. Theodore P. Kane, 20 March 1912–25 September 1912

1st Lt. Edward B. Cole, 26 September 1912–29 October 1912

1st Lt. William E. Parker, 30 October 1912–7 December 1912

Lt. Col. Theodore P. Kane, 8 December 1912–1 January 1914

1st Lt. William B. Harrison, 2 January 1914–27 February 1914

Col. Ralph Dickens, 28 February 1914–4 October 1914

Capt. Edward B. Cole, 5 October 1914–27 October 1914

2d Lt. Harold C. Daniels, 28 October 1914–4 January 1915

Maj. Newt B. Hall, 5 January 1915–15 August 1915

Capt. Harry O. Smith, 16 August 1915–15 December 1916

Lt. Col. Newt B. Hall, 16 December 1916–14 Sep 1918

Capt. Angus Wilson, 15 Sep 1918–2 December 1918

Capt. Melville J. Shaw, 3 December 1918–1 July 1920

Col. George Van Orden, 2 July 1920–20 Sep 1921

Col. Arthur T. Marix, 21 Sep 1921–25 June 1922

Capt. George F. Adams, 26 June 1922–5 July 1922

Col. Arthur T. Marix, 6 July 1922–14 June 1923

Col. L.M. Gulick, 15 June 1923–4 July 1924

Col. Lawrence Moses, 5 July 1924–31 October 1925

1st Lt. John McQueen, 1 November 1925–31 December 1925

Col. Lawrence Moses, 1 January 1926–31 March 1926

1st Lt. John C. McQueen, 1 April 1926–30 November 1926

Appendix: List of Commanding Officers

Lt. Col. Harry O. Smith, 1 December 1926–15 December 1929

Lt. Col. Willia T. Hoadley, 16 December 1929–17 April 1933

Lt. Col. Frederick A. Barker, 18 April 1933–17 June 1934

Maj. James M. Bain, 30 June 1934–4 November 1934

Col. Frederick A. Barker, 5 November 1934–4 July 1935

Lt. Col. Calhoun Ancrum, 5 July 1935–16 February 1936

Maj. Frederic R. Hoyt, 17 February 1936–13 June 1936

Col. Samuel M. Harrington, 14 June 1936–16 January 1937

Maj. Percy D. Cornell, 17 January 1937–6 February 1937

Col. Samuel M. Harrington, 7 February 1937–19 May 1937

Maj. Percy D. Cornell, 20 May 1937–14 June 1937

Lt. Col. Robert Montague, 15 June 1937–19 January 1938

Lt. Col. Harold C. Pierce, 20 January 1939–29 March 1939

Maj. Hamilton M. Fleming, 30 March 1939–10 April 1939

Lt. Col. Harold C. Pierce, 11 April 1939–29 April 1945

Col. James E. Betts, 30 April 1945–12 December 1945

Col. James H.N. Hudnell, 13 December 1945–17 June 1946

Col. William W. Orr, 18 June 1946–10 June 1949

Lt. Col. William F. Harris, 11 June 1949–10 July 1949

Col. Presley H. Rixey, 11 July 1949–25 May 1951

Lt. Col. Ralph E. Boulton, 26 May 1951–26 June 1951

Col. Paul D. Sherman, 27 June 1951–21 June 1952

Col. Ralph M. King, 22 June 1953–31 May 1956

Lt. Col. Francis X. Beamer, 1 June 1956–15 June 1956

Lt. Col. Richard G. Warga, 16 June 1956–30 June 1956

Col. John A. McAlister, 1 July 1956–7 August 1958

Lt. Col. Richard G. Warga, 8 August 1958–3 Sep 1958

Col. Edward L. Hutchinson, 4 Sep 1958–31 October 1959

Lt. Col. C.H. Cowles, 1 November 1959–12 November 1959

Col. James B. Glennon, Jr., 13 November 1959–27 June 1962

Maj. Frederick S. Knight, 28 June 1962–22 August 1962

Col. Thaddeus P. Wojcik, 23 August 1962–26 May 1965

Lt. Col. William S. Anthony, 27 May 1965–22 July 1965

Col. John T. O'Neill, 23 July 1965–31 May 1967

Col. William G. Dair, Jr., 1 June 1967–12 July 1969

Col. Edward H. Mackel, 13 July 1969–14 October 1971

Lt. Col. John R. Yates, Jr., 15 October 1971–30 June 1974

Chapter Notes

Chapter 1

1. Bruce Catton, "The Marine Tradition," *American Heritage*, February 1959, Vol. 10, No. 2, p. 28.
2. Ibid., p. 75.
3. *Boston Naval Shipyard Architectural and Environmental Inventory*, May 17, 1974, p. 75.
4. Ibid., p. 75.
5. G.R. Evans, *Historic Structure Report: Marine Barracks (Building I), Charlestown*, p. 4.
6. Ibid., p. 5.
7. Ibid., p. 83.
8. Ibid., p. 5.
9. Ibid., p. 83.
10. Ibid., p. 6.
11. Edwin C. Bearss, *Historic Resource Study, Charlestown Navy Yard 1800–1842*, Vol. 1, p. 91(Telecom Simmons to Bearss, July 11, 1976; Brig. Gen. Simmons was director of Marine Corps History).
12. Edwin C. Bearss, *Historic Resource Study, Charlestown Navy Yard 1800–1842*, Vol. 1, p. 163.

Chapter 2

1. Bruce Catton, "The Marine Tradition," *American Heritage*, 1959, Vol. 10, No. 2, p. 25.
2. Ibid., p. 26.
3. Simmons, *The United States Marines, 1775–1975*, p. 24.
4. Edwin C. Bearss, *Historic Resource Study, Charlestown Navy Yard, 1800–1842*, Vol. 2, October 1984, p. 166.
5. *Boston Naval Shipyard Architectural and Environmental Inventory*, May 17, 1974, p. 3.
6. Ibid., p. 75.
7. Ibid., p. 383.
8. *Boston Gazette*, p. 1, September 27, 1819.
9. Black and Bearss, *Charlestown Navy Yard, 1842–1890*, p. 384.
10. Bruce Catton, "The Marine Tradition," *American Heritage*, February 1959, Vol. 10, No. 2, p. 28.
11. Richard S. Collum, Major, USMC, *History of the United States Marine Corps*, Philadelphia, 1890.
12. Ibid.
13. Edwin C. Bearss, *Historic Resource Study, Charlestown Navy Yard, 1800–1842*, Vol. 2, October 1984, p. 747.
14. Edwin C. Bearss, *Historic Resource Study, Charlestown Navy Yard 1800–1842*, Vol. 2, p. 1023.

Chapter 3

1. Edwin C. Bearss, *Historic Resource Study, Charlestown Navy Yard 1800–1842*, Vol. 2, p. 1028.
2. Ibid., p. 1029.
3. G.R. Evans, *Historic Structure Report: Marine Barracks (Building I), Charlestown*, p. 10.
4. Black and Bearss, *Charlestown Navy Yard 1842–1890*, p. 30.
5. Ibid., p. 30.
6. Ibid., p. 30.
7. Ibid., p. 31.
8. Ibid., p. 31.
9. Freeman to Nicholson, July 30, 1842, National Archives, RG 127, 97–1, Letters Sent.
10. Cobb and Pierce to Freeman, Aug. 12, 1842, National Archives, RG 127, 97–1, Letters Sent.
11. Marston to Henderson, Sept. 8, 1843, National Archives, RG 127, 97–1, Letters Sent.
12. Watson to Henderson, Oct. 17, 1843, National Archives, RG 127, 97–1, Letters Sent.
13. Watson to Nicholson, Oct. 4, 1844, National Archives, RG 127, 97–1, Letters Sent.
14. Watson to Henderson, Oct. 16, 1844, National Archives, RG 127, 97–1, Letters Sent.
15. Watson to Henderson, Dec. 9, 1844, National Archives, RG 127, 97–1, Letters Sent.
16. Henderson to Bancroft, Sept. 13, 1845, National Archives, RG 127, 98–1, Letters Received.
17. Henderson to Watson, May 29, 1846, National Archives, RG 127, 97–1, Letters Sent.
18. Henderson to Watson, Aug. 7, 1846, National Archives, RG 127, 97–1, Letters Sent.
19. Henderson to Watson, March 6, 1847, National Archives, RG 127, 97–1, Letters Sent.
20. Brooke to Henderson, June 4, 1847, National Archives, RG 127, 97–1, Letters Sent, Henderson to Brooke, July 9, 1847, National Archives, RG 127, 98–1, Letters Received.
21. Philip N. Pierce and Frank O. Hough, *The Compact History of the United States Marine Corps* (New York: Hawthorne Books, 1969), pp. 82–83.
22. Henderson to Watson, May 18, 1847, National Archives, RG 127, 98–1, Letters Received.
23. Simmons, *The United States Marines, 1775–1975*, p. 48.
24. Gabrielle M. Santelli, *Marines in the Mexican War*, 1991, pp. 34–38.
25. Henderson to Waldron, Feb. 23, Feb. 28, 1848, National Archives, RG 127, 98–1, Letters Received.
26. Black and Bearss, *Charlestown Navy Yard 1842–1890*, p. 36.
27. English to Howle, Dec. 29, 1848, English to Henderson, Jan. 1, 1849, National Archives, RG 127, 79–81, Letters Sent.
28. English to Henderson, April 2, May 4, 1850, National Archives, RG 127, 97–1, Letters Sent.
29. Black and Bearss, *Charlestown Navy Yard 1842–1890*, p. 87.
30. English to Henderson, June 7, 1849, Jan. 19, 1949, Dec. 4, 1850, National Archives, RG 127, 97–1, Letters Sent.

31. English to Henderson, Feb. 27, 1850, Jan. 29, 1851, National Archives, RG 127, 97-2, Letters Sent.
32. English to Lindsay, Oct. 17, 1849, Feb. 11, 1850, National Archives, RG 127, 97-2, Letters Sent.
33. English to Henderson, July 22, 1851, National Archives, RG 127, 97-2, Letters Sent.
34. English to Quartermaster, July 24, Sept. 17, 1849, National Archives, RG 127, 97-2, Letters Sent.
35. Christopher Cox, *Boston Herald*, Book Section, Tuesday, October 17, 1995, pp. 37-38.
36. Reynolds to Quartermaster, Feb. 7, 1861, National Archives, RG 127, 97-2, Letters Sent.
37. Reynolds to Quartermaster, April 22, 1861, National Archives, RG 127, 97-2, Letters Sent.

Chapter 4

1. Lawrence Lader, "New York's Bloodiest Week," *American Heritage*, June 1959, Vol. 10, No. 4, pp. 44-49, 95-98.
2. Reynolds to Harris, Dec. 1, 1862, National Archives, RG 127, 97-2, Letters Sent.
3. Reynolds to Harris, Dec. 9, 1862, National Archives, RG 127, 97-2, Letters Sent.
4. Reynolds to Harris, Dec. 11, 1862, National Archives, RG 127, 97-2, Letters Sent.
5. Reynolds to Mass. Adjutant General, Dec. 15, 1862, National Archives, RG 127, 97-2, Letters Sent.
6. Reynolds to Montgomery, May 11, 1863, National Archives, RG 127, 97-2, Letters Sent.
7. Bruce Catton, "Prison Camps of the Civil War," *American Heritage*, August 1959, Vol. 10, No. 2, p. 5.
8. Gorton Carruth, *The Encyclopedia of American Facts and Dates*, Harper and Row, p. 282.
9. Reynolds to Harris, May 12, 1863, National Archives, RG 127, 97-2, Letters Sent.
10. Reynolds to Harris, May 17, 1863, National Archives, RG 127, 97-2, Letters Sent.
11. Reynolds to Harris, June 17, 1863, National Archives, RG 127, 97-2, Letters Sent.
12. Lawrence Lader, "New York's Bloodiest Week," *American Heritage*, June 1959, Vol. 10, No. 4, 44-49, 95-98.
13. Reynolds to Harris, July 22, 1863, National Archives, RG 127, 97-2, Letters Sent.
14. Reynolds to Marston, Dec. 11, 1863, National Archives, RG 127, 97-2, Letters Sent.
15. Black and Bearss, *Charlestown Navy Yard 1842-1890*, p. 148.
16. Reynolds to Lowry, Feb. 15, 1864, National Archives, RG 127, 97-2, Letters Sent.
17. Marston to Harris, March 26, 1864, National Archives, RG 127, 97-2, Letters Sent.
18. Marston to Augustus Stevens, Selectman of Needham, March 26, 1864, National Archives, RG 127, 97-2, Letters Sent.
19. Marston to Harris, March 30, 1864, National Archives, RG 127, 97-2, Letters Sent.
20. Marston to Harris, April 2, 1864, National Archives, RG 127, 97-2, Letters Sent.
21. Curttis Dahl, "Lincoln Saves a Reformer," *American Heritage*, October 1972, Vol. 23, No. 6, pp. 74-78.
22. *The Boston Herald*, p. 1, June 20, 1864.
23. *The Boston Herald*, p. 1, June 29, 1864.
24. Curtis Dahl, "Lincoln Saves a Reformer," *American Heritage*, October 1972, Vol. 23, No. 6, pp. 74-78.
25. Marston to Zeilin, July 13, 1864, National Archives, RG 127, 97-2, Letters Sent.
26. Marston to Zeilin, July 20, 1864, National Archives, RG 127, 97-2, Letters Sent.
27. Marston to Zeilin, July 22, 1864, National Archives, RG 127, 97-2, Letters Sent.
28. Marston to Zeilin, July 28, 1864, National Archives, RG 127, 97-2, Letters Sent.
29. Marston to Zeilin, August 8, 1864, National Archives, RG 127, 97-2, Letters Sent.
30. Marston to Zeilin, August 22, 1864, National Archives, RG 127, 97-2, Letters Sent.
31. Marston to Zeilin, August 22, 1864, National Archives, RG 127, 97-2, Letters Sent.
32. Sergeant Daniel Stoner to Rear Adm. S.W. Stringham, August 26, 1864, National Archives, RG 127, 97-2, Letters Sent.
33. LCDR R.B. Lowry to Gideon Welles, Secretary of the Navy, September 12, 1864, National Archives, RG 127, 97-2, Letters Sent.
34. Simmons, *The United States Marines, 1775-1975*, p. 67.
35. McCawley to Slack, Quartermaster Marine Corps, December 7, 1865, National Archives, RG 127, 97-2, Letters Sent.
36. McCawley to Zeilin, December 11, 1865, National Archives, RG 127, 97-2, Letters Sent.
37. McCawley to Zeilin, August 14, 1866, National Archives, RG 127, 97-2, Letters Sent.
38. Frederick R. Black, *Cultural Resources Management Study No. 20, Charlestown Navy Yard 1890-1973*, p. 2.
39. McCawley to Zeilin, December 16, 1867, National Archives, RG 127, 97-2, Letters Sent.
40. McCawley to W.B. Slack, Quartermaster Marine Corps, January 7, 1868, National Archives, RG 127, 97-2, Letters Sent.
41. McCawley to W.B. Slack, Quartermaster Marine Corps, March 6, 1868, National Archives, RG 127, 97-2, Letters Sent.
42. McCawley to Zeilin, February 18, 1868, National Archives, RG 127, 97-2, Letters Sent.
43. McCawley to Zeilin, July 23, 1868, National Archives, RG 127, 97-2, Letters Sent.
44. McCawley to Zeilin, October 17, 1868, National Archives, RG 127, 97-2, Letters Sent.

Chapter 5

1. G.R. Evans, *Historic Structure Report: Marine Barracks (Building I), Charlestown*, pp. 10-17.
2. G.R. Evans, *Historic Structure Report: Marine Barracks (Building I), Charlestown*, pp. 10-17.
3. Collum to Jones, November 15, 1872, National Archives, RG 127, 97-2, Letters Sent.
4. Burt to Jones, National Archives, November 20, 1872, National Archives, RG 127, 97-2, Letters Sent.
5. Black and Bearss, *The Charlestown Navy Yard 1842-1890*, p. 347.
6. Ibid.
7. Ibid.
8. Black and Bearss, *The Charlestown Navy Yard 1842-1890*, p. 347.
9. Black and Bearss, *The Charlestown Navy Yard 1842-1890*, p. 348.
10. Black and Bearss, *The Charlestown Navy Yard 1842-1890*, p. 348.
11. Black and Bearss, *The Charlestown Navy Yard, 1842-1890*, p. 348.
12. Black and Bearss, *The Charlestown Navy Yard 1842-1890*, p. 349.
13. Black and Bearss, *The Charlestown Navy Yard 1842-1890*, p. 349.
14. *Boston Naval Shipyard, Architectural and Environmental Inventory*, May 17, 1974.

15. Collum to Zeilin, February 20, 1873, National Archives, RG 127, 97–3, Letters Sent.
16. Pope to Commandant Nichols of Naval Station, Boston, January 26, 1875, National Archives, RG 127, 97–3, Letters Sent.
17. Pope to Commandant Nichols of Naval Station, Boston, National Archives, RG 127, 97–3, Letters Sent.
18. Jones to Slack, Quartermaster Marine Corps, July 15, 1874, National Archives, RG 127, 97–3, Letters Sent.
19. Jones to Quartermaster Slack, March 24, 1875, National Archives, RG 127, 97–3, Letters Sent.
20. General Order No. 56, April 31, 1875, National Archives, RG 127, 99, Orders Received.
21. Jones to Secretary of the Navy George Roberts, November 20, 1876, National Archives, RG 127, 97–3, Letters Sent.
22. Jones to Col. McCawley, June 7, 1877, National Archives, RG 127, 97–3, Letters Sent.
23. Parker to Jones, August 23, 1877, National Archives, RG 127, 97–3, Letters Sent.
24. Jones to Parker, July 24, 1877, National Archives, RG 127, 97–3, Letters Sent.
25. Wallace to Quartermaster Slack, May 5, 1880, National Archives, RG 127, 97–3, Letters Sent.
26. Hebb to Quartermaster Slack, May 20, 1880, National Archives, RG 127, 97–3, Letters Sent.
27. White to Jones, July 25, 1878, National Archives, RG 127, 97–3 (Mr. White was Navy Yard civil engineer), Letters Sent.
28. Black and Bearss, *The Charlestown Navy Yard, 1842–1890*, p. 282.
29. Hebb to McCawley, July 20, 1880, National Archives, RG 127, 97–3, Letters Sent.
30. Hebb to Capt. S.L. Reese, Commanding Officer, *Wabash*, National Archives, RG 127, 97–3, Letters Sent.
31. Hebb to McCawley, April 18, 1881, National Archives, RG 127, 97–3, Letters Sent.
32. Hebb to McCawley, August 13, 1881, National Archives, RG 127, 97–4, Letters Sent.
33. Hebb to McCawley, October 12, 1881, National Archives, RG 127, 97–4, Letters Sent.
34. Hebb to Quartermaster Slack, November 1, 1881, National Archives, RG 127, 97–4, Letters Sent.
35. Hebb to Cmdt. Ranson, November 25, 1881, National Archives, RG 127, 97–4, Letters Sent.
36. Hebb to Secretary of the Navy W.H. Hunt, December 26, 1881, National Archives, RG 127, 97–4, Letters Sent.
37. Hebb to J.S.Knight, Yard Surgeon, January 31, 1882, Hebb to Boston Board of Health, January 31, 1882, Hebb to Private Rosemond, February 4, 1882, National Archives, RG 127, 97–4, Letters Sent.
38. Hebb to McCawley, February 22, 1882, National Archives, RG 127, 97–4, Letters Sent.
39. Hebb to R.C. Badger, Cmdt., Navy Yard, March 22, 1882, National Archives, RG 127, 97–4, Letters Sent.
40. Hebb to McCawley, March 30, 1882, National Archives, RG 127, 97–4, Letters Sent.
41. Hebb to Secretary Garfield, Monument Committee, Washington, D.C., April 10, 1882, National Archives, RG 127, 97–4, Letters Sent.
42. Hebb to McCawley, April 10, 1882, National Archives, RG 127, 97–4, Letters Sent.
43. Hebb to McCawley, April 22, 1882, National Archives, RG 127, 97–4, Letters Sent.
44. Hebb to Quartermaster Slack, May 30, 1882, National Archives, RG 127, 97–4, Letters Sent.
45. Hebb to O.C. Badger, Cmdt., Charlestown Navy Yard, November 16, 1882, National Archives, RG 127, 97–4, Letters Sent.
46. Hebb to O.C. Badger, Cmdt., Charlestown Navy Yard, November 20, 1882, National Archives, RG 127, 97–4, Letters Sent.
47. Hebb to *Boston Herald*, November 21, 1882, National Archives, RG 127, 97–4, Letters Sent.
48. Hebb to McCawley, November 28, 1882, National Archives, RG 127, 97–4, Letters Sent.
49. Hebb to McCawley, December 7, 1882, National Archives, RG 127, 97–4, Letters Sent.
50. Hebb to Secretary of the Navy W.E. Chandler, December 16, 1882, National Archives, RG 127, 97–4, Letters Sent.
51. Hebb to Commandant Badger, Charlestown Navy Yard, February 10, 1883, National Archives, RG 127, 97–4, Letters Sent.
52. Hebb to Quartermaster W.B. Slack, May 3, 1883, National Archives, RG 127, 97–4, Letters Sent.
53. Hebb to C.G. McCawley, May 7, 1883, National Archives, RG 127, 97–4, Letters Sent.
54. Hebb to C.G. McCawley, July 9, 1883, National Archives, RG 127, 97–4, Letters Sent.
55. Zielin to McCawley, May 21, 1869, National Archives, RG 127, 99, Orders Received.
56. Hebb to W.E. Chandler, Secretary of the Navy, July 9, 1883.
57. Hebb to McCawley, July 17, 1883, National Archives, RG 127, 97–4, Letters Sent.
58. Hebb to McCawley. July 24, 1883, National Archives, RG 127, 97–4, Letters Sent.
59. Huntington to Commandant Badger, Charlestown Navy Yard, September 11, 1883, National Archives, RG 127, 97–4, Letters Sent.
60. Hebb to *Boston Herald*, October 10, 1883, National Archives, RG 127, 97–4, Letters Sent.
61. Hebb to C.G.McCawley, October 16, 1883, National Archives, RG 127, 97–4, Letters Sent.
62. Hebb to C.G. McCawley, October 26, 1883, National Archives, RG 127, 97–4, Letters Sent.
63. Hebb to C.G. McCawley, November 20, 1883, National Archives, RG 127, 97–4, Letters Sent.
64. Hebb to C.G. McCawley, November 27, 1883, National Archives, RG 127, 97–4, Letters Sent.
65. Hebb to W.E. Chandler, Secretary of the Navy, February 18, 1884, National Archives, RG 127, 97–4, Letters Sent.
66. Hebb to 1st Lt. Elliott and 1st Lt. Spicer, April 22, 1884, National Archives, RG 127, 97–4, Letters Sent.
67. Hebb to Albert C. Gorgas, Naval Hospital, Chelsea, June 12, 1884, National Archives, RG 127, 97–4, Letters Sent.
68. Hebb to McCawley, June 12, 1884, National Archives, RG 127, 97–4, Letters Sent.
69. Hebb to Commanding Officer, Marine Barracks, Portsmouth, NH, June 28, 1884, National Archives, RG 127, 97–4, Letters Sent.
70. Hebb to McCawley, July 14, 1884, National Archives, RG 127, 97–4, Letters Sent.
71. Hebb to *Boston Herald*, September 15, 1884, National Archives, RG 127, 97–4, Letters Sent.
72. Hebb to O.C. Badger, Cmdt. of the Navy Yard, National Archives, RG 127, 97–4, Letters Sent.
73. Hebb to Secretary of the Navy W.E. Chandler, December 13, 1884, National Archives, RG 127, 97–4, Letters Sent.
74. Hebb to O.C. Badger, Cmdt. of Navy Yard, March 30, 1885, National Archives, RG 127, 97–4, Letters Sent.

Chapter 6

1. Broome to McCawley, February 2, 1885, National Archives, RG 127, 97–4, Letters Sent.

2. Simmons, *The United States Marines 1775–1975*, p. 59.

3. Broome to Secretary of the Navy W.C. Whitney, April 3, 1885, National Archives, RG 127, 97–4, Letters Sent.

4. Black and Bearss, *The Charlestown Navy Yard, 1842–1890*, p. 350.

5. Reid to McCawley, May 19, 1885, National Archives, RG 127, 97–5, Letters Sent.

6. Broome to McCawley, June 6, 1885, National Archives, RG 127, 97–5, Letters Sent.

7. Broome to Capt. Reid, 1st Lt. Jackson, 2d Lt. White, June 15, 1885, National Archives, RG 127, 97–5, Letters Sent.

8. Records of Courts-martial, 1890–1908, Marine Barracks, Boston, National Archives, RG 127, 99–2.

9. Broome to McCawley, June 22, 1885, National Archives, RG 127, 97–5, Letters Sent.

10. Broome to McCawley, July 15, 1885, National Archives, RG 127, 97–5, Letters Sent.

11. Broome to McCawley, July 21, 1885, National Archives, RG 127, 97–5, Letters Sent.

12. Broome to *Boston Herald*, July 27, 1885, National Archives, RG 127, 97–5, Letters Sent.

13. Broome to McCawley, September 30, 1885, National Archives, RG 127, 97–5, Letters Sent.

14. Broome to Charles E. Powers, Pres., Middlesex Railroad Co., 27 Tremont Row, Boston, June 9, 1886, National Archives, RG 127, 97–5, Letters Sent.

15. Broome to L.A. Kimberly, Cmdt. of Navy Yard, November 26, 1886, National Archives, RG 127, 97–5, Letters Sent.

16. Broome to McCawley, December 23, 1886, National Archives, RG 127, 97–5, Letters Sent.

17. Broome to McCawley, December 28, 1886, National Archives, RG 127, 97–5, Letters Sent.

18. Broome to McCawley, Febbruary 10, 1887, National Archives, RG 127, 97–5, Letters Sent.

19. Broome to McCawley, April 16, 1887, National Archives, RG 127, 97–5, Letters Sent.

20. Broome to McCawley, May 18, 1887, National Archives, RG 127, 97–5, Letters Sent.

21. Broome to Quartermaster Marine Corps, May 20, 1887, National Archives, RG 127, 97–5, Letters Sent.

22. Broome to McCawley, May 23, 1887, National Archives, RG 127, 97–5, Letters Sent.

23. Broome to McCawley, June 15, 1887, National Archives, RG 127, 97–5, Letters Sent.

24. Broome to McCawley, June 16, 1887, National Archives, RG 127, 97–5, Letters Sent.

25. Broome to McCawley, August 4, 1887, National Archives, RG 127, 97–5, Letters Sent.

26. Broome to Charlestown Gas Company, August 16, 1887, National Archives, RG 127, 97–5, Letters Sent.

27. Broome to Chief of Police, Jersey City, NJ, September 22, 1887, National Archives, RG 127, 97–5, Letters Sent.

28. Broome to Quartermaster Marine Corps, November 8, 1887, National Archives, RG 127, 97–5, Letters Sent.

29. Broome to McCawley, December 1, 1887, National Archives, RG 127, 97–5, Letters Sent.

30. Broome to Commandant, Charlestown Navy Yard, December 17, 1887, National Archives, RG 127, 97–5, Letters Sent. Broome to Judge Advocate of the Navy, December 9, 1887, National Archives, RG 127, 97–5, Letters Sent.

31. Broome to Commandant, Navy Yard, December 28, 1887, National Archives, RG 127, 97–6, Letters Sent.

32. Broom to McCawley, January 20, 1888, National Archives, RG 127, 97–6, Letters Sent.

33. Broome to Commandant, Navy Yard, Boston, February 28, 1888, National Archives, RG 127, 97–6, Letters Sent.

34. Broome to McCawley, February 27, 1888, National Archives, RG 127, 97–6, Letters Sent.

35. Order from Secretary of the Navy, June 30, 1888, National Archives, RG 127, 99, Orders Received.

36. Broome to McCawley, February 28, 1888, National Archives, RG 127, 97–6, Letters Sent.

37. Houston to McCawley, March 26, 1888, National Archives, RG 127, 97–6, Letters Sent.

38. Houston to Pay Master, USMC, April 25, 1888, National Archives, RG 127, 97–6, Letters Sent.

39. Houston to Col. Cmdt. McCawley, April 20, 1888, National Archives, RG 127, 97–12, Letters Sent.

40. Houston to McCawley, March 27, 1888, National Archives, RG 127, 97–6, Letters Sent.

41. Houston to Pay Master, USMC, October 12, 1888, National Archives, RG 127, 97–6, Letters Sent.

42. Houston to Col. Cmdt. McCawley, April 24, 1888, National Archives, RG 127, 97–12, Letters Sent.

43. Houston to Col. Cmdt. McCawley, October 12, 1888, National Archives, RG 127, 97–12, Letters Sent.

44. Houston to Col. Cmdt. McCawley, May 3, 1888, National Archives, RG 127, 97–12, Letters Sent.

45. Hebb to Quartermaster Marine Corps, May 12, 1889, National Archives, RG 127, 97–6, Letters Sent.

46. Houston to Sgt. Berry, April 29, 1889, National Archives, RG 127, 97–6, Letters Sent.

47. Houston to McCann, Cmdt., Navy Yard, April 29, 1889, National Archives, RG 127, 97–6, Letters Sent.

48. Houston to Secretary of the Navy, June 8, 1889, National Archives, RG 127, 97–6, Letters Sent.

49. Houston to Secretary of the Navy, February 15, 1889, National Archives, RG 127, 97–6, Letters Sent.

50. Houston to Col. Cmdt. McCawley, November 25, 1889, National Archives, RG 127, 97–12, Letters Sent.

51. McCawley to Broome, March 14, 1890, National Archives, RG 127, 99, Orders Received.

52. Hebb to McCawley, September 25, 1890, National Archives, RG 127, 97–6, Letters Sent.

53. Captain L.E. Fagan to Mayor James A. Hart, October 28, 1890, National Archives, RG 127, 97–6, Letters Sent.

54. Captain L.E. Fagan to Cmdt., Navy Yard, October 29, 1890, National Archives, RG 127, 97–6, Letters Sent.

55. Hebb to Uniform Board, Headquarters Marine Corps, January 6, 1891, National Archives, RG 127, 97–6, Letters Sent.

56. Hebb to Quartermaster Marine Corps, April 19, 1890, National Archives, RG 127, 97–6, Letters Sent.

57. Hebb to Quartermaster Marine Corps, August 16, 1890, National Archives, RG 127, 97–6, Letters Sent.

58. Fagan to Quartermaster Marine Corps, October 7, 1890, National Archives, RG 127, 97–6, Letters Sent.

59. Fagan to Quartermaster Marine Corps, November 4, 1890, National Archives, RG 127, 97–6, Letters Sent.

60. Hebb to Secretary of the Navy, May 26, 1892, National Archives, RG 127, 97–6, Letters Sent.

61. Pope to Health Department, July 22, 1892, National Archives, RG 127, 97–6, Letters Sent.

62. Pope to Cmdt., Navy Yard, Charlestown, July 22, 1892, National Archives, RG 127, 97–6, Letters Sent.

63. Pope to Heywood, July 25, 1892, National Archives, RG 127, 97–6, Letters Sent.

64. Pope to Mr. Leo C. Brenner, Exterminator, 279 Myrtle Ave., Brooklyn, NY, National Archives, RG 127, 97–6, Letters Sent.

65. Pope to Isa A. Horn, November 25, 1892, National Archives, RG 127, 97–7, Letters Sent.

66. Pope to Heywood, January 26, 1893, National Archives, RG 127, 97–7, Letters Sent.

67. Pope to Heywood, January 24, 1893, National Archives, RG 127, 97–7, Letters Sent.

68. *Boston Naval Shipyard Architectural and Environmental Inventory*, May 17, 1974.

69. Pope to *Boston Herald*, February 14, 1893, National Archives, RG 127, 97-7, Letters Sent.
70. Pope to Colonel Wm. J. Chase, 233 State St., Boston, MA, June 9, 1893, National Archives, RG 127, 97-7, Letters Sent.
71. Pope to Colonel Wm. J. Chase, 233 State St., Boston, MA, June 18, 1893, National Archives, RG 127, 97-7, Letters Sent.
72. Pope to New England Telephone and Telegraph, July 28, 1893, National Archives, RG 127, 97-7, Letters Sent. Pope to Cmdt., Navy Yard, Charlestown, July 12, 1893, National Archives, RG 127, 97-7, Letters Sent.
73. Pope to Wm. A. Brown, Superintendent of Police, Newark, NJ, July 29, 1893, National Archives, RG 127, 97-7, Letters Sent.
74. Pope to Heywood, September 25, 1893, National Archives, RG 127, 97-7, Letters Sent.
75. Pope to Quartermaster Marine Corps, September 28, 1893, Pope to Heywood, December 7, 1893, National Archives, RG 127, 97-7, Letters Sent.
76. Pope to Harrington, December 15, 1893, National Archives, RG 127, 97-7, Letters Sent.
77. Harrington to Heywood, December 20, 1893, National Archives, RG 127, 97-7, Letters Sent.
78. Harrington to Cmdt., Navy Yard, Charlestown, December 22, 1893, National Archives, RG 127, 97-7, Letters Sent.
79. Harrington to Surgeon E.P. Stone, U.S. Navy, January 12, 1894, National Archives, RG 127, 97-7, Letters Sent.

Chapter 7

1. Meade to Col. Cmdt. Heywood, June 29, 1897, National Archives, RG 127, 97-12, Letters Sent.
2. Meade to NE News, 14 Franklin St., Boston, January 19, 1894, National Archives, RG 127, 97-7, Letters Sent.
3. Meade to Chaplain Alfred L. Royce, U.S. Navy, January 20, 1894, National Archives, RG 127, 97-7, Letters Sent. Barracks Order, January 20, 1894, National Archives, RG 127, 97-7, Letters Sent.
4. Meade to Mr. Fre Helger, 384 Huntington Ave, Boston, February 5, 1894, National Archives, RG 127, 97-7, Letters Sent.
5. Meade to Judge Advocate General, U.S. Navy, February 6, 1894, National Archives, RG 127, 97-7, Letters Sent.
6. Meade to Charles Ruger, James Lee, James McLaughlin, February 18, 21, 1894, Letters Sent.
7. Meade to Mr. W.H. Spencer, 41 Oxford St., Worcester, MA, February 27, 1894, National Archives, RG 127, 97-7, Letters Sent.
8. Meade to Secretary of Agriculture, March 6, 1894, National Archives, RG 127, 97-7, Letters Sent.
9. Meade to Captain M.L. White, 15th Precinct, Charlestown, March 14, 1894, National Archives, RG 127, 97-7, Letters Sent.
10. Meade to Heywood, March 17, 1894, National Archives, RG 127, 97-7, Letters Sent.
11. Meade to Surgeon E.P. Stone, March 21, 1894, National Archives, RG 127, 97-7, Letters Sent.
12. Meade to Heywood, March 28, 1894, National Archives, RG 127, 97-7, Letters Sent.
13. Meade to Heywood, April 4, 1894, National Archives, RG 127, 97-7, Letters Sent.
14. Harrington to Meade, April 5, 1894, National Archives, RG 127, 97-7, Letters Sent.
15. Meade to Heywood, April 4, 1894, National Archives, RG 127, 97-7, Letters Sent.
16. Meade to Heywood, April 20, 1894, National Archives, RG 127, 97-7, Letters Sent.
17. Meade to Heywood, April 24, 1894, National Archives, RG 127, 97-7, Letters Sent.
18. Meade to Heywood, April 25, 1894, National Archives, RG 127, 97-7, Letters Sent.
19. Meade to Hon. W.M. Curtis, U.S. House of Representatives, April 24, 1894, National Archives, RG 127, 97-7, Letters Sent.
20. Meade to Cmdt., Navy Yard, Charlestown, May 29, 1894, National Archives, RG 127, 97-7, Letters Sent.
21. Meade to Heywood, June 1, 1894, National Archives, RG 127, 97-7, Letters Sent.
22. Meade to Heywood, June 19, 1894, National Archives, RG 127, 97-7, Letters Sent.
23. Meade to Cmdt., Navy Yard, Charlestown, July 13, 1894, National Archives, RG 127, 97-7, Letters Sent.
24. Captain of the Yard, General Order, July 14, 1894, July 14, 1894, National Archives, RG 127, 97-7, Letters Sent.
25. Meade to Quartermaster Marine Corps, July 23and 24, 1894, National Archives, RG 127, 97-7, Letters Sent.
26. Meade to Cmdt., Navy Yard, Charlestown, August 22, 1894, National Archives, RG 127, 97-7, Letters Sent.
27. Meade to Heywood, August 29, 1894, National Archives, RG 127, 97-7, Letters Sent.
28. Meade to Cmdt., Charlestown Navy Yard, Sept. 15, 1894, National Archives, RG 127, 97-7, Letters Sent.
29. Meade to Charlestown Gas and Electric, Sept. 16, 1894, National Archives, RG 127, 97-7, Letters Sent.
30. Meade to Messrs. Lynch and Woodward, Sept. 24, 1894, National Archives, RG 127, 97-7, Letters Sent.
31. Meade to Commandant, Charlestown Navy Yard, Oct. 3, 1894, National Archives, RG 127, 97-7, Letters Sent.
32. Meade to Commandant, Charlestown Navy Yard, Oct. 6, 1894, National Archives, RG 127, 97-7, Letters Sent.
33. Meade to Heywood, Oct. 16, 1894, National Archives, RG 127, 97-7, Letters Sent.
34. Meade to Quartermaster Marine Corps, Nov. 3, 1894, National Archives, RG 127, 97-7, Letters Sent.
35. Meade to Quartermaster Marine Corps, Nov. 14, 1894, National Archives, RG 127, 97-7, Letters Sent.
36. Meade to Hon. Wm. Cochrane, Commissioner of Pensions, Washington, D.C., Dec. 3, 1894, National Archives, RG 127, 97-7, Letters Sent.
37. Meade to Frank A. Titus, 143 Main St., Charlestown, Dec. 8, 1894, National Archives, RG 127, 97-7, 97-7, Letters Sent.
38. Meade to Messrs. S.P. Hicks and Sons, 9 Bowker St., Boston, Dec. 10, 1894, National Archives, RG 127, 97-7, Letters Sent.
39. Meade to Cmdt., Charlestown Navy Yard, Jan. 12, 1895, National Archives, RG 127, 97-7, Letters Sent.
40. Meade to Cmdt., Charlestown Navy Yard, Feb. 12, 1895, National Archives, RG 127, 97-7, Letters Sent.
41. Meade to Cmdt., Charlestown Navy Yard, Feb. 25, 1895, National Archives, RG 127, 97-7, Letters Sent.
42. Meade to Heywood, April 22, 1895, National Archives, RG 127, 97-7, Letters Sent.
43. Meade to Superintendent, Deer Island, May 20, 1895, National Archives, RG 127, 97-7, Letters Sent.
44. Meade to Rector, St. Mary's Church, Charlestown, June 4, 1895, National Archives, RG 127, 97-7, Letters Sent.
45. Meade to Heywood, May 29, 1895, National Archives, RG 127, 97-7, Letters Sent.
46. Meade to Heywood, May 29, 1895, National Archives, RG 127, 97-7, Letters Sent.
47. Meade to *Boston Globe*, July 2, 1895, National Archives, RG 127, 97-7, Letters Sent.
48. Meade to Heywood, July 15, 1895, National Archives, RG 127, 97-7, Letters Sent.
49. Meade to Heywood, July 15, 1895, National Archives, RG 127, 97-7, Letters Sent.

50. Meade to Cmdt., Charlestown Navy Yard, July 28, 1895, National Archives, RG 127, 97-7, Letters Sent.
51. Meade to Heywood, August 8, 1895, National Archives, RG 127, 97-7, Letters Sent.
52. Meade to Heywood, August 20, 1895, National Archives, RG 127, 97-7, Letters Sent.
53. Meade to Cmdt., Charlestown Navy Yard, August 24, 1895, National Archives, RG 127, 97-7, Letters Sent.
54. Meade to Heywood, August 30, 1895, National Archives, RG 127, 97-7, Letters Sent.
55. Meade to Heywood, September 9, 1895, National Archives, RG 127, 97-7, Letters Sent.
56. Meade to Cmdt., Charlestown Navy Yard, September 25, 1895, National Archives, RG 127, 97-7, Letters Sent.
57. Meade to Cmdt., Charlestown Navy Yard, October 3, 1895, National Archives, RG 127, 97-7, Letters Sent.
58. Meade to Cmdt., Charlestown Navy Yard, December 25, 1895, National Archives, RG 127, 97-7, Letters Sent.
59. Report of Sanitary Conditions in Marine Barracks and Naval Prison, January 26, 1896, National Archives, RG 127, 97-7, Letters Sent.
60. Meade to Cmdt., Charlestown Navy Yard, April 2, 1896, National Archives, RG 127, 97-7, Letters Sent.
61. Meade to Warren National Bank, Charlestown, April 4, 1896, National Archives, RG 127, 97-7, Letters Sent.
62. Remarks to Accompany Notes of the Surgeon of the Navy Yard, Re: Pvt. George Emerson, USMC, August 17, 1896, National Archives, RG 127, Page 164, Book 4, 97-8, Letters Sent.
63. Heywood to Meade, July 21, 1896, National Archives, RG 127, 98-1, Letters Received.
64. Mead to Lt. Sweet, Ordnance Officer, Mass Naval Militia, August 19, 1896, National Archives, RG 127, 97-8, Letters Sent.
65. Meade to Cmdt., Charlestown Navy Yard, August 4, 1896, National Archives, RG 127, 97-8, Letters Sent.
66. Meade to Cmdt., Charlestown Navy Yard, August 26, 1896, National Archives, RG 127, 97-8, Letters Sent.
67. Meade to Cmdt., Charlestown Navy Yard, August 29, 1896, National Archives, RG 127, 97-8, Letters Sent.
68. Meade to Cmdt., Charlestown Navy Yard, September 3, 1896, National Archives, RG 127, 97-8, Letters Sent.
69. Meade to Cmdt., Charlestown Navy Yard, September 18, 1896, National Archives, RG 127, 97-8, Letters Sent.
70. Secretary of the Navy to Heywood, October 27, 1896, National Archives, RG 127, 97-8, Letters Sent.
71. Meade to Heywood, October 29, 1896, National Archives, RG 127, 97-8, Letters Sent.
72. Notes, Surgeon J.H. Clark, Re: Pvt. John Doyle, October 4, 1896, National Archives, RG 127, 97-8, Letters Sent.
73. Meade to Heywood, October 31, 1896, National Archives, RG 127, 97-8, Letters Sent.
74. Meade to Cmdt., Charlestown Navy Yard, November 3, 1896, National Archives, RG 127, 97-8, Letters Sent.
75. Meade to Heywood, November 5, 1896, National Archives, RG 127, 97-8, Letters Sent.
76. Meade to Hon. H.H. Herbert, Secretary of the Navy, December 10, 1896, National Archives, RG 127, 97-8, Letters Sent.
77. Heywood to Cmdt., Charlestown Navy Yard, January 7, 1897, National Archives, RG 127, 98-1, Letters Received.
78. Heywood to Meade, February 15, 1897, National Archives, RG 127, 98-1, Letters Received.
79. Meade to Sergeant Daniel Sullivan, February 24, 1897, National Archives, RG 127, 97-8, Letters Sent.
80. Meade to Cmdt., Charlestown Navy Yard, March 18, 1897, National Archives, RG 127, 97-8, Letters Sent.
81. Meade to Cmdt., Charlestown Navy Yard, March 26, 1897, National Archives, RG 127, 97-8, Letters Sent.
82. Heywood to Meade, March 20, 1897, National Archives, RG 127, 98-1, Letters Received.
83. Heywood to Meade, March 30, 1897, National Archives, RG 127, 98-1, Letters Received.
84. Meade to Cmdt., Charlestown Navy Yard, April 1, 1897, National Archives, RG 127, 97-8, Letters Sent.
85. Meade to Secretary of the Navy, April 3, 1897, National Archives, RG 127, 97-8, Letters Sent.
86. Major G.C. Reid, Adjutant and Inspector, Headquarters Marine Corps, April 22, 1897, National Archives, RG 127, 98-1, Letters Received.
87. Heywood to Meade, May 5, 1897, National Archives, RG 127, 98-1, Letters Received.
88. Meade to Cmdt., Charlestown Navy Yard, June 5, 1897, National Archives, RG 127, 97-8, Letters Sent.
89. Meade to Cmdt., Charlestown Navy Yard, June 7, 1897, National Archives, RG 127, 97-8, Letters Sent.
90. Meade to Cmdt., Charlestown Navy Yard, July 24, 1897, National Archives, RG 127, 97-8, Letters Sent.
91. Meade to Quartermaster Marine Corps, August 19, 1897, National Archives, RG 127, 97-8, Letters Sent.
92. Meade to Col. Cmdt. Heywood, July 3, 1897, National Archives, RG 127, 97-12, Letters Sent.
93. Mead to Col. Cmdt. Heywood, October 15, 1897, National Archives, RG 127, 97-12, Letters Sent.
94. Meade to Cmdt., Charlestown Navy Yard, September 14, 1897, National Archives, RG 127, 97-8, Letters Sent.
95. Meade to Heywood, October 30, 1897, National Archives, RG 127, 97-8, Letters Sent.
96. Col. Cmdt. Heywood to Meade, September 18, 1897, National Archives, RG 127, 97-8, Letters Sent.
97. Meade to Col. Cmdt. Heywood, October 30, 1897, National Archives, RG 127, 97-12, Letters Sent.
98. Meade to Secretary of the Navy, October 21, 1897, National Archives, RG 127, 97-8, Letters Sent.
99. Meade to Quartermaster Marine Corps, October 29, 1897, National Archives, RG 127, 97-14, Letters Sent.
100. Evans, G.R. *Historic Structure Report:Marine Barracks (Building I), Charlestown*, pp. 20-25.
101. Meade to Charlestown Gas and Electric Co., November 22, 1897, National Archives, RG 127, 97-8, Letters Sent.
102. Heywood to Meade, November 23, 1897, National Archives, RG 127, 98-2, Letters Received.
103. Heywood to Meade, December 4, 1897, National Archives, RG 127, 98-2, Letters Received.
104. Simmons, *The United States Marines, 1775-1975*, p. 83.
105. Max Boot, *The Savage Wars of Peace*, pp. 85-87.
106. Kelton to Sgt. Thomas McCabe, Sgt. Edward Clifford and Cpl. Timoth Sugrue, February 17, 1898, National Archives, RG 127, 97-8, Letters Sent.
107. Heywood to Kelton, January 13, 1898, National Archives, RG 127, 98-2, Letters Received.
108. Kelton to Cmdt., Charlestown Navy Yard, March 4, 1898, National Archives, RG 127, 97-8, Letters Sent.
109. Pope to 1st Lt. T.P. Kane, April 5, 1898, National Archives, RG 127, 97-8, Letters Sent.

Chapter 8

1 Frederick R. Black, *Cultural Resources Management Study No. 20, Charlestown Navy Yard, 1890-1973*, 1988, p. 122.
2. Pope to Sgt. Clark, April 6, 1898, National Archives, RG 127, 97-8, Letters Sent.
3. Pope to Agent, Fall River Line, April 18, 1898, National Archives, RG 127, 97-8, Letters Sent.
4. Pope to Commanding Officer, Marine Barracks,

Brooklyn, NY, April 18, 1898, National Archives, RG 127, 97-8, Letters Sent.
    5. Frederick R. Black, *Cultural Resources Management Study No. 20, Charlestown Navy Yard 1890-1973*, 1988, p. 121.
    6. Kelton to Col. Cmdt. Heywood, January 7, 1898, National Archives, RG 127, 97-12, Letters Sent.
    7. Ibid., p. 123.
    8. Ibid., p. 124.
    9. Pope to Amos J. Cummings, Member of Congress, April 19, 1898, National Archives, RG 127, 97-8, Letters Sent.
    10. Pope to Paymaster, USMC, Washington, D.C., April 20, 1898, National Archives, RG 127, 97-8, Letters Sent.
    11. Pope to Sgt. John Brine, April 22, 1898, National Archives, RG 127, 97-8, Letters Sent.
    12. Lieutenant Commander, U.S. Navy, to Sgt. E.W. Clifford, April 24, 1898, National Archives, RG 127, 97-8, Letters Sent.
    13. Wallach to ticket agent, Penn Railroad, April 27, 1898, National Archives, RG 127, 97-8, Letters Sent.
    14. Wallach to Sgt. Wm. H. Cooper, April 30, 1898, National Archives, RG 127, 97-8, Letters Sent.
    15. Wallach to Sgt. Jackson, May 2, 1898, National Archives, RG 127, 97-8, Letters Sent.
    16. Wallach to Sgt. L. Ebers, May 5, 1898, National Archives, RG 127, Letters Sent.
    17. Wallach to Heywood, May 7, 1898, National Archives, RG 127, 97-8, Letters Sent.
    18. Wallach to Cmdt., Charlestown Navy Yard, May 17, 1898, National Archives, RG 127, 97-8, Letters Sent.
    19. Wallach to Sgt. Daniel Sullivan, May 17, 1898, National Archives, RG 127, 97-8, Letters Sent.
    20. Wallach to *Boston Post* and *Boston Herald*, May 21, 1898, National Archives, RG 127, 97-8, Letters Sent.
    21. Wallach to Agent, Merchants and Miners Line, Boston, June 3, 1898, National Archives, RG 127, 97-8, Letters Sent.
    22. Wallach to Sgt. Augustus Rahn, June 15, 1898, National Archives, RG 127, 97-8, Letters Sent.
    23. Wallach to Cmdt., Charlestown Navy Yard, June 15, 1898, National Archives, RG 127, 97-8, Letters Sent.
    24. Wallach to Thomas H. Armstrong, Esq., June 28, 1898, National Archives, RG 127, 97-8, Letters Sent.
    25. Wallach to Cmdt., Charlestown Navy Yard, June 29, 1898, National Archives, RG 127, 97-8, Letters Sent.
    26. Wallach to Cmdt., Charlestown Navy Yard, August 2, 1898, National Archives, RG 127, 97-8, Letters Sent.
    27. Wallach to Sgt. Wm. McCollam, August 4, 1898, National Archives, RG 127, 97-8, Letters Sent.
    28. Wallach to Cmdt., Charlestown Navy Yard, August 5, 1898, National Archives, RG 127, 97-8, Letters Sent.
    29. Wallach to Cmdt., Charlestown Navy Yard, August 10, 1898, National Archives, RG 127, 97-8, Letters Sent.
    30. Wallach to *Boston Globe* and *Boston Post*, August 26, 1898, National Archives, RG 127, 97-8, Letters Sent.
    31. Pope to Quartermaster Marine Corps, September 12, 1898, National Archives, RG 127, 97-8, Letters Sent.
    32. Pope to Cmdt., Charlestown Navy Yard, September 13, 1898, National Archives, RG 127, 97-8, Letters Sent.
    33. Pope to Cmdt., Charlestown Navy Yard, September 21, 1898, National Archives, RG 127, 97-8, Letters Sent.
    34. Pope to Cmdt., Charlestown Navy Yard, September 21, 1898, National Archives, RG 127, 97-8, Letters Sent.
    35. Pope to Mrs. Cutler, October 7, 1898, National Archives, RG 127, 97-8, Letters Sent.
    36. Pope to Auditor for the Navy Department, October 28, 1898, National Archives, RG 127, 97-8, Letters Sent.
    37. Pope to Cmdt., Charlestown Navy Yard, October 29, 1898, National Archives, RG 127, 97-8, Letters Sent.
    38. Pope to 1st Lt. Long, November 18, 1898, National Archives, RG 127, 97-8, Letters Sent.
    39. Pope to *Boston Globe* and *Boston Herald*, December 8, 1898, National Archives, RG 127, 97-8, Letters Sent.
    40. Pope to Chief of Police, Boston, December 8, 1898, National Archives, RG 127, 97-8, Letters Sent.
    41. Heywood to Pope, January 25, 1899, National Archives, RG 127, 98-2, Letters Received.
    42. Pope to Cmdt., Charlestown Navy Yard, January 6, 1899, National Archives, RG 127, 97-8, Letters Sent.
    43. Heywood to Pope, January 17, 1899, National Archives, RG 127, 98-2, Letters Received.
    44. Pope to Chief of Bureau of Equipment and Recruiting, Navy Department, January 10, 1899, National Archives, RG 127, 97-8, Letters Sent.
    45. Kelton to Pope, April 8, 1899, National Archives, RG 127, 97-8, Letters Sent.
    46. Moses to Commanding Officer, Battalion of Marines, Cavite, PI, April 30, 1899, National Archives, RG 127, 97-8, Letters Sent.
    47. Heywood to Cochrane, May 26, 1899, National Archives, RG 127, 98-2, Letters Received.
    48. Lighthouse Keeper, Newburyport, MA to Commanding Officer, Marine Barracks, Boston, May 9, 1899, National Archives, RG 127, 98-22, Letters Received.
    49. Simmons, *The United States Marines 1775-1975*, pp. 69-70.
    50. Cochrane to Judge Advocate General, Navy Department, and Cmdt., Charlestown Navy Yard, June 10 and June 26, 1899, National Archives, RG 127, 97-8, Letters Sent.
    51. Cochrane to Cmdt., Charlestown Navy Yard, June 19, 1899, National Archives, RG 127, 97-8, Letters Sent.
    52. Cochrane to Journal Newspaper Co., 264 Washington St., Boston, July 25, 1899, National Archives, RG 127, 97-8, Letters Sent.
    53. Cochrane to 2d Lt. Norman G. Burton, USMC, August 8, 1899, National Archives, RG 127, 97-8, Letters Sent.
    54. Cochrane to Asst. Adj. and Inspector of Rifle Practice, Headquarters Marine Corps, August 19, 1899, National Archives, RG 127, 97-8, Letters Sent.
    55. Cochrane to Asst. Adj. and Inspector of Rifle Practice, Headquarters Marine Corps, May 27, 1899, National Archives, RG 127, 97-12, Letters Sent.
    56. Heywood to Cochrane, July 27, 1899, National Archives, RG 127, 98-2, Letters Received.
    57. Cochrane to Cmdt., Charlestown Navy Yard, August 21, 1899, National Archives, RG 127, 97-8, Letters Sent.
    58. Heywood to Cochrane, August 8, 1899, National Archives, RG 127, 98-2, Letters Received.
    59. G.C. Reid to Cochrane, August 14, 1899, National Archives, RG 127, 98-2, Letters Received.
    60. Cochrane to Publisher, *Springfield Republican*, September 9, 1899, National Archives, RG 127, 97-8, Letters Sent.
    61. Cochrane to Brig. Gen. Heywood, October 3, 1899, National Archives, RG 127, 97-12, Letters Sent.
    62. Cochrane to Brig. Gen. Heywood, October 9, 1899, National Archives, RG 127, 97-12, Letters Sent.
    63. Cochrane to Cmdt., Charlestown Navy Yard, November 25, 1899, National Archives, RG 127, 97-8, Letters Sent.
    64. Cochrane to Cmdt., Charlestown Navy Yard, December 8, 1899, National Archives, RG 127, 97-8, Letters Sent.
    65. Cochrane to Cmdt., Charlestown Navy Yard, December 9, 1899, National Archives, RG 127, 97-8, Letters Sent.
    66. Cochrane to 2d Lt. N.G. Burton, USMC, October 29, 1899, National Archives, RG 127, 97-8, Letters Sent.
    67. Cochrane to Capt. L.W. Moses, November 20, 1899, National Archives, RG 127, 97-8, Letters Sent.
    68. Cochrane to 2d Lt. J.N. Wright, USMC, January 6, 1900, National Archives, RG 127, 97-8, Letters Sent.

69. Cochrane to Sgt. E.F. Larkin, January 22, 1900, National Archives, RG 127, 97–8, Letters Sent.
70. Heywood to Cochrane, February 6, 1900, National Archives, RG 127, 98–2, Letters Received.
71. Cochrane to Brig. Gen. Heywood, January 18, 1900, National Archives, RG 127, 97–12, Letters Sent.
72. Cochrane to Brig. Gen. Heywood, January 16, 1900, National Archives, RG 127, 97–12, Letters Sent.
73. Cochrane to Marie Georges, Valley Hotel, Keene, NH, February 1, 1900, National Archives, RG 127, 97–8, Letters Sent.
74. Cochrane to Commanding Officer, Marine Barracks, Washington, D.C., February 8, 1900, National Archives, RG 127, 97–8, Letters Sent.
75. Cochrane to Commanding Officer, Marine Barracks, Washington, D.C., March 15, 1900, National Archives, RG 127, 97–8, Letters Sent.
76. Cochrane to Brig. Gen. Heywood, March 17, 1900, National Archives, RG 127, 97–12, Letters Sent.
77. Cochrane to Brig. Gen. Heywood, April 16, 1900, National Archives, RG 127, 97–12, Letters Sent.
78. Cochrane to Cmdt., Charlestown Navy Yard, April 18, 1900, National Archives, RG 127, 97–8, Letters Sent.
79. Cochrane to Cmdt., Charlestown Navy Yard, May 2, 1900, National Archives, RG 127, 97–8, Letters Sent.
80. Cochrane to Cmdt., Charlestown Navy Yard, May 20, 1900, National Archives, RG 127, 97–8, Letters Sent.
81. Cochrane to Cmdt., Charlestown Navy Yard, June 1, 1900, National Archives, RG 127, 97–8, Letters Sent.
82. Pope to Cmdt., Charlestown Navy Yard, June 19, 1900, National Archives, RG 127, 97–8, Letters Sent.
83. Pope to Sgt. H.J. Bray, USMC, June 21, 1900, National Archives, RG 127, 97–8, Letters Sent.
84. Pope to Cmdt., Charlestown Navy Yard, June 21, 1900, National Archives, RG 127, 97–8, Letters Sent.
85. Cochrane to 2d Lt. D.C. McDougal, USMC, June 15, 1900, National Archives, RG 127, 97–8, Letters Sent.
86. Cochrane to Brig. Gen. Heywood, June 26, 1900, National Archives, RG 127, 97–12, Letters Sent.
87. Cochrane to Brig. Gen. Heywood, June 28, 1900, National Archives, RG 127, 97–12, Letters Sent.
88. Cochrane to Mary McCabe, June 28, 1900, National Archives, RG 127, 97–8, Letters Sent.
89. Cochrane to Mary McCabe, July 4, 1900, National Archives, RG 127, 97–8, Letters Sent.
90. Pope to Mary McCabe, July 15, 1900, National Archives, RG 127, 97–8, Letters Sent.
91. Cochrane to Cmdt., Charlestown Navy Yard, July 9, 1900, National Archives, RG 127, 97–8, Letters Sent.
92. Pope to Commanding Officer, Marine Barracks, Newport, RI, July 31, 1900, National Archives, RG 127, 97–8, Letters Sent.
93. Heywood to Cochrane, July 16, 1900, National Archives, RG 127, 98–2, Letters Received.
94. Cochrane to Brig. Gen. Heywood, July 26, 1900, National Archives, RG 127, 97–12, Letters Sent.

Chapter 9

1. Pope to Brig. Gen. Heywood, August 4, 1900, National Archives, RG 127, 97–12, Letters Sent.
2. Pope to Cmdt., Charlestown Navy Yard, August 7, 1900, National Archives, RG 127, 97–8, Letters Sent.
3. Pope to G.C. Brenner, 25 Crown St., Brooklyn, NY, August 31, 1900, National Archives, RG 127, 97–8, Letters Sent.
4. Pope to Messrs J.E. Lewis and Co., Chelsea, MA, September 10, 1900, National Archives, RG 127, 97–8, Letters Sent.
5. Pope to Cpl. J.H. Underwood, USMC, September 20, 1900, National Archives, RG 127, 97–8, Letters Sent.
6. Heywood to Pope, September 18, 1900, National Archives, RG 127, 98–3, Letters Received.
7. Pope to Cmdt., Charlestown Navy Yard, September 21, 1900, National Archives, RG 127, 97–8, Letters Sent.
8. Pope to Brig. Gen. Heywood, September 6, 1900, National Archives, RG 127, 97–12, Letters Sent.
9. Pope to Brig. Gen. Heywood, September 8, 1900, National Archives, RG 127, 97–12, Letters Sent.
10. Pope to New England Telephone and Telegraph, 125 High St., Boston, October 6, 1900, National Archives, RG 127, 97–8, Letters Sent.
11. Pope to Cmdt., Charlestown Navy Yard, October 9, 1900, National Archives, RG 127, 97–8, Letters Sent.
12. Pope to Capt. E.S. Houston, U.S. Navy, Commanding Officer, USS *Amphitrite*, October 11, 1900, National Archives, RG 127, 97–8, Letters Sent.
13. Capt. John A. Lejeune to Col. Pope, October 12, 1900, National Archives, RG 127, 98–22, Letters Received.
14. Simmons, *The United States Marines, 1775–1975*, p. 115, p. 135.
15. Heywood to Pope, October 18, 1900, National Archives, RG 127, 98–3, Letters Received.
16. Pope to Superintendent of Streets, City of Boston, November 7, 1900, National Archives, RG 127, 97–8, Letters Sent.
17. Pope to Mr. G.M. Elliott, Brunswick, ME, November 12, 1900, National Archives, RG 127, 97–8, Letters Sent.
18. Pope to Cmdt., Charlestown Navy Yard, November 17, 1900, National Archives, RG 127, 97–8, Letters Sent.
19. Pope to Cmdt., Charlestown Navy Yard, November 30, 1900, National Archives, RG 127, 97–8, Letters Sent.
20. Pope to Col. H. Clay Cochrane, December 17, 1900, National Archives, RG 127, 97–8, Letters Sent.
21. Pope to Waltham Chemical Co., December 28, 1900, National Archives, RG 127, 97–8, Letters Sent.
22. Pope to Brig. Gen. Heywood, December 20, 1900, National Archives, RG 127, 97–12, Letters Sent.
23. Pope to Cmdt., Charlestown Navy Yard, January 26, 1901, National Archives, RG 127, 97–8, Letters Sent.
24. Pope to Brig. Gen. Heywood, January 30, 1901, National Archives, RG 127, 97–12, Letters Sent.
25. Pope to Brig. Gen. Heywood, February 1, 1901.
26. Col. G.C. Reid, Adjutant and Inspector, USMC, to Pope, February 4, 1901, National Archives, RG 127, 98–3, Letters Received.
27. Pope to Brig. Gen. Heywood, February 7, 1901, National Archives, RG 127, 97–12, Letters Sent.
28. Pope to Cmdt., Charlestown Navy Yard, February 11, 1901, National Archives, RG 127, 97–8, Letters Sent.
29. Pope to Cmdt., Charlestown Navy Yard, May 15, 1901, National Archives, RG 127, 97–8, Letters Sent.
30. Heywood to Pope, March 8, 1902, National Archives, RG 127, 98–3, Letters Received.
31. Heywood to Pope, April 6, 1901, National Archives, RG 127, 98–3, Letters Received.
32. Transfer List, Marine Barracks, Boston, April 10, 1901, National Archives, RG 127, 97–8, Letters Sent.
33. Pope to Waltham Chemical Co., May 25, 1901, National Archives, RG 127, 97–8, Letters Sent.
34. Pope to Cmdt., Charlestown Navy Yard, April 12, 1901, National Archives, RG 127, 97–8, Letters Sent.
35. Pope to Cmdt., Charlestown Navy Yard, April 17, 1901, National Archives, RG 127, 97–8, Letters Sent.
36. Pope to Cmdt., Charlestown Navy Yard, April 18, 1901, National Archives, RG 127, 97–8, Letters Sent.
37. Pope to Brig. Gen. Heywood, May 2, 1901, National Archives, RG 127, 97–12, Letters Sent.

38. Pope to Brig. Gen. Heywood, May 9, 1901, National Archives, RG 127, 97-12, Letters Sent.
39. Pope to Brig. Gen. Heywood, June 10, 1901, National Archives, RG 127, 97-12, Letters Sent.
40. Pope to Cpl. Michael J. O'Day, USMC, May 10, 1901, National Archives, RG 127, 97-9, Letters Sent.
41. Pope to Waltham Chemical Co., May 10, 1901, National Archives, RG 127, 97-9, Letters Sent.
42. Pope to Cmdt., Charlestown Navy Yard, May 13, 1901, National Archives, RG 127, 97-9, Letters Sent.
43. Pope to Cmdt., Charlestown Navy Yard, May 20, 1901, National Archives, RG 127, 97-9, Letters Sent.
44. Pope to Cmdr. W.F. Sinclair, Gen. R.S. MacKenzie Assoc., 1161 Washington St., Boston, May 23, 1901, National Archives, RG 127, 97-9, Letters Sent.
45. Pope to various Memorial Day committees, May 25, 1901, National Archives, RG 127, 97-9, Letters Sent.
46. Pope to Mr. Harold Hutchinson, Massachusetts Rifle Association, 53 Devonshire St., Boston, May 23, 1901, National Archives, RG 127, 97-9, Letters Sent.
47. Pope to Cmdt., Charlestown Navy Yard, May 25, 1901, National Archives, RG 127, 97-9, Letters Sent.
48. Pope to Cmdt., Charlestown Navy Yard, May 25, 1901, National Archives, RG 127, 97-9, Letters Sent.
49. Pope to Capt. Clark, Company E, 5th Regt., MVM, May 28, 1901, National Archives, RG 127, 97-9, Letters Sent.
50. Pope to Cmdt., Charlestown Navy Yard, May 29, 1901, National Archives, RG 127, 97-9, Letters Sent.
51. Report of Prisoners, Naval Prison, Charlestown Navy Yard, June 1, 1901, National Archives, RG 127, 97-9, Letters Sent.
52. Pope to Secretary, Board of Prisons, Middlesex County, June 10, 1901, National Archives, RG 127, 97-9, Letters Sent.
53. Heywood to Pope, June 18, 1901, National Archives, RG 127, 98-3, Letters Received.
54. Pope to Charlestown Gas and Electric Co., June 21, 1901, National Archives, RG 127, 97-9, Letters Sent.
55. Pope to Waltahm Chemical Co., June 24, 1901, National Archives, RG 127, 97-9, Letters Sent.
56. Pope to Cmdt., Charlestown Navy Yard, June 25, 1901, National Archives, RG 127, 97-9, Letters Sent.
57. Pope to Mr. D.L. Chase, President, Massachusetts Rifle Association, July 30, 1901, National Archives, RG 127, 97-9, Letters Sent.
58. Report of Prisoners, Naval Prison, Charlestown Navy Yard, August 5, 1901, National Archives, RG 127, 97-9, Letters Sent.
59. Pope to Sgt. W.G. Smith, USMC, August 8, 1901, National Archives, RG 127, 97-9, Letters Sent.
60. Col. G.C. Reid, Adj. and Inspector, Headquarters Marine Corps, August 15, 1901, National Archives, RG 127, 98-3, Letters Received.
61. Pope to Cmdt., Charlestown Navy Yard, August 22, 1901, National Archives, RG 127, 97-9, Letters Sent.
62. Pope to Cmdt., Charlestown Navy Yard, August 24, 1901, National Archives, RG 127, 97-9, Letters Sent.
63. Pope to Waltham Chemical Co., September 4, 1901, National Archives, RG 127, 97-9, Letters Sent.
64. Pope to Waltham Chemical Co., October 16, 1901, National Archives, RG 127, 97-9, Letters Sent.
65. Pope to Washington Avenue Street Car Line, Chelsea, November 11, 1901, National Archives, RG 127, 97-9, Letters Sent.
66. Heywood to Pope, November 29, 1901, National Archives, RG 127, 98-3, Letters Received.
67. Civil Engineer to Cmdt., Charlestown Navy Yard, December 3, 1901, National Archives, RG 127, 97-9, Letters Sent.
68. Pope to Cmdt., Charlestown Navy Yard, December 8, 1901, National Archives, RG 127, 97-9, Letters Sent.
69. Col. G.C. Reid, Adj. and Inspector, Headquarters Marine Corps, to Pope, December 11, 1901, National Archives, RG 127, 98-3, Letters Received.
70. Report of Prisoners, Naval Prison, Charlestown Navy Yard, January 25, 1902, National Archives, RG 127, 97-9, Letters Sent.
71. Report of Prisoners, Naval Prison, Charlestown Navy Yard, March 15, 1902, National Archives, RG 127, 97-9, Letters Sent.
72 Heywood to Pope, February 13, 1902, National Archives, RG 127, 98-3, Letters Received.
73 Max Boot, *The Savage Wars of Peace*, pp. 64, 65.
74 Pope to Capt. Dion Williams, USMC, March 18, 1902, National Archives, RG 127, 97-9, Letters Sent.
75 Pope to Gy. Sgt. John A. Logan, USMC, March 22, 1902, National Archives, RG 127, 97-9, Letters Sent.
76 Pope to Cmdt., Charlestown Navy Yard, March 25, 1902, National Archives, RG 127, 97-9, Letters Sent.
77. Pope to Capt. Dion Williams, USMC, April 2, 1902, National Archives, RG 127, 97-9, Letters Sent.
78. Pope to Mr. Fred Pettigrove, Chairman, Prison Commission, 24 Statehouse, Boston, April 2, 1902, National Archives, RG 127, 97-9, Letters Sent.
79. Pope to Mr. Fred Pettigrove, Chairman, Prison Commission, 24 Statehouse, Boston, April 4, 1902, National Archives, RG 127, 97-9, Letters Sent.
80. Pope to Commanding Officer, USS *Wabash*, April 14, 1902, National Archives, RG 127, 97-9, Letters Sent.
81. Williams to Cmdt., Charlestown Navy Yard, April 21, 1902, National Archives, RG 127, 97-9, Letters Sent.
82. Williams to Mr. George H. Champlin and Co., 181 Tremont Street, Boston, May 3, 1902, National Archives, RG 127, 97-9, Letters Sent.
83. Williams to Mrs. J.E. Mason, 10 Lundberg St., Lowell, MA, May 6, 1902, National Archives, RG 127, 97-9, Letters Sent.
84. Pope to Cmdt., Charlestown Navy Yard, May 10, 1902, National Archives, RG 127, 97-9, Letters Sent.
85. Pope to Cmdt., Charlestown Navy Yard, May 12, 1902, National Archives, RG 127, 97-9, Letters Sent.
86. Pope to Commanding Officer, Marine Barracks, Newport, RI, May 29, 1902, National Archives, RG 127, 97-9, Letters Sent.
87. Pope to Mrs. Edward Flagg, 108 2nd St., NW, Washington, D.C., May 29, 1902, National Archives, RG 127, 97-9, Letters Sent.
88. Pope to Sgt. Michael O'Day, USMC, June 11, 1902, National Archives, RG 127, 97-9, Letters Sent.
89. Pope to Cmdt., Charlestown Navy Yard, June 16, 1902, National Archives, RG 127, 97-9, Letters Sent.
90. Pope to Commanding Officer, Marine Barracks, Brooklyn, NY, June 28, 1902, National Archives, RG 127, 97-9, Letters Sent.
91. Heywood to Pope, July 11, 1902, National Archives, RG 127, 98-3, Letters Received.
92. Pope to Cmdt., Charlestown Navy Yard, July 23, 1902, National Archives, RG 127, 97-9, Letters Sent.
93. Williams to Mr. A.P. Gardner, Hamilton, MA, August 7, 1902, National Archives, RG 127, 97-9, Letters Sent.
94. Col. G.C. Reid, Adj. and Inspector, Headquarters Marine Corps, to Pope, August 6, 1902, National Archives, RG 127, 98-3, Letters Received.
95. Report of Prisoners, Naval Prison, Charlestown Navy Yard, August 31, 1902, National Archives, RG 127, 97-9, Letters Sent.
96. Report of Prisoners, Naval Prison, Charlestown Navy Yard, November 2, 1902, National Archives, RG 127, 97-9, Letters Sent.
97. Report of Prisoners, Naval Prison, Charlestown Navy

Yard, November 15, 1902, National Archives, RG 127, 97–9, Letters Sent.
98. Report of Prisoners, Naval Prison, Charlestown Navy Yard, November 29, 1902, National Archives, RG 127, 97–9, Letters Sent.
99. Capt. Charles Long, USMC, to Cmdt., Charlestown Navy Yard, December 3, 1902, National Archives, RG 127, 97–9, Letters Sent.
100. Col. G.C. Reid, Adj. and Inspector, Headquarters Marine Corps, September 22, 1902, National Archives, RG 127, 98–3, Letters Received.
101. Capt. Charles Long, USMC to Cmdt., Charlestown Navy Yard, December 3, 1902, National Archives, RG 127, 97–9, Letters Sent.
102. Long to Maj. Gen. Heywood, December 11, 1902, National Archives, RG 127, 97–13, Letters Sent.
103. Long to Maj. Gen. Heywood, December 19, 1902, National Archives, RG 127, 97–13, Letters Sent.
104. Col. G.C. Reid, Adj. and Inspector, Headquarters Marine Corps, December 22, 1902, Letters Received.
105. Heywood to Pope, December 22, 1902, National Archives, RG 127, 98–2, Letters Received.
106. Pope to Cmdt., Charlestown Navy Yard, January 16, 1903, National Archives, RG 127, 97–9, Letters Sent.
107. Pope to Commanding Officer, Marine Barracks, Washington, D.C., January 17, 1903, National Archives, RG 127, 97–9, Letters Sent.
108. Pope to Cmdt., Charlestown Navy Yard, January 24, 1903, National Archives, RG 127, 97–9, Letters Sent.
109. Col. G.C. Reid, Adjutant and Inspector, Headquarters Marine Corps, to Pope, January 29, 1903, National Archives, RG 127, 98–22, Letters Received.
110. Pope to Cmdt., Charlestown Navy Yard, January 30, 1903, National Archives, RG 127, 97–9, Letters Sent.
111. Capt. George Pigman, Commanding Officer, USRS *Southery*, to Pope, February 6, 1903, National Archives, RG 127, 98–23, Letters Received.
112. Pope to Cmdt., Charlestown Navy Yard, February 10, 1903, National Archives, RG 127, 97–9, Letters Sent.
113. Telegram, Heywood to Captain R.M. Gibson, OIC, Recruiting Office, Worcester, MA, February 17, 1903, National Archives, RG 127, 98–3, Letters Received.
114. Col. Denny, Quartermaster Marine Corps, October 22, 1903, National Archives, RG 127, 98–3, Letters Received.
115. Brig. Gen. Elliott to Pope, October 31, 1903, National Archives, RG 127, 98–3, Letters Received.
116. Brig. Gen. Elliot to Kelton, December 16, 1903, National Archives, RG 127, 98–3, Letters Received.
117. Pope to Mrs. Willis Hadley, Trident Avenue, Winthrop, MA, February 21, 1903, National Archives, RG 127, 97–9, Letters Sent.
118. Pope to Cmdt., Charlestown Navy Yard, February 26, 1903, National Archives,RG 127, 97–9, Letters Sent.

Chapter 10

1. Heywood to Pope, March 27, 1903, National Archives, RG 127, 98–3, Letters Received.
2. Heywood to Pope, April 6, 1903, National Archives, RG 127, 98–3, Letters Received.
3. Pope to Sgt. Samuel F. McCauley, USMC, April 1, 1903, National Archives, RG 127, 97–9, Letters Sent.
4. Extract from military records of Sergeant Arthur Lahar, USMC, April 7, 1903, National Archives, RG 127, 97–9, Letters Sent.
5. Pope to Mayor, City of Lynn, April 9, 1903, National Archives, RG 127, 97–9, Letters Sent.
6. Pope to Sergeant George Bernard, USMC, April 10, 1903, National Archives, RG 127, 97–9, Letters Sent.
7. Colonel G.C. Reid, Asst. CMC, to Pope, April 6, 1903, National Archives, RG 127, 98–3, Letters Received.
8. Pope to Cmdt., Charlestown Navy Yard, April 10, 1903, National Archives, RG 127, 97–9, Letters Sent.
9. Pope to Cmdt., Charlestown Navy Yard, April 16, 1903, National Archives, RG 127, 97–9, Letters Sent.
10. Pope to Captain Charles T. Hilliker, State Armory, Lynn, MA, April 17, 1903, National Archives, RG 127, 97–9, Letters Sent.
11. Pope to Chairman, Board of Public Works, City of Lynn, MA, May 14, 1903, National Archives, RG 127, 97–9, Letters Sent.
12. Pope to Colonel James G. White, IG for Rifle Practice, Statehouse, Boston, MA, May 14, 1903, National Archives, RG 127, 97–9, Letters Sent.
13. Pope to Maj. Gen. Heywood, May 10, 1903, National Archives, RG 127, 97–13, Letters Sent.
14. Pope to Cmdt., Charlestown Navy Yard, May 15, 1903, National Archives, RG 127, 97–9, Letters Sent.
15. Pope to Cmdt., Charlestown Navy Yard, May 26, 1903, National Archives, RG 127, 97–9, Letters Sent.
16. Pope to Private Ocie E. Batten, USMC, June 8, 1903, National Archives, RG 127, 97–9, Letters Sent.
17. Pope to Cmdt., Charlestown Navy Yard, June 13, 1903. National Archives, RG 127, 97–9, Letters Sent.
18. Pope to Messrs. Ganey and Burke, 4 Alden St., Boston, June 16, 1903, National Archives, RG 127, 97–9, Letters Sent.
19. Pope to Messrs Huey Bros., 35 Hartford St., Boston, June 16, 1903, National Archives, RG 127, 97–9, Letters Sent.
20. Pope to JAG, Dept. of the Navy, July 6, 1903, National Archives, RG 127, 97–9, Letters Sent.
21. Pope to Cmdt., Charlestown Navy Yard, July 13, 1903, National Archives, RG 127, 97–9, Letters Sent.
22. Report of Prisoners, Naval Prison, Charlestown Navy Yard, July 24, 1903, National Archives, RG 127, 97–9, Letters Sent.
23. Pope to Maj. Gen. Heywood, August 5, 1903, National Archives, RG 127, 97–13, Letters Sent.
24. Pope to Cmdt., Charlestown Navy Yard, August 19, 1903, National Archives, RG 127, 97–9, Letters Sent.
25. Pope to Maj. Gen. Heywood, August 31, 1903, National Archives, RG 127, 97–12, Letters Sent.
26. Pope to Captain, Station No.15, Charlestown, October 21, 1903, National Archives, RG 127, 97–13, Letters Sent.
27. Pope to Sgt. James L. Culliton, USMC, October 21, 1903, National Archives, RG 127, 97–9, Letters Sent.
28. Pope to 1st Lt. Frank J. Schwable, USMC, October 22, 1903, National Archives, RG 127, 97–9, Letters Sent.
29. Kelton to Secretary of the Navy, November 12, 1903, National Archives, RG 127, 97–9, Letters Sent.
30. Report of Prisoners, Naval Prison, Charlestown Navy Yard, November 14, 1903, National Archives, RG 127, 97–9, Letters Sent.
31. Kelton to Mr. Dennis H. Finn, November 16, 1903, National Archives, RG 127, 97–9, Letters Sent.
32. Kelton to Commanding Officer, USS *Aretusa*, November 19, 1903, National Archives, RG 127, 97–9, Letters Sent.
33. Kelton to Cmdt., Charlestown Navy Yard, November 28, 1903, National Archives, RG 127, 97–9, Letters Sent.
34. Kelton to Cmdt., Charlestown Navy Yard, November 30, 1903, National Archives, RG 127, 97–9, Letters Sent.
35. Kelton to Major F.J. Moses, December 7, 1903, National Archives, RG 127, 97–9, Letters Sent.
36. Kelton to Mr. John F. Watkins, 1745 Eighteenth Street, NW, Washington, D.C., December 7, 1903, National Archives, RG 127, 97–9, Letters Sent.
37. Kelton to Mrs. M.Carwin, 341 Preston St., Dallas, TX, December 14, 1903, National Archives, RG 127, 97–9, Letters Sent.

38. Kelton to Captain George C. Reid, USMC, December 25, 1903, National Archives, RG 127, 97–9, Letters Sent.
39. Kelton to Captain Sam G. Lemly, USN, JAG, Washington, D.C., December 16, 1903, National Archives, RG 127, 97–9, Letters Sent.
40. Kelton to Cmdt., Charlestown Navy Yard, January 22, 1904, National Archives, RG 127, 97–9, Letters Sent.
41. Kelton to Cmdt., Charlestown Navy Yard, January 22, 1904, National Archives, RG 127, 97–9, Letters Sent.
42. Kelton to Dr. H.S. Flynn, Providence, RI, January 25, 1904, National Archives, RG 127, 97–9, Letters Sent.
43. Kelton to Chairman, Board of Public Works, Lynn, MA, February 4, 1904, National Archives, RG 127, 97–9, Letters Sent.
44. Kelton to Judge Advocate General, Navy Department, Washington, D.C., National Archives, RG 127, 97–9, Letters Sent.
45. Kelton to Mr. John E. Sawyer, Postmaster, Methuen Station, Lawrence, MA, February 24, 1904, National Archives, RG 127, 97–9, Letters Sent.
46. Postmaster John E. Sawyer to Brig. Gen. Commandant Elliott, October 3, 1904, National Archives, RG 127, 98, Letters Received.
47. Major Magill, Asst Adj & Insp, Headquarters Marine Corps to Kelton, May 18, 1904, National Archives, RG 127, 98–23, Letters Received.
48. Mordecai T. Endicott, Chief Bureau of Yards and Docks to Cmdt., Charlestown Navy Yard, August 24, 1904, National Archives, RG 127, 98–23, Letters Received.
49. Kelton to Cmdt., Charlestown Navy Yard, October 28, 1904, National Archives, RG 127, 97–9, Letters Sent.
50. Kelton to Commanding Officer, USTBD *Hull*, October 31, 1904, National Archives, RG 127, 97–9, Letters Sent.
51. Captain G.N. Reid, USMC, to Captain John A. Blanchard, 1st Corps of Cadets, MVM, No.39 Court Street, Room 26, Boston, MA, November 2, 1904, National Archives, RG 127, 97–9, Letters Sent.
52. Captain G.N. Reid, USMC, to Cpl. James Hall, USMC, November 28, 1904, National Archives, RG 127, 97–9, Letters Sent.
53. Maj. Magill, Asst. Adj. and Insp., Headquarters Marine Corps, to Capt. G.N. Reid, November 23, 1904, National Archives, RG 127, 98–23, Letters Received.
54. Captain G.N. Reid, USMC, to Cmdt., Charlestown Navy Yard, November 21, 1904, National Archives, RG 127, 97–9, Letters Sent.
55. Captain G.N. Reid, USMC, to Cmdt., Charlestown Navy Yard, November 21, 1904, National Archives, RG 127, 97–9, Letters Sent.
56. Captain G.N. Reid, USMC, to Mrs. J.S. Groom, 466 West Broad Street, Savannah, GA, November 29, 1904, National Archives, RG 127, 97–9, Letters Sent.
57. Captain G.N. Reid, USMC, to Cmdt., Charlestown Navy Yard, December 1, 1904, National Archives, RG 127, 97–9, Letters Sent.
58. Captain C.S. Hatch, USMC, to Cmdt., Charlestown Navy Yard, December 9, 1904, National Archives, RG 127, 97–9, Letters Sent.
59. Captain C.S. Hatch, USMC, to Wellington-Wild Coal Co., 7 Central St., Boston, MA, December 13, 1904, National Archives, RG 127, 97–9, Letters Sent.
60. Captain C.S. Hatch, USMC, to Mr. James Moynahan, 839 Dix Avenue, Detroit, MI, December 24, 1904, National Archives, RG 127, 97–9, Letters Sent.
61. Captain C.S. Hatch, USMC, to Mrs. A. Hurlbut, Holland Patent, NJ, December 30, 1904, National Archives, RG 127, 97–9, Letters Sent.
62. Captain C.S. Hatch, USMC, to Cmdt., Charlestown Navy Yard, January 5, 1905, National Archives, RG 127, 97–9, Letters Sent.
63. Captain C.S. Hatch, USMC, to Panama Steamship Co., New York, NY, January 7, 1905, National Archives, RG 127, 97–9, Letters Sent.
64. Captain L.W. Little, USMC, to Private David M. Dow, USMC, January 14, 1905, National Archives, RG 127, 97–9, Letters Sent.
65. Captain L.W. Little, USMC, to Mr. Henry Wessell, 38 Morris Street, Charleston, SC, January 16, 1905, National Archives, RG 127, 97–9, Letters Sent.
66. Kelton to Cmdt., Charlestown Navy Yard, January 20, 1905, National Archives, RG 127, 97–9, Letters Sent.
67. Kelton to Insinger Company, Stanton Avenue, Wagner Junction, Philadephia, PA, January 20, 1905, National Archives, RG 127, 97–9.
68. Kelton to Commanding Officer, Marine Barracks, Brooklyn, NY, January 20, 1905, National Archives, RG 127, 97–9, Letters Sent.
69. Kelton to Sgt. Maj. John F. Lawler, USMC, January 21, 1905, National Archives, RG 127, 97–9, Letters Sent.
70. Kelton to Chief, Yards and Docks, Navy Department, Washington, D.C., January 25, 1905, National Archives, RG 127, Letters Sent.
71. British Consulate General, New York, to Col. Kelton, February 6, 1905, National Archives, RG 127, 98–24, Letters Received.

Chapter 11

1. Col. Raucheimer, Adj. and Insp., Headquarters Marine Corps, to Col. Kelton, February 8, 1905, National Archives, RG 127, 98–24, Letters Received.
2. Kelton to Mrs. Thomas P. Naylor, Falls City, Nebraska, February 15, 1905, National Archives, RG 127, 97–9, Letters Sent.
3. Second endorsement, Sgt. R.S. Nau, USMC, from Quartermaster Marine Corps, September 29, 1904, National Archives, RG 127, 97–16 (Endorsements), Letters Sent.
4. Fourth endorsement, Kelton to Quartermaster Marine Corps, February 9, 1905, National Archives, RG 127, 97–16 (Endorsements), Letters Sent.
5. Kelton to Brig. Gen. Elliott, February 16, 1905, National Archives, RG 127, 97–13, Letters Sent.
6. Kelton to Mr. M.K. Pollock, Insingler Co., Stanton Ave., P.O. Box G, Philadelphia, PA, February 23, 1905, National Archives, RG 127, 97–9, Letters Sent.
7. Kelton to Brig. Gen. Elliott, March 15, 1905, National Archives, RG 127, 98, Letters Received.
8. Col. Raucheimer, Adj. and Insp., Headquarters Marine Corps, to Col. Kelton, March 11, 1905, National Archives, RG 127, 98–24, Letters Received.
9 Kelton to Brig. Gen. Elliott, March 22, 1905, National Archives, RG 127, 97–13, Letters Sent.
10. Kelton to Brig. Gen. Elliott, March 14, 1905, National Archives, RG 127, 97–13, Letters Sent.
11. Kelton to JAG, Navy Department, Washington, D.C., March 22, 1905, National Archives, RG 127, 97–9, Letters Sent.
12. Kelton to 1st Lt. John A. Hugghes, USMC, March 23, 1905, National Archives, RG 127, 97–9, Letters Sent.
13. Kelton to Captain S.W.B. Diehl, USN, JAG, Navy Department, Washington, D.C., April 18, 1905, National Archives, RG 127, 97–9, Letters Sent.
14. Kelton to Captain of the Yard, May 11, 1905, National Archives, RG 127, 97–10, Letters Sent.
15. Kelton to Capt. H.T. Harris, Bureau of Supplies and Account, Navy Department, May 11, 1905, National Archives, RG 127, 97–10, Letters Sent.
16. Kelton to Gen. Elliott, June 15, 1905, National Archives, RG 127, 97–10, Letters Sent.

17. Kelton to 1st Lt. Hughes, 2d Lt. White, June 24, 1905, National Archives, RG 127, 97-10, Letters Sent.
18. Kelton to Quartermaster Marine Corps, June 24, 1905, National Archives, RG 127, 97-10, Letters Sent.
19. Kelton to Quartermaster Marine Corps, June 26, 1905, National Archives, RG 127, 97-10, Letters Sent.
20. Kelton to Brig. Gen. Elliott, July 6, 1905, National Archives, RG 127, 97-10, Letters Sent.
21. Kelton to Brig. Gen. Elliott, July 17, 1905, National Archives, RG 127, 97-10, Letters Sent.
22. Kelton to Brig. Gen. Elliott, July 20, 1905, National Archives, RG 127, 97-10, Letters Sent.
23. Kelton to Quartermaster Marine Corps, August 15, 1905, National Archives, RG 127, 97-10, Letters Sent.
24. Kelton to 2d Lts. J.H. White and E.P. Moses, August 15, 1905, National Archives, RG 127, 97-10, Letters Sent.
25. Kelton to Starbird and Johnson, 292 Main Street, Charlestown, August 18, 1905, National Archives, RG 127, 97-10, Letters Sent.
26. Kelton to Brig. Gen. Elliott, September 1, 1905, National Archives, RG 127, 97-10, Letters Sent.
27. Elliott to Kelton, October 25, 1905, National Archives, RG 127, 98, Letters Received.
28. Elliott to Kelton, November 18, 1905, National Archives, RG 127, 98, Letters Received.
29. G.M. Kincade, AAQM, to Union Bureau of News, 32 E. Clapier St., Germanton, PA, June 23, 1906, National Archives, RG 127, 97-17, Letters Sent.
30. 1st Lt. Kincade to Commanding Officer, Marine Barracks, Boston, July 7, 1906, National Archives, RG 127, 97-17, Letters Sent.
31. Maj. A.S. McLemore, Asst. Adj. and Insp., to Wood, August 22, 1906, National Archives, RG 127, 98-25, Letters Received.
32. Capt. F.L. Boadman, AAQM, to C.W. York Company, 120 Border St., East Boston, September 20, 1906, National Archives, RG 127, 97-17, Letters Sent.
33. Wood to JAG, Navy Department, November 19, 1906, 97-15 (Naval Prison), Letters Sent.
34. Wood to Cmdt., Charlestown Navy Yard, April 25, 1907, National Archives, RG 127, 97-10, Letters Sent.
35. Wood to Cmdt., Charlestown Navy Yard, May 9, 1907, National Archives, RG 127, 97-10, Letters Sent.
36. Wood to Cmdt., Charlestown Navy Yard, May 6, 1907, National Archives, RG 127, 97-10, Letters Sent.
37. Wood to Metropolitan Park Commission, May 8, 1907, National Archives, RG 127, 97-10, Letters Sent.
38. Wood to Brig. Gen. Elliott, May 21, 1907, National Archives, RG 127, 97-10, Letters Sent.
39. Wood to Cmdt., Charlestown Navy Yard, May 23, 1907, National Archives, RG 127, 97-10, Letters Sent.
40. Wood to Cmdt., Charlestown Navy Yard, May 26, 1907, National Archives, RG 127, 97-10, Letters Sent.
41. Wood to Cmdt., Charlestown Navy Yard, June 7, 1907, National Archives, RG 127, 97-10, Letters Sent.
42. Brig. Gen. Elliott to Wood, June 17, 1907, National Archives, RG 127, 98-14, Letters Received.
43. Wood to Brig. Gen. Elliott, June 24, 1907, National Archives, RG 127, 97-10, Letters Sent.
44. Brig. Gen. Elliott to Wood, June 28, 1907, National Archives, RG 127, 97-14, Letters Received.
45. Wood to Cmdt., Charlestown Navy Yard, July 1, 1907, National Archives, RG 127, 97-10, Letters Sent.
46. E.P. Moses to Commanding Officer, Marine Barracks, Boston, July 13, 1907, National Archives, RG 127, 97-17, Letters Sent.
47. 1st Lt. Munzell to Mrs. Hurst Sebbens, 484 Humphrey St., Swampscott, MA, August 6, 1907, National Archives, RG 127, 97-10, Letters Sent.
48. Wood to Capt. Thomas F. Lyons, USMC, September 5, 1907, National Archives, RG 127, 97-10, Letters Sent.
49. E.P. Moses, PQM, to Passenger Agent, Boston and Northern Street Railroad Co., September 26, 1907, National Archives, RG 127, 97-17, Letters Sent.
50. Wood to Brig. Gen. Elliott, September 7, 1907, National Archives, RG 127, 97-10, Letters Sent.
51. Wood to Brig. Gen. Elliott, September 16, 1907, National Archives, RG 127, 97-10, Letters Sent.
52. Wood to Capt. Thomas F. Lyons, September 26, 1907, National Archives, RG 127, 97-10, Letters Sent.
53. Wood to Brig. Gen. Elliott, October 16, 1907, National Archives, RG 127, 97-10, Letters Sent.
54. Brig. Gen. Elliott to Wood, January 8, 1908, National Archives, RG 127, 98-15, Letters Received.
55. Brig. Gen. Elliott to Wood, January 31, 1908, National Archives, RG 127, 98-15, Letters Received.
56. Wood to Brig. Gen. Elliott, February 4, 1908, National Archives, RG 127, 97-10, Letters Sent.
57. Wood to *Boston Globe*, February 5, 1908, National Archives, RG 127, 97-10, Letters Sent.
58. Wood to Brig. Gen. Elliott, February 27, 1908, National Archives, RG 127, 97-10, Letters Sent.
59. Wood to Brig. Gen. Elliott, March 7, 1908, National Archives, RG 127, 97-10, Letters Sent.
60. Wood to Brig. Gen. Elliott, March 9, 1908, National Archives, RG 127, 97-10, Letters Sent.
61. Wood to Rabbi Nathan Blechman, Sec. Passover Society, 36 Gaston St., Roxbury, MA, April 2, 1908, National Archives, RG 127, 97-10, Letters Sent.
62. Maj. Gen. Elliott to Wood, May 29, 1908, National Archives, RG 127, 98-15, Letters Received.
63. Wood to Messrs. Bruce, Price and DeSibour, 527 Fifth Ave., NY, June 7, 1908, National Archives, RG 127, 97-10, Letters Sent.
64. Wood to Cmdt., Charlestown Navy Yard, June 18, 1908, National Archives, RG 127, 97-10, Letters Sent.
65. Wood to Brig. Gen. Elliott, June 19, 1908, National Archives, RG 127, 97-10, Letters Sent.
66. Wood to Commanding Officer, Chelsea Naval Hospital, June 22, 1908, National Archives, RG 127, 97-10, Letters Sent.
67. Wood to Brig. Gen. Elliott, July 16, 1908, National Archives, RG 127, 97-10, Letters Sent.
68. Capt. C.H. Hill to Cmdt., Charlestown Navy Yard, April 13, 1908, National Archives, RG 127, 97-10, Letters Sent.

Chapter 12

1. Col. F.L. Denny, Quartermaster Marine Corps, June 1, 1908, National Archives, RG 127, 98-32, Letters Received.
2. Col. F.L. Denny, Quartermaster Marine Corps, August 20, 1908, National Archives, RG 127, 98-32, Letters Received.
3. Wood to Brig. Gen. Elliott, August 14, 1908, National Archives, RG 127, 97-10, Letters Sent.
4. Maj. C.S. Hill to Brig. Gen. Elliott, August 29, 1908, National Archives, RG 127, 97-10, Letters Sent.
5. Maj. C.S. Hill to Brig. Gen. Elliott, August 29, 1908, National Archives, RG 127, 97-10, Letters Sent.
6. Wood to Mrs. J.H. Mitton, 2003 Monroe St., Toledo, OH, September 4, 1908, National Archives, RG 127, 97-10, Letters Sent.
7. Wood to Maj. Gen. Elliott, September 4, 1908, National Archives, RG 127, 97-10, Letters Sent.
8. Wood to Commanding Officer, USRS *Wabash*, September 10, 1908, National Archives, RG 127, 97-10, Letters Sent.

27. Maj. Gen. Biddle to Wood, April 24, 1911, National Archives, RG 127, 98–18, Letters Received.
28. Wood to Maj. Gen. Biddle, March 31, 1911, National Archives, RG 127, 97–11, Letters Sent.
29. Wood to Maj. Gen., Biddle, April 8, 1911, National Archives, RG 127, 97–11, Letters Sent.
30. Wood to Cmdt., Charlestown Navy Yard, April 9, 1911, National Archives, RG 127, 97–11, Letters Sent.
31. Wood to Maj. Gen. Biddle, April 25, 1911, National Archives, RG 127, 97–11, Letters Sent.
32. Wood to Secretary of the Navy, May 25, 1911, National Archives, RG 127, 97–11, Letters Sent.
33. Moses to Maj. Gen. Biddle, July 4, 1911, National Archives, RG 127, 97–11, Letters Sent.
34. Moses to Maj. Gen. Biddle, July 6, 1911, National Archives, RG 127, 97–11, Letters Sent.
35. Moses to Adjutant and Inspector's Department, Headquarters Marine Corps, July 8, 1911, National Archives, RG 127, 97–11, Letters Sent.
36. Moses to Capt. Fay, Headquarters Marine Corps, July 12, 1911, National Archives, RG 127, 97–11, Letters Sent.
37. Moses to Maj. Gen. Biddle, July 12, 1911, National Archives, RG 127, 97–11, Letters Sent.
38. Moses to Capt. Fay, July 17, 1911, National Archives, RG 127, 97–11, Letters Sent.
39. Moses to Col. McCawley, Quartermaster Marine Corps, July 20, 1911, National Archives, RG 127, 97–11, Letters Sent.
40. Moses to 1st Lt. Edw. A. Osterman, 2d Lt. Leander A. Clapp, July 21, 1911, National Archives, RG 127, 97–11, Letters Sent.
41. Moses to Capt. Fay, Headquarters Marine Corps, August 2, 1911, National Archives, RG 127, 97–11, Letters Sent.
42. Moses to 1st Sgt. Victor H. Czegka, August 3, 1911, National Archives, RG 127, 97–11, Letters Sent.
43. Board of Protection to Cmdt., Charlestown Navy Yard, August 3, 1911, National Archives, RG 127, 97–11, Letters Sent.
44. Moses to Cmdt., Charlestown Navy Yard, August 11, 1911, National Archives, RG 127, 97–11, Letters Sent.
45. Moses to Maj. Gen. Biddle, August 23, 1911, National Archives, RG 127, 97–11, Letters Sent.
46. Moses to Cpl. Luther C. Spiers, September 19, 1911, National Archives, RG 127, 97–11, Letters Sent.
47. Moses to Cpl. John Baker, September 23, 1911, National Archives, RG 127, 97–11, Letters Sent.
48. Moses to Maj. Gen. Biddle, September 21, 1911, National Archives, RG 127, 97–11, Letters Sent.
49. Moses to Clerk of Superior Court, September 25, 1911, National Archives, RG 127, 97–11, Letters Sent.
50. Moses to Maj. Gen. Biddle, September 30, 1911, National Archives, RG 127, 97–11, Letters Sent.
51. Marine Barracks Order, October 26, 1911, National Archives, RG 127, 97–15, Orders by Commanding Officer, Letters Sent.
52. Moses to Maj. Gen. Biddle, November 12, 1911, National Archives, RG 127, 97–11, Letters Sent.
53. Simmons, *The United States Marines, 1775–1975*, p. 83.
54. Ibid., p. 103.
55. Max Boot, *The Savage Wars of Peace*, p. 163.
56. Simmons, *The United States Marines, 1775–1975*, p. 112.
57. Maj. Gen. Biddle to Moses, November 28, 1911, National Archives, RG 127, 98–20, Letters Received.
58. Secretary of the Navy, Dir. 28267-8, to CMC, August 24, 1911, National Archives, RG 127, 98–20, Letters Received.
59. Asst. Secretary of the Navy to Cmdt., Charlestown Navy Yard, August 29, 1911, September 7, 1911, September 25, 1911, September 25, 1912, October 18, 1912, November 14, 1912, April 25, 1913, May 19, 1913, August 25, 1913, September 25, 1913, National Archives, RG 127, 98–21, Letters Received.
60. Cmdt., Charlestown Navy Yard, to Kane, November 22, 1913, National Archives, RG 181, File 6153, Box 155.
61. Col. McCawley, Quartermaster Marine Corps, to Capt. Coffman, Cmdt., Charlestown Navy Yard, September 18, 1913, National Archives, RG 181, File 6153, Box 155.
62. Preliminary plans for junior officers' quarters alterations, National Archives, RG 181, File 6153, Box 269.
63. R.E. Bakenhus to Maj. Gen. Cmdt., May 29, 1914, National Archives, RG 181, File 6153.

Chapter 15

1. Simmons, *The United States Marines, 1775–1975*, p. 82.
2. Rear Adm. W.R. Rush to Maj. Gen. Cmdt., January 25, 1915, National Archives, RG 181, File 6153.
3. Maj. Gen. Barnett to Rear Adm. Rush, January 28, 1915, National Archives, RG 181, File 6153.
4. R.E. Bakenhus, Yard Civil Engineer, to Cmdt., Charlestown Navy Yard, February 13, 1915, National Archives, RG 181, File 6153.
5. Bureau of Yards and Docks to Cmdt., Charlestown Navy Yard, June 11, 1915, National Archives, RG 181, File 6153.
6. Maj. Gen. Cmdt. to Bureau of Supplies and Accounts, September 1, 1915, National Archives, RG 181, File 6153.
7. Simmons, *The United States Marines, 1775–1975*, p. 104.
8. W.R. Rush to Maj. Gen. Cmdt., August 4, 1915, National Archives, RG 181, File 6153, Box 267.
9. Cmdt., Charlestown Navy Yard, to Maj. Hall, May 2, 1916, National Archives, RG 181, File 6153, Box 326.
10. Frederick R. Black, *Cultural Resources Management Study No. 20, Charlestown Navy Yard, 1890–1973*, 1988, p. 305.
11. Ibid., p. 305.
12. Ibid., p. 307.
13. Ibid., p. 309.
14. Ibid., p. 311.
15. Ibid., p. 311.
16. Ibid., p. 311.
17. Ibid., p. 311.
18. 1st Lt. J.Q. Adams to Lt. Col. N.T. Hall, March 9, 1917, National Archives, RG 181, File 6153, Box 409.
19. Ens. M. Griswold to Mr. O.A. Thayer, 89 Franklyn St., Boston, April 25, 1918, National Archives, RG 181, File 6153, Box 530.
20. Black, *Cultural Resources Management Study No. 20, Charlestown Navy Yard 1842–1973*, p. 354.
21. Ibid., p. 404.
22. Ibid., p. 406.
23. Simmons, *The United States Marines, 1775–1975*, p. 102.
24. Col. Magill, Assistant Adjutant and Inspector, to Commanding Officer, Marine Barracks, Boston, January 27.
25. Post Quartermaster to Post Warrant Officer, Charlestown Navy Yard, June 21, 1920, National Archives, RG 181, File 6153, Box 734.
26. Endorsement, Col. Van Orden, to Major H.O. Smith, July 5, 1920, National Archives, RG 181, File 6153, Box 734.
27. Post Quartermaster to Quartermaster Marine Corps, August 27, 1920, National Archives, RG 181, File 6153, Box 734.
28. Commanding Officer to Maj. Gen. Cmdt., August 30, 1920, National Archives, RG 181, File 6153, Box 734.
29. Post Quartermaster to Quartermaster Marine Corps,

August 24, 1920, National Archives RG 181, File 6153, Box 734.

30. Post Quartermaster to Quartermaster Marine Corps, August 26, 1920, National Archives, RG 181, File 6153, Box 734.

31. Maj. R.B. Creecy, Assistant Adjutant and Inspector, to Maj. Gen. Cmdt., November 15, 1922, National Archives, RG 181, File 6153, Box 796.

32. Cmdt. of Yard to Bureau of Yards and Docks, March 2, 1923, National Archives, RG 181, File 6153, Box 901.

33. Cmdt. of Yard to Bureau of Yards and Docks, June 21, 1923, National Archives, RG 181, File 6153, Box 901.

34. Fifth End. of Rear Adm. de Steiguer to Maj. Gen. Cmdt., April 1, 1924, National Archives, RG 181, File 6153, Box 944.

35. Sixth End., Quartermaster Marine Corps, to Chief Bureau Yards and Docks, April 9, 1924, National Archives, RG 181, File 6153, Box 944.

36. Cmdt., Charlestown Navy Yard, to Bureau of Yards and Docks, February 13, 1924, National Archives, RG 181, File 6153, Box 944.

37. Bureau of Yards and Docks to Cmdt., Charlestown Navy Yard, June 11, 1924, National Archives, RG 181, File 6153, Box 944.

38. Personal observations, Lt. Col. John R. Yates, Jr.

39. Message 22DNAGGUT, Cmdt. 1st Naval District, to Commanding Officer, Marine Barracks, Boston, 30 March 1926.

40. Maj. Gen. Fuller to Cmdt., 1st Naval District, July 31, 1931, National Archives, RG 181, Box 133, KK, Letters Received.

41. Officer in Charge, Marine Corps Reserve, to Commanding Officer, Marine Barracks, Boston, National Archives, RG 181, KW, Letters Received.

42. Maj. Gen. Cmdt. to Commanding Officer, 2d Bn, FMCR, March 9, 1935, National Archives, RG 181, KW, Letters Received.

43. Ibid.

44. Frederick R. Black, *Cultural Resources Management Study No. 20, Charlestown Navy Yard 1890–1973*, p. 520.

45. John J. Carey, *A Marine From Boston* (Maryland: Garrett Press, 2000), pp. 357–361.

Chapter 16

1. Personal observations, John R. Yates, Jr.
2. Personal observations, Thomas Yates.

Bibliography

Primary Sources

National Archives, Waltham, Massachusetts.
Series 127, Record of Marine Barracks, Boston Navy Yard
Entry 97 Marine Barracks, Boston: Letters Sent, November 1828–March 1912
Entry 98 Marine Barracks, Boston: Letters Received, June 1896–December 1913
Entry 99 Marine Barracks, Boston: Orders Received and Issued, January 1867–November 1905
Entry 99A Marine Barracks, Boston: Guard Post Regulations, 1938
Entry 100 Marine Barracks, Boston: Muster Rolls, January 1833–October 1911
Entry 100A Marine Barracks, Boston: Muster Rolls, February 1930–June 1936
Entry 101 Marine Barracks, Boston: Reports, November 1816–February 1913
Entry 102 Marine Barracks, Boston: Records of Summary Courts-martial, September 1870–January 1875
Entry 102A Marine Barracks, Boston: Muster Rolls and Pay Rolls, April 1841–January 1848
Entry 102B Marine Barracks, Boston: Reports, 1820 to 1873
Series 181, Record of First Naval District

Secondary Sources

Published Works—General History

Bearss, Edwin C. *Historic Resource Study, Charlestown Navy Yard 1800–1842*. Vols. I and II, Boston National Historic Park, U.S. Department of the Interior/National Park Service, October 1984.

Black, Frederick R. *Cultural Resources Management Study No. 20, Charlestown Navy Yard 1890–1973*. Boston National Historic Park, U.S. Department of the Interior/National Park Service, 1988.

Black, Frederick R., and Edwin C. Bearss. *The Charlestown Navy Yard 1842–1890*. Boston National Historic Park, U.S. Department of the Interior/National Park Service, July 1993.

Boot, Max. *The Savage Wars of Peace*. Basic Books, 2002.

Carey, John J. *A Marine from Boston*. Garrett Park Press, P.O. Box 190, Garrett Park, MD 20896, Library of Congress Number 00-090079.

Carruth, Gorton. *The Encyclopedia of American Facts and Dates*. New York: Harper and Row.

Catton, Bruce. "The Marine Tradition." *American Heritage*, Vol. 10, February 1959. Catton, Bruce. "*Prison Camps of the Civil War*." *American Heritage*, Vol. 10, August 1959.

Collum, Richard S. *History of the United States Marine Corps*. Philadelphia, 1890.

Dahl, Curtis. "Lincoln Saves a Reformer." *American Heritage*, Vol. 23, October 1972.

Evans, G. Rodger. *Historic Structure Report: Marine Barracks (Building 1), Charlestown Navy Yard*. Architectural Data, Boston National Historical Park, U.S. Department of the Interior/National Park Service, October 1978.

Lader, Lawrence. "New York's Bloodiest Week." *American Heritage*, Vol. 10, June 1959.

Mooney, James L., ed. *Dictionary of American Fighting Ships*. Naval Historical Center, Department of the Navy, 1981.

Pierce, Philip N., and Frank O. Hough. *The Compact History of the United States Marine Corps*. New York: Hawthorne Books, 1969.

Roberts, Shelley K., and Audrey Marie. *Historic Structure Report, Building 136*, Architectural Data and Archeological Data Sections, Charlestown Navy Yard, Boston Historical Park, Massachusetts, August 1982.

Santelli, Gabrielle M. *Marines in the Mexican War*. 1991.

Simmons, Edwin H., *The United States Marines, 1775–1975*. New York: Viking Press, 1974.

Utt, Ronald D. *Ships of Oak Guns of Iron*. Regnary History, 2012.

Records of Boston Naval Shipyard

Boston Naval Shipyard Architectural and Environmental Inventory, May 17, 1974, Boston National Historic Park, U.S. Department of the Interior/National Park Service.

Newspapers

The Boston Herald, One Herald Square, Boston, MA 02106.
The Boston Gazette, 13 Congress Street, Boston, MA (1795–1822).
The Boston Globe, 135 Morrissey Boulevard, Boston, MA 02107.

Index

Abbot, Frank E. 119
Adams, John Quincy 19
Adams, Lt. John Quincy 154, 175
Alabama 19
Alamo 24
Alden St. 120
Alexander the Great 94
Alexandria, Egypt 94
Alexandria, VA 13
Allied Cuban Guerrillas 209
American Legation at Peking 103, 136
American Samoa 109
Ames, Howard F. 142
USS *Amphitrite* 102
Annapolis, MD 107, 145, 149
Annapolis Officer's School 97
Apia 109
Arabi Pasha 94–95
USS *Aretusa* 122
Arizona 24
Arkansas 88
Armistead 33
Armistice Day 183
Armstrong, Thomas H. 190
Army and Navy Register 67
Arthur, Chester A. 157
Arundel 129
Associated Press 144
USS *Atlanta* 120
Augusta, GA 19
Augustine 18
Australian Light Horse 129
Austria-Hungary 84

Bader, Charles 103
Badger, Commandant 49
Bailey, Archibald 153
Bainbridge, William 15, 25
Bakenhus, R.E. 172–173
Baker, Joseph E. 44
Baker, William 32
Baltimore 35, 61
USS *Baltimore* 102
Bancroft, Secretary of the Navy George 23
Barber, Private 91
Barnett, Corporal 76
Barnett, Major General 173–174
Barrett, George H. 163

Barrett, James S. 90
Basey 160
Basoni, Joseph 153
Bassert, Morgan 153
Batten, Ocie E. 120
Battery G, 7th U.S. Artillery 204
Battle of Belleau Woods 151
Baxter 36
Bay State Military Rifle Association 139
Bay State Military Rifle Range 125
Beacon St. 119
Becker, J.C. 107
Belgium 59
Belknap, R.R. 119
Bell, Alexander Graham 48
Belleau Wood 171
Benson, William I. 144
Bernard, George 119
Berry, Sgt. 61
Bickford, Charles E. 116
Biddle, General 165–167, 169–170
Big Dig 188
Blanchard, John A. 125
Blechman, Rabbi Nathan 139
Blush, Charles W. 64
Boadman, F.L. 136
Boar War 128
Board of Prisons Commission 106
Bobb, H.P. 163
Boers 128–129
Bon Home Richard 14
Boston and Northern Street Railroad Company 138
Boston City Hall 40
Boston Common 58
Boston Globe 66, 68, 74, 79, 91–92, 139
Boston Herald 35, 49, 52–53, 56, 65, 67, 89, 92, 156
Boston Ice Company 137
Boston Post 89
Boston Roma Band 182–183
Boston Transcript 156
Bowen, William H. 122
Boxer Rebellion 3, 85, 100, 103, 136, 162, 170–171, 173
Boyle, Hugh 113
Boylston 85
Bradlee and Chatman Co. 178

Brady, J.J. 126
Bray, Henry J. 100
Breed's Hill 6, 9
Breen, Thomas 112
Brenner, G.C. 101
Brett, Thomas 153
Brevort. A.N. 27–28, 49
Brigade Armory 166
British Consulate General 128
British Mediterranean Fleet 94
British Troops 129–130
Broad St. 40
Broadhead 85
Brooke, Benjamin E. 25–28
USS *Brooklyn* 16, 78
Brooklyn, NY 26, 35–36, 54, 95, 98, 100–101, 104–105, 113, 121, 127
Brooklyn Navy Yard 19
Brooks, John 10, 18, 20
Broom, James R. 20, 23, 24
Broome, J.L. 53–59
Broomfield, Frank 68, 69
Brown, Frank 153
Brown, Peter F. 163–164
Bruns, Lucas I. 179
Brunswick, ME 103
Bruse, Price, and DeSibour 140, 142
Brussels, Belgium 58
Bryan, William Jennings 79
Bryant, William 74
Buckley, Eugene 66
Buffalo, NY 105
Buick Sports Wagon 186
Building 5 145
Building 24 116
Building 30 153
Building 34 126
Building 36 174
Building 38 3, 56
Building 40 132
Building 77 97
Building 109 158
Building 136 153, 155
Bull Run 58
Bunker Hill 6, 9
Bunker Hill Day 35, 55, 57, 70, 99, 120
Bunker Hill Monument 192

217

Bunker Hill National Bank 90
Bunker Hill St. 152
Burke, Private 50
Burns, Anthony 29–30
Burroughs, Gale 26
Burt, William L. 41
Burton 42
Bush, William 22, 23
Butler, Smedley 170
Buttrick, J.T. 144
Byrd, Richard 158

Cain, Pvt. 74
Caldwell, Henry 8–9, 13
California 24, 44, 100
Call of Duty: Black Ops 2 171
Cambridge, MA 35, 191
Camp Curtis Guild 147
Camp Elliott 138
Camp Heywood 107
Camp Lejeune 103, 185
Camp Perry 168
Camp Roosevelt 122
Campbell, B.H. 149
Campbell, Maurice 134
USS *Canadaigua* 37
Canal St. 65–67, 178
Cape Colony 128
Cape Horn 25, 44, 54
Carman 36
Carpenter, Charles G. 140
Carr, William I. 108
Carroll, James 98
Carroll, Private 144
Carter, Lucy 147
Carwin, Mrs. M. 123
USS *Cassin Young* 4
Cassious, Joseph M. 59–60
USS *Castine* 94
Castle Island 7
Castle of Juan de Ullo 46
Catholic Church 73, 101
Catlin, Albertus W. 149, 151, 153, 155, 159, 162
Cavite 93, 95, 98, 102, 104, 119, 159
Central Ave. 141
Central Europe 5
Central Powers 174
Centre St. 40, 126
Chapultepec Castle 26–27, 47
Charles, MD 139
Charles River 10, 60
Charles Street Jail 150
Charlestown Exchange of the New England Telephone and Telegraph 143
Charlestown Gas and Electric Company 71, 84, 106, 108
Charlestown Gas Company 58
Charlestown State Prison 27, 28, 99
Chase, William J. 65
Chelsea, MA 143
Chelsea Bridge 92, 97, 107
Chelsea Creek 141

Chelsea Naval Hospital 47, 49, 51, 55, 69, 96, 99, 121, 126, 130, 140, 144
Chelsea Re 147
Chelsea Square 141
Cherry Point, NC 185
Chevalier, Eugene 98
Chicago World's Fair 64
Chien Men Gate 171
China 84, 100, 103, 108, 136, 142, 191
Chinese Arsenal 95
Cholera 45, 55
Cienfuegos 96, 162
City of Chelsea 186
The City of Taunton 118
Civil War 3, 14, 59, 106, 169
Clapp, Leander A. 168
Clark 106
Clark, Harry 157
Clifford, Edward 89
Cobb, Cyrus 22
Cochran, William 72
Cochrane, Henry Clay 78, 94–100, 104
Coggin, Joseph W. 163–164
Collum, Richard S. 40–41, 43, 85
Coloenso 129
Colombian Forces 54
Colon 54
Colonial Auto Company 167
Colorado 24
Colt machine gun 159
Columbus 87
Colvcoressess, H. 104
Combat Zone 186
Commodore's Hill 56
Communism 86
Conant, Levi S. 143
Condon, D. 175
Confederate 35
Conger, U.S. Minister to China B.M. 103
Congregation Adath Joshua 144
USS *Congress* 13
Congress Ave. 141
Conlan, Frank 120–121
Connecticut 5
Connecticut State Prison 100
Connell, Patrick 153
Connor, Robert E. 149
Conscription Act 32
USS *Constellation* 8
USS *Constitution* 4, 7, 13, 15, 22, 80, 91, 97, 190–192
Constitutional Centennial Celebration 120
Conway, Mary 145
Conway, Walter 73
Conway, William H. 66
Cooney 50
Corbett, Laurence F. 149
Court St. 68, 74, 103
Cox 34
Cranith, W.D. 97
Creecy, Richard B. 178

Creek peoples 19
Crowley, Jeremiah 98
Crown St. 101
Cuba 18, 87, 91–92, 95, 106, 116, 125, 145, 162
Cudder, Henry J. 145
Culebra Island 122
USS *Cumberland* 22
Cummings, Congressman 89
Cummings, Samuel 23
Curtis, George P. 116
Curtis, W.M. 69
Custer, George Armstrong 159
Cutler, Fred S. 92
Cutler, Mrs. 92
Czegka, Victor H. 168

D Company 154
D-Day 101
Daley, P.J. 163–164
Dallas, TX 123
Daly, Daniel 108, 170–171
Davis, Henry W. 108
Davis, James 81
Day, Robert 144
De Bock, Louis 53, 58–59
Decoma W.F. 127–128
Decoration Day 57
De La Doer, John 77
Delaney, Thomas 158
Delano, Frederick H. 121
Denny, F.L. 142, 154
Derby, CT 119
Derr, E.Z. 125
Desert Storm 88
De Steiguer, L.R. 180
USS *Detroit* 136
Detroit, Michigan 127
Detroit Free Press 67
Devon 36
Dewey, George 96–97, 157
Diehl, S.W.B. USN 132
diphtheria 104
District of Columbia National Guard 166
Dix Ave. 127
Dixon, Blacksmith 69
Dock St. 168
Doherty 107
USS *Dolphin* 157
Dominican Republic 3, 174
Dora, Mount 53
Dougherty, Bernard 98
Downes 19, 28, 50
Downey, Martin 69
Doyle, John 75, 78–79, 86
Drummond, Secret Service Detective 60
Duckworth, Alfred H. 122
Duddy, Bernard 59
Dulany, Jane 45–46
Dulany, William 45, 91
Duncan, James 125
Dutton, Captain 133
Dyer, J.F. 144

Eaker AFB 88
Eastern Penitentiary in Philadelphia 69
Ebers, Louis 89
Edgar, John M. 144
Edwardian Era 135
Edwards, Harry J. 165
Edwards, John G. 119
Egypt 38, 94–95
Electric Light and Gas Company 62
Elizabeth I 3
Ellery St. 92
Elliot, G.F. 102
Elliot, G.M. 103
Elliot, Jesse D. 18
Elliot, Lt. 52
Elliott, Brigadier General 117, 124, 131, 133–134, 137–138, 147, 155, 163
Emerson, George 77
Empire of Spain 92
England 129
Engle, Alonzo 43–44
English, Thomas T. 27–28, 50, 53
English, T.S. 18
USS *Erie* 21
Essex St. 141
Esther 147
Europe 169
Evan 14
Evans, F.E. 98
Evans, Prisoner 76

Fagan, Captain 62
Fairburn, John R. 106
Fall River, MA 102
Fargo Building 185
Farragut, David Glasgow 14, 54
Fay, Captain 167
Fealy, Michael J. 170
Federal Penitentiary at Atlanta, GA 137
Federal St. 35
Ferris, Donald E. 97
Field, Oscar J. 150
5th Ave. 140
Finch, William 25
Finley, John 170
Finn, Dennis H. 122
First Philippine Republic 101
Fisk, Oscar V. 136
Fitzgerald, Pvt. 144
Flagg, Mrs. Edward 112
Flamborough Head 22
Flintlocks 29
Florida 18–20, 53
Flowers, Thomas E. 116, 136
Flynn, H.S. 124
Fort Banks 155
Fort Bayard 120
Fort Dade 20
Fort Hamilton 26
Fort Independence 7
Fort Juan de Ulloa 26
Fort McHenry 14, 21

Fort Mitchell 19
Fort Pillow 59
Fort Sumter 31–32, 37, 67
Fort Warren 34–35, 155
Foster, George 153
Fox, Francis M. 66
France 5, 18, 24, 84, 151
Franklin, William 145
Fraser, Alexander C. 156
Frederick, Peter F. 153
Freedom Trail 192
Freeman 19, 21–22, 34, 36–37
French, Edwin 34
French and Indian War 5
Fugitive Slave Act of 1854 29
Fuller, Ben 81

Galvin, Owen D. 125
Ganey and Burke 120
USS *Ganges* 17
Garfield, James A. 48
Gaston, William 40, 77
Gaston St. 139
George H. Champlin & Company 110
George's Island 34–35
Georgia 18–19
Germany 31, 84, 109
Gettysburg 94
Gibbons, Floyd 171
Gibraltar 23
Gibson, R.M. 117–119
Glen, Harry 159
Glidden, Harvey L. 149, 151
Globe Theater 43
Gloucester, MA 157
Gosport 26
Government Hospital for the Insane at Anacostia 109
Governor's Island 25
Grand Army of the Republic (GAR) 57, 70, 106
Grant, Frank M. 71
Grant, U.S. 33, 59
Grealy, M.J. 149
Great Boston Fire of 1872 40, 75
Great Britain 5, 7, 18, 51
Great Chelsea Fire of April 1908 141
Great Chelsea Fire of 1973 187
Great Turkish War 5
Great White Navy 173, 193
Greeneleaf, Richard 14
Griffin, Patrick J. 99
Griffin, Thomas A. 100
Grimes, Senator 35
Griswold, Ensign M. 175
Groll, Francis 41
Groom, Mrs. J.S. 126
Guam 91–93, 95, 113
Guantanamo Bay 91, 125, 137, 165
HMS *Guerriere* 15, 92
Guyor, Louis 58

Habsburg Spain 3
Hadley, Mrs. Willis 117

Haggerty, Jeremiah 98
Haines, H.C. 59
Haines, Henry C. 171
Haiti 3, 171, 174, 176
Hall, James 125
Hall, Lt. Col. 175
Hall, Major 174
Hall, Newt B. 173
Hamilton Place 167
Hancock St. 167
Hanna, Charles L. 13
Hanna, George B. 78
USS *Hannibal* 143
Hanover St. 46, 98
Harbaugh 163
Harllee, William C. 119
Harnan, James 78
Harrington, Francis 66–69
Harris, H.T. 133
Harris, John 8, 12–13, 33, 57, 118
Harrison, William Henry 48
Hart, Privat 126
Hartford St. 120
Hart's yard 8, 15
Harvard 99
USS *Harvard* 89, 130
Harvard Square 191
Hatch, Captain 126–127
Hatch, Charles S. 149
Haut Obispo 123
Hay, Andre 50
Hay-Herran Treaty 114
Hayes, John F. 66
Haymarket Square 46, 152
Hebb, Clement C. 43, 45–54, 61–63
Helger, Fred 67
Henderson, Archibald 13, 19–28, 32, 35, 37, 39–40, 42–45, 48–51
Henley, J.R. 166
Henley, John R. 167
Herbert, H.A., Jr. 104
Herrington, Corporal 72, 79
Heywood, Colonel 72, 75, 77, 79–80, 84, 102, 104, 107–108, 110, 113, 116–118, 120–121
Hicks, S.P. 71
Higgins, Peter 51–52
Hill, Charles S. 141–142, 144
Hilliker, Charles T. 119
Hilton, Henry 107
Hilton Trophy 107
Hingham, MA 150, 169
Hingle, Sgt. 167
Hingle Gallery Device 168
Hirshinger, H.J. 149, 151
Hispanola 174
Hogan, John H. 145
Holcomb, Thomas, Jr. 167
Holland Patent, NJ 127
Holmes, Parker H. 179
Holt, Herbert E. 136
Hong Kong 84
Hoover, Herbert 85
Hoover, Lou Henry 85
Horn, Frank 64

Horn, Isa A. 64
Houston, E.S. 103
Houston, George P. 60–61
Howard, Royal D. 179
Howlett, Private 79
Huey Brothers 120
Hughes, J.A. 133–134
Hughes, John 48, 66
USTBD *Hull* 125
Hull, D. 165
Hull, Isaac 23
Huntington 83, 95
Hurlbut, Mrs. A. 127

Indian Removal Act 19
Insinger Company 127
Iowa 35
Iraq 129
Israeli, Phineas 144
Isthmus of Panama 140
Italy 84
Iwana 166

Jackson, Andrew 19
Jackson, Lt. 55
Jackson, Samuel 62
Jackson, Sgt. 152
Japan 31, 84, 101
J.E. Lewis & Co. 101
Jersey City 58
Jersey Shore 48
Jewell, Ernest A. 164
Jewell, Ernest E. 151
Johannesburg 128
USS *John Adams* 13, 20
Johnson, Martin J. 175
Johnston, Norman 136
Jones, James 41, 44–46, 87–89, 91
Jones, John Paul 14
Journal Newspaper Co. 95
Joyce, Thomas 132–133
Judson, Howard C. 312
Julian, James 145
Junkin, W.D.A. 104

Kane, Theodore 81, 86
Kansas 55
Kantz, Albert 70
USS *Kearsage* 37
Keene 8, 13
Kelleher, Micheal 94
Kelly, Father 149
Kelton, Allen C. 86–88, 92, 121–125, 127, 130–134
Kelton, Theodore 81
Kennedy, John F. 48
Kennedy Building 190
Kenny 48
Kenny, Nicholas 73
Kensel, Frederic 151
Key West 95
Keyser, Ralph S. 167
Kimberley 128
Kimberly, L.A. 56
Kimberly Brothers 46–47, 56
Kincade, G.M. 157

Kincade, Lt. 135
King, Daniel 144
King Edward 135
Kinzie 36
Kissinger, Henry 191
Kneller, George 136
Korea 3
Korean War 27
Kroll 36
Kuchnester, Herman W. 96
Kyle, Joshua 36

Lacross, Walter A. 168
Ladysmith 128
Lafayette 18
Lahar, Arthur 119
Lake, George H. 150
Lake Erie 168
Lamont, Harry B. 116
Lanang 160–161
Lanang River 160
USS *Lancaster* 84, 89, 94
Lang, Edward F. 137
Langille, Fred 166
Laucheimer, Colonel 157
Lawler, John L. 125, 128
Lawless, G.F. 124
Lawless, Margaret 124
Lawrence, MA 117, 122, 124
Lawson, Lawrence 134
Leach, E.M. Company 150
League Island, PA 123
Leahy, William 158
Lechmere Point 18
Lee, Arthur E. 169
Lee, James 144
Lee Straight pull rifle 95–96, 113
Lejeune, Major General 180
Lejune, John A. 103
Lemly, Sam G., USN 123
Lewis, Ward 148
Light House Service 153
Lincoln, Abraham 35, 48, 94, 164
Lincoln Ave. 168
Little, Captain 127
Little Big Horn 159
Logan, John A. 109
London Illustrated News 67
Long, Charles H. 114–115
Long, Charles S. 92
Long, Private 59
Looke, Frank P. 116–117
Louisiana Purchase 24
Lovell's Island 70–71, 96, 106, 119, 138, 148
Low, Mr. 144
Lowell, MA 25
Lowny 34
Lowry R.B. 36
Lucy-le-Bocage 171
Lyman, C.H. 150–152
Lyman, Charles H. 147
Lynch and Woodward 70–72
Lynn, MA 65, 117, 119–120, 125, 166
Lynn Public Works 124

Lyons, Thomas F. 137–138

Mackel, Edward H. 185
Mafeking 128
Magill, Louis J. 153, 176
Mahon, Ralph 122
Maine 6, 100
USS *Maine* 87–88, 151
Malabar 23
Mall of America 165
Manifest destiny 24
Manila 96–98, 102
Manila Hemp 159
Mannion, John 149
Manzanillo Harbor, Cuba 116, 125
USS *Marblehead* 93, 96, 162
Mare Island 50, 137
Marine Camp for Rifle Instruction 150–151, 154
Marine's Hymn 183
Marston, Ward 22, 34, 61–63, 67, 68
Martha's Vineyard 186
Marxism 86
Mary 147
Mason-Dixon line 31
USS *Massachusetts* 100, 120
Massachusetts Naval Militia1 67
Massachusetts Rifle Association 106
Massachusetts Society of the Prevention of Cruelty to Children 146
Mather 36
Matthews, Calvin T. 145
Maverick St. 141
McAughre, Henry 53
McCabe, Mary 100
McCabe, Thomas 86, 100
McCafferty, James 122, 125
McCalla, B.H. 96
McCauley, Samuel F. 119
McCawley, Charles G. 36–38, 42, 46, 50–51, 56, 58
McCawley, Colonel 168
McClure, C. 155
McCrossin, Hugh 162
McDougal, Douglas C. 98, 100, 167
McFadden, Hugh 63
McGovern, George 191
McKean, James M. 165
McKendry, James 50
McKenna, Micheal 66
McKeough, Charles 89
McKim, James 13
McKinley, William 79, 83, 87
McKinnon, John 190
McLaughlin, James 144
McLaughlin, John T. 20
McLemore, A.S. 135
McLittle, L. 133
McNulty, John S. 179
McQuade, Private 90
McSwinney, Brian 119, 121
Meade, Robert C. 52, 67–86, 100

Mechanical Accountant Company 165
Medal of Honor 162, 170
Mediterranean Sea 112
Melaney, Michael 119
Melrose, MA 154
Melrose Police 154
Melvin, Edward L. 148, 169
Memorial Day 106
Merchants and Miners Transportation Company 86, 109, 112, 130
Merrimac River 94
Methuen, MA 124
Mexican-American War 3, 29, 32, 37
Mexico 24–26, 37, 57, 174
Mexico City 26–27, 29
Mickken, Martin 132
Middle East 174
Middlesex County 18; jail 106, 108
Middlesex Railroad Company 115
Milk St. 40
Millican, Edward 130
Miniham, James 64
USS *Minnesota* 46
Minnesota State Prison 155
Mississippi River 19, 23
Missouri 31
USS *Missouri* 22–23, 126, 152
Mitchener, Thomas H. 115
Mitten, J.H. 142
Montgomery, A.B. 146
Moody, William Henry 157
Mooney, John 137
Moore, Herbert S. 79
Moore, Yandell 104
Morse, Joseph A. 60
Moses, Captain 93, 99
Moses, E.P. 134, 136–138, 144
Moses, F.J. 122
Moses, Laurence H. 100, 166–170
Moynahan, James 127
Muir, Captain 133
Murphy, James 97–98
Murphy, John A. 108
Murphy, Thomas 72
Murray, J.C. 112
Murray, Michael 148
Murray, Timothy 153
Myers, John 173
Mystic Ball Park 162
Mystic River 55–56, 99, 167–188
Mystic River Bridge 65, 97, 187–188, 191

Nashua, NH 164
USS *Nashville* 162
Natal 128
National Museum 164
National Palace 48
National Rifle Association 107
Nau, R.S. 130
Naval Academy 149
Naval Magazine, Hingham, MA 163, 169
Naval Powder Depot 150

Naval Prison 149, 152
Navigation Bureau 70
Naylor, Marshall T. 130
Needham 34
Nevada 42
Neveleta 102
New England Telephone and Telegraph Company 65, 147
New Hampshire 6, 29
USS *New Hampshire* 56, 58
USS *New Jersey* 152
New London 6
New Mexico 42, 120
New Orleans 5, 54
New Spain 18
USS *New York* 136
New York City 19, 33, 58, 60, 61, 140, 149, 157
New York Herald 67
New York Times 118
USS *Newark* 89, 116, 173
Newburyport 94
Newport, RI 6, 78, 104, 110, 125, 134, 152, 167
Newport Marine Barracks 78
Newton 13
Nichols 44
Nicholson 9–10, 22, 35, 36
Nicholson, Adjutant-Inspector Major 49
Nixon, Richard M. 186, 191
Norfolk, VA 21, 36, 89, 98, 130, 132, 134
Norfolk Navy Yard 149
North Vietnam 191
Nueces River 24

O'Byrne, John 49
O'Day, Michael 107, 112
Ohio 32, 51, 57, 68, 76, 78, 85
USS *Ohio* 21–22, 37, 40, 43
O'Keefe, John J. 92
O'Loughlin, John 155
USS *Omaha* 55
Ontario 130
Orfant, Harry C. 145
O'Riordan, P. 137
O'Rourke, Thomas F. 62
O'Shea, John 38
Osterman, Edmund A. 167–168
O'Toole, P.T. 52–53
Ottoman Empire 174
Overlook, Dr. 168
Owen, C.S. 149

Paine Furniture Company 154
Pan-American Exposition in Buffalo, NY 105, 107
Panama 3, 54–55, 114, 123, 127, 138
Panama Battalion 153
Panama Canal 25
Panama Canal Zone 132, 138
Panama Steamship Co. 127
Pancho Villa 174
USS *Panther* 95
Paris Exposition of 1889 61

Paris Exposition of 1900 98
Park Square 167
Parker, Commandant 26, 42, 44
Parker House 85
Parris Island 169
Passover 130
Passover Society 139
Patches 189
Patterson, S.A.W. 98–99
Pawtucket 6
Payne's Landing 19
Peabody, MA 113
Pearl Harbor 31, 88, 101
Peddocks Island 99
Peking, China 85, 103, 170
Pemberton Square 169
Pennsylvania 120
Pensacola 18
Perry, John E. 44
Pershing, John J. 174
Pettgrove, Fred 10
Philadelphia, PA 11, 14, 26, 35, 38, 45, 58, 63, 69, 127, 149, 162, 178
Philippine Insurrection 3
Philippines 91, 93, 94, 97–98, 100–102, 104, 106, 108–109, 113, 115–116, 119, 121, 127, 142, 153, 159, 162
Philips, Reuben J. 108
Pierce, Caleb 21–22, 37
Pierce, Franklin 26, 29
Pierce, Henry 43
Pierce, Lt. Col. 183
Pilgrim Auto Company 167
The Pilot 67, 142
Piscataqua River 120
Plum Island 94
Plymouth 118
Plymouth 5
Polk, James 24–25, 43
Pope, Percival C. 44, 49, 63–66, 86, 89–93, 101–114, 116–117, 119–122
Port-au-Prince 176
Port Royal, SC 130, 149, 167, 169, 171
Portal, John M. 138
Porter, Captain 160–161
Portland, ME 6
Portsmouth, NH 6, 34, 98, 100, 104, 120, 123, 128, 132–133, 138, 145, 149, 151–152, 157, 165, 170–171, 176, 182
Portsmouth Marine Barracks 52
Portsmouth Naval Prison 132, 171
Portsmouth Naval Shipyard 90, 120
Portugal 90
Post Exchange (PX) 81–82
Powers, Charles 56
USS *Powhatan* 43
Preston St. 123
Pretoria 129
Price, Andrew 77–78
Prince, Lt. Col. 154
Prince of Wales Light Horse 128

Princeton St. 96
Prisoners of War 191
Priviater, Henry 158
Providence, RI 124, 165
Provisional Company A 123
Puerto Rico 91, 122
Puritan Auto Company 167

Quantico, VA 182
Queen, H.W. 21
Queen Victoria 135
Quick, John H. 159
Quigley, John G. 78
Quinapundan 119
Quinn, Corporal 137
Quinn, Mr. and Mrs. Patrick 61

Rackliff, Private 61
Ransom, George M. 46
Rapp, Henry W. 122
Ratcliff, Arthur 64
Rauchiemer, Colonel 132
Raupp 37
Raynor, Sidney N. 155, 167
Reading, MA 154
Reardon 36
Reed, Willis 157
Reid, E.C. 55–56
Reid, George C. 104, 123, 125–127, 131
Republic of Texas 24
Revere Drive-In Theater 186
Reynolds 29–30, 32–34, 36, 61, 65–66
Reynolds, George 125
Reynolds, James 114–115
Rhode Island 6
Richards, Miss 62
Rio Grande 24
Robinson, Philip 52
Robison, S.S. 176
Rodgers 166
Rogers, Surgeon 77
Roosevelt, Franklin D. 158
Roosevelt, Theodore 79, 82–84
Rosemond 47
Rosengarten 142
Roxbury, MA 139, 144
Royce, Chaplin 67
Royer, Alfred L. 142
Ruger, Charles 144
Rush, W.R. 173
Russia 31, 84–85, 191
Russo-Japanese War 157
Ryan, Matthew B. 63

Sabine 36
St. Augustine 30
St. Marks 30
St. Mary's Church 73, 149, 157
St. Paul's Church 62
Sal 182–183
Salem, MA 65, 117
Salem Cadet Band 57
Salem Turnpike 9, 65
Samar 119, 153, 159–160

Samar 171
Samoa 3, 108, 113, 121
San Diego 165
USS *San Francisco* 110
San Juan 122
Sandy Hook, NY 64
Sanjule, Eugene 153
Santiago, Cuba 130
Santo Domingo 14, 174
USS *Saratoga* 47
SAT Team 190
Savannah, GA 126, 130
Sawyer 67
Sawyer, Edwin L. 124
Sawyer, Fireman 108
Sawyer, John E. 124
Saxon, J.P. 128–129
Sayre, Prisoner 76
Scannell, David J. 108
Schererhern 35
School of Application 96
School St. 40
Scott, Dred 29
Scott, Joseph F. 162
Scott, Winfield 26
Seavey's Island 123
Secret Service 125
Seminole 18–20
Seminole Wars 18–21, 26
Serapis 14
Serrine, Charles 43
Seven Years War 18
Shailer 85
Shaw, Thaddeus P. 119
Shawmut Ave. 35
Shea, Joseph M. 165
Shenandoah 127
USS *Shenandoah* 52
Sherburne, J.H. 40, 78
Sicard 83
Sightseeing Auto Company 167
Sigsbee, Charles D. 87
Sinclair, Charles G. 167
Sisters of Charity 18
6th Marines 151
Slack, W.B. 37, 46, 50
smallpox 47
Smith, Benjamin G. 35
Smith, Billy 109
Smith, Eugene 100
Smith, Franklyn W. 35
Smith, Harry L. 166
Smith, H.O. 149–151, 178
Smith, Jacob 159
Smith, John 73
Smith, W.G. 107
Smith, William 28
Smith, Prother & Co. 35
Snow, Elliot 146
Sohoton Cliffs 159
Sojoton River 159
Somme River 174
South Africa 128–129
South Boston Annex 175
South Carolina 19
South Pacific 93

South Pole 158
USPS *Southery* 109–110, 113, 116, 119–120, 152, 186
Spain 18–19, 54, 87–88, 97–98, 113
Spanish-American War 3, 14, 92, 95–96, 113, 116, 122, 142, 151, 162, 175
Spanish Fleet 97
Spanish Florida 19
Speers, Private 80
Spicer, 1 Lt. 52
Springfield 97
Springfield Republican 97
Standard Oil 141
Stanton Avenue 127
Star Theater 143
Starbird and Johnson 134
Stenberg, Gustaf W. 112
Stewart, Peter 108
Stoddert, Benjamin 7
Stokes, A. 163
Stone, E.P. 68
Stoner, Daniel 36
Strauss, Ernest 163
Stringham, S.W. 36
Strongberger Automatic Telephone System 145
Suez Canal 54, 94
Sugrue, Timothy 86
Summer St. 40
Sumner, Charles 35
Sweeney, John 91
Sweeney, Smith 191

Tactical Police Force (TPF) 191
Taft, William H. 79
Tallapoosa 98
Taylor, Charles B. 100
Taylor, Zachary 24
Tennessee 59
USS *Tennessee* 47
Tesch, Herman R. 136
Texas 24
Thayer, O.A. 175
3rd Field Artillery 154
Thirty Years War 5
Thompson, Captain 10
Thompson, Secretary of the Navy 46
301st Company of the Marine Corps Reserve 182
Tielsch, George P. 163–164
Tientsin 84–85, 95, 106, 173
Tietze, Alfred 108
Titus, Frank A. 155
Tobin Bridge 187
Toledo, OH 168
Topsfield, MA 192
Tourist Auto Company 167
Trail of Tears 19
Transvaal 128
Trask, Oliver B. 24
Treaty of Paris 18
Treffethen, Fred 125
Tremont St. 40, 62, 85
Tribon, Chaplin 75

Index

Tripartite Convention of 1899 109
Turner 21
Tutuilla 121
Tyler, John 24

Udell, F. 104
Uniform Board 62
Union Bureau of News 135
United Kingdom 184
USS *United States* 23
U.S. Army 154; Company C 159
U.S. Naval Disciplinary Barracks 169, 171
U.S. Naval Home 127
Upshur, Abel 22
Ursuline Convent 18
Utah 24

Vaal River 128
Valentine's Day 1892 134
Van Orden, Col. George 176, 178
Varnum 18
Vera Cruz 26, 37, 151
Verdun 174
Veteran Marine Association 153
Vietnam 3, 62, 102, 159, 185, 191
Virginia 32, 48

USRS *Wabash* 46, 55–56, 67, 75–76, 112–113, 127, 143, 152, 158, 186
Wadleigh, John W. 163–164, 166
Wadleigh, Lt. 100
Wagner Junction 127
Wainwright, Robert D. 17–18
Wakefield 125, 139, 147, 150, 152, 154, 162
Waldron 27
Walker, James 44–46, 89, 91
Wallace, William 40–41, 43–45, 49
Wallach, Captain 89–92
Waller, Littleton W.T., Jr. 167

Waller, L.W.T. 113, 160–161
Walnut Hill 106
Walsh, Robert H. 60–61
Walsh, Thomas M. 65
Waltham Chemical Company 104–105, 107
Wapping St. 137
War Department 20, 62
War of 1812 18
Ward 37
Ward, William 26
Wardee, Levasco 152
Warren National Savings Bank 77
Warren Street 165
USS *Washington* 176
Washington Barracks 32
Washington, D.C. 11, 98, 102, 109, 121, 123
Washington Street Bridge 52
Watkins, John F. 123
Watson, Samuel 21, 23–29, 37
Webster, Frank 36
Weigand, John 37
Welles, George M. 40, 75, 77, 78
Welles, Gideon 36
Wellington-Wild Coal Company 126
Wesley, Henry 126
Wessell, Private 127
West, Edward S. 21
West, George 50
West Cambridge 106
West Indian Campaign Medals 116, 125, 130
Weston, Gilbert 126
Wethersfield, CT 100, 136
Wharter, Private 154
Wharton, Franklin 9–10, 13–18, 20, 23
White, Capt. 68
White, Francis B. 25, 26
White, James G. 120
White, J.H. 133–134

White, Lt. 55, 60
White Star Steamship Company 158
Whiting, Homer C. 146
Whitney, W.C. 59
Williams, A.S. 144
Williams, Dion 104, 110
Williams, Lt. 160–161
Williamson, Sarsfield 155
Wills, George 48
Wilson, John C. 150
Wiltse, F.S. 104
Winslow, Herbert 143
Winslow, Surgeon 50
Winthrop, MA 117
Wiscasset, ME 6
USS *Wisconsin* 152
Woburn, MA 120, 138
Wood, Abel J. 33
Wood, Thomas N. 135–150, 152–159, 162–166
Wood, William W. 164
Woodrow 150, 151, 153
Woods, James 153
Woog, Lt. 110
Worcester, MA 116, 168
World War I 129, 151, 157, 171, 174–175, 182, 192
World War II 7, 192
Wylie, Adm. J.C. 190
Wyoma, Lynn 120, 124

Yates, Edward 76
Yates, John R., Jr. 186–189, 191–193
Yates, Virginia 186
York, C.W. Co. 136
USS *Yosemite* 93

Zedong, Mao 85
Zeilin, Brigadier General 36–38, 42, 51
Zion, William 108

www.ingramcontent.com/pod-product-compliance
Lightning Source LLC
Chambersburg PA
CBHW081554300426
44116CB00015B/2874